MW00800701

Ordering Independence

Britain and the World

Edited by The British Scholar Society

Editors: **James Onley**, University of Exeter, UK; **A. G. Hopkins**, University of Texas at Austin, USA; **Gregory Barton**, The Australian National University, Australia; and **Bryan Glass**, Texas State University, USA

Other titles in the Britain and the World *series include*:

Benjamin Grob-Fitzgibbon
IMPERIAL ENDGAME
Britain's Dirty Wars and the End of Empire

Brett Bennett and Joseph M. Hodge (*editors*)
SCIENCE AND EMPIRE
Knowledge and Networks of Science across the British Empire, 1850–1970

John Fisher
BRITISH DIPLOMACY AND THE DESCENT INTO CHAOS
The Career of Jack Garnett, 1902–1919

Forthcoming titles include:

Richard Scully
BRITISH IMAGES OF GERMANY
Admiration, Antagonism and Ambivalence, 1860–1914

Joe Eaton
THE ANGLO-AMERICAN PAPER WAR
Debates about the New Republic, 1800–1825

Christopher Hagerman
BRITAIN'S IMPERIAL MUSE
The Classics and Britain's Indian Empire, 1784–1914

Martin Farr and Xavier Guégan (*editors*)
THE BRITISH ABROAD SINCE THE EIGHTEENTH CENTURY
Vol. 1: Travellers and Tourists
Vol. 2: Experiencing Imperialism

John Griffiths
THE SOUL OF THE EMPIRE
Australian and New Zealand Cities in the British World c.1880–1939

Barry Gough
THE PAX BRITANNICA
Royal Navy and the Rise and Fall of the British Empire

Britain and the World
Series Standing Order ISBN 978–0–230–24650–8 (hardcover) and
ISBN 978–0–230–24651–5 (paperback)
(*outside North America only*)

You can receive future titles in this series as they are published by placing a standing order. Please contact your bookseller, or write to us at the address below with your name and address, the title of the series and one or both of the ISBNs quoted above.

Customer Services Department, Macmillan Distribution Ltd, Houndmills, Basingstoke, Hampshire RG21 6XS, England

---

Ordering Independence

The End of Empire in the Anglophone Caribbean, 1947–1969

Spencer Mawby

Associate Professor, Department of History, University of Nottingham, UK

First published 2012 by
PALGRAVE MACMILLAN

Palgrave Macmillan in the UK is an imprint of Macmillan Publishers Limited,
registered in England, company number 785998, of Houndmills, Basingstoke,
Hampshire RG21 6XS.

Palgrave Macmillan in the US is a division of St Martin's Press LLC,
175 Fifth Avenue, New York, NY 10010.

Palgrave Macmillan is the global academic imprint of the above companies
and has companies and representatives throughout the world.

Palgrave® and Macmillan® are registered trademarks in the United States,
the United Kingdom, Europe and other countries.

ISBN 978–0–230–27818–9

This book is printed on paper suitable for recycling and made from fully
managed and sustained forest sources. Logging, pulping and manufacturing
processes are expected to conform to the environmental regulations of the
country of origin.

A catalogue record for this book is available from the British Library.

A catalog record for this book is available from the Library of Congress.

10   9   8   7   6   5   4   3   2   1
21 20 19 18 17 16 15 14 13 12

Transferred to Digital Printing in 2014

Contents

Series Editors' Preface

Spencer Mawby's *Ordering Independence: The End of Empire in the Anglophone Caribbean, 1947–1969* is the fourth book in the *Britain and the World* series, edited by The British Scholar Society and published by Palgrave Macmillan. From the sixteenth century onward, Britain's influence on the world became progressively profound and far-reaching, in time touching every continent and subject, from Africa to South America and archaeology to zoology. Although the histories of Britain and the world became increasingly intertwined, mainstream British history still neglects the world's influence upon domestic developments and British overseas history remains largely confined to the study of the British Empire. This series takes a broader approach to British history, seeking to investigate the full extent of the world's influence on Britain and Britain's influence on the world.

Ordering Independence examines the process of decolonisation in the British West Indies: the character of local nationalism, constitutional developments, and British policy-making. It studies the negotiations leading to the West Indian Federation's establishment, the federation's short life (1958–62), its aftermath and the separate discussions with individual colonies that took place concurrently, which ultimately led to independence. It also considers the economic and racial tensions that threatened the process of orderly decolonisation. *Ordering Independence* is the most comprehensive study of the end of empire in the Anglophone Caribbean yet written. We hope you will enjoy reading it.

Editors, *Britain and the World*:

James Onley, University of Exeter, UK
A. G. Hopkins, University of Texas at Austin, USA
Gregory Barton, The Australian National University, Australia
Bryan Glass, Texas State University, USA

Acknowledgements

The acknowledgements are almost always the last item to be completed in preparing a book and are often the first to be scrutinised by the reader. They therefore provide an opportune moment to say that although history books like this one are commonly described in the parlance of modern universities as the product of a 'lone researcher', the authors are dependent on the time, patience and knowledge of many people. The cooperation of those working in archives is essential and in that regard I would like to thank all the archivists and librarians at the institutions listed in the primary source section of the bibliography. In particular, the British National Archives has offered increasingly efficient assistance to researchers over the years. The various archives located in the Anglophone Caribbean also provide good service despite obvious budgetary constraints. For those studying the politics of the 1950s and 1960s the most useful resource in the region is the W. I. Federal Archives Centre at Cave Hill, Barbados, where I received a huge amount of useful advice from Cherri-Ann Beckles and Halcyon Wiltshire.

Of course one also has to get to the archives and in that regard the assistance of all those workers who keep various forms of transport on the rails, the roads and in the skies are greatly appreciated. During my trip to Jamaica I was dependent on private transport and in that regard I need to offer special thanks to Kevin Thompson who drove me back and forth between Kingston and Spanish Town in the midst of the State of Emergency. Birte Timm offered essential guidance in planning the trip and drew my attention to the work of Help Jamaica! (helpjamaica.org). Hotel chains sometimes proved less welcoming than locally run businesses, but Johnsons Guest House in Port of Spain, Trinidad and Tobago; the Pax Guest House in St. Augustine, Trinidad and Tobago; and Altamont Court in Kingston, Jamaica, each provided a haven during research trips to the region, for which I am grateful to the staff and owners.

The process of preparing this book for publication has been a relatively smooth and painless one, for me at least. I am therefore indebted to the editorial team at Palgrave and the series editors of the *Britain and the World* volumes. Michael Strang commissioned the book, Ruth Ireland took it up and Jenny McCall as well as Clare Mence have been very solicitous in preparing the final text for publication. James Onley was extremely kind in welcoming me aboard the *Britain and the World* series. Devasena Vedamurthi and her team were accommodating during the always complicated task of preparing the final text.

As a consequence of various foreseen and unforeseen circumstances very few people have read this book in draft. The one person who did conduct a detailed study of the text was Bryan White. He has taken on this task twice before and once again made a great job of it, even though we never did come up with a suitable entry for 'x' in the index. My former PhD supervisor, John Kent, is owed an acknowledgement for the last book on Aden which he actually suggested, so belated thanks are due to him both for that piece of productive advice and for providing a roof over my head during some of my trips to London during the research for this one.

More broadly any book is a product of the environment in which it is written and I really do owe a great deal to those who have sustained morale in the Department of History at the University of Nottingham, UK. The efforts of those staff and students who still seem willing to defend academic values against the encroachment of what might most diplomatically be described as non-academic values had a restorative effect. Anybody with the slightest acquaintance with work in a modern university knows that the role of the head of a department really is an impossible job. Fortunately for me, the three heads I worked with while I was conducting this research proved exceptionally sympathetic and understanding and so thanks are due to Professor Colin Heywood, Professor Elizabeth Harvey and Professor John Young.

Oddly enough, having an academic for a son does not seem to have made my mother, Sheila Mawby, wonder too often whether it would have been better to discourage my nascent bookishness and for that, and for her good advice, I really am very grateful.

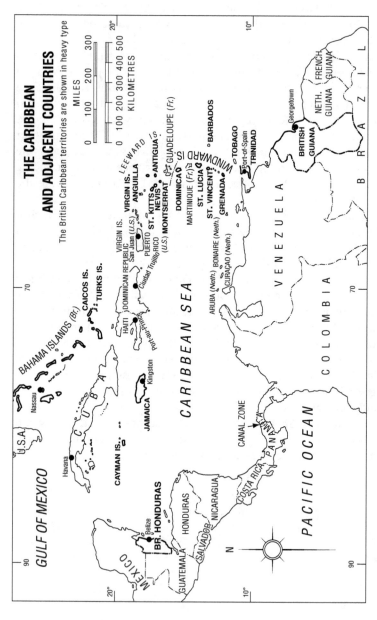

The Anglophone Caribbean in 1953, adapted from a map available at the National Archives, Kew, CO 1031/751.

1
Introduction

On 23 May 2010 the Jamaican Prime Minister, Bruce Golding, declared a State of Emergency in the midst of violent confrontations between the residents of Tivoli Gardens in Kingston and the security forces. The cause of the outbreak of urban warfare was Golding's decision to cooperate with American requests to extradite Christopher 'Dudus' Coke, who was suspected of playing a leading role in the trading of drugs and arms between Jamaica and the United States. He was also reputedly a client of Golding's Jamaica Labour Party (JLP) which had for many years collaborated with criminal gangs in order to consolidate its electoral support in West Kingston. The consequences for the people of Tivoli Gardens were catastrophic: estimates vary but it is certain that more than 70 people were killed in the fighting. In a thoughtful article which was published on 13 June 2010 by the *Jamaica Gleaner*, Kevin O'Brien Chang sought to place the violence in its historical context. His starting point was the recorded murder rate in Jamaica of 3.9 per thousand at independence in 1962; this had risen to 62.2 since then. He noted that Britain had been seen as 'a "gentler" colonial master than Germany, Spain or France' but not so gentle that it had not opened fire on ordinary people during the strikes of 1938. There was a tradition of the use of brute force against civilians which had been inherited from the colonial period. However, O'Brien Chang rejected the notion that the rise in violence after the transfer of power to Jamaican political parties was a consequence of 'British overlordship democracy'. He argued that while the leaders of the Jamaican independence movement, such as Alexander Bustamante and Norman Manley, had recognised the requirement for restraint, their successors had recklessly embraced a violent political culture.[1] Unlike some of his compatriots he did not suggest that British authority was necessary to contain the latent conflicts which

1

existed in Jamaican society, but his article was typical in urging the need for a greater sense of local political accountability. In situating the fighting in Tivoli Gardens amidst the history of imperialism but shifting culpability away from the failings of the British and towards the inadequacies of those who were responsible for directing the nation's affairs after 1962, the *Gleaner* article reflected some trends in the historiography of the end of empire in the Anglophone Caribbean that give the British credit for arranging an orderly decolonisation and attribute subsequent unrest and dissatisfaction to the failings of Caribbean nationalism.

Aside from their inability to stem rising levels of criminality, another common complaint which Caribbean people level against the region's politicians is their failure to improve economic conditions in the region. Much of this criticism focuses on the ineffectiveness of the Caribbean Community (CARICOM) which has been unable to fully implement plans for a Single Market and Economy (SME). In July 2010, as the State of Emergency continued in Kingston, the CARICOM Heads of Government gathered for their annual meeting 80 miles to the northwest in Montego Bay. It turned out to be a typical example of the organisation's indecisiveness. No progress was made with the abiding issue of how to ensure that member states implemented measures for the liberalisation of trade and the free movement of people. In February 2011 R. E. Guyson Mayers reflected on the troubled history of efforts to achieve cooperation across the Caribbean in his column in the *Barbados Advocate*. His thoughts were prompted by the continuing inaction of CARICOM, the revolutionary changes occurring in Middle Eastern societies and the suggestion that the Royal Navy would end warship patrols in the Caribbean for the first time since the Second World War. In his view these developments illustrated the lassitude and inauthenticity of Caribbean politics which was particularly evident in the realm of regional integration. He noted that for years 'Caribbean leaders have worked to build a level of cooperation among regional States with the hope that this would redound to the benefit of the peoples of the region.' The only time when such ideas were enacted was during the four years of federation at the end of the British empire; in the post-independence era of CARICOM and other regional organisations, the results 'were never as productive as the flowery words that came to be associated with their meetings.' Guyson Mayers concluded that 'the federation reached as far as it did because of the efforts of the British and since our mentality has not changed, there will be no successful union among us unless Britain or

America command us to do it. We have the ability to build, but we are better at criticising, complaining and dismantling.'[2] As in the case of O'Brien Chang, the *Barbados Advocate*'s columnist turned to the era just before independence as a vantage point from which later generations of Caribbean leaders could be chastised.

The general sense of frustration expressed in these columns is very widespread in the contemporary Caribbean and there are exceptionally good reasons why the people of the region should be discontented with the state of its politics. As columnists, O'Brien Chang and Guyson Mayers were justified in challenging the worst instincts of contemporary political leaders and neither argued for a return to an era when it was for British officials to judge what was in the best interests of the people of Jamaica, Barbados and the other colonial territories. What jars about the opinions they expressed is that they employed history in a way which misrepresented the era of decolonisation by exaggerating the stability of the colonial condition. The task of trying to rectify this imbalance is a delicate one, but it may be useful to state the counterargument with the minimum of qualification at the outset. In the 20 years before independence, British policymakers prioritised the notion of an orderly transition in a way that pointlessly delayed the implementation of constitutional reform, encouraged the development of authoritarian politics and neglected the economic conditions which stimulated local discontent. Although the eventual demission of power was largely peaceful, the British were engaged in a genuine kind of confrontational politics with nationalist leaders who prioritised independence and autonomy and came to regard metropolitan policymaking as equivocating, negligent and obstructive. Viewed from this perspective the issues addressed in the newspaper columns look very different. In the case of the rise of violent criminality in Jamaica one can say that the British bear significant responsibility for the emergence of an increasingly violent political conflict between the JLP and the People's Nationalist Party (PNP) that predates the era of independence. And on the question of the politics of unity, it is necessary to remember that the form in which the federation emerged in 1958 was not the outcome of British design but of ongoing disagreements between nationalist leaders and metropolitan officials, and its demise had as much to do with the attitudes of the latter as with the failings of the former. Before examining these arguments in detail, a swift tour of some geographical, demographic, economic and cultural features of the region ought to be helpful in providing some basic context.

Characterising the Anglophone Caribbean

The subtitle of this book refers to the 'Anglophone Caribbean' and in the text this term is usually, although not invariably, used instead of the 'West Indies'. This requires some justification, particularly because, when a federation was established in the region, it was deliberately called The West Indies. The principal rationale for the use of 'Anglophone Caribbean' is the greater conceptual clarity which is offered by a term which identifies more distinctly the territories under discussion. Although there is a great deal of linguistic diversity in those places which once formed part of the British Empire, the English language forms their most important bond. By contrast, the term 'West Indies' has been used by many, most notably C. L. R. James, to identify all the islands of the region, whether they were subject to conquest by the British, French, Spanish, Danish or Dutch. Furthermore, the adjective 'West Indian' was for centuries associated particularly with the white European settlers and, although its appropriation by black Caribbean migrants to Britain had a liberating effect, the reversing of the racial character of the term means that its usage is still laden with ambiguities.[3] One further geographical anomaly is unresolved by either appellation. Although the term 'Anglophone Caribbean' neatly picks out British Honduras or Belize to the west, Jamaica to the north, Trinidad and the English-speaking islands of the Windwards and Leewards to the east, in cartographical terms, the Guyanese territories of mainland South America, which were conquered by the French, British and Dutch, lie outside the frame provided by the Caribbean littoral. However, the history of British Guiana has been shaped to a much greater degree by contact with British imperialism than by any influences from the Hispanophone or Lusophone countries of the continent. The most conspicuous evidence of this was the establishment of a large East-Indian population, brought to Guiana as indentured labourers in the nineteenth century.

The concept of an Anglophone Caribbean also usefully draws attention to the importance of the Caribbean Sea itself, which forms a branch of the Atlantic Ocean and constitutes one of the larger deep-water seas in the world. It is circumscribed by a chain of larger islands to the north, numerous smaller islands to the east, the mainland of South America and the Panamanian isthmus to the south and Central America to the west. In contrast to the pre-Columbian peoples of these territories, who came to the islands after the initial encounter between European and American civilisation at the end of the fifteenth century, the more recent immigrants did not develop a seafaring tradition, no doubt because for many of them the naval history of the region was intrinsic to the history of death and suffering associated with the slave trade. Nevertheless, its maritime rather than continental character was evident in the ease with which the Caribbean islands could and can be penetrated by external influences; this is manifest in the record of frequent conquest and reconquest by the European powers in the seventeenth and eighteenth centuries and in the constant transmission of a range of cultural influences to and from the region, which have generated its familiar and influential creole character.

Turning from the sea to the land, the richness and fecundity of the environment gives the appearance of hospitability to human habitation, but the geography of the region also makes life intermittently hazardous. At various times these physical dangers have had major effects on the economic and social life of the inhabitants. Those who live in the Anglophone Caribbean have generally accommodated themselves to the inherent risks but they have also propagated a broader psychological sense of unease which sometimes appears to feed metropolitan neuroses about the political stability of the region. Perhaps the most notorious dangers are those posed by the occasional hurricanes which pass westwards and northwards across the Caribbean, usually in the second half of the calendar year. The most dramatic example of human vulnerability to the winds taken from the period of this study occurred in 1961 when hundreds of residents of Belize City were killed by a hurricane and the subsequent storm surge which effectively destroyed the urban infrastructure.[4] Even during those years when weather conditions are relatively benign, heavy downpours and flooding during the rainy season are at best an inconvenience and at worst a threat to life. The Caribbean also sits on its own tectonic plate whose edges roughly describe the perimeter of the region. The very existence of the land is a product of the ancient folding of the earth's crust and the eruptions which take place along these fault lines; these in turn generate perils for the residents in the form of earthquakes and erupting volcanoes. In historical terms Jamaica has suffered the worst consequences of seismic activity: in 1692 over half of Port Royal was engulfed by the sea as a consequence of devastating tremors, while in 1907 nearly every building in Kingston was damaged by a major quake which set the city ablaze. The active volcanoes in the region are concentrated in the eastern islands; it was the French colony of Martinique which in 1902 witnessed perhaps the greatest natural disaster in the entire history of the region when an estimated 30,000 people were killed in the aftermath of the eruption of

Mount Pelée.[5] From 1995 volcanic activity in the Soufrière Hills posed an ongoing and continuous danger to the population of Montserrat that eventually led to the evacuation of the majority of the inhabitants in an operation which caused an early but minor political crisis at the start of Tony Blair's British premiership.[6]

Perhaps partly as a consequence of the unpredictability of an environment which intermittently called upon the Treasury to take up the costs of disaster relief, post-war British governments have often disclaimed the notion that they had any financial interest in the retention of the Anglophone Caribbean. These assertions marked a discontinuity, because for centuries the region had played a central role in the economic history of the British Empire. If the early generations of European settlers could do nothing about the climate or geology of the region, they could and did transform the ecology and demography to suit their commercial purposes. The catalyst which revolutionised every other aspect of life in the region was the sugar revolution of the mid-seventeenth century which began in Barbados and rapidly spread to the rest of Britain's nascent Caribbean empire.[7] It entailed the transformation of the landscape, as the majority of agricultural land was given over to a crop which originated in Asia, together with an expansion of the population, as increasing numbers of chattel slaves were transported to the region from West Africa. The profits of the sugar industry were dependent on the coercion of labour and the existence of markets willing to pay high prices for what was, at least at the outset, a luxury product rather than a staple. The subsistence of the local people required large-scale food importation and as a consequence the economy exhibited an extreme form of dependency and its fortunes fluctuated regularly. Its period of greatest success was probably the third quarter of the seventeenth century. The increase in sugar prices during those years meant that by some estimates St Kitts in the Leeward Islands was the richest colony in the empire.[8] Its wealth, and that of the other territories, continued to depend on an army of enslaved workers from Africa which reached six times the size of the white population across the Anglophone Caribbean in 1748 and 12 times the size in 1815. In Demerara in British Guiana it has been estimated that the ratio was 37 to 1 at the later date.[9] Some greater variety in agricultural production did occur and by the early twentieth century the territories were also exporting coffee, bananas and citrus fruits. Subsequently a further measure of diversification arose in the form of bauxite mining in Jamaica and Guiana and oil extraction in Trinidad, but the economies of the region rested on an exceptionally narrow and insecure base of commodity exports. One of the most compelling arguments of nationalist politicians was that the British were morally obliged to offer financial recompense for the deformation of the local economy during these centuries of imperial exploitation. Despite its persuasiveness this reasoning was rejected by metropolitan policymakers on the grounds that candidates for statehood must demonstrate their financial fitness for statehood.

Alongside the material deprivation which it entailed, by bringing people from all over the world to live in the Caribbean plantation agriculture contributed to a preoccupation with issues of skin colour in the Anglophone Caribbean which was and is inescapable. Prior to the era of decolonisation it had only been possible to justify the gross economic inequalities perpetuated by imperialism on the basis of doctrines of racial superiority, which accounted for the supremacy of white Europeans, and racial inferiority, which was deployed to defend the callous treatment of non-whites living in Asia, Africa and America. On the brink of independence, Trinidad's first Prime Minister, Eric Williams, lectured the youth of the country on their obligation to overcome this legacy of colonialism by educating their parents about the necessity of judging their fellow citizens on merit rather than skin pigmentation, while his former political rival, Albert Gomes, later insisted that his own career as a Trinidadian politician of Portuguese descent had constituted a not always successful attempt to navigate a way through the maze of the island's morbid racial prejudices.[10] Liberal injunctions to transcend the racial categories inherited from the imperial past generated an antithesis in the form of ideologies of black empowerment, as articulated in the writings and speeches of the Jamaican political activist Marcus Garvey and later the Guyanese historian, Walter Rodney. From this perspective demands for racial harmony constituted a threadbare attempt to camouflage the unmissable and persistent correlation between race and power which had not weakened in the era of decolonisation and then independence. The racial character of the Anglophone Caribbean was shaped by three historical developments: the extermination of almost the entire Amerindian population during the early colonial phase; a constant process of coerced and voluntary migration to and from Africa, Europe and Asia; and the subsequent miscegenation which rendered attempts to offer a demographic analysis based on binary classifications wholly futile. The unstable and mutable character of the categories available to describe the population ensured that the social and political force of arguments about race relied on comparative measures of 'blackness' and 'whiteness'. George E. Eaton gave some sense of the gradations and their connections to social hierarchy in Jamaica:

At the apex of the social system were the whites...in descending order there were near-whites or mustefinos, mustays of swarthy complexion but lighter than the brown-skinned mulattos, who in turn were subject to an almost endless variety of groups.... Further down the social ladder, the lower echelons grew progressively darker, passing through 'sambo' to black at the base.[11]

In more crudely political terms the free coloured population which came into existence as a consequence of sexual relationships between male European masters and female African slaves was the first to occupy the intermediary spaces between the white elites and the black masses.[12] Their political, social and economic advancement did not constitute a challenge to European political control until the early twentieth century. Before that time the existence of a class which was lighter skinned and more privileged than the black majority and darker skinned and less privileged than the white minority served as confirmation of the apparently inextricable connection between skin colour and power.

As well as the physical mixing of races, a combining of different cultural traditions took place in the Caribbean and this has had an astonishing global impact. The end of the European empires was accompanied almost everywhere by cultural renaissance and in the Anglophone Caribbean this took two potent forms: during the second trimester of the twentieth century the region became both a sporting and literary superpower by adapting European cultural practices for their own purposes. To the delight of the Caribbean public in 1950 the touring West Indies cricket team, which included Walcott, Worrell, Weekes and Ramadhin, defeated England in a Test series 3–1. With their bowling attack subsequently reinforced by Hall, Gibbs and Sobers they established a sporting superiority over England which was to last for 40 years and which became a durable source of regional pride.[13] More recently the reverence in which cricketers were once held has been transferred to track-and-field athletes. The early success of Don Quarrie, Hasely Crawford and Merlene Ottey at Olympic and World Championships has reached its culmination with Usain Bolt's unprecedented dominance of the sprint events. While the region's sportsmen have demonstrated a discipline and physical prowess which has frequently outmatched that of the old colonial powers, Caribbean writers have posed an intellectual challenge to imperial complacency. A short list of notable figures includes authors as diverse as Jean Rhys, Roger Mais, E. R. Braithwaite, Sam Selvon, George Lamming, Sylvia Wynter, Derek

Walcott, Kamau Brathwaite, V. S. Naipaul and Jamaica Kincaid. Whether it was Braithwaite's direct attack on bigotry in the imperial metropolis; Naipaul's magnification of the banal failure to establish a stable, alternative identity to that imposed by the European colonisers; or Wynter's emphasis on the way in which British influence pushed the peoples of the region to the margins of their own culture and society, the attitudes on display in their work have constituted a disavowal of the misleading but edifying narrative of an orderly process of decolonisation.[14] At a popular level, Caribbean music has also often been infused with ideological content: both Jamaican reggae and Trinidadian calypso are well adapted to the transmission of political messages. During the era of independence musicians such as Bob Marley and Mighty Sparrow provided a commentary on events in Jamaica and Trinidad respectively. As a consequence of migration to the old imperial metropolis ska and reggae have had a particular influence on British popular music since the 1960s and have carried much of their political content with them.

Themes in the history of the Anglophone Caribbean

Before turning to the history of individual territories, it seems important to note that the experience of colonialism across the Anglophone Caribbean is broadly comparable. It is this measure of historical uniformity which provides coherence to the general argument which follows. From the seventeenth century onwards, developments in the whole of the Anglophone Caribbean were governed by two sets of binary relationships: the shifting balance of power between metropolitan and peripheral interests, on the one hand, and the entrenched and unequal division between a local oligarchy and the labouring classes within the periphery, on the other. The intercourse between peripheral and metropolitan elites was mediated by constitutional and legislative action, and the key themes were the peripheral elite's defence of their economic privileges and political liberty and the metropolitan elite's concern with the ramifications of West Indian policy on the British domestic economy and other overseas interests. By the late eighteenth century the debate had cohered around a clash between advocates of slavery and protectionism and those who supported emancipation and free trade. Although the Caribbean oligarchs were defeated in this contest they retained some residual influence in Westminster in the middle of the twentieth century. By contrast, relations between the colonial oligarchs and the labouring classes were regulated entirely by coercive means. The continued political and economic subordination of most of the people was, as the oligarchs themselves argued in their disputes with the metropolitan authorities, essential to the profitability of their enterprises. However, it also necessitated a constant defence of order, which was synonymous with the status quo. Oligarchical neuroses about proletarian insurrection were fully justified by the plentiful and ongoing evidence of quotidian resistance on the plantations and intermittent popular rebellions.[15] Although it is more difficult to recover the views of the majority of the people who lived in the Caribbean under colonialism, the extent of resistance illustrates that disorder, in the form of either non-cooperation or violent counter-attacks against colonial rule, was a means of challenging the perpetuation of exploitation and disenfranchisement.

Gross disparities in political influence and economic power were a persistent feature of the region from the establishment of a British colonial presence in the Caribbean during the first half of the seventeenth century to the present day but there have also been conspicuous changes in the social and political life of the region since that time. It is possible to identify three particularly significant phases. The first began with the establishment of the plantation system after the initial acquisitions of the early seventeenth century and was marked by increased capital investment in the newly acquired territories, the gradual replacement of free and indentured labour by slave labour and the ever-growing commitment to the export of sugar as the defining purpose of the territories. During this period West Indian planters exercised increasing influence in the metropolis and used it to guarantee preferential access to the British market and a reliable supply of unfree workers from Africa. The second phase began with the rise of abolitionist sentiment in Britain in the late eighteenth century and was characterised by efforts to circumscribe the influence of the Caribbean plantocracy. The key events of the period were the decision of the British Parliament to abolish the trade in slaves in 1807 and then to enforce a policy of emancipation in 1833–1834. These years also yield plentiful evidence of the extent of resistance on the part of Caribbean labour, which continued after abolition as former slaves discovered that the change in their legal status did not end their impoverishment or marginality. The continuation of the plantation system as the dominant form of activity narrowed the range of options for the newly freed people of the region and led to significant attacks on the estates themselves in Dominica in 1844, St Vincent in 1862 and Jamaica in 1865. In the metropolis there was a widespread belief that the uncompromising attitude of the planters was responsible for much of the disorder in the Anglophone Caribbean;

this led the British government to abolish the representative system on Jamaica and the other islands and to extend the Crown Colony system of government, which had already been established on the territories that had been ceded by France during the previous century. The eradication of the political influence of the oligarchs was not completed until the third phase during which nascent trade unions and political parties demanded democratic reform and the alleviation of working conditions. The emergence of liberationist ideas in the Anglophone Caribbean in the early twentieth century was a product of various ideological influences, including elements of European liberalism and socialism as well as more Afrocentric, communalist notions of black empowerment. Nationalists articulated the connections between political and economic grievances and Bell has argued that for them 'political independence was largely the means of attaining the legitimate power to try to transform society so as to achieve social justice.'[16] The metropolitan government reluctantly conceded universal adult suffrage and the expansion of popular representation in both the executive and the legislature but remained sceptical of ambitious nationalist plans to diversify the economy and distribute the wealth of the territories on a more equal basis. Nevertheless popular participation in politics, which had gathered pace in the surrounding Hispanophone and Francophone territories long before, was an unprecedented development in the Anglophone Caribbean.

Barbados is an obvious place to start examining the question of how these developments affected particular territories, because the Barbadian oligarchs were deservedly famous for the tenacity with which they defended their interests against metropolitan interference and the thoroughness with which they colonised the island with sugar plantations. The first elected General Assembly of freeholders was established in 1639 and the plantocracy clung on to a representative system of government for the next 300 years even when other islands became Crown Colonies in the late nineteenth century.[17] Their constitutional supremacy partly reflected their reputation for greater economic efficiency, which was in turn a consequence of higher levels of residency that contrasted with the Leewards where absenteeism prevailed. Alongside the vigorous defence of their material interests the local oligarchy also promoted an ideology of Barbadian exceptionalism which was based on the intimacy of their ties to the British metropolis. The notion of Barbados as a 'Little England' ready to leap to the defence of 'Big England' was memorably described in George Lamming's novel *In the Castle of My Skin*.[18] What Lamming also portrayed were the consequences of the popular uprising of 1937 for a small village and the plantation to which it was attached. The rebellion of that year was the culmination of a counter-tradition of popular resistance on Barbados which, because of the scarcity and partiality of much of the source material describing the lives of the island's workers, is difficult to uncover. In his book *Natural Rebels*, Hilary Beckles uses the sources which are available to describe how women working on plantations in Barbados during the era of slavery engaged in non-violent resistance, flight from the workplace, attacks on the economic infrastructure and even armed insurrection.[19] Both the Anglophilia and insurrectionary traditions of Barbadian political life continued to be represented in the mid-twentieth century era of demotic politics by Grantley Adams, whose ambition was to transplant Asquithian liberal traditions to the region, and by Clennell Wickham, who urged a policy of organised resistance to the continuing dominance of the plantocracy.[20]

Like Barbados and the other Anglophone territories, Jamaica's past has been defined by the history of slavery and sugar production but it has often been differentiated from them on the basis of two superlatives: it is the largest island and the one furthest from the others. Philip Sherlock has pointed out that Jamaican isolationist sentiment, which was expressed in the 1961 referendum which rejected continued participation in the West Indian federation, was not only a product of distance but also of the geography of the island itself. Whereas the inhabitants of the smaller islands had no choice but to face the sea, Sherlock argued that Jamaicans relished the prospect of a retreat to the mountainous interior and turned to them for moral uplift. As well as being a source of spiritual sustenance the highlands were also a place of refuge for those wishing to challenge colonial authority, most famously the Maroons.[21] As the name indicates, the tradition of *marronage* or flight from the plantations began in the era of Spanish colonialism which ended with the British conquest in 1655. By this time, the Maroons had already established their own settlements and posed a continuous challenge to British efforts to extend their administrative control. During 1739–1740 an unstable modus vivendi was established in the form of a number of treaties but at the outset of the French Revolutionary Wars, the British decided to eradicate the Maroon villages because they were a potential source of insurrection. In 1796 after months of fighting, a policy of enforced deportations was implemented which obliterated their culture. If the Maroons are generally taken to be symbols of Jamaican resistance to British imperialism, the free coloured people of the island are sometimes associated with a tradition of collaborationism. Some were able to obtain a degree of economic independence by becoming shopkeepers or engaging in artisanal work such as millinery but they were excluded from the rights of full citizenship. When the nationalist movement emerged in the twentieth century it inherited Jamaican society's acute consciousness of the fine gradations of skin colour and was hampered by notions that a lighter skinned or brown middle class dominated the movement at the expense of darker-skinned or black working class people. One of the oddities of the conflict between Norman Manley and Alexander Bustamante was that although the two men were cousins and of a mixed but common ancestry Manley was often seen as a spokesman for the former group and Bustamante for the latter.

Identifying the members of the Leeward Islands has sometimes been problematic. They constitute the northwestern outposts of the Lesser Antilles and are named in recognition of the fact that they are reached by the trade winds after they have crossed the Windwards, but these basic geographical facts do not establish where the frontiers of the group might lie. Dominica to the south was once governed as part of the Leewards before being transferred to the Windwards. The American Virgin Islands to the northwest constituted part of the Anglophone Caribbean but were never annexed to the British West Indies, and established closer links with the American mainland than the other islands. As non-Anglophone members of the Leeward Islands St Martin, St Barthelemy and Guadeloupe contribute to the linguistic diversity of the sub-region. Of the Anglophone group, the small territories of the British Virgin Islands, Montserrat, Nevis and Anguilla were the subject of constantly mutating administrative arrangements. What is clear and has been apparent since the seventeenth century is that Antigua and St Christopher are the core members of the Anglophone Leewards. It is the latter island, which is universally known as St Kitts, whose experience of decolonisation will be examined in more detail. Three aspects of its past had a particular effect on the way in which the imperial episode ended. The first is that, after Thomas Warner was commissioned by Charles I to colonise the island in the 1620s, sugar interests prevailed even more completely in the history of the island than in Barbados or neighbouring Antigua; whereas in the latter two territories a more diverse economy began to emerge in the first half of the twentieth century, imperial reservations about the economic viability of St Kitts in the 1960s and 1970s were sustained by its continuing and complete dependence on sugar exports as a source of revenue. Secondly, St Kitts had a complex constitutional relationship with the other territories of the Leewards. In 1816 the British government divided the group into two administrative sub-units, one of which comprised St Kitts, Nevis, Anguilla and the Virgin Islands. Following many further reorganisations, in 1882 the first three of these territories became a single Presidency within the Leewards federation which had been established 11 years earlier. Because the Presidency was administered from the Kittitian capital of Basseterre it was perhaps inevitable that secessionist sentiment should develop to some degree on neighbouring Nevis and even more strongly on the more distant and smaller island of Anguilla. The constitutional controversies which ensued culminated in 1969 with a full-blown late imperial crisis. Thirdly, as a consequence of their role in the labour rebellions of the 1930s, Kittitians acquired a reputation for labour militancy. The 1948 strike on the island which will be examined in the next chapter evoked memories of the confrontation between the estate workers and the local oligarchy in 1935, when three workers were killed by local defence forces.[22]

Grenada, which is the most southerly of the Windwards grouping to the south of the Leewards, was the island least affected by the popular rebellions of the 1930s. As in the case of the other territories in the group, namely Dominica, St Lucia and St Vincent, Grenada fell under British control as a consequence of victory in the eighteenth-century wars with France. The Treaty of Paris of 1763 which ceded the island to Britain was the prelude to further struggles for control of Grenada, but by the end of the Napoleonic wars the British had strengthened their hold and in the following century, it was anglicised to a greater extent than the other Windward territories. Migration became a common experience for many Grenadians in the late nineteenth and twentieth centuries and, because of its proximity, Trinidad was a common destination.[23] One of the primary factors influencing the outflow of people was the unemployment and underemployment associated with Grenada's relatively high population density. As a consequence the culture of the island was closely tied to that of the larger Anglophone territories as well as to the United States and Great Britain which eventually became alternative destinations for Grenadian migrants. The export of labour abroad and the decision of many local oligarchs to forsake sugar production ameliorated some of the tensions caused by land scarcity. The relatively peaceful circumstances of the 1930s generated a certain smugness on behalf of local elites but, even though the precise circumstances were different, the class divisions on the island were as sharp as anywhere else. George Brizan, who was a Grenadian historian and politician, noted that by 1950 'Grenada remained a society dominated by a tiny clique of planter-merchants and professionals... the Grenadian peasantry was one of the largest in the Caribbean relative to size, young, predominantly black, largely illiterate.'[24] Despite the supposed social insulation provided by the existence of an independent peasantry and the diversification of production into cocoa, nutmeg and bananas, conditions of disease, poor housing and penury in the countryside made an eventual challenge to the status quo inevitable; the specific form it took under the leadership of Eric Gairy was wholly unexpected.

Like Grenada, Trinidad had experience of other forms of European colonialism. It was a Spanish colony for three centuries after 1498, which was longer than the period of British imperial control. Its first Prime Minister, Eric Williams, offered a damning judgement on the conclusion of Madrid's control in 1797: 'Spanish colonialism on its death bed had ended in nothing.'[25] Williams's assessment is true to the extent that in the nineteenth century the political and social life of the colony was utterly transformed by British imperialism and not much remained of Hispanic influence, with some exceptions such as the names of places and the character of the island's traditional folk music. In the middle of the nineteenth century the economic supremacy of the Trinidad oligarchy was threatened by a combination of increased labour costs as a consequence of emancipation and downward pressure on sugar prices because of competition from European beet sugar. They responded by transporting large numbers of indentured labourers from South Asia. It has been estimated that 143,900 contract labourers migrated to Trinidad between 1838 and 1918.[26] The great majority of these were East Indians and, as the former African slave population and their descendants increasingly sought employment in the towns, they occupied the bottom rung of the status ladder in their capacity as low-wage workers tied to the plantations. When organised opposition to the perpetuation of British colonial control emerged, it confronted the problem of how to reconcile African, East Indian and European populations who generally lived apart from one another. After being elected to the island's legislature in 1925, Arthur Andrew Cipriani became a legendary figure in the political history of Trinidad precisely because of his success in transcending these divisions: as a Corsican he represented European influence but he aligned himself with Indian Trinidadians campaigning for improved conditions on the plantations and with the nationalist movement that was developing among middle-class African-Trinidadians. His reputation was consolidated by the success of C. L. R. James's early biography which was written while Cipriani was still alive. Less fortunately, the lionising of Cipriani formed part of a tradition of personalist politics in Trinidad which inhibited the emergence of an effective party system. It also infected metropolitan thinking and became manifest in the British obsession with questions of political leadership, which was frequently accompanied by a disregard for wider socioeconomic conditions. In the case of Trinidad the British assumed that Eric Williams was the candidate best qualified to maintain order on the island.

Unlike the islands, the two mainland territories of British Honduras and British Guiana stood outside the West Indies Federation when it was created in 1958. The former was psychologically isolated from the Anglophone Caribbean and this reflected both its geographical distance from the Eastern Caribbean and its distinctive economic history which was dominated by the logwood industry. It has a small but distinctive historiography, much of it the product of energetic research by Nigel Bolland.[27] In order to draw out the broader themes the focus of this analysis will be on the other continental territory, British Guiana. When the distinguished Guianese historian Walter Rodney undertook a detailed history of his own country he gave greater emphasis to environmental factors than was evident in his earlier work on African colonial history. The defence of the Guianese coastal strip, along which the majority of the population lived, required the local plantocracy to maintain an infrastructure of damming and drainage. Rodney estimated that in establishing a viable agricultural system, slaves in Guiana moved '100 million tons of heavy water logged clay with shovel in hand, while enduring conditions of perpetual mud and water.' Despite these exhausting precautions the coast remained vulnerable to flooding and drought.[28] The grim conditions on the plantations encouraged migration to the towns after emancipation and, as in the case of Trinidad, indentured workers were imported, first from Portuguese Madeira and then from South Asia, to remedy the labour shortage. In 1905 African workers in towns and Indian labourers in the countryside rebelled in protest at conditions of work, low wages and irregular employment. Plantation workers on the sugar estates, domestic servants, dock workers and the unemployed all participated. The uprising had little ideological coherence, and much of the anger was directed at the small Portuguese bourgeoisie rather than at the colonial administration.[29] It failed to dent the power wielded by a handful of corporations which was satirised in the appellation of 'Booker's Guiana', in reference to the pervasive influence of the British-based company of Booker-McConnell. The company had been founded by Josias Booker in the early nineteenth century and dominated Guianese sugar production. This tendency towards monopoly was subsequently replicated in bauxite extraction: during the twentieth century the Canadian company Alcan established a dominant position in Guianese mining. At the outset of the 1950s Cheddi Jagan and Forbes Burnham finally offered an ideological programme which would channel resentment at the exploitation of both African and East Indian workers by a tiny economic and political elite which repatriated profits to Britain and North America. The conflict between commercial interests backed by London and Washington and a nationalist movement which eventually fractured along racial lines made the Guianese episode one of the most tragic in the story of British decolonisation.

Interpreting the end of empire in the Anglophone Caribbean

The end of British political control was a seminal event in the history of the Anglophone Caribbean and some differences have emerged over how it ought to be interpreted. Four broad strands in the historiography can be identified: firstly, a set of vindicatory writings authored either by British officials themselves or those sympathetic to them; secondly, inculpatory accounts by critics of the nationalist leadership of the independent Caribbean; thirdly, what might be called contextual interpretations which stress international factors, including the influence of the United States and the Cold War; and, finally, critical narratives which focus explicitly on the inadequacies of British policymaking. There is obviously some overlap between these categories: the vindicatory narratives, for example, may stress the role of international factors, such as the Cold War, and the internationalist accounts may be critical of British policymaking. However, it is the fourth of these which has proved the least robust and the substantive chapters of this book constitute an effort to revive it.

John Mordecai's book *The West Indies: The Federal Negotiations* is an informed, intelligent account and also the founding document of the vindicatory tradition. Mordecai was a colonial civil servant who rose to become deputy to the Governor General of the federation, Lord Hailes, and the sense of affiliation he felt for Hailes personally and for the federation as a concept is evident in their unpublished correspondence.[30] One notable problem with attempting to summarise the purpose of his book is that Mordecai does not itemise the themes and arguments in either an introduction or a conclusion. What his narrative offers is a lucid analysis of the quotidian problems which emerged in establishing and maintaining the federation. The relentless detail he provides about the many disagreements between Caribbean politicians serves to magnify their role in the troubled constitutional history of the era, while leaving the influence of British officials and politicians out of focus at the margins. There is, for example, no mention at all of the British Secretary of State for the Colonies between 1954 and 1959, Alan Lennox-Boyd.[31] Mordecai's version may be supplemented with the memoirs of two of the most influential Caribbean Governors of the time, Hugh Foot and Kenneth Blackburne. The former expresses some sympathy for the nationalist leaders of the region while carefully itemising their failings; the latter evinces a distaste for what he came to regard as the rowdy and destructive politics of the region.[32] At the end of the 1970s, Elizabeth Wallace augmented the vindicatory tradition. In her analysis of Britain's role in the Caribbean she reiterated the familiar theme that 'by establishing liberal political institutions it implanted a tradition of respect for parliamentary democracy.' As a supplement to this view she suggested that social failures were largely a consequence of demographic pressures which outran determined imperial efforts to improve health and education.[33] Even the more balanced analysis provided by Ashton and Killingray in their introductory essay to an invaluable compendium of primary sources from the period veered perilously close to assimilating the official view expressed in the documents collected. Although they acknowledged the 'patrician disdain' with which small island leaders like William H. Bramble of Montserrat were treated by metropolitan policymakers, they argued:

> By and large CO officials were reasonably understanding of the problems encountered by West Indian politicians and the way in which they were handled...although the constant bickering and the rifts that opened up between rival personalities tended to strain the patience of officials who had spent a long time trying to create the federation and get it off the ground.[34]

One might expect arguments of this kind to spark a radical counter-tradition in which the role of local actors in promoting the ideals of unity, liberation and equality are reasserted. However the one thing which the leading figures on the Caribbean left have had in common with Mordecai and Wallace is a determination to highlight the negligence of the nationalist leadership. Numerous writer-activists from the region, including C. L. R. James, Trevor Munroe and Richard Hart, have argued that the corruption and inequality of the post-independence era was a consequence of the inadequacies of the first and second generation of union and party leaders. In four volumes Richard Hart has provided a comprehensive alternative history of the end of empire, which deals principally with Jamaica but also, on occasions, with other territories in the Caribbean, including Guiana.[35] Although part of his purpose is to expose the hypocrisy of British colonialism, many of Hart's harshest criticisms in the final volume were reserved for the two largest political parties and particularly the PNP from which he had been expelled by Manley. His attacks on the PNP leadership were echoed by Trevor Munroe who argued that the party represented only bourgeois interests and embraced a 'fundamentally British' form of politics.[36] This historiographical tendency to indict the nationalist leadership is reinforced by the teleological approach adopted by Marable and Bolland in searching for the origins of Caribbean authoritarianism and its transmission from the colonial period. Bolland examines the manner in which the necessary struggle for better working conditions undertaken by the trade union movement established a tradition of autocratic leadership.[37] Marable's acknowledgement of the liberationist elements in nationalist thinking is, at best, grudging. He argues that bourgeois nationalists 'frequently assimilated the authoritarian style of the former colonial bureaucrats, but under specific conditions, fractions could also advance egalitarian and democratic agendas, which, at least rhetorically were consistent with the anti-colonial agitation of the 1940s and 1950s.'[38] Most of these inculpatory accounts of the rise of Caribbean nationalism do not take the rhetorical commitment to popular liberation seriously despite the success of nationalists in obtaining trade union recognition, universal suffrage and popular control of first the legislative and then the executive functions of government. When the emphasis placed on collaborationism between the elites of the metropolis and the periphery entirely displaces the confrontational aspects of the struggle for independence, the record is in danger of becoming distorted.

While both the vindicatory and inculpatory traditions were already becoming entrenched as the Anglophone Caribbean moved towards independence, the most significant historiographical development of the last decade has been a new focus on international factors, and in particular on the role of the United States. Cary Fraser established this tradition with a book whose title, *Ambivalent Anti-Colonialism*, summarised his assessment of the attitudes struck by American policymakers in dealing with the region.[39] In the last 10 years, Rabe on British Guiana, Parker on Jamaica and Trinidad and Cox-Alomar on the Eastern Caribbean have all stressed the significance of Washington's influence which was exercised either directly, through economic, intelligence and diplomatic agencies, or indirectly, by asserting their commanding position in the Cold War alliance with Britain.[40] Perhaps because of the distancing effect of the Atlantic Ocean, this tradition of scholarship has been rather sceptical of the justifications provided by British policymakers for their actions. Parker, for example, has highlighted the manner in which the conspicuous inadequacy of imperial administration raised issues both for American security, which would be threatened by the violent upheavals which might result if social conditions did not improve, and for American domestic politics, because of the ties between political activism in the United States and the Caribbean. Rabe has exhibited the hostile response which the emergence of opposition to their authority in Guiana elicited from the imperial authorities. More specifically he exposed British complicity in the plot to unseat Cheddi Jagan which originated inside the Kennedy administration and finally reached fruition in 1964. The stress which these works place on transatlantic collaboration and occasional conflict has been important in establishing the Cold War context in which British policy operated. They also suggested that American involvement in the Anglophone Caribbean was episodic; as a consequence, these authors have been less preoccupied with the continuous conflicts between nationalists and imperial administrators over constitutional reform that is the concern of the final group.

The basis for this fourth, critical tradition of writing on the end of empire in the region can be found in the indictments of British policymakers contained in the memoirs of nationalist politicians. In this sense Mordecai's attempt to justify the British policies he upheld as an imperial official through a demonstration of the failings of regional nationalism has its equivalent in a parallel set of writings which provide a perspective from the other side of the political conflict. However, as though to validate Mordecai's views on the divisiveness of anti-colonial politics, the attack on the British colonial record in these works has been almost drowned out by the deafening roar of old scores being settled. This tendency reached heroic levels in the case of the autobiographies of

Patrick Solomon in Trinidad and Wynter Crawford in Barbados, significant parts of which were devoted to attacking the respective records of their political foes, Albert Gomes and Grantley Adams.[41] Eric Williams's more detailed and analytical account of what he described as his political education, *Inward Hunger*, is not free from this tendency either and is made less persuasive because of his willingness to unleash the egocentric elements of his character at every opportunity.[42] As a consequence, it has been left to the biographers of some of the key nationalist leaders to provide a more rounded and less partisan treatment. Particularly sympathetic discussions can be found in Sherlock's book about Norman Manley and Hoyos's admiring narrative of Grantley Adams's life.[43] Williams's numerous biographers have usually struck a reasonable balance between critical distance and sympathetic analysis.[44] Although such works deal incidentally with the confrontations between peripheral and metropolitan actors, the most effective critique of British policy in the Caribbean remains Gordon Lewis's *The Growth of the Modern West Indies* which was published in 1968.[45] Since Lewis's book there has been no attempt to relate the deficiencies of British policymaking to the conflict which they engendered with anti-colonialism across the territories of the Anglophone Caribbean. This inevitably raises the question of whether, in an odd reversal of the usual historiographical trend in imperial history, British policymakers have been robbed of agency, or more tellingly, of responsibility.

Themes and arguments

At the outset of this introductory chapter some of the key arguments of the book were set out in unvarnished fashion, and it is now time to enter some caveats while elaborating further on the central thesis. The purpose of this book is not to rehabilitate the reputations of the governments of the independent Anglophone Caribbean. At their worst, such as the cases of Gairy in Grenada and Burnham in Guyana, the newly independent states of the region proved even more repressive than the colonial state which they replaced. Even in those countries which have received praise for retaining democratic traditions and achieving a measure of economic development, such as Barbados, the post-independence governments have been unable to establish an egalitarian society free from the autocratic tendencies of the past. What is required is an effort to balance an account of the intrinsic flaws of the anti-colonial movement with some acknowledgement of its achievement in pressing the case for the enfranchisement of the people, the demission of power to local representatives and the promulgation of new economic policies which would address the inadequacies of an imperial system that kept the majority of the population in penury. It is only possible to sustain such an interpretation by bringing British policy at the end of empire into sharper focus, and this also has a number of risks. Over the last 30 years, scholars have been engaged in the essential task of restoring agency to colonial subjects. In this context, a project which requires that closer attention be paid to what British officials and politicians said to one another about these subjects may appear atavistic. In the case of the Anglophone Caribbean it can be justified on three grounds. The first derives from what has already been said about the extant picture of collaborative decolonisation which can only be redrawn by offering a clearer sense of the attitudes which metropolitan and peripheral actors expressed and which were considerably more hostile than has so far been allowed. The second is historiographical: there has been no detailed account of British policymaking in the region to compare with the numerous studies of, for example, the Attlee government's policies towards India, the role of the Eden government in the Suez crisis or the later evolution of British policy towards the Central African Federation and Southern Rhodesia. There is no Caribbean equivalent to the work of R. J. Moore, Scott Lucas or Philip Murphy, with the single and notable exception of the long, analytical introduction to the relevant volume of the *British Documents on the End of Empires* series written by Ashton and Killingray.[46] Thirdly, in theory, it ought to be possible to study the records of the imperial centre without assimilating the views expressed in them. Whether this can be achieved in practice is another question but one that can only be answered by attempting it.

The hostility between nationalism and late imperialism can be illustrated by examining some of the different ideas about order and independence which prevailed at the end of empire. Metropolitan policymakers had a developmentalist view which portrayed the achievement of independence as analogous to a child's attainment of maturity after a period of careful schooling. The colonial power took on a paternal role which necessitated disciplinary action in cases of insubordinate behaviour. When the British resorted to coercion in Guiana in 1953 or in Anguilla in 1969, it was justified as a regrettable response to the puerile behaviour of nationalist politicians. Although this can appear as a caricature of official thinking, the files of the Colonial Office are replete with references to the callowness and irrationality of the Caribbean's leading nationalist politicians. The condescension is as evident in the views of those who wished to encourage Britain's colonial wards by offering constitutional advance as an inducement as in those of unreconstructed imperialists. In 1952 during his time as Governor of the Leewards, Kenneth Blackburne attempted to persuade a sceptical Colonial Office that they really should show some trust in their colonial wards. He advised: 'it is absolutely vital that we should stick to my policy of giving these people as much responsibility as possible and accepting their proposals even if we believe them to be wrong – unless of course they put up some proposal which involves breach of faith or some essential principle.' According to Blackburne this method had been successful in Antigua where, following the first elections under universal suffrage, the newly elected nationalists were 'extremely careful not to put up silly proposals – and indeed have not done so for the past ten months.' The principle ought, he proposed, to be extended to St Kitts but Blackburne acknowledged that the labour leader in that territory, Robert Bradshaw, was 'a man of such incredible conceit (really an acute inferiority complex) that he is always liable to do some crazy thing.'[47]

Some of the first generation of anti-colonial activists in the periphery were accustomed to the lofty disdain of imperial thinking and even assimilated the notion that gratitude was due to the imperial power for concessions obtained from the metropolitan centre. Men such as Cipriani, T. A. Marryshow and Hubert Critchlow initiated campaigns for democratisation and trade union reform in Trinidad, Grenada and Guiana, and were sufficiently appreciative of the meliorist reforms which were eventually offered that in their later careers they baulked at the implications of demolishing the entire imperial edifice. Gordon Lewis has noted how the Guianese leader's attitude to universal suffrage changed: 'even there the father of Guyanese unionism, Hubert Critchlow, whose British Guiana Labour Union had advocated the reform as far back as 1925, himself came to feel some wavering doubts late in the day about giving the vote to people who might be fooled, as he saw it, by any kind of thing.'[48] The generation which followed Critchlow were more explicit in emphasising the liberationist and egalitarian connotations of independence. This was perhaps most evident in those movements which promoted the reinvigoration of the black African heritage of the Caribbean. After his return to Jamaica in 1957, Claudius Henry exposed his followers 'to the unapologetic militant, anti-colonialism in Rastafarian ideology.'[49] By 1960 Henry's African Reformed Church was engaged in an armed confrontation with Jamaica's security forces. Although Henry was operating at the margins of Jamaican anti-colonialism by this stage scepticism about imperial apologetics and the requirement for a liberation which extended to social, cultural and economic fields was common currency among revolutionary Marxists, reformist Fabians and even cautious liberals. It was possible for Eric Williams, whose People's National Movement represented prudent middle-class sentiment on Trinidad, to affirm the requirement for a cultural renaissance in a speech to an audience in Woodford Square in August 1955: 'The Negro, or the Indian for that matter, will not achieve moral status until he achieves economic and political status.... Only a few years ago, Nehru's status was that of a political gaolbird, India's status that of a colony. Today India, having achieved economic and political status, enjoys moral status.'[50] As the South Asian precedent suggested, Caribbean nationalists believed that to achieve their ambition of autonomy a confrontation with British imperialism was necessary.

For the British, the agonist thinking of the new generation of political leaders imperilled plans for a collaborative transition to independence. The labour rebellions of the late 1930s portended that rising discontent with the inegalitarian economic system might sweep away the political status quo in a flood of anti-imperialist sentiment. In some respects this worked to the advantage of the nationalist leadership: metropolitan vigilance against potential insurgency could make even radical nationalist politicians appear as worthwhile collaborators. Furthermore, although they were populist figures themselves and committed to a liberationist form of politics, many of those advocating constitutional reform were nervous about the consequences of metropolitan overreaction in the face of anti-colonial protests. The potential for the emergence of a more revolutionary politics based on ideals of communism or black empowerment challenged the assumption that mainstream nationalist parties were the only possible inheritors of the authority once exercised by the British. Thus it was Norman Manley who first expelled the Marxist faction from the PNP in 1952 and then dealt with the apparent threat posed to a stable transition to independence by raiding the camps of Claudius Henry's Rastafarian supporters in 1960. Such actions have fed the historiographical tradition that emphasises the collaborationist attitude of local nationalism. However the politics of order was more complicated than has sometimes been acknowledged and differences became manifest in five distinct areas of concern: regional unity, labour disputes, potential racial conflict, the Cold War and development economics.

The establishment in 1958 of a new federal polity called The West Indies was the culmination of 10 years of negotiation about what form political integration should take. The capitalisation of the definite article was deliberate: this was to be a single country united by a common Caribbean culture set on a course towards independence, at which point it would have the collective material resources to act as an effective guarantor of regional stability. While such hopes were widely shared they were given a different emphasis by different actors. For politicians in the Caribbean the overwhelming desire was to ensure independence from colonial control and when it became evident that federation was slowing rather than expediting this process, centrifugal tendencies were reinforced. The absence of any guarantees of federal independence buttressed Caribbean parochialism, as represented by Bustamante in Jamaica, and resulted in the defeat of the regional cosmopolitanism promoted by the majority of the nationalist leadership. For the British the maintenance of order and good government in the federation provided a warrant for the next stage in the process of decolonisation. This generated an equivocating attitude among metropolitan policymakers who both feared that an early demission of power would lead to chaos in the region and recognised that the slow, incrementalist approach to constitutional reform which they championed risked generating resentment and an upsurge in isolationist sentiment on the islands. As the Jamaican referendum of 1961 and the failure of negotiations for an Eastern Caribbean federation showed they were overly vigilant in their concern for the former and paid insufficient attention to the latter possibility.

The continuation of industrial relations controversies into the postwar era provided, on the British account, both compelling evidence of the dangers entailed in transferring power to the periphery and a rationale for doing so. Memories of the riots of the late 1930s persisted and became an enduring source of apprehension in the metropolis. Strikes in St Kitts in 1948 and Grenada in 1951 augmented metropolitan neuroses. The British were reluctant to devolve authority to labour leaders who they regarded as irresponsible but expected constitutional advance to mitigate the anti-imperialist tone of labour protests. Some of the most earnest tutorials they offered nationalist politicians during the course of their apprenticeship pertained to the necessity of containing industrial unrest. Following a period of supervision British policymakers hoped that labour leaders would increasingly be forced to take account of the interests of overseas capital on which the region was still dependent. Nevertheless, they remained sceptical that nationalist leaders would assimilate the lesson and they relied increasingly on the handful of politicians, often at the periphery of the labour movement, whom they regarded as responsible, most notably Norman Manley. Even more, conservative nationalist leaders such as Manley argued that political independence required that greater attention be paid to the inegalitarianism of Caribbean society and that labour was entitled to some recompense for centuries of economic exploitation. From their perspective the riots of the 1930s had played a decisive role in forcing the imperial power to finally pay some attention to the requirements of economic justice and constitutional advance.

The politics of race, both in terms of the racial attitudes of British policymakers and the racial divisions within particular societies, were another potential source of disorder. Caribbean politicians and writers have been a good deal more ingenuous than their British counterparts in discussing the role which assumptions about race have played in shaping their societies. In Jamaica the differences between the brown middle class and a black proletariat remained a preoccupation, while in Guiana and Trinidad the Indian and African populations increasingly divided along party lines from the 1950s onwards. Although British imperial administrators prided themselves on the greater racial tolerance which was evident in the Anglophone Caribbean compared to the United States, elite attitudes were underpinned by racial presuppositions. In December 1942, the American representative on the Caribbean Commission, Charles Taussig met Winston Churchill for a general discussion on Caribbean and international affairs. The British Prime Minister expatiated very broadly on the racial politics of empire and explained: 'We will not let the Hottentots by popular vote throw the white people into the sea, nor let the Syrians by popular vote throw out the Jews.'[51] Although Churchill did not take a great interest in the affairs of the Caribbean it was during his 1951–1955 premiership that a debate began over restrictions on immigration from the empire, which revealed a great deal about British assumptions and became entangled with the fate of the Caribbean federation. While frequently accusing Caribbean politicians of 'anti-white' prejudice, metropolitan discussions of such issues were themselves predicated on the assumption that the mixing of races was likely to lead to disorder.

The politics of the Cold War has become the subject of some historiographical interest, but it was not the foremost consideration of British policymakers in the region. For one relatively brief period in 1952–1953 an outbreak of McCarthyite panic gripped the Anglophone Caribbean; with this exception, British imperial strategists tended to be sanguine about the difficulties which seemed certain to attend any effort by Moscow to promote communism in the region. By contrast, Washington's influence was inescapable and was particularly evident in the economy, where Texaco, for example, developed a significant role in the nascent oil industry of Trinidad, and in the defence field, where the United States acquired bases across the region during the Second World War. Direct American pressure was evident in the disputes over the leadership of Trinidad and British Guiana where both Eric Williams and Cheddi Jagan were identified in Washington as troublemakers. The former was provided with a degree of protection by British policymakers who regarded him as a potential ally against the forces of disorder, while the latter was sacrificed, at least partly to appease the Kennedy administration. More broadly the British were also concerned that the process of decolonisation should be endorsed by the United Nations and one of the reasons for their advocacy of federation was their concern that the smaller territories would not be welcomed into the UN or the Commonwealth. When the federation collapsed they adopted a policy of Associated Statehood for these territories on the basis that it was a method of decolonisation approved by the UN.

The fifth aspect of the politics of order and independence in the Anglophone Caribbean concerns the relationship between metropolitan and peripheral economies which were characterised by the dependence of the latter on the former. British officials and politicians, who were preoccupied with guaranteeing economic and political continuity at the end of empire, also regarded decolonisation as an opportunity to pursue domestic retrenchment by curtailing financial assistance directed overseas. A countervailing tendency was evident in efforts to uphold the principle that the economic conditions which led to the upheavals of the 1930s required a programme of development which necessitated an injection of metropolitan capital in the form of development funding. Although the British government was anxious to avoid additional burdens on the Treasury, they feared that the underdevelopment of some of the smaller territories meant that they would never adequately obtain genuine independence outside a federation. The question of whether and to what extent this funding should be extended into the independence period also exposed tensions in anti-colonial thinking. Despite constant demands that the constitutional privileges enjoyed by the metropolitan authorities should be eliminated, anti-colonial nationalists asserted that Britain had an obligation to continue to provide grants and loans. This appeared to compromise the ideas of autonomy which they espoused in other spheres. For the nationalists, contemporary

British obligations to offer financial support were justified on the basis of the record of colonialism which demonstrated that the people of the region had been coerced into a position of economic dependency. It was impossible for the new nation states of the region to plan for an independent future in a competitive global economic system without some transitional financial aid. An adequate understanding of the economic aspects of decolonisation, such as the analysis of regional integration, labour unrest, the Cold War and race, needs to be grounded in a detailed account of the events which took place in the region and having established the foundations of the analysis it is time to turn to that task.

2
The Struggle for Independence 1947–1952

The Montego Bay conference of September 1947 was intended to provide the basis for the establishment of a new nation state in the Anglophone Caribbean. After gathering in Jamaica, delegates from across the region passed 15 resolutions for the future of the region. The first affirmed their support for a federation of the various individual territories; the fifteenth resolution humbly expressed their loyalty and allegiance to George VI who responded by affirming his 'deep interest in their welfare.'[1] Despite some intemperate exchanges over how a federation was to be funded, a political programme entailing greater unity between the islands and continuing loyalty to British traditions seemed to presage a relatively smooth path to independence for the West Indies, at a time when events in Palestine and India proved that dissolving an empire could be a bloody and acrimonious process. During the following two decades, and with the significant exception of the mainland territory of British Guiana, the story of decolonisation in the region gave at least the appearance of incremental progress towards a harmonious transfer of authority from British imperial officials to the region's nationalist politicians. Fifty years after independence it is evident that the apparent reconciliation between nationalism and imperialism offered rather inadequate camouflage for two incompatible sets of preoccupations. West Indian nationalists were seeking to develop a sense of common nationhood in a region where geography and history made this an exceptionally difficult task. A lack of territorial contiguity between the islands and the mainland territories and a history in which any sense of cultural, political and economic achievement was attenuated by the human suffering endured on the plantations, constituted obstacles to the nation-building project. Given the urgency of the problems confronting them, nationalists believed that yet more years of British tutelage would not assist the process of constructing a new identity which transcended the grimness of the past. In some senses the British had wider horizons because they were handling similar problems across the globe but this broader perspective actually blurred their vision of the regional obstacles to unity. The goal in the Caribbean as elsewhere was to secure an orderly transition to independence and events were constantly refracted through this lens. When British notions of orderliness were unpacked they were found to contain a formidable list of criteria for independence: guarantees against unrest, budgetary parsimony, constitutional probity, potential for economic development and allegiance to British or Western cultural values. Although metropolitan politicians and officials accepted that such standards could not be permanently guaranteed they wished to entrench various constitutional, social and financial safeguards before independence was granted and this necessitated delay. During the Montego Bay negotiations they assumed that George VI and his descendants would require the loyalty and obedience of the Caribbean people for some years to come. Over the next five years this presupposition was challenged by the emergence of a regionalist trade-union movement, the articulation of a powerful local nationalism in Jamaica and labour disputes in the Leewards and Windwards.

Standing closer in the Caribbean

While metropolitan policymakers and nationalist politicians concurred that a federation consisting of all or most of the Anglophone countries of the region was a laudable goal, for two decades after 1945, discussions of the more detailed issues revealed many differences between the protagonists. The often divergent interests of each particular territory generated recurring controversies among the nationalists over the practical matters of federal revenue, customs union and freedom of movement. Such squabbles served to conceal the more fundamental conflicts between anti-colonial actors from the Caribbean, who were eager to utilise the federation as a means of obtaining early independence, and imperial administrators, whose habitual response was one of extreme caution regarding matters of constitutional reform. Colonial Office reserve was founded on a conviction that the peoples of the Anglophone Caribbean remained in a dangerous state of discontent which required them to handle local affairs with great delicacy. At times they acknowledged that the turbulence of local politics was a consequence of the grim economic circumstances in which most of the people of the region still lived but they also believed in the existence of a Caribbean sensibility which was prone to irrationality and violence. In principle they favoured federation because it would leash these instincts to a sturdier political order than if the territories achieved unilateral independence. The rational planning of economic development required greater cooperation and any measure of political reform undertaken in one place inevitably had ramifications elsewhere which had to be considered when making constitutional calculations. Regional integration also offered the prospect of relieving the British Exchequer of the burden of financial support for the territories. Despite these apparent incentives, British officials constantly urged vigilance and caution in the debates about Caribbean decolonisation and this attitude eventually proved debilitating for the federal project. They were particularly wary about the more radical ideas expressed by the Caribbean Labour Congress (CLC).

The CLC was one forum in which nationalists discussed plans for greater regional unity and its fortunes rose and fell with their sponsorship of the federal idea. Perhaps surprisingly the origins of the organisation lay in British Guiana which did not join the federation when it was finally formed in 1958. In the 1920s Guianese trade unionists were in the forefront of workers' organisation partly due to the influence of Hubert Critchlow, who in 1905 at the age of 21 had led a strike for better wages by waterfront workers which precipitated disturbances across the colony.[2] Union activity was to varying degrees illegal across the Anglophone Caribbean until the late 1930s and labour leaders had a common interest in securing recognition of their role as legitimate representatives of workers' grievances. In 1926 Critchlow hosted a conference in Georgetown which led to the formation of the Guianese and West Indian Federation of Trade Unions and Labour Parties (GWIFTULP).[3] Among those who attended was a Trinidadian of Corsican descent called Arthur Andrew Cipriani who, in recognition of his service in the First World War, was universally addressed as Captain Cipriani. The programme of his Trinidad Workingmen's Association, which later became the Trinidad Labour Party, fused proposals for constitutional reform with demands for better working conditions. Cipriani was also a supporter of federalism and introduced a motion proposing regional unity at the 1926 Georgetown conference.[4] Despite Cipriani's enthusiasm for regional integration the influence of the GWIFTULP was restricted to Trinidad, Guiana and Surinam and it was superseded by the CLC which held its first conference in Barbados in 1945. The CLC had a much wider geographical reach than the old GWIFTULP and its adoption of the Cipriani thesis that a federation of the Anglophone territories would benefit labour, marked a significant step towards greater unity. Despite the consensus in favour of political integration, the new organisation was divided between the increasing conservatism of the old labour leaders, like Critchlow and T. A. Marryshow of Grenada, who took on the positions of Vice-President and President respectively, and a younger grouping of radicals, including Richard Hart of Jamaica and Robert Bradshaw of St Kitts.

The radical case for federation, which alarmed both the British and the senior leadership of the CLC, encompassed a critique of the current order in its economic, constitutional and international manifestations along with the reconfiguring of conceptions of independence. In economic terms the CLC radicals diverged from the classical liberal orthodoxy which the Colonial Office were determined to maintain, by advocating import substitution and local capital accumulation rather than export promotion and external capital investment. The Statement of Economic Development and Federation approved at the Barbados conference criticised the extant monoculture centred on sugar production as an imperialist imposition which 'had resulted in the importation of food and in failure to establish many local manufacturers capable of development.' Dependence on external capital was also regarded as enervating because local people did not receive the full benefit of their economic production. On this account British imperialism was an exercise in economic exploitation and greater regional unity was a means of challenging imperialism in its economic and political aspects. It was evident that the smaller territories of the region were vulnerable to external influences and federation was a prerequisite for greater autarchy.[5] Economic independence was intimately connected to political independence which was, in many respects, a more straightforward matter. The Trinidadian trade unionist, Ralph Mentor, told the Barbados delegates: 'What was wanted was the transfer to the West Indies of the political power at present exercised in Downing Street'.[6]

Although there was unanimity on the need for a loosening of political ties to Britain, CLC leaders were also apprehensive about the rise of American influence. At the moment when Caribbean labour was formulating a programme for independence, they felt exposed to the unrestrained capitalism and Jim Crow racial attitudes exported from the United States. In 1940 Roosevelt had acquired bases in Bermuda, the Bahamas, Jamaica, Antigua, St Lucia, British Guiana and Trinidad as part of a deal to supply 50 near-obsolescent destroyers to the Royal Navy.

Harvey Neptune has demonstrated that, in the case of Trinidad at least, the response of the local population to the arrival of the American forces was ambivalent rather than universally hostile, but it is clear that labour leaders were appalled at the potential replacement of British imperialism with American neo-colonialism.[7] Among the older leaders there was still a residual loyalty to the nascent British Commonwealth which Marryshow suggested was a potential bulwark against American interference in the region's affairs. Speaking for the younger generation Robert Bradshaw declared in 1946 that he was relieved that the Americans had not come to his home island of St Kitts: 'We have had no Yankees and we want none. Forward to federated British West Indies.' In referring to the discriminatory measures imposed in the base areas he expressed astonishment at the 'shameful atrocities committed against blacks in these islands by the same Yankees since we have been forced to share our island homes with them.'[8]

To the sensibilities of Whitehall the least uncongenial aspect of the CLC prospectus was the determination to resist American influence. During the Second World War British policymakers argued with their American counterparts about the future of the region in the forum provided by the Anglo-American Caribbean Commission. This organisation was established in 1942 because the Roosevelt administration insisted that their support for the region's development must be conditional upon consultation over the process of political and economic reform.[9] After its establishment British officials came to share many of the reservations of Caribbean labour leaders about the potentially disruptive role of an expanded American presence.[10] Scepticism about Washington's motives was interpreted in London as sensible and prudent, but when local nationalists expressed aspirations for greater economic independence and early dominion status for a West Indian federation they merely reinforced preconceived British ideas about the immaturity of Caribbean political thinking. Consideration of some measure of political unity among their scattered possessions in the Caribbean had been a part of metropolitan debates about the region's future since the middle of the nineteenth century but had stalled following the failure to reach agreement on a confederal plan at Barbados in 1876. The official debate on federation recommenced with a message from the Colonial Secretary, Oliver Stanley, to West Indian Governors on 14 March 1945. Stanley's despatch offered a parenthetical dismissal of the goal of economic autarchy: 'It will no doubt be generally appreciated that financial stability (which is of course very different from economic self-sufficiency) is an essential accompaniment of full self-government and that the latter cannot be a reality without the former.' A federation built on British design would be one in which the imperial power would continue to act as a warden against financial irresponsibility and which would be disqualified for independence until the accounting books were balanced. In the interim the people of the region were advised to exercise their political instincts in the development of local self-government and community work.[11] There are at least two potentially divergent interpretations of this programme: one suggests that the principal British concern was with the strain which economic subsidies to their Caribbean colonies was placing on metropolitan finances which required the Colonial Office to enforce a policy of budgetary retrenchment before discarding entirely the burden of empire as rapidly as possible; the other proceeds on the assumption that the emphasis on economic incontinence was a product and a symbol of British convictions regarding the ingrained political immaturity of the Caribbean colonies which disqualified the people of the region from obtaining early independence. The latter seems a more convincing portrayal in the context of ongoing equivocations during the debate about federal independence which took place after the Montego Bay conference, persistent reservations about self-government in the most advanced territory, Jamaica, and the continuing fear of labour unrest, which is evident from an analysis of developments in some of the smaller islands.

The founding CLC conference at Barbados in 1945 and the Stanley despatch of the same year established that British officials and Caribbean politicians were on common ground in supporting federalism. It soon became evident that they had reached the same conclusion by different routes and that the difference in rationale would generate controversy, particularly regarding the relationship between federalism and independence. The Colonial Office spent much of their time deducing gloomy conclusions about the nature of what they termed 'the West Indian mind' from a set of premises about the region's political problems. This tendency was particularly conspicuous in the debate between metropolitan officials and imperial administrators which occurred once the Labour Colonial Secretary, Arthur Creech Jones, recommended in February 1947 the holding of a conference to discuss federation. This initiative precipitated expressions of scepticism from some British representatives in the region who doubted whether ambitious plans for a closer association across the whole of the Anglophone Caribbean were feasible. The proposed conference interrupted British efforts to expand the existing Leeward Islands federation by increments, with the incorporation of the Windward Islands as a first step. Brian Freeston, the Governor of the Leewards, recorded his opposition to a pan-Caribbean federation because 'it appears very doubtful whether public opinion has yet been educated to a point where the conception can be usefully discussed on a practical basis.' He suggested that the recent failure of local leaders to coordinate plans for participation in the Caribbean Commission demonstrated 'the inability of West Indian politicians to think together'. Another Governor, Arthur Grimble of the Windwards, was aggrieved that the delays which would accompany the formulation of any grand plan for integration across the whole of the Anglophone Caribbean would interrupt more practical efforts to promote a series of local political unions. Officials in Whitehall agreed that the creation of a large federation would be accompanied by many disagreements between local politicians but seemed comforted by the expected lethargic pace of constitutional change. Robert Arundell who was a member of the Anglo-American Caribbean Commission and succeeded Grimble to the Governorship of the Windwards in 1948, received reassuring messages from the Colonial Office explaining that they did not expect much progress to be made at the impending Montego Bay conference and that 'even if the principle is accepted it would probably take years to elaborate.'[12]

Delegates to the second Caribbean Labour Congress which met in Kingston between 2 and 9 September 1947 were in much more of a hurry and their haste distressed the Caribbean oligarchy which had previously dominated local politics and continued to control the economy. Gordon Lewis noted that CLC delegates set themselves at odds with local commercial interests in developing an 'advanced programme' at Kingston which intended federation 'as a vehicle for democratic social growth'.[13] The defence of the status quo devolved to Alexander Bustamante's Jamaica Labour Party (JLP) which, despite its origins in the labour protests of the 1930s, adopted an increasingly conservative position over the next two decades and became the party of Jamaican business. One of the first portents of these future developments was Bustamante's condemnation of CLC radicalism and his refusal to attend the Kingston conference despite its location in the capital city of the island of which he was Chief Minister.[14] The *Gleaner* provided detailed reports of the riotous enthusiasm of the delegates inside Coke Hall for federation and against Bustamante and imperialism. The meeting began with the Trinidadian Albert Gomes 'hitting out' at Bustamante on the first day and Marryshow invoking the spirit of Admiral Collingwood on the second with the injunction: 'Gentlemen let us do something today that the world will talk of hereafter.' Bustamante responded by denouncing the 'loud mouthed people' who had insufficient patience to await the impending talks at Montego Bay. The CLC conference culminated with Gomes prematurely declaring, 'we are on the threshold of creating a West Indian nation.'[15] This was the closest that the federal cause ever came to establishing itself as a populist movement but in the longer term the rivalries between island leaders which were already evident in Kingston and the stifling effect of British procrastination would cause a decade of delay. Having set himself at odds with Bustamante at Kingston, Gomes continued to prove his talent as a controversialist by alienating almost every other labour leader in the Caribbean during the course of his long career. Nevertheless his memoirs accurately evoke the hesitant reaction of the British to plans for a federation. He recalled: 'the British had to cloak their enthusiasm in cagey ambivalence. They wanted it if we wanted it; but they wouldn't press it if we didn't want it.' During a discussion with the Colonial Secretary about federation, Gomes noted that Creech Jones wanted 'reassurance that if he acted the reaction in the West Indies would not be such as to cause retardation rather than advance of the cause.'[16]

One means of illustrating the extent of the differences alluded to by Gomes is to compare the programme agreed to by the CLC delegates with Colonial Office briefing papers for the Montego Bay conference which began two days after the Kingston meeting ended. The former called for the early establishment of a federation encompassing all the Anglophone islands and the mainland territories of British Guiana and British Honduras and the granting of dominion status to the new polity. The CLC also recommended that simultaneously with the acquisition of dominion status, the units of the federation should each obtain internal self-government and electoral systems based on universal adult suffrage. By contrast Colonial Office memoranda emphasised that the Montego Bay meeting was unlikely to produce a federal constitution, despite the fact that the CLC had drafted one, and that they should aim instead, to make progress towards a customs union and the establishment of a working party to prepare a scheme for closer political association. Perfunctory British efforts to sketch the future federal constitution were indicative of the extreme caution with which metropolitan policymakers approached the possible demission of power in the Anglophone Caribbean. Although the Jamaican constitution of 1944 had led to conflicts because of the extensive executive authority retained by British appointees, the Colonial Office suggested it might provide a model for the federation.[17] Given that metropolitan policymakers were expecting a long interval before the institution of the federation, the imposition of a constitutional system based on a model devised during the Second World War would ensure that elected politicians could exercise greater authority at the level of the units than at the federal centre. In other words, the inevitable consequence of Colonial Office wariness was that legislators and ministers in unit governments would have wider powers than their equivalents in the federal government. The attempt to coordinate constitutional progress at these different levels remained a debilitating factor in all future discussions of federation and undermined efforts to recruit local politicians to the federal Parliament after its final establishment in 1958.

On 11 September 1947 elected and official members of the governments of the Anglophone Caribbean met with representatives of the Colonial Office at the coastal resort of Montego Bay in Jamaica to try and reconcile their views about the constitutional architecture of any future federation. British reluctance to establish a federal centre in which their own authority would be greatly diminished and the determination of nationalist leaders to prevent the federal project from inhibiting their efforts to secure greater powers in their home territories ensured that the notion of uneven constitutional progress was given official sanction by delegates. Resolution 2 of the conference specified that political development in the units 'must be pursued as an aim in itself without prejudice and in no way subordinate to progress towards federation.'[18] As Mordecai later acknowledged, in his long defence of the evolution of official policy, this was a 'fateful decision'. He suggested that this resolution was one of three obstacles which came into clearer view at Montego Bay; the others were Bustamante's inconvenient sloganeering about a 'federation of paupers' and Creech Jones's 'subtle opposition to the CLC approach.'[19] Gomes shared this analysis in his own reminiscences, although he portrayed the situation more dramatically by claiming that Bustamante 'injected the poison into the foetus which killed the infant'.[20] Even aside from this unpleasant rhetorical flourish, the views of Mordecai and Gomes overstate the case and were influenced by hindsight. While it is evident, in retrospect, that some of the problems which would dog the federation for the next decade first achieved prominence at Montego Bay, on the question of relations between the units and the future federal centre, it was not feasible to retard local constitutional progress during the federal negotiations. The motions adopted at Montego Bay reflected existing conditions and the decision made there to establish a Standing Closer Association Committee (SCAC) provided a forum to resolve emerging disagreements. Much more problematic was the reluctance of the Colonial Office over the next decade to concede that the new federation might obtain early self-government and this only became evident when the SCAC began detailed constitutional drafting under the chairmanship of Hubert Rance in 1949.

SCAC meetings provided an opportunity for the new generation of nationalist politicians to debate the details of a federal constitution with Colonial Office representatives. Grantley Adams of Barbados attempted to defend the CLC concept of a federation with Dominion status, but his opposition to the incrementalist approach of the Colonial Office was flattened by British officials. They wished to ensure that the constitutional structure of the new West Indian state would follow the apprenticeship model which would give the imperial power sufficient authority to guide and if necessary curb the inclinations of locally elected federal representatives. Some labour leaders, such as Vere Bird of Antigua, whose unyielding demands for economic justice had established their reputation as political radicals in their home territories, were remarkably forbearing of British sensitivities on regional constitutional issues. Writing to Richard Hart after the first two SCAC meetings Bird reported, with no sense of rancour, 'it seems that the decision will be that to go from an extreme of Crown Colonies to Dominion Status will be rash. Too much of an extreme to go from one extreme to another in one jump.'[21] Bird's appreciation of the metropolitan perspective caused him to moderate his position sufficiently that at the end of the talks, he was commended by Rance as one of only two members of the committee 'who were genuinely interested in Federation for its own sake.' The condemnation of Bird's non-cooperative colleagues reflected a broader British sensibility which denigrated the capacities of Caribbean political leadership as unfit for the responsibilities of independence. Rance had been transferred to the Caribbean shortly after his tenure as the last British Governor of Burma and from the outset he expressed some disdain for the capacities of the people of the region. Even before he had chaired the first Committee meetings Rance endorsed the view that 'West Indians are not notable for a strong sense of relevance.' At the end of the negotiations he offered a schoolmaster's report on Adams, who would later become the first Prime Minister of the Federation: 'He displayed the fact that he had not studied his papers, that on any point of detail his mind is essentially a woolly one, that he lacks intellectual courage, and that he is obsessed with points of appearance rather than of substance.'[22]

The prejudices of the British participants in the discussions could be regarded as a trivial matter but they ramified, and had a particular influence on discussions of the balance of constitutional powers between the appointed Governor and the elected representatives in the putative federation. During the meetings of SCAC, the right of the British Governor to control defence and foreign affairs, and to assume emergency powers went unquestioned; the only time when nationalist resistance to ongoing imperial supervision was mounted occurred when the question of the federal budget was raised. The repetitive invocation of financial insolvency as a bar to political independence for the Caribbean territories appears incongruous because in the late 1940s Britain was itself dependent on an enormous loan from the United States to avoid bankruptcy but the emphasis given to it by Rance and the Colonial Office was entirely consistent with the historical tradition of trusteeship thinking. Arguments about whether the West Indian people were inherently unsuited for self-government or whether they would at some point in the future graduate from their colonial apprenticeship and become capable of genuine autonomy had numerous precedents, including the Wood Report of 1922.[23] The particular form which they took in the late 1940s focused on the incapacities of contemporary politicians to provide an effective administration which would balance the books of any new nation state. Initially the CLC representatives on the SCAC argued in favour of the Ceylonese constitution which had brought the island to the brink of independence in 1946 but Rance emphasised that any British Governor would require greater powers to deal with the fact that the Caribbean islands were not as financially stable as Ceylon.[24] After the second SCAC meeting in Trinidad in March 1949 the Colonial Office expressed confidence that Caribbean politicians had assimilated the argument that they would inevitably be dependent on budgetary assistance from Britain and that if they did 'concede the link, they must concede the S. of S. [Secretary of State] ultimate control in financial matters.'[25] This confidence was misplaced, and at the third meeting in Barbados, Adams was able to eliminate from the draft report those passages granting the Governor reserved powers in the field of finance. A future Governor could still exercise financial control by refusing to assent to bills which required spending and by extending the previous year's financial measures in the case of a budgetary crisis but this was still insufficient to reassure officials in Whitehall. During the concluding drafting sessions, Rance reimposed measures granting the

Governor powers to legislate on any occasion when elected representatives undertook action which might appear 'gravely to imperil financial stability'.[26]

The importance which was accorded to these detailed technical arguments attests to the continued nervousness of British policymakers about whether a future federation would be financially solvent; analysis of the reportage which accompanied the negotiations demonstrates that this was matched by a sour pessimism regarding the process of constitution-building itself. While Rance presided over the SCAC meetings, much of the detailed drafting was undertaken by another Colonial Office official, Charles Carstairs, who, acting in his capacity as Secretary of SCAC, also provided Whitehall with a commentary on events. In April 1949 he reported that the Caribbean politicians with whom he was dealing were 'an idle lot' and that his goal was to 'get them to face squarely the logic of the situation, particularly the political and constitutional consequences of economic instability and financial dependency.'[27] Five months later, and before the issuing of the final report, Carstairs predicted that the proposals on which he was working would prove unacceptable to the territorial governments. This pessimistic conclusion was founded on the premise of Caribbean contrarianism which ensured that any proposal emanating from the precincts of British officialdom was automatically mistrusted. Such attitudes, according to Carstairs, derived 'not from the behaviour of HMG at all but from the prevailing low standards of political morality in the region.'[28] When Caribbean Governors and Administrators met in November 1949 to discuss the likelihood of SCAC plans being endorsed by territorial legislatures they took the opportunity to exchange discouraging forecasts. Representing the Colonial Office in his capacity as Assistant Under-Secretary, George Seel went as far as to suggest that 'it seemed impossible at this stage to make any assumption that the area would become self-dependent financially and economically'.[29] Such a bald statement of short- and medium-term dependency was anathema to Caribbean nationalists.

The publication of the Rance report in March 1950 provided an opportunity for a new nationalist critique of metropolitan thinking. Although its recommendations were widely regarded as inadequate the chance to adumbrate a more progressive alternative was missed because of continuing dissension between Caribbean politicians. Inevitably the lack of a coherent response served to ratify Colonial Office prejudices about the inadequacy of local leadership, particularly on the smaller islands. Rance's intention was to force territorial legislatures to declare their position on the federal issue; this purpose was frustrated by the inevitable lack of enthusiasm for such timid proposals which appeared to portend an extended period of continued British control, and by further disagreements among the local political actors. After 12 months, only the legislatures of Trinidad and the Windward Islands had debated the recommendations. In Jamaica, Bustamante remained sceptical about regional integration. His unwillingness to support federation encouraged labour leaders in the Eastern Caribbean to consider whether they should form a political union of their own. Proposals emanating from Robert Bradshaw in St Kitts for a 'nuclear federation' of Trinidad, the Windwards and the Leewards foreshadowed the discussions which would occur in the aftermath of the Jamaican secession in 1961. On both occasions metropolitan policymakers reacted by emphasising the role of the federation in curbing the disorderliness of small island politics. Federalist sentiment in the Windwards and Leewards was attributed by Stephen Luke, the Assistant Under-Secretary responsible for Caribbean affairs at the Colonial Office, to a 'rather pathetic belief in Federation as offering a way out from the frustrations of their economic and political limitations'.[30] Bradshaw's 'nuclear federation' also prompted a revealing discussion of the role of big-island leadership. The Governor of the Leewards, Kenneth Blackburne, was obsessed with the requirement to remedy the irresponsibility of politicians in territories like St Kitts and Antigua. He remarked: 'If we are to avoid "boss rule" in these little islands (and we have nearly got it already) then we must enable more experienced West Indian leaders to take control as soon as possible'. Luke concurred that federation ought to broaden the outlook of the small islands and 'subject them to more sober and responsible West Indian leaders'.[31] The notion of the nuclear federation was eventually rejected by the Colonial Office in favour of a policy of 'studious neutrality' towards the squabbles between Bustamante and the Eastern Caribbean leaders.[32] The impasse was broken in August 1951 when Bustamante adopted a motion in the Jamaican Executive Council cautiously endorsing the principle of federation and calling for a conference in London to discuss how the Rance recommendations could be made more palatable. The centrality of Jamaica as the biggest of the big islands was evident from the gratified reaction in Whitehall but this new initiative set the stage for a new round of federal wrangling in anticipation of the commencement of the London conference in 1953.[33] Before turning to these developments in the next chapter, it will be useful to examine first, the state of Jamaican politics in the years after the introduction of the 1944 constitution and, second, to attend to the nature of small island politics, using the cases of St Kitts and Grenada to analyse why they were regarded by metropolitan policymakers as a danger to the process of decolonisation.

Manley, Bustamante and constitutional reform in Jamaica

Arguments about the design of the federation highlighted the irregularity of the many different territorial constitutions in the Anglophone Caribbean. There could be no one Colonial Office blueprint for reforming the governments which would become the units of the federation because Jamaica, Trinidad, Barbados, the Windwards, the Leewards and the mainland territories were each at a different stage of constitutional development. When constitutions were revised in particular localities it was in reaction to the contingencies facing Governors and Administrators at a local level and this tended to amplify existing disparities. British policymakers dealt with issues of constitutional reform with an impressive degree of ingenuity and subtlety but the purpose to which they put this inventiveness was to delay the moment at which Britain's regional empire was to be dissolved. Whereas they were frequently bewildered by industrial relation conflicts in the Anglophone Caribbean, they had extensive knowledge of the design of political systems for imperial territories which they put to good use in assembling small packages of incremental reform for each of the territories. The drawback of this ingenuity was that the various bespoke constitutions exacerbated discontent among nationalist politicians who felt they were lagging behind their rivals elsewhere: for this reason it is useful to analyse the case of Jamaica which in 1944 had been granted the most advanced constitution in the region. What an examination of British strategy demonstrates is that the purpose of all this tactical manoeuvring was to place impediments along the path to independence which the nationalists would find it difficult to circumnavigate. Even though the British eventually invested a great deal of trust in the Jamaican politician Norman Manley as the future leader of a wider Caribbean federation and denigrated small island leaders for not living up to the standards set on the larger islands, they resisted demands for further measures of constitutional reform for which the nationalists in Jamaica were pressing.

The nationalist programme exhibited a significant degree of uniformity across the Anglophone Caribbean. Its focus was on democratisation which required first, the concession of universal suffrage; secondly, the replacement of officials and nominees in local legislatures by elected representatives; and thirdly, the transfer of executive power from British-appointed Governors to Chief Ministers, Prime Ministers or Premiers who derived their authority from the people through the electoral process. In the aftermath of the labour riots of the late 1930s the British government recognised that universal suffrage was a necessary conduit for the peaceful expression of popular opinion and, within a decade of the first elections held under such a system in Jamaica in 1944, all the territories had enfranchised the adult population. They were more reluctant to concede wholly elected legislatures: under the 1944 Jamaican constitution the Colonial Secretary, the Attorney General, the Financial Secretary, the Treasurer, two other appointed British officials and ten nominees still sat on the Legislative Council which constituted the upper house of the local parliament. As we shall see demands for the removal of officials and nominees from the legislature would remain a source of controversy in Jamaica and the other territories. It was perhaps inevitable that the greatest struggle of the nationalists should be to gain effective control of the executive. The expedient employed by the Colonial Office to prolong this process was to offer local politicians a measure of executive responsibility through the so-called committee system which entailed the creation of pseudo-Cabinets in which British administrators continued to sit, and elected members remained under the supervision of the colonial bureaucracy. In Jamaica five members of the elected House of Assembly attended the Executive Council. Even more prized and contentious was the reservation of powers to Governors which varied from territory to territory but nearly always included the right to call a State of Emergency, to conduct foreign relations and to veto legislation, particularly if it entailed public expenditure.

One of the most significant features of Jamaican politics was the early emergence of a rigid, personalist two-party system. The conflict between the People's National Party (PNP) and the JLP was associated in everybody's minds with the rivalry between the cousins Norman Manley and Alexander Bustamante. When it seemed certain that one of these men would become the first Prime Minister of an independent Jamaica, British officials began to weigh their admiration for Manley's character against lingering concerns about the leftist orientation of his politics and their distrust of Bustamante's unpredictable, authoritarian personality against his willingness to defend the status quo from the criticisms of Caribbean socialists. Perhaps no other nationalist politician in the periphery of empire attracted quite so much praise from the British as Manley. In 1961, towards the end of his career and after his campaign for an affirmative vote in the referendum on Jamaican membership of the federation was defeated, the Governor of Jamaica, Kenneth Blackburne lamented: 'He is a remarkable man, but he is taking too much on himself – and out of himself. He gets far too little support from his Ministers. I only hope he can last out.'[34] Blackburne's predecessor, Hugh Foot had a predilection for writing effusive letters of praise to Manley but offered a more nuanced view in his memoirs which noted that he could be 'offensive' in negotiations. Nevertheless, Foot concluded that 'whatever failings he may have are far outweighed by his positive qualities – a commanding and constructive mind and a courageous determination to stand by his beliefs and an unquestioned personal integrity of the highest order.'[35] The qualities which enamoured him of the British were, as the journalist Theodore Sealy explained, the 'product of many crises'.[36] His father, mother and brother all died early in his life. He was particularly affected by the loss of his brother during the third battle of Ypres while Manley was serving with him on the Western Front. His remarkable achievements were based on the diligence with which he cultivated his formidable physical and mental abilities. He established himself as one of Jamaica's leading sportsmen, won a Rhodes scholarship and became the most famous lawyer in the country. Although he excelled at cricket, football and shooting, his greatest sporting success was setting a national record for the 100 yards in 1912 which stood for three decades. The demotic view of Manley's numerous victories in court was summed up in the prudential advice of the 1920s: 'If you commit murder, Manley is the lawyer to save you from hanging.'[37] In the midst of the labour uprisings of 1938 he founded the PNP which called for universal suffrage in a campaign which Rex Nettleford described as having 'started the English speaking Caribbean on the road to political modernisation.'[38]

Alexander Bustamante was born almost a decade before Norman Manley, and was in his fifties when he came to national prominence with the series of audacious letters he wrote to the *Gleaner* after 1934 condemning the inequalities of Jamaican society.[39] One of the few certainties about his life before this time was that he changed his surname from Clarke to Bustamante during a series of adventures in the Hispanophone regions of the world. He claimed that he had served with the Spanish army fighting Abd-el Krim in Morocco and, although these tales were greeted with scepticism by many, including Manley, others wondered whether they were too extraordinary to have been entirely invented.[40] In the absence of the formal education which Manley had obtained, the stories provided Bustamante with a unique rhetorical repertoire, allowing him, for example, to compare a political opponent to 'a wolf baying [sic] in the Atlas mountains'.[41] His ethos appealed to a popular audience and the autobiographical elements sustained his own assertions that he was of Spanish descent, without 'a drop of coloured blood in my veins.' After the failure of Garvey's campaign for Negro empowerment a new approach in which the light-skinned Bustamante would defend the black proletariat against the oppression of both the brown bourgeoisie and the white oligarchy proved appealing to many Jamaican workers.[42] His embrace of the paternal role of 'the Chief' and his magnetic appeal to the Jamaican crowd seemed to his opponents to presage an incipient Bustamante dictatorship. Such apprehensions were magnified when the JLP won the 1944 elections only a year after the party was founded as a rival to the PNP, and by his ongoing role as president for life of the Bustamante Industrial Trade Union (BITU), the name of which suggested an egocentric and personalist approach to trade union politics. Many thought such pretentions were the prelude to autocratic rule. In 1939 the Colonial Office's Labour Advisor, Granville Orde-Brown, endorsed the view of Manley's British ally, the socialist politician, Stafford Cripps, that Bustamante was 'a thoroughly irresponsible agitator'. Orde-Brown added his own assessment that Bustamante was an 'unbalanced demagogue', although one who could possibly be rehabilitated.[43] When the Jamaican Governor, John Huggins, complained about Bustamante's conduct after his 1944 election victory, the Colonial Office advised that there was little prospect of getting rid of him because he would summon up his 'mob oratory' to win any future election. At this stage British officials were still undecided as to whether they preferred Bustamante and the JLP to Manley and the PNP. Seel recorded that the former was 'apt to lose all self-control when excited and has ... led his followers into acts of violence.' However, the PNP was 'more doctrinaire', with potential Marxist influences.[44] The events of the 1950s and 1960s would transform these opinions as Bustamante was characterised as a more benign, conservative figure who was a guarantor rather than threat to Jamaican democracy and Manley was identified as a statesman who, it was hoped, might ensure an orderly transition of power across the Anglophone Caribbean.

These changing views reflected the rightward drift of Jamaican politics which was congenial to metropolitan policymakers and confirmed their preference for 'big island' leadership. However, it did not prevent a series of confrontations over constitutional reform. Manley was a democratic socialist who would have been content in the Labour party of Attlee or Gaitskell. The meaning of Jamaican socialism changed for Manley and Rex Nettleford has gone as far as to suggest that the concept gradually degraded from a programmatic belief in public ownership of the means of production to a mere 'label'.[45] For British officialdom what this amounted to was a partial domestication of the PNP after a period in the 1940s when the party had appeared willing to countenance the notion that liberating the country from dependence on international capital was a necessary corollary to freeing Jamaica from British political control. The most overt demonstration of Manley's increasing conservatism was the decision he made in 1952 to expel the most prominent left-wing members of the PNP, including the brothers Ken and Frank Hill, Richard Hart and Arthur Henry. The removal of Marxist influence within the party enabled Manley to endorse a more liberal economic manifesto. By the time of his election victory in 1955 he had concluded that the only means of reducing Jamaican unemployment was to attract international capital at a time when local finance was scarce. He expressed admiration for Munoz Marin's Operation Bootstrap programme in Puerto Rico, which he described as having 'the best leadership in the world'.[46] Bustamante was less interested in the abstract notions which underpinned rival economic positions and scoffed at political theorising. The very haziness of his ideological vision allowed him to shift position from the champion of labour to the booster of Jamaican commercial interests while claiming that his essential views remained unchanged. His amanuensis, adviser and future wife, Gladys Bustamante née Longbridge, has explained his attitude in terms which make clear that his position was one of exceptionally cautious reformism: 'We too believed in self-government, but we did not want to reach that goal by a scrambling short-cut which without material and intellectual resources, could end in chaos, frustration and even further disappointment for the masses. Instead, we advocated as a first step a strong, enlightened and healthy working- and middle-class upon which to build.'[47] The JLP's focus on 'bread and butter issues' at the expense of reordering the relationship between Britain and Jamaica, distinguished it from the PNP which, after the success of its campaign for universal suffrage, was principally responsible for forcing constitutional concessions from the British. The one abstraction about which Bustamante could be passionate was the importance of British traditions to Jamaica. When he went to London in 1948 to conduct negotiations on constitutional reform he declared: 'No one knows the weakness and bad things about England as well as I do. But in spite of all these weaknesses and all the bad, the breaking up of the British Empire would mean the end of democracy, the end of everything good on this earth.'[48] Such sentiments were reassuring to British policymakers who nevertheless remained concerned that, despite this attachment to British institutions, Bustamante's reliance on the Jamaican crowd as a source of power and influence could produce mob rule in the country.

Colonial Office neuroticism on the subject of Jamaican independence was expressed in fretting about Bustamante's demagoguery but, given their concerns about the potential disorderliness of decolonisation, British policymakers showed a surprising degree of tolerance for the rising political violence in Jamaica in the 1940s. Although they found the coercive tactics of the two main parties distasteful it was manageable so long as they were employing such tactics against one another rather than targeting the British administration. Amanda Sives has noted: 'The failure of the colonial state to ensure the political arena was equally open to both political parties created a context within which they could claim the need to "defend" themselves.' The PNP's resort to violence 'could be partly explained by their relationship with a colonial state which was suspicious of their socialist ideology.'[49] After his 1944 election victory Bustamante and the JLP were in a formidably strong position. In institutional terms he was the leader of the largest party in the elected House but had very limited executive authority. However, by virtue of his position as head of the BITU he could call on the support of labour in a crisis. Furthermore, after his election as mayor of Kingston, he also had the resources of the capital's municipal government at his disposal. When frustrated by his inability to emasculate the rival Jamaican Trades Union Council (TUC) which was led by Florizel Glasspole of the PNP, he turned to other measures.[50] The most notorious example of this was his personal confrontation with striking nurses at the mental health asylum in 1946. Bustamante summoned his supporters to march on the hospital and a series of violent confrontations between PNP and JLP supporters across Kingston ensued. A State of Emergency was declared and Bustamante was charged with manslaughter for his role in the death of a bystander; after a sensational trial he was acquitted.[51] Although bloody fights between the supporters of the two parties are often thought of as a modern phenomenon in Jamaica, they have their origins in Bustamante's efforts to marginalise the TUC and the belligerent response of the PNP.

In ideological terms Bustamante's outspoken anti-communism was appealing to the British, as was the fact that the JLP was less inclined than the PNP to make the case for the rapid transfer of political authority to the Jamaican people. Disagreements with the Governor, John Huggins, over quotidian matters of policy brought to Bustamante's notice the way in which current constitutional arrangements operated to the disadvantage of elected representatives. In theory the reforms of

1944 bridged the gap between the executive and legislative branches but the novel manner in which the system functioned in Jamaica ensured that British officials rather than nationalist politicians remained in control. Although described as a ministerial system, the operation of the constitution denied elected ministers effective responsibility because all executive actions had to be channelled through the Colonial Secretary and the Governor. After three years of mounting animosity in 1947 Bustamante launched a series of personal attacks against Huggins who complained: 'Mr Bustamante's outbursts have become more frequent and his periods of intervening common sense of shorter duration.'[52] By the time of his visit to London in July 1948 Bustamante was distrustful of Huggins and intensely suspicious of proposals that the Governor should acquire additional reserved powers as a prelude to any further constitutional progress. During the London talks Bustamante went as far as to argue that the plan to transfer control over the reserved powers from the Executive Council to the Governor 'savoured of Hitlerism'; the outburst confirmed Colonial Office views regarding his unfitness for government.[53]

Had Bustamante known of the internal debates between British policymakers his worst fears about the Governor's proposals would have been confirmed. Huggins' correspondence with the Colonial Office's constitutional expert, Sydney Caine, revealed just how limited the effect of the 1944 reforms had been. While Huggins accepted that it was not feasible to retreat from the system introduced in 1944, he argued that only minimal concessions should be offered to nationalist sentiment in Jamaica. He explained: 'Judged by the knowledge available to the public the embryo ministerial system has been a success. That success has been more apparent than real.' What was actually happening, according to Huggins, was that elected ministers were unwilling and unable to exercise any real power. They had titular responsibility for executive policy but had almost no control over its direction. Huggins proposed to resolve this anomalous situation by removing the right of British officials to vote in the Executive Council but transferring the reserved powers which it currently possessed to the Governor. His price for conceding an increase in the number of elected politicians on the Executive Council was the strengthening of the authority of the Governor who was an appointee of the British government. Caine was unconvinced that this kind of constitutional contrivance would work and suggested that changes to the voting system on the Executive Council were unlikely to have much practical effect. He was more concerned with the 'great oddity' that Jamaican ministers had 'no real responsibility for the control of the Department with which they are associated, and are apparently not even allowed access to the files of those departments except as a favour.' Although Caine was one of the most radical thinkers in the Colonial Office even he did not endorse the case for Jamaican self-government. Instead he argued for a new package of reforms which would at least constitute a penultimate step towards this goal. Caine concluded: 'we have put up a handsome facade of transfer of power to local representatives but have really kept the whole administrative machine entirely out of their grasp. I would prefer to see rather less formal transfer but the admission of the unofficials to more real authority in the details of government.'[54]

For Manley and the PNP, the conspicuous problems which were inherent in the 1944 constitution provided an opportunity to begin a battle on two fronts: the first, against Bustamante and the JLP, whose appeal to isolationist and imperialist sentimentalism inside Jamaica was hindering progress towards federation and self-government, and the second, against the Colonial Office whose cautiousness on constitutional matters appeared to presuppose that independence could be postponed indefinitely. The blame which Manley later received for the failure of the federation has contributed to neglect in the historiography of his role in expediting constitutional reform in Jamaica. One of the PNP expellees of 1952, Richard Hart argued in his comprehensive history of the period that Manley essentially collaborated with British efforts to turn the federation into a 'glorified Crown Colony.'[55] Elsewhere Manley has been widely criticised for refusing to stand for election to the federal parliament in 1958 and then for calling the referendum which led to Jamaican withdrawal in 1961.[56] What this leaves out of account is the earlier catalysing effect which the PNP had on the debate about Jamaican independence at a period when the issue appeared moribund. In July 1948, from his position outside the Legislative Council, Manley reached the cynical conclusion that the Colonial Office would let Bustamante 'have at present undisclosed constitutional amendments but not to go so far as they do not hold the ultimate power in their hands.'[57] Manley's assumption that the British would not relinquish 'ultimate power' was correct but his prediction that some measure of substantive reform would occur proved mistaken. For the next three years the debate on constitutional reform stalled and when it resumed the prevailing caution of the 1947–1948 years was again evident in British policymaking circles. After the Colonial Office failed to establish a consensus in favour of Huggins's proposed reforms to the Executive Council, a Select Committee of the Jamaican House of Representatives re-examined the constitution. It had the misfortune to report as both parties were preparing for the 1949 elections; neither the JLP nor the PNP was willing to consider any significant reform of the Executive Council until they knew who the newly empowered ministers were likely to be. The outcome of the election, in which the PNP increased its representation in the House to 13, left the JLP with a slim majority and guaranteed that any further measures would be the subject of dispute between the two parties. The slowing of an already dilatory process gratified the Colonial Office. The Permanent Under-Secretary, Thomas Lloyd, suggested they advise the Governor that they did not want to expedite reform. The Minister of State, Lord Listowel, emphasised: 'We should move slowly about constitutional change in Jamaica and reasons for delay are desirable.'[58]

It was the resumption of the PNP campaign for self-government and the arrival of a new Governor, Hugh Foot, which eventually restarted serious discussions of constitutional reform but even measures short of self-government were met with resistance on the basis that local politicians were not sufficiently responsible to exercise ministerial authority. After his appointment, Foot persuaded the Labour Colonial Secretary, James Griffiths, that the elected members should form a majority on the Executive Council and assume effective control of their departments for the first time. In return for these concessions Foot suggested the nationalists would have to accept a strengthening of the Governor's powers. Following the Conservative victory in the British general election of October 1951 British ministers became still more sceptical about any further demission of power to the elected element, even though Foot's proposals largely replicated those put forward by Huggins in 1948. Listowel's replacement as Minister of State at the Colonial Office, Alan Lennox Boyd, was critical of Foot's suggestion that greater responsibility should be given to elected members of the Executive Council and their numbers increased. Although Griffiths had previously authorised discussions on this basis, Lennox-Boyd was 'disturbed' by the assumption that such reforms were inevitable. Lord Munster, the new Parliamentary Under-Secretary, seconded these concerns and declared: 'I think it is a case of more haste less speed.'[59]

Reform in Jamaica was delayed for two years as Foot sought to reconcile the caution of British politicians and administrators with local demands for greater autonomy. Numerous anxious minutes were scribbled by the former group in support of an extension of the reserved powers of the Governor, even though it was, as one official, Heinemann, acknowledged 'in a sense a retrogressive move and will be represented as such in Jamaica.' Despite this the Colonial Office argued that, because of the instability and disorderliness of Jamaican politics, the Governor 'must always be in a position to take over the engine.' Lloyd relished the task of scattering obstacles along the path to independence around Britain's global empire. He argued that Jamaica should not advance any further than Trinidad, where recent constitutional reforms had left the Governor with the power to certify legislation.[60] The trading of a limited increase in the executive power of elected ministers in return for greater licence for the Governor was, as Foot pointed out, unlikely to be attractive in Jamaica where the PNP was campaigning for the abolition of the upper house or Legislative Council, which consisted of the Governor's nominees and officials, an increase in the numbers of elected politicians on the Executive Council and the removal of the right of officials to vote on policy matters. Although some of these proposals had been considered viable in 1948, they caused irritation in the Colonial Office four years later. The West India department composed a note suggesting that Manley's demand that appointed officials should lose their voting rights was divisive and would merely increase the likelihood of the Governor employing his reserved powers to frustrate the Executive Council. It was agreed that Munster should visit Jamaica to investigate the controversy. The most revealing comments on his mission were supplied by the Conservative Colonial Secretary, Oliver Lyttelton, who urged Munster to pursue 'a Fabian policy in the true sense'. He recommended that Munster should maintain 'a strong and of course impartial bias in favour of officials retaining their votes.'[61] The inclusion of numerous constitutional safeguards in the reform package proposed by Munster in April 1952 was predictable: he endorsed the notion that the Governor should be the 'sole judge' of when to exercise his newly strengthened reserve powers and recommended that nominated officials on the Executive Council should be 'full members' with voting rights. In return for this bolstering of imperial authority the nationalists were to be offered an increase in the numbers of elected members on the Executive Council. They would also finally obtain effective ministerial responsibility in their own departments.[62]

In response to the Munster proposals Norman Manley rallied his supporters in the PNP behind the cause of Jamaican self-government. The start of the campaign in July 1952 was recorded by his wife, Edna Manley: 'Norman's old dynamism seems to have returned, and in the house and on the streets he has launched a great campaign to seize the dynamic in the country again.'[63] Although his efforts were interrupted by the great natural disaster of Hurricane Charlie, which struck

Jamaica during the 1952 storm season, Manley utilised the strengthened position of the PNP in the House of Representatives to revitalise the case for self-government which had been effectively moribund since the end of the war. While Foot had been examining the Nigerian constitution as a model for Jamaica, Manley devoted himself to an analysis of the independent constitution of Ceylon and took the nationalist campaign on that island as the blueprint for an early peaceful transfer of power.[64] When they initially discussed the reform package of the Colonial Office, Foot reported that Manley was 'critical' but agreed that the proposals 'represented a big step forward.'[65] This proved an overly optimistic assessment of Manley's attitude. Frustrated with the glacial pace of decolonisation Manley attacked the Munster proposals in the House of Representatives. In one of the most significant speeches of his career he outlined the damaging consequences of continued dependence on Britain which was manifested in the package of reforms negotiated by Bustamante and the Colonial Office; by contrast a policy of genuine self-government would set a beneficial precedent for the rest of the empire. He argued that 'even the most liberal-minded members of a world-governing country do not believe in the effectiveness of any colonial people to govern themselves, except peradventure where they are people of their own race.' It was the duty of Jamaicans, Manley declared, 'to press forward as fast as we can' with constitutional reform so that they could demonstrate their capacity to govern their own affairs.[66]

Manley's speech was a significant moment in the history of decolonisation in the Caribbean: in the short term, it precipitated only minor concessions from the Colonial Office but in the medium term it established the basis for a populist campaign for independence which contributed towards the PNP's victory in the 1955 election, while in the longer term the momentum towards greater autonomy in Jamaica, which culminated in effective self-government in 1959 and independence in 1962, set precedents for the nationalist campaigns in the other territories. Initially, Foot expressed alarm that Manley had been too persuasive, and dismay that JLP resistance to the idea of a more advanced constitution appeared comparatively feeble. Faced with the possibility of defeat in the House of Representatives, Foot and Bustamante conceded to Manley's demand for the establishment of a new committee to formulate proposals for full self-government. Back in Whitehall, the Colonial Office were impressed both by Foot's adroit manoeuvring, which succeeded in getting the reforms passed, but also by Manley's 'considerable Parliamentary triumph.' More significantly they restated their commitment to Lyttelton's Fabian tactics. Lloyd made clear that if Bustamante exploited the success of Manley's new campaign for constitutional advance in order to accrue greater powers for the elected executive he would be resisted.[67] When the constitutional reordering finally took place in May 1953 the only significant change from the Munster proposals was a provision allowing the Chief Minister to advise the Governor on the appointment of seven newly empowered ministerial positions.[68] The securing of a majority for the elected representatives on the Executive Council seemed a limited achievement, in the context of the six-year debate which had preceded it. The outcome reflected continuing Colonial Office determination to conceive the smallest viable increment of constitutional reform; this in turn reflected their suspicion about the capacity of local Jamaican politicians, and Bustamante in particular, to administer the affairs of the territory. Somewhat paradoxically the skill with which Manley conducted the campaign for self-government, combined with the reassurance he offered by expelling the Marxist left of the PNP in 1952 established his reputation as a more reliable potential collaborator in the process of decolonisation. He increasingly seemed the candidate most likely to contain rather than exacerbate the social tensions which were an inevitable consequence of the overlapping racial and social fractures not just in Jamaica but elsewhere in the Anglophone Caribbean. These divisions appeared to be even more conspicuous in the smaller islands of the Leewards and the Windwards.

Small island turmoil

The pedestrianism of constitutional talks in the aftermath of Montego Bay contrasted with the rapid pace of social and economic change across the region. One of the most significant phenomena of the period was the triumph of labour on the small islands which British policymakers accepted as inevitable, while fretting about its consequences for decolonisation. Strikes on the islands of St Kitts in 1948, Antigua and Grenada in 1951 and St Lucia in 1957 were climacteric events in the history of the islands. In each case the newly organised forces of the trade union movement won at least partial victories over the employers.[69] Metropolitan policymakers tended to apportion the blame for such disputes equally between employers for their intransigence and the workers for their recklessness. This reflected a broader ambivalence about the role of trade unions. The Colonial Office encouraged unionisation as a safe channel for labour discontent but feared that workers might become imbued with sentiments of racial assertiveness or communist sympathy. While the ideological conservatism of the first generation of labour leaders like Critchlow in British Guiana, Bustamante in Jamaica and Uriah Butler in Trinidad offered some reassurance on the latter point, there was one inherent aspect of trade unionism that caused ongoing uneasiness among British officials: the mobilisation of large numbers of ordinary people which manifested itself in mass meetings, demonstrations and the coordinated withdrawal of labour. From a British perspective the politicisation of workers threatened renewed turbulence and the danger was aggravated by the antediluvian attitudes of the local plantocracy in the Caribbean who were determined to resist any erosion of their authority. The new generation of labour leaders, including Robert Bradshaw on St Kitts, Vere Bird on Antigua, Eric Gairy on Grenada and George Charles on St Lucia, built their reputations on success in alleviating the poverty of the workers. Their initial challenge was largely confined to the sphere of industrial relations but in each case quickly ramified into organised party-political activities. This development, which entailed utilising popular discontent with social conditions in order to achieve constitutional advance, was generally interpreted by the metropolitan power as a significant threat to the orderly process of decolonisation. The best which could be hoped to achieve in the circumstances was to contain union radicalism while constructing a safe constitutional environment in which longer-term stability could be achieved.

St Kitts

In common with almost all Kittitians of his and previous generations, the personal fortunes of Robert Bradshaw were tied to those of the island's sugar industry right from his birth in 1916. His father worked as a blacksmith on one of the sugar estates and he recalled: 'Ours is a poor family – still poor – because if you go to the village today, you will still find some of my relations working in the cane fields. So to the extent that blood is blood, I have not quite left the fields. I am still attached to the earth.' After his upbringing on the estate Bradshaw escaped field labour and went to work instead in the sugar factory at Basseterre. He became concerned at an early stage both with the lack of autonomy and injustice imposed by the arduous working conditions in the factory and on the plantations. It was evident to him that the rural labourers 'were not quite free' and he was infuriated when he found a document in a waste-paper bin which detailed the profits being made by the factory's owners.[70] In the 1930s workers' organisations were more advanced on St Kitts than on many of the other small islands, due partly to the initiative of the first generation of leaders including the cousins, Thomas Manchester and Edgar Challenger. Although it is difficult to make a fine judgement about the degree of immiseration on each of the territories, discontent on St Kitts certainly reflected the extent of economic distress on the island which was exceptionally acute even by West Indian standards.[71] Bradshaw joined the Workers League of Manchester and Challenger which became the St Kitts-Nevis Labour Union following the industrial relations legislation which legalised union activity in the aftermath of the Moyne Commission report of 1939. He was under 30 when he became President in 1944 and by 1947 the membership of the union had increased to over 8,000 workers.[72]

In the years after he had established his dominance over Kittitian politics, Bradshaw's sartorial dandyism, oenophilia and antiquarianism made him vulnerable to charges of being one of Naipaul's 'mimic men', whose attempts to emulate English aristocratic culture transformed them into comical figures. Despite these affectations, Bradshaw's political hegemony in St Kitts was founded on a remarkable achievement in finally overcoming the power of the sugar oligarchy on the island. His later electoral success would have been impossible had he not husbanded the workers through the traumatic confrontation of 1948. Like the earlier generation of labour leaders Bradshaw was both pro-federalist and anti-communist. His union supported the newly formed International Confederation of Free Trade Unions (ICFTU) which was formed by British, American and Dutch unionists as a rival to the World Federation of Trade Unions (WFTU) which they claimed was dominated by Soviet surrogates.[73] Bradshaw's support for the ICFTU aligned him with the West in the Cold War, while the consistent backing he gave to the cause of federal unity at a regional level eventually garnered some praise from imperial bureaucrats. The Vincentian Fred Phillips, who was Administrator of the island 20 years after the 1948 strike, claimed to be often bewildered by Bradshaw's policies but found him to be exceptionally courteous and regarded him as 'a man of high principles'.[74] In the late 1940s and early 1950s British officials regarded Bradshaw's role quite differently. His confrontational approach to industrial relations ensured that his name was added to the growing list of potentially dangerous militants who could unsettle the process of orderly decolonisation. The Administrator of St Kitts, Leslie Greening, complained about Bradshaw's personal attacks and bemoaned the absence of an effective class of collaborators in the process of reform. His reports to the Colonial Office lamented the absence of a middle class to mediate between workers and employers. On 3 December 1947 he explained the rise of Bradshaw in these terms: 'unlike the larger islands, there is no vocal or active body willing to present and argue the other side of the question. In the result a noisy, abusive, persistent nobody can soon collect a following of the ignorant who are unable to understand and who are unlikely to comprehend, until too late, the consequences of believing the lies told to them and of following such leadership.'[75] These comments reflected the distaste many British officials felt for the working-class Trade Union leadership on the small islands and took little account of their ideological orientation or the circumstances in which Kittitian politics was conducted.

The extreme monoculture of St Kitts was evident from the trade figures of the colony: in 1950 sugar exports generated revenues of BWI $ 5.5 million, while the value of cotton exports, which was the next most remunerative commodity, was estimated to be only BWI $ 0.3 million.[76] The historic legacy of sugar was to divide the island into one large class of workers, on the estates and in the factory, who were wholly dependent on cultivating and processing cane for employment and one much smaller class of managers, investors and landowners who dominated the political and economic life of the colony. When he visited the island after the Second World War, Patrick Leigh Fermor found that it had 'an undeniably patrician air' which he attributed to the aristocratic origins of the early French and British settlers.[77] Noble interests and values had long been marginalised by the crude dictates of commercial calculation which led to the consolidation of estates and the associated rise of a new mercantile class but the changing character of the local oligarchy had not ended their tradition of secluded superiority. Their reaction to the demotic challenge posed by the union movement was uncompromising. Incremental improvements in the terms and conditions of the sugar workers on St Kitts made in the aftermath of the 1935 uprising failed to mitigate the sense that a final confrontation between workers and employers was inevitable. Bradshaw announced that he was 'sick and tired of seeing the people in rags, bare-footed, living in places which no decent man would house his horse.' At the outset of the 1948 dispute he promised that the strike would be a 'big step in this march towards our economic emancipation'.[78] The employers remained unreconciled to the existence of workers' organisations which fell outside their auspices and argued that improving conditions for workers would be costly to their businesses at a time when the economic prospects of the island were endangered by competition in the international market for sugar. British officials in the region made clear their distaste for the employers' indifference to the social conditions in which most islanders lived. The Colonial Secretary of the Leeward Islands, William Macnie, who frequently took on the role of Acting Governor, noted that 'the attitude of the Sugar Producers' Association of St Kitts may be described as the "last ditch stand" of the old "plantocracy" of the West Indies.' He condemned the 'careless attitudes' of the employers to workers' conditions and suggested that 'racial and social antagonism in St Kitts appears to be worse than in any other Colony in the Caribbean.'[79] Despite levelling charges of atavism against the sugar magnates, the Colonial Office blamed the 1948 strike on what they regarded as the unreasonable demands put forward by Bradshaw's union which at the end of the previous year had proposed an increase of 75% in wages.[80] The union's submission was accompanied by a number of ancillary demands and the subsequent strike became entangled in a range of grievances including whether the union should be able to maintain a closed shop.

What was clear from the outset was that Bradshaw's criticisms of the employers were grounded in the quotidian experiences of cultivating cane and, more particularly, of harvesting it in the fields and processing it in the factory. Perhaps the most important of the disagreements concerned the issue of how much cane a person could be expected to cut in a day. Variations in the fertility of the soil, the inclination of the land and other geographical factors made it more difficult for some workers than others to cut similar quantities of cane. Bradshaw was emphatic that the only equitable solution was to pay the same amount for each line of cane harvested by the worker rather than each ton weighed by the overseer. The end of payments based on weight would leave the workers less vulnerable to sleight of hand by employers because workers knew how many lines had been cut but had no confidence in the weighing machines used by the employers. At the other end of the production line was the factory, in which Bradshaw had worked. Because cane spoiled quickly once cut, sugar processing had always been dependent on the existence of another set of workers in close proximity to the cutters who coordinated their labour with that of those in the field. They manned the machinery which crushed or comminuted the cane fibres in order to extract a sugar liquid, and the vats which heated this substance to generate a crude form of sucrose sufficiently stable to be preserved for further processing.[81] Although pay was better in the factory than in the field, the work was dangerous and Bradshaw persisted with his campaign to have it nationalised both during and after the strike. However, the sugar processing operation on St Kitts was judged to be one of the most efficient and profitable in the Caribbean by the Soulbury commission, which was chaired by a former Conservative MP and whose findings were sympathetic to the employers.[82]

Grievances over conditions, rates of pay and the role of the union, rather than over broader political questions about nationalisation, led to a breakdown of negotiations with employers on 5 January 1948. As a consequence the workers refused to cut cane at the start of the harvesting season two weeks later. Employees at the sugar factory came out on strike at the same time. On 22 January Macnie reported that no work was being done in the factories or the fields but that the union was willing to submit all issues in dispute to arbitration with the single exception of their demand for payment by the line. Despite these early signs of compromise, Macnie was sceptical about the prospects for a resolution because of the prevalent culture of the union which included an 'appalling distrust of "Englishmen".' Racial considerations of this kind probably did not account for the Colonial Office's decision to dispatch a Welsh labour advisor, Edgar Parry, from Britain to the island to investigate the causes of the strike. Parry seems to have been bewildered by the intensity of the dispute: the employers were attempting to starve the workers into submission and they retaliated by setting fire to the cane fields. Although appalled at the manner in which both sides conducted the strike, he considered that it was the union's actions which were more reprehensible. While he accepted that Bradshaw was 'straightforward and frank' and that the demands of the union were not unreasonable, the gist of his oral briefing for Colonial Office officials on 19 March was thoroughly alarmist. Bradshaw was accused by Parry of possessing 'a "messianic" belief in the inspiration of his views' and of ambitions to become 'dictator of St Kitts'. The workers were condemned for failing to give adequate notice of the strike action, neglecting the animals on the estates and for attempting to enforce the 'closed shop'.[83]

From the union's perspective the danger of Parry's intervention was that it would erode traditional metropolitan scepticism about the employers' case at a time when the owners of the estates were planning to starve their employees back to work. Bradshaw noted that during his visit Parry seemed 'so fed up with the whole affair' that he almost expected him to abandon his mission. On Bradshaw's account Parry went as far as claiming that had he known how bad the situation was, 'no one would have got me out of London'. For the union the resulting report was a catastrophe which prompted the employers to redouble their anti-union propaganda campaign.[84] In his role as Secretary of the Caribbean Labour Congress, Hart was less confident than Bradshaw about a successful outcome. In correspondence with Grantley Adams, Hart aired the possibility that 'the Sugar Producers Assn may have decided to sacrifice the 1948 crop in order to break the union through the starvation of the local population.' As a well-known moderate and a favourite of the Colonial Office, Adams was a suitable candidate for the role of conciliator. He was persuaded to take up negotiations on behalf of the St Kitts sugar workers and in this capacity pursued Hart's compromise proposals that they accept a 15% increase in wages and another investigation of the issue of payment by the line.[85] By this stage it was evident that the sugar producers were expecting a comprehensive victory but their obstinacy lost them some of the gains made by Parry's intervention in their favour. In the middle of March Macnie recorded that, while the union was showing signs of flexibility, the employers were convinced they would prevail and were 'definitely not prepared to compromise in any way.'[86] Following Adams's mission at the end of the month a deal was effectively imposed by Macnie which saved most of the 1948 crop, secured an increase in wages and provided for further consultations which eventually moderated the system of payment by weight. Bradshaw persisted with his campaign to nationalise the factory so that its earnings could be utilised for the purposes of development on the islands rather than repatriated by its overseas owners but he was unable to persuade the metropolitan authorities of the merits of his case. Although Creech Jones as Colonial Secretary acknowledged that nationalisation might ameliorate local resentment, the Colonial Office believed it would jeopardise the efficiency of production on the island.[87]

Both the unions and the employers of St Kitts had their champions in the British Parliament whose opinions were illustrative of broader attitudes to Caribbean politics in the metropolis. For the right-wing MPs, Ernest Taylor and Alfred Bossom, strike action on St Kitts portended a possible race war. Taylor forwarded a letter to Creech Jones from a constituent who was 'naturally very anxious as regards the safety of the white people in St Kitts'. A similar theme emerged from Bossom's interventions. He 'appeared very excited' during a meeting at the Colonial Office in March and the following month asked the Under-Secretary of State, Christopher Mayhew, whether the government was 'satisfied that the forces now existing on the island of St Kitts are entirely capable of protecting members of the white population against further industrial trouble.'[88] By contrast, the Labour MP Hyacinth Morgan blamed the employers for the strike. He supported Bradshaw's campaign for the nationalisation of the sugar factory and pressed the case for public control once again in two letters to Creech Jones written in early 1949. His advocacy of the workers' case put him at odds with MPs like Taylor and Bossom but he shared their belief that the tensions between different classes and races could generate further violence. Morgan told Creech Jones that, if he were resident in the West Indies, he would 'be on my knees praying for constitutional and peaceful methods' and that he had 'grave apprehension' for the lives of even his political opponents in the region.[89] A decade after the labour unrest of the 1930s industrial disputes in the West Indies were still perceived in the metropolis as containing the potential for insurrection or race war.

The leaders of the labour movement on St Kitts were principally concerned with improving the conditions of workers but Bradshaw perceived the connections between economic and political autonomy and took any opportunities provided to harry the British for greater control over the island's government. The popular campaign for constitutional reform culminated with the launch of Operation BLACKBURNE in 1950 which sparked lively demonstrations in protest against the appointment of the Governor of that name. The protests were a reaction to two related but separate developments which to Kittitians illustrated Colonial Office disdain for opinion on the smaller islands: the formulation of a minimalist package of constitutional change and the dismissal of Oliver Baldwin as Governor of the Leewards. In January 1948 the five elected members of the Kittitian Legislative Council had sponsored a resolution calling for reform of the political system, including an elected majority on the Executive Council which at that time consisted entirely of officials and nominees. Reporting from the Leewards, Greening and Macnie expressed concern about the possibility of the labour leaders taking control of the executive in the aftermath of the strike.[90] In July 1948 Seel opined that significant constitutional reform was 'the last thing we want to do in the case of these ridiculously small communities, and particularly in a place like St Kitts, where recently we have escaped serious trouble by a narrow margin and where matters would have been infinitely more difficult if the Administrator had had a Legislative Council, with a majority of people like Mr Bradshaw.' Sydney Caine, despite his reputation as a progressive, agreed that they needed to delay the transfer of political authority in the Leewards.[91]

The problem for the Colonial Office was that constitutional reform in the Leewards was also being sponsored by the Governor, Oliver Baldwin, who was the son of the former Prime Minister, Stanley Baldwin. His socialist views were at variance with those of his father and he was elected as a Labour MP in the landslide victory of 1945. On his father's death in 1947 he automatically became a member of the House of Lords and in the following year Attlee appointed him Governor. He proved an idiosyncratic representative of British imperial interests. His flouting of the usual proprieties of the office led him into constant conflict with the metropolitan government. Aside from the breaches of cultural form arising from a refusal to disguise his homosexuality and his incommunicativeness, which was manifest in a persistent refusal to respond promptly to urgent telegrams, the advanced political views he espoused scandalised the local plantocracy and irritated the Colonial Office.[92] The new politicians rising out of the union movement were less concerned about this case of administrative anomie than with the fact that Baldwin demonstrated a paternalist sympathy with their cause. He established a particularly close alliance with Bird on Antigua. In the case of St Kitts Baldwin proposed universal adult suffrage, a wholly elected Legislative Council and the introduction of a committee system which would give local politicians a role in the executive.[93] Although willing to concede the first point, officials in Whitehall resisted the other two. Creech Jones authorised a less generous package of reforms than that proposed by Baldwin. In order to induce Bradshaw to cooperate the Colonial Office offered to institute the committee system, which they had initially opposed, but only on the condition that Baldwin was not credited with accomplishing this change of policy. They feared that if the Governor received the acclaim of the Kittitian population for having 'won concessions' which strengthened the position of elected representatives, it would only further encourage the 'demonstration psychology' on the island.[94]

In November 1949 Bradshaw condemned the Colonial Office proposals as 'a shockingly scandalous far cry from what was demanded by the Council.'[95] Six months later it was announced that the implementation of the new constitution would be overseen by Kenneth Blackburne who replaced Baldwin as Governor. Blackburne's arrival therefore provided an opportunity for the union movement to protest against metropolitan resistance to further democratisation. In October 1950 numerous islanders turned out to bang pots and pans and boo the new Governor and this no doubt reinforced the perception in Whitehall that a 'demonstration psychology' existed on St Kitts. Blackburne himself never seems to have forgiven what he described as 'the rabble' who booed him when he made his first visit to the island.[96] When he settled down to write his memoirs he entitled one of the chapters 'Boos and Booze' in a specific reference to his introduction to Kittitian politics.[97] In his memory the protests symbolised the truculence of many of the small islanders. A year later, after another visit to St Kitts to discuss the constitution he complained: 'If any one of these pathetic little places is not giving trouble then the other one is!' His letters home and his later memoirs placed responsibility for the problems on the people of the Leeward Islands who he described as 'too stiff necked' but most particularly on the labour leaders who were 'so filled with conceit that they cannot stand having been refused anything.'[98] Rather than symptomatic of any inherent truculence the local enthusiasm for Operation BLACKBURNE is best understood in the context of the imposition of a new Governor who was expected to be more subservient to the Colonial Office and the lagging behind of the small islands in the process of constitutional reform. The eventual measures which were implemented in 1953 ensured elected representatives in St Kitts still exercised less authority than those who participated in the Jamaican system introduced in 1944: in contrast to the wholly elected Jamaican House, three officials and three nominees continued to sit in the Legislative Council in St Kitts and the elected members of the Executive Council, like their counterparts in Jamaica, remained corralled by the bureaucratic constraints of the committee system. The discounting of these issues and the emphasis on personalities and emotion in British criticisms of Kittitian politics is significant because it cast ideological issues into the shadows; the same tendency was evident in the British discussion of events in Grenada but in this second case one differentiating factor was the influence of the Cold War.

Grenada

Among the smaller islands, in terms of both socio-economic circumstances and scholarly attention, Grenada is at the opposite pole to St Kitts. The American invasion of 1983 precipitated a mini-publishing boom on the subject of Grenada's history and politics which contrasts sharply with the exiguous literature available to students of Kittitian affairs. Although much of the post-invasion writing was concerned with the proximate causes of the American intervention, most also at least glanced at the twentieth-century history of the colony and acknowledged the strike of 1951 as a transformative event.[99] Prior to that year the island had been notable for its political quiescence which was usually attributed to the fact that, unlike their counterparts on St Kitts, many peasants and estate workers owned small plots of land which gave them greater economic security and social independence. This in turn was a consequence of historical developments which had generated a slightly more diverse economy than existed on some of the other small islands. During the mid-nineteenth century many landowners in Grenada had abandoned sugar cultivation in favour of cocoa. A few years later the export of nutmeg and its by-product, mace, became a new source of revenue for the Grenadian estates. Production methods in the new sectors of the economy were less punishing than in the cane fields. Although workers remained tied to employers by various instruments, including the 'contracting out' or Metayer system which obliged them to devote a portion of land to growing export crops on behalf of the landowners, many Grenadians were able to supplement their low wages by cultivating food crops.[100] The key area of commonality with the other territories in the Anglophone Caribbean was that, despite the plurality of production methods evident in cocoa, nutmeg and sugar cultivation, Grenada was dependent on the international market for the commodities it produced. When international prices fell employers attempted to cut wages, while a sharp rise in prices resulted in changes to social relations because, when the value of land increased, estates were often sold to new owners at a profit.[101] The connections between economic dependency and social protest were even clearer in the case of Grenada than in the case of St Kitts.

The acknowledged leader of the new workers' movement of 1950–1951 was Eric Matthew Gairy whose political ascent has garnered historiographical attention as an unparalleled, if unfortunate, example of the salience of charisma in Caribbean politics.[102] Gairy's ideological position was so parochial, not to say incoherent, that he did not offer a strategic threat to British interests in the region, despite the success of his tactics in challenging the imperial bureaucracy at a local level. His programme contained elements of socialism, spirituality, paternalism and self-aggrandisement with the last probably forming the largest portion of the mix. His methods attracted particular attention and this is warranted to the extent that the legends associated with the impact of 'Hurricane Gairy' in the 1950s, the uncovering of 'Squandermania' in the 1960s and the enforcement tactics of the 'Mongoose Gang' in the 1970s are unlikely to fade, not least because of the resonance of the labels attached to what became new forms of corruption in Grenadian political life. At the outset of his career Gairy appeared to fit the pattern of populist union agitation established by Bustamante, Bradshaw and Butler. After a short period of teacher-training in Grenada, Gairy sought new opportunities first at the American base in Trinidad, where he worked on the construction site, and then as a clerk in the oil industry of Aruba, where he participated in union work for the first time. On returning to Grenada at the end of 1949 he utilised his experience of organising expatriate workers in the Dutch colony in order to mobilise the agricultural workers who had hitherto lacked any effective union representation. The strikes he led on Grenada were more decisively successful than Bradshaw's and provided the popular base for the bizarre political career which culminated when he became the first Prime Minister of an independent Grenada in 1974. Despite his role in securing better conditions for workers, Gairy's excesses frequently alienated his supporters and he suffered both electoral defeat and eventually revolutionary overthrow during the course of his career. However, as a number of authors have insisted, the unusual events of Gairy's life must be placed in the context of the social, economic and political circumstances of Grenada at mid-century.[103]

Prior to Gairy's emergence the journalist T. Albert Marryshow led the opposition to the Grenadian oligarchy. In alliance with his comrade, the Trinidadian Arthur Andrew Cipriani, he became the leading proponent of constitutional reform and regional cooperation in the Anglophone Caribbean during the inter-war period. Gordon Lewis has noted that Marryshow's political programme was limited because his 'staunch Whig constitutionalism never permitted him to fight the colonial power except on its own polite terms.'[104] In contrast to Grantley Adams in Barbados, who shared his liberal reformist ideology, Marryshow failed to recognise that trade unions would inevitably play an integral role in reshaping Caribbean society at a time when both the local mercantile elite and the imperial power were in slow decline. Legal opportunities for organising the workers which emerged after the passage of the Trade Union Ordinance of 1934 were almost wholly neglected on Grenada; it fell to the colonial authorities after the promptings of the Moyne Commission to encourage the organisation of labour during the 1940s.[105] By the end of the decade the St John's Labour Party (General Workers' Union) and the Grenada Workers' Union had merged to form the Trades Union Council (TUC) but neither offered any effective representation for agricultural workers. The expected benefits of a series of wage increases during the 1940s were attenuated because of price inflation. Rises in the cost of living were a consequence of increased commodity prices in overseas markets which generated a local economic boom.

Popular attention was also directed, as in St Kitts, to the profits being generated by estate owners at a time of economic success. The official Colonial Office analysis of the disturbances focused largely on the faults of the union but acknowledged: 'That there is considerable poverty there can be no doubt, but it appears discontent was not very marked until Gairy started his campaign, encouraged by the high prices being obtained for cocoa and nutmeg.'[106] The leading Grenadian historian and future Prime Minister, George Brizan, has illustrated what the Colonial Office meant by 'considerable poverty' by offering some detailed analysis of the slum my living conditions and cases of infant malnutrition which prevailed on the island in the 1940s.[107]

Gairy's first intervention in Grenadian labour politics appears to have been his organising role in some short-lived agitation among the proto-peasantry who worked the Metayer system in the nutmeg industry in March 1950.[108] Four months later he registered the Grenada Manual and Mental Workers' Union (GMMWU), whose title bespoke of the need for class alliances against the oligarchy but which recruited many more agricultural labourers than urban shop and office workers. Gairy's initial success occurred in the island's residual sugar industry. On 31 July 1950 the GMMWU demanded a 50% wage increase and improvements in other terms and conditions on the remaining sugar estates. The employers disputed the right of the GMMWU to represent the workers but the Colonial Office's labour adviser acknowledged the legitimacy of Gairy's claim to be their spokesman. A strike in late August was resolved by arbitration which awarded the workers a 25% wage increase, seven days statutory vacation for those employed for 200 days or more and double time for work on public holidays.[109] This was a notable success and agricultural labourers flocked to join Gairy's new union which recruited 5,000 members in its first year.[110]

The expansion in membership encouraged Gairy to confront the owners of the cocoa plantations. He chose the La Sagesse estate, where there was strong support for the GMMWU, as the battleground for recognition of the union. Having visited the estate on 29 January 1951, on 8 February he submitted demands for a 45% increase in wages. The extension of the GMMWU's influence across all sectors of the agricultural economy was resisted by the employers who still hoped to deal with the more accommodating TUC. The insistence of the owners of La Sagesse and two other estates that they would only negotiate with the TUC led Gairy to call a general strike on 19 February.[111] Workers' resentment was exacerbated by the unyielding attitude of the employers who, as in St Kitts, regarded the strike as an opportunity to emasculate the new union movement. The colonial authorities swung backwards and forwards between a policy of repression and appeasement. Their immediate reaction to the strike was to declare a state of emergency, intern Gairy and call up a warship, HMS Devonshire, to the Grenadian coast. By 6 March it had become evident that the strikers could not be coerced into returning to work and Gairy was released. The violent unrest which had marked the strike continued and on 16 March two men and a woman were killed after police from Trinidad fired on a crowd who were protesting about the arrest of eight workers charged with stealing from the cocoa plantations.[112] On 4 April the colonial administration, the GMMWU and the employers agreed to establish a Wages Council and Gairy promised to encourage union members to return to work. The final settlement which increased the minimum wage and introduced seven days' annual holiday with pay, was effectively imposed on the Grenadian business leaders. The Colonial Office's labour adviser, Ernest Barltrop, noted that he 'had, if anything more difficulty in negotiating with the employers than with Mr Gairy.'[113] The government estimated that at least 80 estates had been affected by the disturbances and nearly £ 200,000 of damage had been caused.[114] After their effective defeat the old plantocracy blamed the colonial authorities for doing insufficient to protect their interests and in September the Governor, Robert Arundell, even reported rumours that they had devised a 'fantastic plot' to abduct him and utilise the ensuing chaos to gun down the leading participants in the strike.

Nothing came of the alleged plot but in the Cold War atmosphere generated by the escalation of the Korean War accusations of communist penetration of the island were given some credence. Although it took place on the other side of the world, the North Korean invasion and subsequent Chinese intervention sparked the gravest crises of the Cold War and a global search by the Western powers for other potential centres of subversion. As his subsequent career attested, Gairy was an exceptionally unlikely candidate for membership of the Soviet bloc and most colonial administrators were sceptical of claims that he was a communist. Other influential figures were absolutely convinced that he was under the influence of Marxism; the most insistent of these groups were the local employers' organisations. During a meeting with businessmen on 7 March, W. E. Julien of the Chambers of Commerce told the Governor 'this is not a strike – it is stark naked communism laid bare.' Dennis Henry of the Employers' Association asserted that Gairyism 'bears all the hallmarks of Communism.' British officials were insufficiently credulous to believe this testimony but they were not invulnerable to Cold War paranoia. Barltrop judged it 'very difficult to say whether Gairy is consciously communist in thought' but was convinced that some of his advisers were. He also reported that Gairy's acolytes were touring the island proclaiming 'Stalin for King'.[115] As in the Kittitian case the employers discovered a Westminster route into Whitehall deliberations. A former Grenadian estate owner with current capital investments in the island, George Duncan, wrote to the Conservative MP, Tufton Beamish, who forwarded his comments to the Colonial Secretary with the gloss that the letter 'contains a number of important points which I think are worthy of comment at the highest level.' Duncan's most pressing concern was that the 'coloured, good chaps' in the police force, who were loyal to the monarch, would be unable to maintain order 'against 70,000 chaps who've gone a little mad; they're just like a lot of children and I'm sure that half or more of the cause of this has been intimidation.'[116] Inside the House of Commons, the earlier concerns expressed about industrial unrest in St Kitts were greatly amplified by news from Grenada. On 26 February 1951 Anthony Eden pressed the Opposition view that 'The first task is to restore law and order so that the merits of the dispute can be examined.'[117] Other Conservative MPs criticised the Labour Colonial Secretary, Griffiths, for his failure to protect the property of Grenadian employers. Henderson Stewart and Harry Legge-Bourke disseminated the employers' assertions that the strikes were directed by communists. The latter claimed to have detected the influence of John La Rose of Trinidad whose organisation, the Workers' Freedom Movement, was assessed by the Colonial Office as being 'tainted' by communism rather than defined by it.[118]

Metropolitan reactions to the violence that accompanied and continued after the strike illustrated their jumpiness about the new demotic politics of their Caribbean empire. In the imagination of British officialdom Grenada was transformed by Gairy's actions from being one of the most comfortable and salubrious outposts in the Caribbean to a crucible for class conflict and racial antagonism. On 17 March Arundell wrote despairingly that 'we have been sitting on an active volcano here for some time' and that: 'Lawlessness was increasing and planters throughout the island were becoming more and more hysterical.'[119] At the end of April he provided a briefing for Griffiths about the current situation on the island: 'The whole atmosphere of Grenada has changed for the worse. Good manners and friendliness have tended to give way to scowls and churlishness. One feels that a spark could set the whole thing off again.' This prediction was either prescient or self-fulfilling; on 5 May

Arundell requested that British troops be sent to the island to deal with potential disturbances after the 'megalomaniac' Gairy was charged with the use of threatening language. Following the dispatch of a company of Royal Welsh Fusiliers, Gairy was convicted and bound over for six months. This minor setback did not hinder his broader campaign which now focused on the first election in Grenada's history to be held under a system of universal adult suffrage.[120]

The new Grenadian constitution introduced on 1 August 1951 was part of a wider and long-planned reform which took place across the Windwards. Its provisions included the introduction of universal suffrage, the liberalisation of qualifications for membership of the Legislative Council and the reorganisation of the Executive Council. However, it was the fourth measure, the establishment of an elected majority on the Legislative Council, which provided Gairy with an opportunity to confront the colonial government.[121] He formed the Grenada United Labour Party (GULP) which contested all eight of the elected seats on the Council. The Colonial Office had not imagined the future impact of 'Hurricane Gairy' when they designed the new constitution and the prospect of his victory at the polls caused them to immediately consider suspending aspects of its implementation. Arundell warned as early as March that he had 'grave doubts' about holding an election in the aftermath of the strike. A visit to the Colonial Office by one of the planters represented on the current Legislative Council, T. E. Noble Smith, caused the metropolitan authorities to pause. He warned that any election would be 'farcical' and Stephen Luke reported that 'there was little exaggeration in his alarming picture of conditions in Grenada.' These hesitations did not, in the end, lead to the cancellation of the elections. Luke's superior, Thomas Lloyd, believed any such move would antagonise the island's labour force. In August Arundell dispatched a more sanguine report which indicated that he expected candidates opposed to Gairy to win four of the eight seats, with the other four going to the GULP.[122] This proved overly optimistic: in the election held on 10 October 1951, Gairy's candidates obtained 63% of the votes and six seats which gave them a majority on the Legislative Council.[123] Although he later suffered setbacks in the 1954 and 1957 elections, Gairy's eventual triumph at the polls in 1961, following further constitutional advance, established him as Chief Minister of Grenada. During these years he became the incarnation of everything the British liked least and feared most about 'small island politics'. His continued influence on Grenada's political life can be traced back to the initial impact of the strikes of

1950–1951 which convinced the general population and the colonial authorities that life on the island would never be the same again.

Conclusion

In the aftermath of the Montego Bay conference the nationalist vision of Caribbean politicians was competing on three fronts with the cautious incrementalist strategies of British imperialism. The first was located at the point of confrontation between workers and employers where the need to redress the degrading conditions of the region's labour force ensured a continuation of the struggles of the 1930s. In Grenada the potential for violence and disorder was manifest in Gairy's campaign. In many respects, the situation on that island was untypical of the rest of the Anglophone Caribbean, most notably because of oligarchical complacency resulting from the absence of major disturbances in the 1930s; but the violence which accompanied the 1951 strike was taken by the British as confirmation of the dangers which would accompany the process of decolonisation across the region. As events in St Kitts illustrated, the Colonial Office were more sympathetic to economic grievances than to political ones and this typified a tradition of paternalism and trusteeship. Consequently, on the second front, where the argument over self-government was being conducted, the British pursued an excessively cautious policy which sought to delay and dilute each successive package of reform. Jamaica is a particularly illuminating case study because the island had a greater measure of economic viability than most of the other territories and Manley was increasingly seen as a potentially reliable collaborator; but even in this instance the British were reluctant to expedite the transfer of power. Their scepticism about the preparedness of the island for self-government, which was confirmed by the ongoing disputes between Bustamante and the British Governors, Huggins and Foot, prompted the PNP to relaunch their campaign for Jamaican constitutional advance in 1952. At that point Manley revived a process that had atrophied under the influence of Bustamante's innate conservatism and the Colonial Office's captiousness. Such demands for territorial self-government had the potential to divert nationalist energies away from the third front which was that of West Indian nation-building; it was here that the gap between the functional approach of the British and the declared ambitions of the nationalists was at its widest. Despite their ostensible commitment to federalism, local politicians proved less persistent in pressing their case at the regional level as their capitulation in the SCAC talks illustrated. After the celebratory CLC meeting in Kingston in 1947 enthusiasm for federation dissipated and Rance's report was imprinted with Colonial Office scepticism about the capacities of the people of the region to run their own affairs. When the new nation of the West Indies was eventually established in 1958 its constitution still reflected the equivocations of British policymaking. By this time the Cold War had impinged further on the calculations of the participants and, in some of the islands the politics of race and migration had become still more prominent and perplexing.

3
Ordering the Islands 1952–1958

The 1950s witnessed the flourishing of a rowdy, demotic form of politics in the Anglophone Caribbean. Although this populist tendency was particularly conspicuous during the many elections in which the newly enfranchised descendants of slaves and indentured labourers could now participate, the campaign for independence extended beyond the contests for seats on various legislative councils. Jamaica was in the vanguard of party formation and during the 1940s the majority of the population enlisted in the cause either of Manley's PNP or Bustamante's JLP. In the early 1950s Gairy in Grenada and Jagan in Guiana mobilised agricultural workers who engaged in strikes and demonstrations in order to secure improvements in their working conditions; in both instances demands for social and economic justice were soon supplemented by campaigns for greater political independence. Trinidad witnessed one of the most innovative examples of populist politics as Eric Williams initiated a programme of mass adult education in what he called the University of Woodford Square. The extreme didacticism of Williams's university 'curriculum' was evident from the focus in his lectures on the historical record of imperialism and the current sterility of colonial politics but, despite the apparent dryness of some of the lessons, many ordinary Trinidadians attended.[1] The People's National Movement (PNM), which became the political embodiment of the spirit engendered in Woodford Square, established itself as the dominant party in the island's politics. By the end of the decade the recondite complexities of federal constitutional arrangements attracted sufficient interest across the region to fill the letters pages of the *Guardian*, the *Gleaner* and the *Advocate* with readers' opinions about issues such as freedom of movement and customs union. In 1961 the fate of the federation became the subject of the ultimate manifestation of popular

will: a plebiscite in Jamaica which led to a victory for the secessionists. The response of the metropolitan authorities to these developments
was ambivalent: they accepted the necessity for universal suffrage but
were dismayed that nationalist campaigning had become a permanent
rather than an occasional feature of local politics. They interpreted
the actions of the nationalist leaders in articulating popular discontent as evidence of irresponsibility. More particularly local Governors,
like Hugh Foot in Jamaica, Patrick Renison in Barbados and Edward
Beetham in Trinidad, feared that popular politics betokened class or
racial conflict. Previous stereotypes regarding the passivity of West
Indian people were displaced by visions of violent insurrection in the
name of either communism or racial exclusivity. In the former case, the
colonial authorities constructed a Cold War justification for extending
surveillance and restricting habeas corpus, while in the latter their com-
mentaries about the racial proclivities of imperial subjects generated
heightened vigilance and precautionary measures designed to subdue
actual and potential dissidents.

The Cold War in the Caribbean

In its generalities the mental picture which British policymakers drew
of the communist 'threat' in the Anglophone Caribbean was similar to
the image they held of it in the rest of the empire: it depicted the naive
but deprived masses being menaced by the machinations of exogenous
political actors who had joined hands with a handful of indigenous
Marxists. It is in its specificities, however, that an examination of the
workings of the imperial imagination in the Anglophone Caribbean
offers new insight into the politics of the 1950s: British administrators believed that the World Federation of Trade Unions (WFTU) was
propagating communist doctrines throughout the region and that there
were only a handful of committed indigenous Marxists who were capable of taking effective action to undermine British colonialism but that
the residents of the sugar estates and urban centres like Kingston and
Georgetown, who did not understand the realities of the Cold War,
might be sufficiently reckless to leap aboard the communist band-
wagon unless prophylactic action was taken. The anti-communist tactics
adopted by the British in Jamaica, Trinidad and Guiana varied according
to their perception of local circumstances. There was an open confrontation with Marxist politicians in Guiana and covert campaigns in
Jamaica and Trinidad but in each instance the elimination of the danger
of disorder promoted by the left was a prerequisite for decolonisation.

The Colonial Office and their representatives made their calculations in the context of the global Cold War and events in East Asia and East Africa were regarded as particularly ominous. Reports from Trinidad indicated that the most effective anti-colonial propaganda was a pamphlet condemning American tactics in Korea entitled 'The Napalm Killers Passed This Way'.[2] In Jamaica there was disquiet about the impact the communist victory in the Chinese Civil War would have upon Jamaican-Chinese residents. Events in Africa were also widely reported and in 1953 the Watson report on Caribbean communism noted that the most insidious propaganda was the material which focused on colonial topics including the Mau Mau insurgency. As a consequence, local police were instructed to monitor communications with Kenya.[3] Overshadowing all these developments were the direct ties which local activists like Ferdinand Smith, Richard Hart and Cheddi Jagan had established with international communist organisations.

Jamaica

At the end of the Cold War the Jamaican political philosopher and activist, Trevor Munroe, offered a deliberately under-theorised account of the defeat of the Jamaican left in the 1950s, based on a close reading of British and American documents. His purpose was to examine the way in which 'state structures, civil society and political culture were in large measure, manipulated and shaped by anti-communist priorities'.[4] The resulting book, *The Cold War and the Jamaican Left*, offered new evidence of the feebleness of the support offered by the eastern-bloc countries for Jamaican communists, the occasional misalignment of British and American views and the potential popular support which the left had during the 1950s, but its most startling conclusion was also its most questionable, namely that 'on occasion the "reactionary" Colonial Office took up positions in advance of the "progressive" anti-colonial leadership.'[5] The example which Munroe cites in order to support this analysis is the British refusal to comply with Bustamante's efforts to ban communist organisations in 1953. Despite Munroe's partial exoneration of the British, the full record suggests that they could easily rival Bustamante's enthusiasm for authoritarianism. The resistance of the Colonial Office to Bustamante's proposals was based on a belief that fighting the Cold War in the Caribbean required a sophisticated and indirect strategy if it were not to stir up the passions of the local population, and that Bustamante's gauche and clumsy efforts simply to ban communism generated their own dangers of autocracy or boss rule. The British instigated their own extensive anti-communist campaign comprising intrusive intelligence-gathering, restrictions on freedom of movement and the harassment of local leftists.

Two events in 1952 had a decisive influence on British attitudes to the Jamaican Cold War. The first was Norman Manley's decision to expel the Marxist grouping in the PNP. This arose from a dual conflict between Richard Hart and Wills Isaacs inside the party and between Ken Hill and Noel Nethersole within the party's union affiliates.[6] Following an internal investigation Manley was persuaded that the left, represented by Hill and Hart, had 'been engaged in propagating communism and building up a communist cell' inside the TUC and that this warranted expulsions from the party.[7] During a special PNP conference in March, Hill questioned the validity of the internal enquiry but was unable to prevent what was effectively an anti-communist purge. After his expulsion he formed the National Labour Party but its effectiveness was hampered by further disagreements between Hill and the other prominent expellee, Hart. This fragmentation among the radicals ought to have delighted British officials who feared that the era of decolonisation would provide new opportunities for the left but it actually marked the onset of the paranoid era in Jamaican politics. The unprecedented concern with communism which marked the next two years was a consequence of the second key event of 1952 which was the return of Ferdinand Smith to the Caribbean. The story of the British hounding of Smith has been detailed by his colleague Richard Hart and the historian Gerald Horne.[8] Smith was the quondam Secretary of the National Maritime Union of the United States. Shortly after the PNP split he held a meeting with other leftist leaders in Trinidad before reporting on the state of Caribbean communism to the WFTU in Vienna. He then travelled back to his home island of Jamaica in July 1952 with, according to British intelligence, a sum of £ 700 to be used for the purposes of extending communist influence in the region. In August 1953 the Colonial Secretary, Oliver Lyttelton, wrote to Caribbean Governors to alert them to the existence of a Soviet-backed political offensive in the region and listed Smith's return a year earlier, alongside the importing of communist literature and liaison between Caribbean leftist groups and international front organisations, as one of the three principal causes of the extension of the Cold War to the Anglophone Caribbean.[9] A Joint Intelligence Committee (JIC) report completed in that same month concluded that Smith's activities 'strengthened the hands of those Jamaican trade unionists who already had communist leanings and it coincided with the open declarations of Communist sympathies by the other leading trade unionists', including John Rojas in Trinidad and Cheddi Jagan in British Guiana. In examining the prospects for communism in the region the JIC identified two potential sources of trouble: on the one hand, 'in most of the territories economic and social conditions are conducive to periodic unrest and disorder', while on the other there was a possibility that, even at times when economic discontent was not prevalent, it could be fomented by 'the personal and political ambitions of a single individual'.[10]

Those Cold Warriors located in the Caribbean were even more anxious than Whitehall planners to take early action to curtail the influence of Marxist activists, such as Smith and Jagan. The two most influential exponents of this unvarnished anti-Communism were the Commander-in Chief of British forces in the Caribbean, A. C. F. Jackson, and the Governor of Jamaica, Hugh Foot. As early as June 1952 Jackson reported that 'a determined attempt is being launched to exploit the very fertile field provided by the politically immature population' of the Caribbean. As evidence he adduced the activities of Smith and the head of the London branch of the CLC, Billy Strachan, which he suggested were designed to secure communist control of unions affiliated to the Jamaican TUC. On Jackson's account the visits of the Trinidadian, John Rojas, and the Guianese, Cheddi Jagan, to Eastern Europe and ongoing Guatemalan subversion in British Honduras formed the other fronts in the left's regional offensive. At this early stage, the Colonial Office brushed aside Jackson's warnings but later in the year he returned to the attack. In November he suggested to the Ministry of Defence that the prospect of Jagan and his communist allies gaining control of the bauxite resources of British Guiana necessitated the suspension of plans for constitutional advance in that territory. This anticipated the actions of British ministers a year later but at this stage the Colonial Office responded by explaining that the local population was incapable of 'forming well-disciplined political parties with precise programmes' and that the establishment of an effective communist organisation by Jagan was unlikely.[11]

If Jackson was a gadfly that was easy to ignore, Hugh Foot was a much more considerable figure who, as Governor of Jamaica, was able to implement the most thoroughgoing anti-communist campaign in the Anglophone Caribbean. Many of the punitive actions which Foot recommended were never implemented because of fears that such repressive measures would establish the foundations of a future autocracy in Jamaica but he did instigate a policy of state harassment of leftist activists. By 1954, partly as a consequence of Foot's policy of surveillance and intimidation, Marxist fortunes were in steep decline. Two years earlier Foot had not been confident that the communist challenge could be contained. During a visit to the Colonial Office in December 1952 he expressed consternation at the prospects of a leftward shift in Jamaican politics.[12] The American consulate reported that the local police estimated that there might be as many as 500 communists in Jamaica.[13] Over the course of the following year Foot put a range of suggestions to the metropolitan government all based on the alarmist premise that Ferdinand Smith, with the assistance of funds from the WFTU, would be able to exploit socio-economic grievances in order to undermine governmental authority. When N.D. Watson of the Foreign Office's newly formed Information Research Department was despatched to the region to investigate the rise in communist activity, Foot presented a bundle of counter-measures to him, each of which was designed to demonstrate that the local government 'regards Communists as natural enemies.' He proposed compiling a list of local communists whose movements should be restricted, the banning of literature, refusal of passports, the interception of communications and the purging of communist supporters from the higher echelons of the Civil Service. The Jamaican authorities seem to have been transfixed by the potential impact of Mao's revolution on the Chinese community in the country. Five measures were aimed specifically at this group: refusing entry to Chinese communists, depriving naturalised citizens of nationality, photographing and fingerprinting all Chinese entrants, keeping 'a special watch' on those suspected of opium and arms smuggling and offering encouragement to Chinese nationalist organisations to resist communism. Foot told Watson that 'there would be need for continuing consultation on "repressive" measures as the situation developed and, more important, also on "constructive" actions against communism.'[14]

Foot's advocacy of discriminatory measures against the Chinese population and a McCarthyite witch hunt in the civil service were not welcomed by the British government. Only his proposal to restrict the freedom of movement of suspected subversives was incorporated into the Colonial Office's wider regional campaign against communism. On 1 November 1952 the government of Barbados had banned Ferdinand Smith from entering the country in order to attend a meeting of the CLC left organised by Hart. Other representatives of the Caribbean left were admitted and in response the Colonial Office sought to devise a more systematic policy regarding restrictions on freedom of movement.[15] The Security Liaison Officers in Jamaica and Trinidad conferred with Special Branches from the other territories to draw up a list of 11 Marxists who could potentially be banned from entering other territories. The list included Janet Jagan from British Guiana, John Rojas and John La Rose from Trinidad and Smith and Hart from Jamaica. In retrospect the most surprising name on the list was that of the popular and charismatic trade union leader from St Vincent, Ebenezer Joshua, who later spent a decade as Chief Minister of the island. Cheddi Jagan and Sydney King were excluded because they were members of the Guianese government. It was thought too embarrassing for the metropolitan government to restrict the movements of elected representatives who possessed ministerial status.[16]

The illiberal measures undertaken by Foot and the other Governors focused on monitoring and restricting potential contacts between Caribbean radicals and international communist organisations. For example, in October 1953 the Jamaican authorities refused passports to two alleged communists who were intent on travelling to Vienna for a meeting of the WFTU.[17] The British Minister of State, Henry Hopkinson, also urged 'everything possible to be done to limit Mr Smith's freedom of movement' but he and Hart continued to attend WFTU meetings in Vienna because they already had valid passports.[18] When Smith's passport eventually expired in 1957 the Jamaican government refused to renew it. The authorities were able to target communists more effectively because they had a surfeit of intelligence about the CLC and Richard Hart's newly formed People's Educational Organisation (PEO). The interception of post and cable communications between the islands was a widespread practice and members of the Special Branch read private letters sent between La Rose in Trinidad and Hart in Jamaica.[19] Labour and political organisations were penetrated by British informers, one of whom was in attendance at the Barbados meeting of November 1952 where it was noted that, although 'the group suspected the servants, they did not discover the identity of the real observer.'[20] The Permanent Under-Secretary at the Colonial Office, Thomas Lloyd, suggested that Grantley Adams would be shocked if he discovered the extent of British penetration of the CLC.[21] Suspected communists in Jamaica were subject to a regime of police raids, monitoring and harassment which was designed to demoralise them.[22] Although the 'lesser satellites' of the movement were singled out for particularly rough treatment on the grounds that they would probably be less steadfast, Richard Hart, who was certainly a major satellite, recalled that he frequently found police cars watching his house and was repeatedly tailed by policemen.[23]

British resistance to Bustamante's desire to effectively ban communism must be placed in the context of this extensive campaign of repression and the fear that future Jamaican governments would make irresponsible use of the authoritarian powers of the colonial state. Bustamante's attention was directed towards the communist 'menace' following the efforts of Smith and Hart to establish a new union in rural Jamaica. The formation of the Sugar and Agricultural Workers' Union (SAWU) created another rival to Bustamante's own trade union which had always been particularly strong in the Jamaican country-side. British officials recognised that the Chief Minister's opposition to SAWU was self-interested and interpreted the stridency of his campaign against it as further evidence of the potential for conflict between an authoritarian post-colonial leadership and a rebellious population. When SAWU applied to the Ministry of Labour for permission to act as representatives of the sugar workers on a number of estates in December 1953, Bustamante's government made clear it would oppose any form of recognition. Foot was sympathetic to Bustamante but he feared that proposals to give the Jamaican Executive Council new powers to effectively ban communism on the island were impractical and 'might in future be abused'. One of the other Caribbean Governors, Patrick Renison, was so alarmed that he entered the debate even though it had no relevance to his British Honduran patrimony. He viewed Bustamante as a potential dictator and warned 'decent parliamentary government is at least as gravely menaced by temptations of boss rule as by communism.'[24] British policymakers in Whitehall were divided in their reactions: on the one hand, they wished 'good luck' to any policy which might 'kill Ferdinand Smith's unions', while on the other they feared that the precedent might constitute 'a rod in pickle' which could be used to coerce non-Marxist political opponents in the future. Foot informed Bustamante on 27 January 1954 that he could not support his proposals for new legislation which 'would enable whatever political power was in power to proscribe its rivals', but the administrative action taken against SAWU was allowed to stand.[25]

The arbitrary refusal to recognise SAWU, which breached precedents requiring employers to negotiate with unions who had the support of local workers, did not prevent Smith from taking industrial action. In February 1954 he organised strikes in St Elizabeth and Hanover. This infuriated Bustamante who wrote to Foot to ask: 'Why don't you agree with Elected Ministers to outlaw communism in this country?' Foot told the Colonial Office he was 'very concerned about all this' and appeared to be particularly irritated by the possibility that his own anti-communist campaign was to be trumped by his Chief Minister's.

Following numerous public statements by Bustamante about the dangers of communism, Foot gave a speech to the Chambers of Commerce which amounted to a diatribe against the leftist threat from within Jamaica. Having told the story of the Trojan horse he declared the 'Moscow horse has arrived in Jamaica'. He went on to characterise communism as an insidious foreign threat: 'It is foreign to all we believe in and foreign to every good tradition which has grown up in this Island.... The money which made it possible for a small clique of persons who worship the false foreign god of communist materialism to make any start at all in Jamaica is foreign money.'[26] As well as demonstrating that they were capable of matching Jamaican politicians in McCarthyite rhetoric, British officials could also summon up almost as much enthusiasm as Bustamante for new laws to contain the spread of communism. They believed the Chief Minister was 'no democrat', that the arbitrary nature of his proposals reflected his own political interests and, in pursuing them, his government had neglected the need for legislation to control societies and extend emergency powers, without which the authorities would 'be almost powerless to deal with militant Communism'. The Conservative Minister of State in the Colonial Office, Henry Hopkinson, even went as far as to acknowledge that 'the growth of Communist trade unions in the Caribbean may prove to be a problem incapable of solution on accepted lines.'[27]

Colonial Office sponsorship of new legislation to control societies and stipulate emergency powers and Bustamante's desire to prohibit communist activity of any kind effectively cancelled one another out during the course of 1954. Foot relied instead on detailed intelligence-gathering and informal measures of persecution to impede the organisational efforts of Smith and Hart. The Governor expected the Chief Minister to consider emergency powers legislation at an Executive Council meeting on 18 March but found him in 'a bad frame of mind to say the least'.[28] After Bustamante's direct rejection of the more nuanced Colonial Office approach Foot proposed a Communist Money Bill which would enable the government to take action against any local organisation receiving overseas funding for subversive activities. The Colonial Office thought Foot was 'right to recognise these activities as the cloud on the horizon no bigger than a man's hand' and initially evinced some support for the proposal. However, the bill was shelved after it caused consternation among the British government's legal advisers who thought it unprecedented. Foot himself opposed the Colonial Office's proposals for stricter regulation of societies because he believed they would generate administrative chaos. With Bustamante still resolved not to compromise on his own demands for an outright ban, the legal situation in Jamaica was left unchanged by a year of wrangling among the anti-communists.[29] This immobilism did not hinder the efforts of the Jamaican planters and police to thwart political and union activity by communists. The SAWU strikes in the sugar industry were decisively defeated by an alliance between the employers, the government and the two established labour unions, BITU and the TUC.[30] On the political front, agents inside the PEO recorded that 'confusion and a modicum of fear have also been created in the ranks due to the fact that it is realised the police are getting regular and authentic information on every move that is made.'[31] In September 1955 Foot notified the American consulate that he estimated there were only 140 communists in Jamaica and that 'communism is now at its lowest ebb in this island.'[32] During the 1960s the son of Norman Manley and leader of the National Workers' Union, Michael Manley, emerged as the voice of the new left in Jamaica but the 1950s were a decade of successful Cold War containment for the British in the Caribbean. Whereas Foot had used indirect methods to defuse the threat posed by Smith and Hart, in British Guiana the Conservative government in London resorted to overt intervention in order to circumvent the challenge posed by Cheddi Jagan and the People's Progressive Party (PPP).

British Guiana

Decolonisation in British Guiana has attracted more scholarly interest than any of the other territories in the Anglophone Caribbean, at least in part because in its case the road to independence was more obviously, as one of the key secondary sources indicates in its title, 'a Cold War story'.[33] The rapid growth of the historiography during the last decade has produced new insights regarding the involvement of the CIA and the American trade union movement in destabilising the PPP government in the early 1960s and changing British attitudes towards the two key nationalist leaders, Cheddi Jagan and Forbes Burnham. Although this recent work has clarified some important points of detail for the later period, in re-examining the events which led the British to suspend the constitution and eject the first PPP government in 1953 three aspects have either been neglected or at least need further emphasis. The first is the phenomenon already noted in the last section, namely the launch of a British counter-offensive against communism in 1952, which was a year before the PPP came to power in British Guiana. The territory constituted the most important theatre of Cold War conflict in the region but events there need to be judged in the context of developments else-where in the Anglophone Caribbean. The second point qualifies and elaborates on the first: although the British believed communism was a threat in British Guiana they were uncertain about whether the PPP was a Marxist-Leninist party of the type approved by Moscow. This equivocation might be better described in terms of the distinctions British policymakers made regarding the convictions of the PPP leaders. Sydney King and Janet Jagan were identified as committed communists before 1953; by contrast British uncertainty regarding Cheddi Jagan's political orientation continued into the 1960s, while Forbes Burnham was initially portrayed as an anti-communist. In retrospect this appears to be a misjudgement because it was Burnham who moved the country towards an alliance with the Soviet Union in the 1970s. The third theme which emerges relates to a wider phenomenon which was observable across the Anglophone Caribbean: the decisive factor in the process of decolonisation was the way in which actors interpreted the relationship between constitutional reform and independence, on the one hand, and socio-economic divisions and the threat to internal stability, on the other. British Guiana's route to independence was unusually complex and controversial but the same factors were at play as on the islands, principally the British conviction that a labile and immature population needed an extended period of political apprenticeship which was pitted against a nationalist argument that true independence necessitated economic as well as political emancipation. For the former, the sharp class and racial divisions in the region were a reason to delay, while for the latter, early independence was a prerequisite for overcoming the restraints of imperial control and the class divisions which British rule had established.

In 1966, the year in which Guyana gained independence, Cheddi Jagan attempted to convict British policymakers of the political crimes of Machiavellianism, cupidity and neglect in his book *The West on Trial*. Jagan's case for the prosecution became somewhat monotonous as he painstakingly accumulated evidence of British iniquity from each successive episode in the story of Guianese decolonisation. However, his laborious endeavours have proved useful as a counter-balance to the even weightier official British record, as detailed in the numerous parliamentary Command Papers devoted to events in Guiana during the 1950s and 1960s. One enlightening aspect of Jagan's account is the description he offers of the circumstances in which ordinary Guianese were living after nearly two centuries of British domination. Growing up on the plantations of Port Morant he thought the 'sugar planters seemed to own the world. They owned the cane fields and the factories; even the small pieces of land rented to some of the workers for family food production belonged to them. They owned the mansions occupied by senior staff, and the cottages occupied by dispensers, chemists, engineers, bookkeepers and drivers. They owned the logies (ranges) and huts where the labourers lived, the hospitals and every other important building.'[34] Although Jagan's family did not occupy the lowest rungs of the estate's status ladder because his father was a driver rather than a cutter, he still recalled that the poverty was sufficiently intense that he had to undertake small jobs from an early age because 'the combined income of my parents from work in the fields was inadequate even to meet the barest necessities of life'.[35] The circumstances of his upbringing required Jagan to give careful consideration to the relationship between the country's constitutional status and its economic conditions. His conclusion that British economic interests were the key obstacle to emancipation derived from his experiences rather than from the study of Marxist theory. Socialist thinking offered Jagan both an interpretation of the brutal economic facts of Guianese life and a practical programme for change. During the Legislative Council debates on Waddington's political reforms in January 1952, Jagan explained that the key test was 'whether or not we are going to get the opportunity under this new Constitution to make any basic changes in the economy of the country.' He criticised Waddington's Commission for implicitly assuming that 'our Constitution must be so formed as not to scare capital which would come from outside. I would rather have a Government and Constitution with real powers so that we can rearrange the economy of this country and get the necessary capital out of it for its development. That can be done if we have real powers.'[36]

Jagan escaped from the cane fields by travelling to the United States to study dentistry. The attainment of professional status was a remarkable achievement for the son of an estate worker at a time when most remained illiterate. Jagan chose the distinctly unglamorous profession of dentist rather than lawyer because he believed his nervousness and reserve would be less exposed in the examination of patients' teeth than in the cross-examination of witnesses.[37] In later years his innate shyness and polite manner surprised those who knew of his reputation for radicalism. V. S. Naipaul saw evidence of this when he met Jagan's mother at their home in 1960: 'The only photograph of interest was one Dr Jagan had sent back from America while he was a student: a studio portrait by an unimaginative photographer of a dazzlingly handsome young man looking over his shoulder, not unaware of his looks:

not the face of a politician or a man who was to go to jail for plotting to burn down Georgetown.'[38] Maternal pride in this portrait reflected Cheddi Jagan's success in joining the Caribbean educational elite but, in contrast to those who safeguarded their gains by adopting a conservative and defensive political position, he derived from his travels an awareness of the global socio-economic forces which shaped both the conditions of Guianese sugar estates and the lives of those living in urban America. This was partly a matter of closer acquaintance with examples of overt racism and economic inequality. When domiciled in Washington and Chicago Jagan came to recognise that his education was not as wide or as liberal as he had believed; he read Nehru and Marx and debated with students from around the world.[39] His most important encounter was with an American, Janet Rosenberg, who was a member of the Young Communist League of Chicago.[40] Their relationship subsequently became the subject of prurient speculation by British and American observers but their affection for one another and a common view on the most important political issues sustained a marriage of over 50 years. After his return in 1943 Cheddi Jagan established himself in a dental practice but also began to campaign for the political and economic emancipation of Guiana. He won a seat on the Legislative Council in 1947 and founded the People's Progressive Party (PPP) in 1950. The precedent the Jagans were following in naming the PPP was that set by the Progressive Party of Henry Wallace and Paul Robeson rather than by Marcus Garvey's Jamaican party of the same name.[41] The central goal of the PPP was to combat British colonial control and in Guianese conditions this necessitated alliances between residents of African and East Indian ancestry.

Cheddi Jagan acquired real, if still circumscribed, power when the PPP won British Guiana's first election held under universal adult suffrage in April 1953. The dramatic early success of the party mirrored that of the JLP in Jamaica nine years earlier and the PNM in Trinidad three years later. Dynamic and controversial figures like Cheddi and Janet Jagan, Alexander Bustamante and Eric Williams derived their warrant to transform moribund colonial politics from electoral success. Jagan's opportunity was provided by the Waddington report of 1951. Although Jagan had criticised Waddington's proposed reforms during debates in the Legislative Council, the new Guianese constitution signalled a more dramatic shift in political authority than either the Governor or the Colonial Office had intended when they began considering the matter in August 1948. In that month Theo Lee, who was an elected member of the Legislative Council and a participant in the Caribbean Labour

Congress, proposed a motion calling for universal adult suffrage and internal self-government within five years.[42] Aspects of the Colonial Office reaction were predictable; Creech Jones wrote to the Governor, Charles Woolley, to insist 'we ought to do all we can to avoid being rushed over this question.'[43] The origins of the ensuing British miscalculations can be traced to their fixation with the racial tensions which were self-evidently a part of Guianese society. Colonial Office officials set off on an irregular constitutional course in British Guiana because they assumed that voting would take place entirely along racial lines. Their psephological analysis was accurate in identifying that the conferral of universal suffrage would enhance the position of the previously marginalised community who were the descendants of the indentured East Indian labourers. What the Colonial Office failed to envisage was that a multiracial party like the PPP could draw support from both East Indian and black African-Guianese voters. Woolley explained that the extension of the franchise implied by the removal of the literacy test would change the racial composition of the electorate because 44% of Indians were illiterate compared to 3% of Africans.[44] The Indians lived in the coastal regions and it was argued that they were likely to ignore the interests of the interior territories, where remnants of the indigenous Indian population lived, and that they would inevitably come into conflict with the urbanised black Guianese population who had attained a greater degree of social advancement. In the Colonial Office the Assistant Under-Secretary, George Seel, commented that the newly enfranchised would be 'coast dwellers with no knowledge of and no interest in the interior and torn by racial dissension.'[45]

The second British error was also a product of their apprehensions regarding potential conflict between racial groups inside British Guiana. Woolley predicted that African-Guianese leaders would oppose the abolition of the literacy test which would be enthusiastically supported by the Indian-Guianese population. For this reason he recommended that the issue should be resolved by the appointment of British arbitrators. This was an unusual procedure and was opposed by the Permanent Under-Secretary of the Colonial Office, Thomas Lloyd. However, Creech Jones accepted that the Governor was the best judge of the situation inside Guiana and endorsed Woolley's argument by listing the problems which were said to distinguish Guianese politics from those elsewhere in the empire: 'the sharp division between people of Indian & African origin, the difficulty of agreement about constitutional advance, the need for a new mind to be on the political scene & see if deadlock can be broken.'[46] Such considerations also ruled out the appointment of 'any coloured West Indian' to the Commission.[47] As a consequence, the Constitutional Commission comprised three white members: the Oxford historian Vincent Harlow, who had supervised Eric Williams's doctoral thesis; Rita Hinden, who had worked with Creech Jones in the Fabian Colonial Bureau; and the chairman, John Waddington, who had been Governor of Barbados and British Guiana for a short time before the Second World War. On constitutional matters this was a surprisingly liberal group and their report recommended the conferral of universal adult suffrage and the establishment of elected majorities in both the legislature and the executive. They were unable to agree on the question of whether to create a second chamber which was often a controversial issue in Caribbean politics.[48] In this instance, the majority recommendations of Hinden and Harlow in favour of bicameralism prevailed, with support from the Colonial Office, against the objections of Waddington and Woolley. The latter argued that the increased influence of the elected element in the legislature could be checked far more effectively by strengthening the Governor's powers than by appointing nominees to a weak second chamber. Woolley questioned whether the limited powers of the second chamber would 'effectively provide those checks and balances which the Commission considers essential and rightly point out are integral feature of democratic Government as western civilisation understands it.' Woolley's reservations were disregarded by the Colonial Secretary Griffiths who approved the majority report on 6 October 1951 in one of his last acts before the defeat of the Attlee government.[49]

As they debated the Waddington recommendations all parties began to ponder the likely outcome of the first general election under the new constitution and what might occur if Jagan's newly formed PPP won. Their predictions were determined less by their views about the influence of communism in the party than by their assessment of the administrative competence of Guiana's politicians. Even before the appointment of the Waddington Commission, the Colonial Office complained it would be difficult to persuade capitalist investors 'that a Government where politicians of the present calibre have effective power is one in which they can place serious confidence.' The production of the report then prompted some grumbling that Hinden, in particular, seemed keen to ease the PPP into power and that the colonial bureaucracy would have grave difficulty accommodating 'a Jaganite ministry'.[50] Woolley liked to claim that Cheddi and Janet Jagan were the only two communists in British Guiana but during the debates on the Waddington reforms he placed greater emphasis on the immaturity of Guianese politicians, who were soon to invade both the legislature and the executive, than on the influence of a familial Jaganite cell. On 20 September 1951 he wrote: 'My greater concern is... whether with universal suffrage the general elections will throw up real leaders and sufficient members of the right calibre for Ministerial office here.'[51]

In assessing the ideological orientation of the PPP, British policymakers were influenced by the intensification of the Cold War atmosphere caused by the escalation of the Korean conflict and their scorn for local politics and politicians but they were also sceptical of alarmist intelligence emanating from Guiana. Many in the metropolis believed that sophisticated ideological commitments were beyond the capacity of people inside a country which was socially and economically underdeveloped. A detailed analysis of the PPP written by the Guianese Commissioner of Police, Orrett, struck the first note of crisis in April 1951. He correctly predicted that the organisational drive of the PPP leadership and Janet Jagan in particular would give them a majority in the Legislative Council. Despite the accuracy of his electoral calculations, Orrett's forebodings that a PPP victory would constitute 'a serious threat to the internal security of the Colony' have the appearance of a self-fulfilling prophecy. Orrett's assertion that the PPP had 'identical' views to the Jamaican PNP, which was justified on the basis of 'their views and Communist methods', appeared particularly unconvincing, given Manley's imminent purge of the left. The Colonial Office did not find his analysis persuasive and succumbed to only minor jitters. Vernon, who headed the West India Department, responded by accepting that 'any Communist affiliates must be closely watched'; but he also accused Orrett of exaggerating the dangers and noted that the Security Services had 'checked' the Jagans and concluded they were not communists.[52] Similarly, the Colonial Office were infuriated when Britain's leading Caribbean Cold Warrior, Jackson, who had begun the pursuit of Ferdinand Smith, insisted that the PPP should not be allowed to gain control of Guiana's bauxite resources. Stephen Luke, the Colonial Office Under-Secretary who was soon to become Comptroller for Development in the Caribbean Commission, wrote to the War Office in January 1953 to explain: 'It might be inferred from Brigadier Jackson's report that there is a well-organised communist Party in British Guiana. That is not the case. The people of British Guiana so far have shown themselves incapable of forming well-disciplined political parties with precise programmes, and we have no reason to believe that Dr Jagan is capable of building up a political party in this sense, at any rate in the foreseeable future.' Officials in the Colonial Office expressed doubts as to whether Jagan would even be able to achieve a majority in the 1953 elections.[53]

Participating in their first election under universal suffrage on 27 April the people of British Guiana elected 18 PPP candidates and six from other parties. Affiliation to the PPP trumped racial considerations: a black African-Guianese woman, Jane Phillips-Gay, was victorious standing for Enmore, where most of the voters were Indian plantation labourers, and the Indian-Guianese Chandra Persaud was elected in Mahaica with the support of black workers.[54] The extent of the PPP triumph attracted the attention of the British Prime Minister, Winston Churchill. He interpreted the election entirely in Cold War terms and recommended coordination with the United States in order to 'break the communist teeth in British Guiana.' As 'a joke' he even suggested the American contribution might be to dispatch Senator McCarthy to the country. Four months later the Colonial Secretary, Oliver Lyttelton, would authorise an intervention to remove the PPP from power but at this stage he sought to contain the Prime Minister's pugnacity by offering a more balanced appraisal: he informed Churchill that the leaders of the PPP had visited Iron-Curtain countries and might be in touch with Soviet agencies but their programme was not communist in nature and they accepted the need for the investment of overseas capital. They would be given an opportunity to govern.[55]

Colonial Office assessments of the PPP in government were continuous with those of the PPP in opposition. Concerns about the party's connections to the Comintern's international-front organisations increased during the summer months but it was more common for British policymakers to divide the leaders into 'extremists' and 'moderates' rather than into communists and non-communists. The moderates were those who seemed disposed to compromise on their demands for the redistribution of resources and early self-government while the extremists were those judged willing to exacerbate social, racial and class tensions in order to achieve victory in the confrontation with British imperialism. At the outset the ministerial moderates were identified as Ashton Chase, Jai Narine Singh and Forbes Burnham and the extremists as Cheddi Jagan, Sydney King and Joseph Prayal Lachmansingh. The greatest hazard during the first phase of PPP government was less that the communist elements in the party would stage a coup and more that an ideological clash between the leaders of the two factions would lead to a physical clash between their supporters. After the first month of PPP administration the new Governor, Alfred Savage, reported that the two factions had nearly split over the issue of ministerial portfolios and

expressed relief that they had reached a compromise which had prevented 'a very serious security situation'.[56] Despite his supposed leadership of the extremist faction Jagan was still regarded by many as a 'fellow
traveller' rather than as a Soviet surrogate. The head of the Guianese
Special Branch indicated in July that although Jagan could have caused
chaos in the sugar industry he had refrained from doing so. At this stage
it was estimated that the PPP had no plans to disrupt the economy but
that 'unrest could arise over matters which the Party executive have
no control, resulting from rash promises made in election days and irresponsible action by Ministers and Members of the House of Assembly'.[57]

Eventual British intervention was more a consequence of alarm at
the stridency of Sydney King's anti-imperialism and acute disillusionment with Forbes Burnham, who had been identified as the leader of
the moderates, than with Jagan's policies. By August political reports
from Georgetown indicated that Burnham was 'proving the most serious disappointment' and had shown 'himself to be viciously anti-British
and to be lacking in balance and judgement.' King and Janet Jagan were
accused of attempting to deliberately undermine the administration of
the country in order to bring about a revolutionary conflagration which
could lead to the establishment of a pro-Soviet government. It was predicted they 'will do everything possible to precipitate a breakdown in
the operation of the Constitution but it is not clear whether Jagan or
Burnham would support such action in the immediate future.' Reports
such as these caused the Colonial Office to reassess the likelihood of
a communist takeover. Having previously treated talk of a communist
putsch as fantastic, Whitehall decision-makers began fantasising about
British Guiana as a pro-Soviet bastion in the region. The Prinicipal of one
of the West Indian departments in the Colonial Office, J. W. Vernon,
even suggested that the PPP might be aping the tactics used successfully by communists in the Balkans.[58] Evidence of contact between PPP
leaders and communist organisations in Eastern Europe was obtained
by surveillance and the interception of cables.[59] The information which
seems to have most alarmed the Colonial Office was probably obtained
by the Secret Intelligence Service (SIS) in Vienna and was passed on to
Savage on 7 July 1953. It comprised a message from King to the WFTU
and was interpreted as proof that King was working in the interests of
international communism.[60]

By this stage, Savage was in the midst of a significant row with the
Colonial Office who accused him of failing to curb the PPP extremists. Propaganda had emerged as the main front in the battle against
communism in British Guiana, so when Savage acquiesced in the PPP's

decisions to revoke the Undesirable Publication Ordinance and lift the ban on the entry of Ferdinand Smith and other leaders of the Caribbean left, he might have anticipated the horrified reaction of the Colonial Office. The subsequent wrangle was aggravated by the fact that Lloyd had written to Savage warning him that Janet Jagan intended to flood the country with communist literature obtained during her trip to Eastern Europe in June. Lloyd explained that the Colonial Office were formulating a coordinated anti-communist policy across the Anglophone Caribbean and urged the Governor not to sell the pass in British Guiana. Unfortunately, the message arrived after Savage had already accepted Jagan's proposed liberalisation. Amidst the subsequent recriminations in Whitehall, Lyttelton opined that Savage's behaviour constituted 'serious signs of weakness and wind'. In apparent anticipation of the action he would authorise two months later, on 20 July he minuted: 'I am much disturbed and expect the situation to deteriorate and not to improve as they appear to think possible.'[61] Before resorting to open intervention, the SIS advocated 'covert work' and an intensification of pro-British propaganda in the Colony. Some of the documents pertaining to the ensuing information campaign are partially redacted but the programme assembled as a result of cooperation between British intelligence agencies, the Information Research Department of the Foreign Office and the Colonial Office included the sponsorship of anti-Communist articles in the British and Guianese press, the establishment of a local front organisation 'as a means of stimulating resistance to Communism by infiltrating a reasonable degree of politics' and encouragement of opposition parties which probably entailed financial subsidy.[62] One particularly significant element was the recruitment of Bookers, who owned the majority of the sugar estates, to the cause of the anti-communist campaign: the company's own propaganda extolling the virtues of the British connection was regarded as one of the best means of responding to the WFTU literature which Janet Jagan and other PPP leaders were distributing.[63]

The decision to suspend the constitution occurred once British officials concluded that even the moderates possessed an incapacity for efficient government and that the radicals had been too successful in cultivating Guianese insubordination. A strike in the sugar industry and reports that King wanted to hold a conference of Caribbean communists provided the pretext for the dispatch of British troops. Although the British press, with some encouragement from the government, emphasised the 'red peril' elements of the story, the invasion was actually a consequence of metropolitan fantasies about an outbreak of anarchy in the colony. Lyttelton reminded the Cabinet on 13 October: 'We didn't act for fear of Comm[unist] *coup* as some press say: but to secure law & order while Comm[unist] Ministers were removed.'[64] A month earlier Savage had issued his gloomiest report to date. He asserted that PPP Ministers were motivated by the 'deepest bitterness', that this was exacerbated by 'a fanatical hatred by the African Ministers of the white race' and that Janet Jagan and King 'appear to believe that by creating disorder and economic chaos they would force the issue of self-government earlier.' The more specific and immediate cause for alarm was the suborning of the police and the civil service. Lyttelton declared that 'a halt must now be called' which would require the deployment of British troops, the arrest of the most dangerous leaders and the publication of an emergency Order-in-Council suspending the constitution.[65] He explained that this programme of action had not been recommended by the Governor but that it was essential 'before morale of police crumbles'.[66] His policy was endorsed by Churchill who, in a conversation with his doctor, singled out British Guiana as a country in which, during his convalescence from a stroke, the Cabinet had 'taken things lying down'. The Prime Minister expressed relish for the 'bloody row' which the British intervention would occasion.[67]

On 30 September the Chiefs of Staff were told that the situation in British Guiana was 'rapidly deteriorating' and that they should make arrangements to send troops to the colony as soon as possible.[68] The arrival of the soldiers on 8 October was greeted with incredulity because there was no immediate emergency which justified the intervention. It had been intended that the landings should be accomplished before any public announcement was made but, after rumours swept through the British and Guianese press, Lyttelton complained on 6 October that 'the element of surprise had now been lost' and the Cabinet authorised a preemptive declaration of intent.[69] Jagan recalled his initial belief that speculation about the imminent arrival of British troops was 'too fantastic' only to be confounded first by a BBC broadcast and then by a raid on his home conducted while he was still dressed in his pyjamas.[70] The public rationale for the suspension of the constitution was expounded by Savage on 9 October and focused on the gradual deterioration of political conditions which threatened public order in the medium term. Savage explained that Jagan's government had undertaken 'a planned and continuous programme of strengthening links with communist countries with a view to making British Guiana a servile state where people are compelled, under intimidation to give up those freedoms which we all cherish.' The story that the intervention was necessary to avert a plot to burn down Georgetown did not feature at this stage; it was fabricated on the basis of reports, issued by Savage after the deployment of troops, that PPP supporters without cars were buying large quantities of petrol.[71] The notion of an impending outbreak of incendiarism was incorporated into the subsequent White Paper which justified the intervention to the British parliament.[72] Jagan refuted these claims in a short book, *Forbidden Freedom* which was published the following year. He noted the Churchill government's admission, elicited by the prominent Labour MP Fenner Brockway and later pursued by Michael Foot and James Chuter-Ede, that the arson plot had first been reported on 7 October, weeks after arrangements to assume emergency powers had been prepared and only a day before the troops arrived.[73] Jagan's speculation that American pressure had influenced British thinking were less convincing: the Cabinet agreed to notify the Eisenhower administration only after the news of the intervention appeared in the press, while in Washington State Department officials complained that they lacked authoritative information on what was happening in Guiana.[74]

It is often forgotten that, in terms of British party politics, the Guianese intervention occurred at a wholly propitious moment for Churchill's administration: the Conservative Party united in support of an effective Cold War intervention, while the divisions between the Bevanites and Gaitskellites in the Labour Party were exposed. In the midst of their feud over the evacuation of the Suez base, Conservative MPs united to condemn Jagan and praise the decisive action of their leaders. Lyttelton's suggestion that, as a consequence of the intervention, his 'position in the Conservative Party was strengthened and reinforced' was triumphalist and self-congratulatory but accurate. His account emphasised the contrast between the disarray in the Labour Party during the debate on 22 October which endorsed the suspension of the constitution and the delight on the government's backbenches: 'Parliamentary parties are prepared to support drastic and unpopular action if they think it right but when that action gives them a happy experience they positively purr.'[75] Among the purring Conservatives was the future Governor of Bermuda, Roland Robinson, who blamed 'the American communist-woman Mrs Jagan' for introducing the Anglophobic epithet 'limey' into the political discourse of British Guiana and Philip Bell, who declared that events in Guiana demonstrated that 'power without experience leads by a quick and short way to murder, plunder and riot.' For Labour, Thomas Reid declared that the PPP was 'a thorough bad lot' which was trying 'to set up a totalitarian

Communist state'. His remarks were echoed by the former Independent Labour Party member, John McGovern, who insisted 'Dr Jagan and his party are a menace.'[76] Although some of Aneurin Bevan's supporters offered lukewarm backing for the PPP, the labour movement as a whole showed little fraternal feeling for the party. Jagan recalled his own shock at the prejudicial headlines which greeted his arrival in London: from the *Daily Mirror*, 'Janet Britain-Hater – Hatred of Britain is Mainspring that Makes Mrs Jagan Tick'; from the *Herald*, 'Jagan Men Had Plot to Set Capital on Fire'; and from the *Express*, 'Jagans Aped Mau Mau Terror'. Sitting in the gallery of the House of Commons he then endured the attacks of the Parliamentary Labour Party on the PPP's record.[77] Nothing better illustrates the differences between metropolitan and peripheral perspectives on the economic and political aspects of decolonisation than the British labour movement's hostility to Cheddi Jagan in October 1953. Leaders of British trade-unionism believed that since its election victory the PPP had advanced the interests of the Guianese Industrial Workers Union (GIWU), which had been formed in 1948, at the expense of the older Manpower Citizens Association (MPCA). They argued that strike action undertaken by the GIWU during the course of 1953 had been sponsored by communists and that they were pursuing political domination rather than a resolution to industrial relations problems. When Jagan and Burnham met British trade unionists, Alice Horan of the General and Municipal Workers Union condemned the PPP's sponsorship of the GIWU, which she claimed was supported by the WFTU. Vincent Tewson, the British TUC's General Secretary, asked whether Ferdinand Smith had played a role in the recent strikes. After the cross-examination was over, Labour MPs claimed Jagan and Burnham had been 'evasive and with an answer for everything.'[78] These attitudes reflected the anti-communism of the British trade union movement but were also suggestive of the limits which liberation movements in the periphery of empire had to observe if they were to be tolerated in the metropolis where many liberals and socialists believed that orderly decolonisation was imperilled by the irresponsibility of the colonised rather than by the authoritarianism of late imperialism.

In the decade after 1953 the policy of confrontation with Jagan gave way to a tacit accommodation. Before making the transition to a potential partner in the decolonisation process, Jagan was, like almost every other prominent anti-colonial politician in the British Empire, arrested and imprisoned. Lyttelton and Churchill had pressed for his internment when the constitution was suspended but had bowed to

Savage's objections.[79] They awaited a fresh opportunity which was provided in April 1954 by the imposition and then the immediate breaking
of restriction orders confining Jagan to Georgetown. Janet Jagan gave
an account of the atmosphere in British Guiana at this time to Hart:
'Police raids, arrests and all that goes with it is as natural as blink-
ing your eyes these days. Hardly a day goes by when a Comrade isn't
raided ... I'm so sophisticated I hardly look to see if I am being trailed.'[80]
She was arrested just before her husband's release in September 1954
and spent four months in gaol.[81] Her own imprisonment coincided
with the Churchill government's final and comprehensive indictment
of the PPP which was provided by a new Constitutional Commission, headed by the erstwhile Civil Secretary of the Sudan government,
James Robertson. The Robertson Commission concluded that a period
of 'marking time' was necessary because the 'immature and undiscrim-
inating electorate' of British Guiana were unwilling to provide a check
on the country's irresponsible leaders.[82] During the ensuing interlude
it became evident that both the policy of cultivating opposition to the
PPP inside Guiana and containing Jagan's influence within the confines
of a federation were either counter-productive or impractical. Recent
research has demonstrated the extent of British efforts to propagate
rivalry within the leadership of the PPP and it is now evident that the
Colonial Office helped to engineer a breakaway by Burnham's faction
in 1955.[83] The formation of Burnham's rival party, which became the
People's National Congress (PNC), aggravated racial tensions because
so many African-Guianese members left the multi-racial PPP after the
split. However, Burnham's defection also had the paradoxical effect of
assisting Jagan's return to power because it laid the basis for two-party
politics which was a prerequisite for the further measure of constitutional advance which was agreed to in 1956. It also contributed towards
British disillusionment with Burnham which had been presaged by
Savage in 1953. British officials would by the early 1960s express a
consistent preference for the PPP government over Burnham's PNC
opposition.

A better option from the British perspective than the dominance
of either of these two parties was to have Guianese affairs guided
by politicians from elsewhere in the Anglophone Caribbean through
the country's participation in a federation. When Lyttelton's successor
Lennox-Boyd informed the Cabinet in April 1956 of his intention to
introduce a constitution providing for new elections, he suggested that
the real safeguard for the long term was Guianese membership of the

West Indies federation.[84] Guianese politicians were suspicious of federation precisely because it threatened to curtail their independence and they refused to participate in the federal negotiations. After Jagan's 1957 election victory he reaffirmed the PPP's opposition to Guianese membership of the federation. Despite this disappointment, a *modus vivendi* was established which, as Jagan admitted, was 'tantamount to a coalition of the People's Progressive Party and the Colonial Office'.[85] British offers of incremental reform and the possibility of a repeat of the events of 1953 caused the PPP leadership to moderate their criticisms of the colonial regime. Given the lingering bitterness engendered by military intervention, a permanent accommodation between the British and the PPP appeared unlikely but the ineffectiveness of the various expedients taken to erode popular support for the party led to a grudging British acceptance that Jagan was likely to become the first leader of an independent Guiana. Such an outcome was only averted because of the sudden and forceful intervention of the Kennedy administration in 1962.

Politics, race and reform in Barbados and Trinidad

During the 1950s, amidst the ideological conflict of the Cold War, race became a global political issue in a way which was unprecedented. India had achieved its independence in 1947 and established itself as the first non-white state in the Commonwealth and an influential anti-colonial voice at the United Nations. Ghana became the first independent black African nation a decade later. Many of the leaders of the newly decolonised countries, including Nehru and Nkrumah, viewed colonial matters such as the Mau Mau war and the extension of Apartheid in South Africa as different fronts in a liberationist struggle against European dominance. Even outside of the imperial periphery, the greater publicity attending to segregationist policies in the United States as a consequence of the flourishing of the civil-rights campaign made it a Cold War issue, particularly for those African states who chose to remain non-aligned. In Britain arguments about race became tied to discussions of immigration from the imperial periphery following riots in London and Nottingham in 1958. Controversy over the introduction of entry restrictions had an obvious impact in the Anglophone Caribbean, where migration of labour was a means of alleviating unemployment, but the racial politics of decolonisation had a much wider resonance. In Trinidad and Guiana for example, there was a tendency for the descendants of indentured labourers from South Asia to look to the example of the Indian National Congress as a precedent for political organisation, while Nkrumah's activities in West Africa assumed much greater salience for those whose ancestors had left the region after being sold into slavery. In the Western Caribbean, Norman Manley consciously encouraged the notion that collaboration between the races in the struggle for Jamaican independence would set an edifying precedent for other liberation movements. From the British perspective, the rising racial consciousness which had been evident since the initial successes of Garveyism in the inter-war period was yet another reason to be gloomy about the prospects for a peaceful transition to independence. The metropolitan government became increasingly apprehensive that the new form of mass-electoral politics would provide an opportunity for the venting of racial grievances. This became evident in the commentary British officials provided on the elections now being held under universal suffrage in Trinidad and Barbados.

Barbados

The two distinguishing features of political life in Barbados were the existence of proportionally the largest white European minority in the Anglophone Caribbean and the continuous retention of a representative parliamentary system. These phenomena were closely related: in contrast to the absenteeism prevalent in a nearby island like St Vincent the plantation owners of Barbados resided in close proximity to their estates and aggressively defended their political privileges. The leader of the radical Congress Party Wynter Crawford recalled in his memoirs: 'Barbados was perhaps the only country in the West Indies that preserved the rigid racial discrimination after emancipation because so many whites remained and controlled the land and commercial enterprises... by and large, colour discrimination was more rampant in Barbados than possibly in any other island in the West Indies.'[86] It was not just nationalist leaders that looked askance at the inegalitarianism and segregationism of Barbadian life. The Governor of the island in the mid-1950s, Robert Arundell, who had previously taken responsibility for the Windward islands, was one of the more conservative British officials in the region and was prepared to argue that the matter of racial prejudice was a complex issue because 'discrimination is more a matter of class and culture than colour'; but even he accepted that 'far more weight is given to colour in Barbados than in most of the rest of the West Indies.'[87] Despite their greater prominence European Barbadians still only constituted just over 5% of the population. Consequently, in an era of popular participation in electoral politics, a shift in power out of the hands of the white minority and into the hands of the black majority was inevitable.

The figure most associated with the reordering of Barbadian politics was Grantley Adams. In 1965, Adams claimed in an interview, transcribed by the American scholar Robert J. Alexander: 'that he changed the whole political climate here. When he first entered the legislature in 1934, the great majority of the black voters voted for their white "betters" and he was one of the three or four blacks in the House of Assembly.... This has now all changed. Now there is only one white member of the House of Assembly'.[88] Adams was a transitional figure in Caribbean nationalism whose views and inclinations were more radical than those of the first generation like Critchlow, Marryshow and Cipriani but more conservative than those of the second generation like Williams and Manley. He shared the imperial sentimentalism of the former and the social progressivism of the latter. In common with many of his fellow citizens he had at least partly assimilated the notion of Barbados as a 'Little England' with greater affinity to 'Big England' than any other territory. Unlike most Barbadians, Adams had experience of English conditions: he won the Barbados-island scholarship and studied at St Catherine's College, Oxford, where his two principal extra-curricular interests were politics and cricket. Aside from keeping wicket for the College he joined the Liberal Party and declared his admiration for the meliorist reformism of Herbert Asquith.[89] This set him against reactionaries in both Britain and the Caribbean but also against more radical socialist prescriptions for change. On his return to the Caribbean in 1925 he worked as a barrister and became ensnared in a conflict with the left rather than with the right. Many Barbadians never forgave him for his lead role in the successful prosecution of a libel suit against the radical journalist Clennell Wickham. Adams's victory in court effectively ended Wickham's career and appeared to establish him as an ally of the privileged. Such expectations were overturned after his election to the Barbadian House of Assembly in 1934. From that point Adams launched what his biographer described as 'a major assault on the oligarchy of the Island.'[90] He campaigned for the extension of the franchise and improvements in working class conditions and became a prominent figure in the new Barbados Labour Party (BLP). When the BLP won the 1946 elections Adams, in amiable partnership with the Governor, Grattan Bushe, advanced a programme of incremental social and constitutional reform. Although for British officials like Bushe the Anglophile, the cricket-loving Adams was congenial company, it became evident during the 1950s that the Colonial Office doubted his capacities as a regional leader. As he grew older Adams was increasingly characterised as lazy and irresolute. British policymakers were also unpersuaded that a Caribbean version of Asquithian liberalism would be sufficiently appealing to obtain populist support in the divisive era of Cold War politics. Despite their abrasive personalities Manley and Williams were greatly preferred to Adams because their industry, dynamism and undiluted nationalism made them more viable alternatives to radicals like Ferdinand Smith or Richard Hart.

Although no Barbadian featured on the Colonial Office's authorised list of Smith's 11 associates, for British officials, the racial tensions evident on Barbados made this another potentially dangerous experiment in decolonisation. The social and political inflexibility of the white European Barbadian elites and the resentment of the black African workers generated a brittle kind of politics which had been unmissable during the disorders of the 1930s and achieved renewed prominence in the December 1951 elections. This was the first poll held on the basis of universal adult suffrage which was an innovation the Colonial Office had nervously supported. Adams's BLP, which effectively represented black Barbadians, won 16 of the 24 seats, while the Electors' Association, which was the party of white and lighter-skinned residents who could claim European descent, won only four seats. Another pillar of the Barbadian establishment, the *Advocate* newspaper, attributed prevailing suspicions of the Electors' Association's manifesto to the difficulty of trying 'to compete against an electorate which has been so consistently taught to believe that white men are, like the ancient Greeks, to be feared, especially when bearing gifts.'[91] Governor Savage, who would later be despatched to Guiana, informed the Colonial Office that the campaign 'was very painful as the colour question predominated *viz* white and coloured versus black.' In offering a prognosis Savage admitted 'the racial issue is my main worry'. He suggested that the situation could be managed effectively, but only if the white elites cooperated with Adams in a process of reform. In London, Luke who was monitoring Barbadian affairs at the Colonial Office predicted that further constitutional advance was the ground on which a racial confrontation was most likely. He expected that Adams would demand a strengthening of the executive powers of the elected element and that 'in their present temper, the white community may regard this issue as vital to their whole future and show no disposition to make any sensible concessions.' Despite expressing some optimism about the possibility of surmounting such dangers, he concluded that Barbadians 'have not previously had to face the need for so drastic and far reaching an adjustment of race relations.'[92]

As in Jamaica and Trinidad, one of the most difficult issues arising during the process of constitutional reform was to redefine the relationship between the legislative and executive branches of government. In the case of Barbados the representative tradition in the legislature had persisted but had been held in check by the executive authority of the Governor. Following the extension of the franchise to the mass of the population, Adams and the BLP were able to argue that executive privilege, which had once restrained the cupidity of the plantation owners, had become a means of frustrating the democratic will of the people. More mundanely, Adams insisted on the institution of a new ministerial system in which the leader of the largest party would become Prime Minister and executive portfolios would be filled by elected members rather than nominees and officials. In March 1952 he told Lloyd that he expected the new constitutional dispensation to become operative within six or seven months.[93] As usual the Colonial Office reacted cautiously and the combination of metropolitan reservations and divisions within the BLP ensured that reform proceeded at a pedestrian pace. Many of the new BLP members elected in 1951, including Errol Barrow and Cameron Tudor, believed that Adams was too hesitant in his pursuit of redistributionist economic policies, and divisions within the party on issues like taxation policy and nationalisation had ramifications for the debates about the constitution. Adams's early history of collaboration with the Barbadian elites and his incrementalist approach to politics were interpreted by many as evidence of ingrained conservatism. The constitutional arena was a place where Adams could more easily prove his nationalist credentials and he constantly pressed the British for both tangible and symbolic concessions in order to bolster his position inside the BLP. The seriousness of the challenge was eventually demonstrated when Barrow resigned from the BLP in order to form the Democratic Labour Party (DLP) in 1955.[94]

The metropolitan authorities were aware that Adams was encircled by the younger members of the BLP to his left and the old conservative European Barbadian elites to his right. They adopted a cautious approach to constitutional reform in an attempt to avert a confrontation between what they perceived as two extremes. When the BLP leaders formally presented their demands for a ministerial system of government in May 1952 Luke again returned to the racial issue. He warned: 'it may well mean handing over political power in full to the coloured majority in a very colour-conscious community; and it will mean handing over power to politicians who apart from Mr Grantley Adams himself, have so far made a very poor showing in the new Barbados House of Assembly.' Savage was also concerned that, although Adams was reliable, the younger generation was not. He informed the Colonial Office of the existence of 'a growing "left" flank' inside the BLP which endangered Adams's leadership. As in the case of Jamaica after the implementation of the 1944 constitution, the Colonial Office decided in September 1952 to 'call a halt' on the reform process, at the bidding of the Conservative Secretary of State, Oliver Lyttelton.[95] It was expected that the period of remission would be a short one. In the interim they conducted a thorough analysis of Barbadian constitutional traditions in order to identify those elements which offered the strongest defence against the potential emergence of a reckless administration dominated by the left of the BLP. From this investigation they established that, in the last resort, British influence rested on the Governor's entitlement, in exceptional circumstances, to reject the advice offered to him by Ministers. When Adams arrived in London in December 1952 he demanded that the Governor should finally be obliged to act on the recommendations of Ministers; the only exceptions he was willing to countenance related to defence and external affairs. For the British this amounted to 'something approaching responsible government' which was inappropriate in a territory where the race and class conflicts of the 1930s remained unburied. In April 1953 they presented Adams with an inelegant formula which retained the Governor's discretionary powers: he 'should, except when it appears to him that grave or exceptional circumstances compel him to act otherwise, accept, in legislative matters the advice of Ministers if they are unanimous.'[96] Adams initially assented but later expressed dissatisfaction with the resulting compromise agreement, which included the retention of nominated members in the Legislative Council. In October he attempted to renegotiate terms with the new Governor, Arundell. Although Arundell disdained the disorderly means by which the BLP conducted their business, he recommended a revised formula specifying that the Governor should act on the advice of the elected Premier rather than on the unanimity of Ministers. This was accepted by Munster, the Conservative Parliamentary Under-Secretary at the Colonial Office, who took the opportunity to reiterate that they only acquiesced 'so long as the Governor has the right to refuse their advice in grave or exceptional circumstances and this I understand is so.'[97] In Barbados, as in Jamaica, the British were tenacious in clinging to the privileges of executive authority against nationalist demands for greater democratic control.

British policymakers displayed a similar avidity in defending the symbols of British paramountcy. Adams later recalled that Lyttelton's reluctance to allow him to assume the title of Prime Minister was an 'amusing' aspect of the negotiations.[98] Oddly, the issue became entangled with the process of African decolonisation. In May 1952 Adams told Savage that his supporters had noted Nkrumah's appointment as Prime Minister of the Gold Coast and were urging him to acquire the same status. The matter of what to call the senior minister remained in abeyance while other constitutional issues were addressed, but it arose again when Adams visited London in December 1952 and argued for the title of Prime Minister, against the advocacy of Chief Minister by the Colonial Office. When Lyttelton wrote to Churchill outlining the constitutional changes, his primary concern was to secure the British Prime Minister's support for the withholding of that title from any elected leader of the Barbadian executive. Despite the intransigence of Lyttelton and Churchill on the matter, in April 1953 the interim Governor, Turner, championed Adams's cause in a peculiar letter which revealed how one official thought about local conceptions of race. Turner argued that Adams's reluctance to accept the title of Chief Minister was understandable in a society where the word 'chief' had connotations of primitive African conditions. As evidence for this he cited the local popularity of the comic book hero *The Phantom*, 'who spends his time accomplishing impossible feats in a sort of American Congo, where the Chiefs always have big bare bellies and wear bone necklaces and dented top hats.' Evidently neither the acting Governor nor the general population wished to be associated with such unsophisticated notions of governance and Turner urged that either Premier or Principal Minister be offered as an alternative to Chief Minister. The Colonial Office adjudged the appellation Premier to be too dignified for Adams and so Principal Minister was initially pressed upon him. It was not until July 1953 that Lyttelton finally conceded that, in the last resort, he would allow Adams to become Premier of Barbados, but not, of course, Prime Minister.[99]

British anxieties that the racial antagonism generated during the 1951 elections would be amplified under a more advanced constitution proved unfounded. Adams tolerated the continuation of racial discrimination on the island and the white Barbadians were compensated for their loss of political power by the retention of their social privileges. A bill which Adams introduced in January 1956 to prevent shops refusing service to customers on racial grounds was prompted not by the

intrinsic merits of such legislation but because it was thought necessary to improve the chances of Bridgetown establishing itself as the
capital of the new federation.[100] A decade later Adams admitted that
'social separation of blacks and whites' was still tolerated, including the
notorious exclusivity of all white social and sporting clubs.[101] On the
political front, the BLP left, whose existence had alarmed Savage in
1952, devoted more of their energies to criticising Adams's failure to
address the problems of unemployment than to an outright assault
on British colonialism. Following their split with Adams in 1955, Errol
Barrow and his supporters in the DLP were decisively defeated in the
1956 elections. Arundell was able to reassure the metropolitan government that the racial rhetoric which had been deployed five years earlier
was much less prevalent. By this stage the greatest concern of British
policymakers was the absence of any obviously reliable successor to
Adams, who they criticised for his failure to groom the younger generation for the responsibilities of office.[102] The next step in the process
of transplanting the Westminster system to Barbados was to strengthen
the power of elected ministers, which required a transfer of authority
from the Executive Committee, on which colonial officials continued
to sit, to a Cabinet. During 1957 Arundell accepted with few qualms the
idea that elected members should acquire control of the Executive and
reported that even the conservatives, who had opposed the introduction
of the ministerial system, accepted that such a development was 'logical
and inevitable.'[103] At the moment when Adams formed his first Cabinet in early 1958, the metropolitan government remained perturbed by
the possibility that the Caribbean islands might become crucibles for
racial conflict but their attention had shifted westwards from Barbados
to Trinidad.

Trinidad

Just as in Barbados, British officials in Trinidad expected that the new era
of democratic politics would aggravate racial tension and in both cases
these fears were revealing of their own assumptions about the character
of different Caribbean ethnic groups. The population in Trinidad was so
inter mingled that the notion of distinct ethnicities was questionable
but subjective appreciations of racial character were an important feature of both popular and elite politics. Significant Chinese, Arab and
Portuguese communities had been established but it was the potential confrontation between the minority group of Indian Trinidadians,
who constituted approximately 35% of the population in 1951, and

the larger black African group, who accounted for 47%, which became a focus of British concern.[104] Cultural divisions were exacerbated by socio-economic differences which had the potential to set poor Indian agricultural workers against the black African working- and middle-classes of San Fernando and Port of Spain. In this context matters such as education policy acquired a racial character; politicians like Simbhoonath Capildeo criticised the colonial government for failing to eradicate illiteracy because its prevalence in the Indian Trinidadian villages was not regarded as sufficiently important either by British officials or by the emerging African Trinidadian elite.[105] The issue which alerted British policymakers in Whitehall to Trinidadian racial tension was the demand of the newly elected Chief Minister, Eric Williams, that his government should take control of the police which was part of the nationalist agenda of his People's National Movement (PNM).

The sociologist Ivar Oxaal has claimed, 'No real grasp of Trinidad politics in the last years of the colonial period can be achieved without understanding the bases of the charismatic authority wielded by Dr Williams.'[106] Certainly none of his contemporaries in the Anglophone Caribbean has garnered as much posthumous commentary from historians and political analysts.[107] There is general agreement that Williams seemed well qualified to fashion a respectable Trinidadian nationalism which would reconcile the island's racial groups and assuage British worries about the economic and political consequences of independence. His continuous battles with British officials after his appointment to the Caribbean Commission in 1948 established his nationalist credentials and provided material for a series of speeches which connected his own struggles with the imperial bureaucracy to the necessity for liberation from colonial rule. Following the termination of his contract with the Commission in June 1955, he began organising a new party with the aim of contesting the elections scheduled for the following year. The PNM was more successful in acquiring popular support than any of the earlier attempts by Trinidadian politicians to establish mass political parties. Williams never lost his reputation as an exceptionally prickly political personality but, from a British perspective his programme, as well as his academic credentials as an Oxford-trained historian, were impeccable. Although the emphasis in his historical work on the material causes of the rise and fall of the transatlantic slave trade showed the influence of Marxism, as a politician he was reconciled to international capitalism. He emphasised that the necessary diversification of the Trinidadian economy would require the courting of international capital.[108] After the PNM victory of 1956,

Williams invited Teodoro Moscoso to advise on how Trinidad could follow the Puerto Rican model of 'Industrialisation by Invitation', which
was sanctioned by Washington.[109] As his biographer Selwyn Ryan has
commented he was 'the first would-be reformer in Trinidad to break
openly with the socialist tradition.'[110] On racial questions, instead of
exploiting the potential division between Trinidadians of African and
Indian descent he argued that their subjection to British imperialism
ought to give them common cause. He admonished both the British
for their use of racism to justify oppression and Trinidadians for their
obsessions with the same issues: 'the absurdity of the ideas expressed
by the world's great scholars and thinkers are a warning to us that our
own racial prejudices and racial stereotypes will appear equally ridicu-
lous and indefensible to future generations.'[111] In a manner similar to
Bustamante in Jamaica, Williams's appearance prompted much speculation about his own racial origins; many believed that he had Indian as
well as African ancestry although Williams asserted that he was of mixed
European and African descent.[112]

Williams's unvarying combativeness led some British and American
officials to claim that he was an anti-white racist. The charge amounted
to a *tu quoque* counter-accusation which was intended to mitigate the
appalling record of European prejudice in the Caribbean; it was particularly pointed in Williams's case because in his most significant book,
Capitalism and Slavery, he argued that racism had been essential to
the rationalisation of the brutalities of the slave trade.[113] In the context of a widespread cultural Anglophilia in the West Indies, Williams
was notable for his scepticism about British rectitude; this tendency
reflected his resentment at the way he was treated at Oxford University, which was a subject to which he frequently reverted. In a letter to
Norman Manley, Williams explicitly stated his belief that he had been
denied a Fellowship on 'racial grounds'.[114] In her diary, Edna Manley
recorded a more dramatic example of his sensitivity. She described how
a power cut appeared to bring out Williams's insecurities: 'in the half
light of the flickering candles, Eric's whole character changed before
our very eyes.... His voice dropped to a sibilant whisper, and he began
to talk of what the English had done to him when he was at Oxford,
of how his letters were opened and messages intercepted'.[115] A more
detailed account of the sense of grievance which Williams expressed
to the Manleys is provided by the chapter of his autobiography *Inward
Hunger* which constitutes an inventory of the racial slights he endured
at Oxford, including the occasions when he was humiliated during an
oral examination and his chilly encounter with an unnamed liberal

author.[116] Like Manley, Williams wanted the colonised to set an example to the colonisers and envisaged the PNM as a vehicle for racial accommodation. He failed in this ambition and by the time of independence in 1962 his party was identified with the defence of the interests of black African Trinidadians. The scarring effects of exposure to racial prejudice were not conducive to generating the liberal idea of colour blindness and, when under pressure, he blundered into crass assumptions about Indian Trinidadians which he vociferously condemned in others. Although this slippage away from his pan-racial ideals was the product of numerous factors, most noticeably the colonial legacy which he analysed in his work, Williams bore significant responsibility for the rising racial tensions of the late 1950s which so alarmed British observers.

The British propensity for panicking about racial controversies was evident during the 1956 election campaign while Williams was still preaching the requirement for racial solidarity. The Governor of Trinidad, Edward Beetham, like Foot when confronted with a potential communist threat in Jamaica and Renison when dealing with the politics of race in Barbados, demonstrated a jumpiness which was at odds with the phlegmatic disposition which was supposed to distinguish British Governors from the local population of the colonies they administered. Although surprised by the absence of lawlessness during the campaign, Beetham predicted that the black African supporters of the PNM would become disenchanted once it became clear that they had not obtained an overwhelming triumph at the polls. He warned that when news of a partial victory reached 'this volatile section of [the] population at the end of a long day [it] may lead to spontaneous disorders particularly in Port of Spain.' Unless sufficient force was available to restrain the rioters, he predicted 'trouble would spread like wildfire and could be very serious.'[117] Beetham proved a poor psephologist and his alarmist predictions about public reaction to the election results were never tested. The PNM's success at the polls was more impressive than had been expected: they won 13 of the 24 seats and obtained 39% of the total votes cast which was twice the number of the second largest party, the People's Democratic Party.[118] Beetham's insistence on calling a warship to the vicinity was ridiculed by Williams who later recalled the prevalence of 'all sorts of rumours of violence and confusion'. On his own account, this alarmism underestimated the command Williams could exercise over his supporters: he recorded Beetham's astonishment at the speed with which crowds dispersed following instructions from him to return to their homes.[119]

Once elected first minister, Williams's priorities were economic growth and constitutional advance. In order to obtain the former he engaged in an urgent search for capital from overseas investors and the British and American governments. On the matter of political reform he advocated a stronger central government for the planned federation and the removal of the confining colonial conventions which limited the freedom of action of elected politicians in the territorial units. During a meeting with Lennox-Boyd in June 1957 he demanded the introduction of a Cabinet system of government in Trinidad. From Williams's perspective this required that the leader of the majority party, in their capacity as Chief Minister, should have the right to appoint and dismiss Ministers, that British colonial officials should lose the right to vote in the Executive Council, and that the Governor's discretionary powers ought to be exercised only on advice from the Chief Minister.[120] Given that Cabinet government had already been established in Jamaica and Barbados, the extension of the system to Trinidad was difficult to resist and Lennox-Boyd sanctioned its introduction. As elsewhere, it was only when the relationship between the powers of an elected first minister and the Governor were examined in detail that the extent of British reservations became clear. In February 1958 Beetham complained that Williams was seeking to undermine the authority of three key officials: the Governor, Chief Secretary and Attorney General. Back in Whitehall, the Assistant Under-Secretary of the Colonial Office, Philip Rogers, and his subordinate in one of the West Indian departments, John Marnham, estimated that it was time to think 'furiously' about the implications of further constitutional change in Trinidad. The latter was dissatisfied with the prospect that the governments of territorial units would acquire additional powers, while the legislative and executive scope of the federal centre remained narrowly circumscribed. He reiterated the familiar and futile Colonial Office orthodoxy that an extension of the powers of elected representatives in one territory ought not to set a precedent for others and argued that the authority of the federal centre should be enhanced before any further demission of power to the units.[121]

What aggravated the argument about constitutional reform in Trinidad was the eruption of racial controversy following the first elections to the newly established federal legislature in March 1958. The outcome was a surprise victory for the newly formed Democratic Labour Party (DLP) which had been established only the year before as an expedient to unite Williams's many enemies. They won six of the 10 seats contested in Trinidad. Albert Gomes, who was one of its architects, described the DLP as a 'rag bag of dissident elements'. He later confessed that the new party appealed to the sense of grievance among the Indian population but argued that in Trinidadian conditions 'in order to pursue an ordinary democratic end, racial rivalries had to be exploited.'[122] This was the attitude which infuriated Williams: the DLP's success in the federal elections seemed to guarantee that the nationalist movement would be divided along racial lines even before the task of eradicating colonialism had been completed. Characteristically these gloomy thoughts drove him to extreme measures of his own. In a speech delivered on 1 April 1958 he denounced what he claimed to be a widely held view among Indian Trinidadians that they owed loyalty to India rather than to Trinidad. In one infamous passage he described Indians in Trinidad as a 'recalcitrant and hostile minority masquerading as the Indian nation, and prostituting the name of India for its selfish, reactionary political ends.' Williams intended to emphasise the need for unity against colonialism but on this occasion his rhetorical embellishments of this nationalist message were as inflammatory as it was possible to imagine. The two leading Indian Trinidadian members of the PNM, Kamaluddin Mohammed and Winston Mahabir, shared the stage with Williams when he delivered his address. Mohammed served in a number of PNM Cabinets and eventually became Deputy Prime Minister and President of the World Health Organisation. Despite his loyalty to Williams he recalled: 'Winston and I were sitting together on the platform and when we heard the speech we turned cold.' The most attractive gloss he could place on the ugly elements of the speech was that what 'Williams was trying to say was that the elections were fought on the basis of race and that the Indian minority, a term I found offensive, were trying to remove him from office.' Mohammed indicated that at a later moment, in a more reflective mood, Williams 'realised it had done a lot of damage.'[123] Mahabir was less forgiving and broke with Williams three years later. He also remembered the 'horrified glances' he exchanged with others as the speech proceeded. Listening to Williams he felt that Indian members of the PNM 'experienced a sudden shattering of all the ideals for which we thought we stood. We felt guilty of all the lies we had preached to the Indians about the genuineness of Williams and our party.'[124]

The rising tensions on Trinidad in the aftermath of Williams's speech influenced the debate over constitutional reform. Beetham was concerned about the effect of Williams's rhetoric. On 9 April he wrote: 'The prognosis for Trinidad...could hardly be worse at the moment of writing. It is however an unpredictable place and anything may happen.' He criticised both the DLP and the PNM for exploiting the race issue and characterised Williams's speech as inflammatory: 'A few sparks (which may well happen during the forthcoming bye-elections for the Leg. Co. [Legislative Council]) and the whole country could become involved, resulting in a state of emergency, troops etc. etc.'[125] The minutes composed by Colonial Office staff in response to Beetham's report accused him of exaggerating but also revealed some startling racial assumptions of their own. Despite the 'nasty bits' of the speech, Marnham's assessment was that it was not 'too awful' and that Beetham was 'feeling the strain.' Another official, Baker, provided a gloss which attended to Williams's peroration which featured the slogan 'seek ye first the kingdom of self-government'. Baker commented: 'I find it a queer mixture of scholarly exposition and demagogic invective, ending with a parody of the New Testament that smells unpleasantly of Africa.'[126] The implication that there was something sinister or repellent about the establishment of independence under a government led by black African Trinidadians informed the subsequent discussion of constitutional reform. On 21 June 1958 Williams's deputy, Patrick Solomon, introduced a motion in the Legislative Council which signalled the PNM's intention to deprive the Governor of the power to legislate. Baxter was responsible for formulating a response in Whitehall and he concluded that the current political tensions in Trinidad required a strengthening, rather than the proposed weakening, of the Governor's powers. He argued that PNM ministers had not shown themselves to be competent and 'a move in the direction of self-government might only inspire them to dictatorial or xenophobic excesses.' These thoughts were endorsed by Marnham who added for good measure that Williams's weakness was his unwillingness to accept 'those self imposed restraints which alone make British type constitutions workable.' However, both he and Rogers reverted to the customary and prudential Colonial Office thought that resistance to proposals emanating from more moderate nationalist leaders was not practical politics.[127]

The disquiet which attended Williams's plans to reduce the Governor's reserved powers was also evident when preparations for the introduction of Cabinet government were discussed. This had already been accepted in principle but became an awkward issue for the Colonial Office because of concerns about racial tensions in Trinidad. Objections to the transfer of responsibility for policing to a locally elected Cabinet Minister came to the attention of Lennox-Boyd when delegations from both the PNM and the DLP visited London in October 1958. On his own account, Solomon, who led the former group and could be almost as acerbic as Williams, made no effort to reassure the Colonial Office. He told Lennox-Boyd that the advance to Cabinet government 'was just a first instalment and that, like Oliver Twist, we would be coming back for more.'[128] Although he offered concessions on some minor constitutional issues, Solomon insisted that the Governor's power to refuse assent to legislation must end and that a member of the elected Cabinet should acquire authority over the police. Such demands elicited the common complaint that the nationalist leadership were displaying dictatorial tendencies. What exacerbated the situation in this instance was the Colonial Office assessment that 'the racial situation in Trinidad is a tense one.' On this point, Lennox-Boyd found the DLP's analysis persuasive. He described himself as 'extremely shaken by the talks we had with the opposition leaders from Trinidad.' Risking the wrath of Williams, he declared his outright opposition to the transfer of responsibilities for policing to a member of the PNM Cabinet.[129] Relations between the colonial authorities and Williams were inflamed further by his campaign against the American military base on Chaguaramas, which will be discussed in the following chapter.

The combined refusal of American and British policymakers to accommodate nationalist demands prompted new bouts of invective from Williams, to which the transatlantic powers responded in different ways. American officials refused to make concessions on the base issue and offered covert encouragement to the DLP; the British government concluded that, despite the difficulties they experienced in working with Williams, he was potentially a capable leader of an independent Trinidad who, in the last resort, had to be appeased. The controversy over ministerial control of the police culminated in a confrontation between Williams and the Parliamentary Under-Secretary of State, Julian Amery, in Trinidad in June 1959. As a trump card, Williams announced that the PNM would not cooperate with the scheduled reopening of Parliament until an elected minister was given authority over policing. His case was strengthened by one positive and one negative development: he had the support of the Governor and he had not repeated the inflammatory remarks about Indian Trinidadians made a year earlier in the aftermath of the federal elections. On 29 June Williams told Amery and Beetham that racial tensions on the island were 'less than in Notting Hill gate'. As a former influential member of the Suez group who delighted in controversy, Amery was one of the least likely Ministers to submit to pressure from colonial nationalists but he recognised that Williams had outmanoeuvred the Governor. Although he reported back to London about the Trinidad police, that 'it should not be forgotten that like PNM they are 90% African', Amery effectively admitted defeat. He reported that Williams was 'aiming at a direct test of strength with UK Government' and suspected that he might precipitate an election on the issues of the police and Chaguaramas which he would certainly win.[130] In order to avoid this, the Colonial Office conceded ministerial control of the police to a PNM minister. Williams made a triumphant radio broadcast on 9 July to declare victory and the establishment of Cabinet government.[131] The following decade was one of continuing racial tension on the island, culminating in Williams's own confrontation with the Black Power movement in 1970. Judged in that context, the Colonial Office had some justification for their reservations about constitutional reform in the late 1950s. In the case of both Barbados and Trinidad, however, the manner in which the metropolitan authorities discussed the racial politics of the islands revealed much about their own subjective appreciation of racial issues and in particular their fear that the domination of Caribbean politics by a mass electorate who were the descendants of African slaves would lead to disorder. These apprehensions reinforced the already prevalent sense of caution about constitutional advance in the territorial units which was also evident during the negotiations to establish a federation.

Building a West Indian State

At the Kingston and Montego Bay conferences of 1947 nationalist politicians had announced their intention to unite the separate territories of the Anglophone Caribbean into a single federation. The Colonial Office had approved of this development but when the details of the constitution were discussed they imposed a set of conservative principles in the Rance report which proved unattractive to the nationalists who, in territories like Trinidad, Barbados and Jamaica, increasingly devoted their energies to obtaining greater legislative and executive authority at a local, territorial level rather than to fostering regional integration. Bustamante, whose prevarication on the federal issue was one of the key reasons for the dilatory progress of federal constitution-building, instituted a new phase in the project when he proposed in August 1951 that a conference should be held to reconsider the Rance plan. As was now customary, this démarche did not produce immediate action but in April 1953 a conference was finally held in London to revise the original recommendations. Preparations for this meeting clarified the terms of the debate about federation: the key disagreements between British officials and the local politicians concerned the balance of constitutional authority and the extent of economic assistance; the issues in dispute among the units were the site of the federal capital, freedom of movement and the source of revenue for the federation. While the British liked to adopt the role of frustrated arbiter, on the matter of their own powers and perquisites they adopted a latitudinarian approach which was designed to entrench their continuing influence.

Those playing the role of constitutional architects in Whitehall and the Caribbean recognised that one of the trickiest aspects of the federal design was the financial structure of the new polity. If their specifications placed too great a financial load on the general population, popular support for federation would almost certainly evaporate. Until Adams suggested the introduction of a federal income tax in 1958, there was unanimity that the best approach was the indirect method of generating revenue from customs. In 1947 the Fiscal Sub-Committee of the Montego Bay conference had proposed that 'any form of federal government should be financed from at least one independent and major source of revenue, in the collection of which it should have complete legislative and administrative control.' They agreed that this source should be customs duties.[132] The idea of making the cost of federation as inconspicuous as possible had political advantages but it inevitably limited the possibilities of what the federation would be able to achieve after it was established. This problem was exacerbated by the British determination to impose the most parsimonious solutions wherever possible. When the Rance committee deliberated further on this matter they concluded that the complete transfer of customs revenue from the units to the centre, as recommended at Montego Bay, would place far too onerous a burden on the former and provide a superfluity of funding for the latter. The portion of customs revenue to be allocated to the federal government was therefore reduced to 25%, with the remainder to be retained by the units. Even this was criticised in the Colonial Office as likely to provide too much budgetary license to the spendthrift federal politicians of the future. Seel, who had been appointed Comptroller of Development and Welfare in the West Indies, considered that 'the financial and economic aspects of the Standing Committee's recommendations... are not the strongest feature of this generally valuable report.'[133]

When in February 1952 Lyttelton contacted the governments of the Anglophone Caribbean territories to urge them to prepare for a new conference on federation in June, his intention was that they should focus their attention on the unsatisfactory financial aspects and on the method of obtaining a customs union.[134] Instead, Lyttelton's initiative inadvertently reopened the debate about the balance of constitutional authority in the putative federation and its connections to the levels of future British assistance. Some local governments were eager both to recast those sections of the current plan dealing with the Governor's reserved powers and secure additional financial guarantees from the British. Bustamante seized the opportunity to demand a minimum of £ 50 million in economic assistance. In July the Jamaican House of Representatives also called for the Rance proposals to be revised in order to secure greater powers for the federation's elected politicians. Manley's PNP demanded that any federation should be fully self-governing.[135] Adams also regarded the Lyttelton dispatch as a means of reviving the more ambitious plans for a federation that had been adumbrated by the Caribbean Labour Congress. Seel complained that Adams and Manley did 'not want federation except on a rigid basis of universal socialism.'[136] One source of comfort for the Colonial Office was the relatively accommodating position of Trinidad. Gomes, who was the dominant figure in the island's politics before the emergence of Williams, campaigned vigorously against proposals emanating from Kingston and Bridgetown for major revisions to the federal plan. The author of that plan, Hubert Rance, who in his new post as Governor of Trinidad had established an informal alliance with Gomes, visited London in June 1952 and cautioned against holding a conference unless the other islands accepted the basic principles which he had affirmed.[137] Although the determination of the Trinidadian government to prevent major revisions harmonised with the cautionary song intoned by the Colonial Office, the dissonance between Bustamante, Adams and Gomes made it impossible to hold Lyttelton's planned federal conference in 1952.

Further complications arose because competing ideas about the relationship between economic development and political autonomy had not been resolved during Rance's chairmanship of the Standing Closer Association Committee (SCAC). One of the advantages of the federation, from the British perspective, was that it would provide a channel for a more rational process of economic planning, leading eventually to the tapering away of financial assistance to the region. British officials were prepared to consider a short-term increase in funding for development in order to secure the longer-term attenuation of their commitment but they argued that estimates of federal requirements emerging from the Caribbean tended to 'gild the SCAC's lily.'[138] In March 1951 the head of the Colonial Office's Finance Department, Henry Bourdillon, produced a detailed report on development policy which recommended that funding be diverted away from 'avoidable recurrent expenditure', by which he meant spending on social welfare in unit territories, towards projects likely to foster economic growth on a regional, federal basis. He also acknowledged that 'until quite recently nothing was done to put money back into these islands in order to expand their economy' and that even recent increases in British funding were 'only scratching the surface of the economic problem.'[139] Nationalist politicians wanted something more than a dent in the hardened veneer of colonial neglect and political subservience. By the early 1950s their demands were eliciting some support from local Governors. Blackburne was so keen to curtail the influence of 'half-baked rabble rousers' in the Leewards that he suggested offering the federation full dominion status on the grounds that the federal authorities would be obliged to curb dissidence on the small islands and undertake rational economic planning.[140] Foot offered a less sweeping solution but suggested that the retention of reserved powers in the field of finance was unnecessary given the constraints which would be imposed on local policymakers once they had to confront the problem of federal indigence. He also recommended that offers of economic aid should be repackaged into a more palatable form to provide a measure of financial inducement to Caribbean politicians to integrate. Even Rance suggested, following some prompting from Gomes, that an offer of additional finance at the outset of any conference 'may well spike the guns of certain people who, while outwardly supporting federation, merely give lip service.'[141]

Disagreements about precisely when to hold the frequently postponed federal conference caused almost as many problems as the substantive issues relating to economics and constitutional authority. A minor crisis broke out in the Colonial Office in February 1953 when Jamaican and Barbadian objections to the scheduling of an 'early' conference seemed certain to reduce the slow progress towards the federal goal to a complete halt. Once the difficulties coordinating timetables were overcome the parties finally assembled in London in April. The most controversial issues during the talks were the constitutional balance of power and finance, where the problems were familiar, and the implementation of freedom of movement, which became an arena of bitter conflict between Trinidad and the other territories. Reginald Maudling, who as Economic Secretary to the Treasury chaired the financial discussions, presented the British position. Despite the prompting of Caribbean Governors to show generosity, the only inducements which he offered were the promise of £ 500,000 towards the cost of constructing federal buildings and the assurance that annual grants to the region would be sustained at their existing levels for the first five years of any federation. Losses of revenue to the units as a consequence of federation were alleviated by reducing the proportion of their customs revenue apportioned to the federation from 25% to 15%, despite the consequential weakening of the federal centre which this entailed. The chair of the constitutional meetings, Lord Munster, accepted some minor amendments to the neo-colonial elements in the Rance report, including a technical change to the financial conditions under which the Governor of the federation was entitled to employ reserved powers and the sub-contracting of emergency powers to the governments of the units. Self-evidently this did not amount to a major redrawing of the federal plan in order to make it more attractive to nationalist politicians. The enthusiasm which they had expressed for such a project at Kingston six years earlier was further dissipated by feuding between them. Adams persuaded the delegates to transfer the subject of freedom of movement from the Concurrent List, where jurisdiction was shared between unit and federal governments, to the Exclusive List, in order to prevent individual units erecting barriers to immigration. This strengthening of federal authority was noisily resisted by Trinidad and, partly as a consequence of the resulting arguments, the conference abandoned plans to locate the federal government on that island in favour of Grenada.[142]

Freedom of movement was important because the ending of restrictions on immigration between the islands after the creation of the federation would allow workers from elsewhere in the Caribbean to enter Trinidad which was experiencing a period of economic growth. In this regard federalism could mitigate the prevalence of unemployment and underemployment elsewhere in the Caribbean. The rise of Trinidad's oil industry made it the region's most dynamic economy but the prospect of an influx of overseas labour, which would inevitably depress wages, provided a disincentive for Trinidadian politicians to accept an open borders policy. By contrast the other territorial governments regarded an end to internal immigration controls as a natural consequence of a federal system and one of its principal attractions. Once again the issue of race impinged on the debate: from the outset many of the leaders of Indian opinion in Trinidad had fretted over their transformation from a large minority on the island to a small minority in a wider federation which did not include the substantial Indian population of British Guiana. The revisions made to the federal plan at London made Trinidad more hesitant still. It took 20 months for the Legislative Council to approve the new reformulated version of federation and only with the qualification that the issues of freedom of movement and the capital site should be reopened. Rance took the alarmist view that unless federal plans were finalised by the time of the September 1955 elections, a new Trinidadian Legislative Council, under the influence of Indian perturbations, might seek to reverse all the decisions made on federation.[143] Trinidad's declining faith in federalism did not initially appear to be balanced by any impairment in Jamaican scepticism. In the Colonial Office, Rogers expressed concern at the 'public talk about Jamaica achieving Dominion status.' The vision of each Caribbean territory attaining independence outside a federation led him to comment: 'I cannot myself for a moment believe that even if it were practicable, which I doubt, it can in any way be considered in the interests of the West Indies.'[144]

British responses to the post-London controversies were continuous with their previous attitudes: half-weary resignation at the contrarian instincts of Caribbean politicians and half-unfettered panic at the prospect that the individual territories might achieve independence outside the constraints imposed by a centralised administration. The more insouciant aspect was evident in the decision to make the arrangement by which the federation was to be established excessively intricate and time-consuming. They opted to follow the precedent set by the Central African Federation which comprised six stages to be completed after the local legislatures had approved the London decisions. When this procedure was outlined to British officials working in the Caribbean, they expressed concern that support for federation would ebb away in the midst of the bureaucratic heavy lifting. In August 1954 Luke warned that the 'dangers of a loss of momentum are obvious'.[145] Three commissions dealing with the civil service, finance and the judiciary were not issued with their terms of reference until June 1955 at which point a new schedule was formulated which entailed another meeting of Caribbean delegates to discuss the commissions' reports in January 1956 and the introduction of enabling legislation in the British Parliament before April 1956. The Colonial Office aimed to finalise a deal before the elections in Trinidad, which had been postponed until September 1956 precisely because it was feared that an anti-federal grouping would be victorious. It was also felt necessary to seek a reaffirmation of the Jamaican commitment to federation following the PNP's election victory in January 1955.[146] In this regard their thinking was misconceived: it was the victors in those two elections, Eric Williams and Norman Manley, who revived the federal project by challenging those anachronistic features of the 1953 plan which appeared to guarantee the federation's irrelevance.

After their electoral successes in 1955–1956, Manley and Williams cooperated to resolve the differences between Trinidad and Jamaica. In retrospect the success of their partnership in promoting federalism in the mid-1950s has been overshadowed by the significant role they played in the later demise of the federation in the early 1960s. However, during the formative period of federal history they reinvigorated a process which the Colonial Office patronised but could not enliven. Manley was much more interested in the potentialities of federation than Bustamante whose first instinct was to ask how much it would cost Jamaica; while Williams was able to mobilise popular sentiment in Trinidad in favour of federation in a way which Gomes had failed to do. Whereas the British regarded federalism as a means to constrain the excesses of the Caribbean character, the two leading nationalist politicians argued that it could serve an emancipatory purpose. In his self-analysis of the public education campaign he launched after leaving the Caribbean Commission, Williams identified the promotion of federalism as one of the key themes of his early political career. He insisted: 'The task of building a West Indian nation is the decisive task of the present and the future.' In instrumental terms it was vital to the linked goals of improving the economic and educational performance of the region.[147] Manley had helped to clarify the purpose of federation at the 1947 Kingston conference where he argued it would provide a venue which could fulfil both the creative and economic potential of the Anglophone Caribbean. It would 'satisfy the growing ambitions of our people for an area of action large enough for their creative energies'; at the same time, the greater political scale would allow for technocratic solutions to political problems, which he described as planning 'for a national future for our people.'[148]

The ascendancy of Manley and Williams suited the Colonial Office in the sense that they were precisely the kind of nationalist politicians with whom they liked to deal: an eminent lawyer and a distinguished historian seemed far more likely to opt for the politics of 'moderation' than firebrand labour leaders such as Alexander Bustamante and his Trinidadian contemporary, Uriah Butler. In another sense they presented a more dangerous ideological challenge because both Manley and Williams had a sense of entitlement and were eager to free the region from the politics of cultural deference and dependency. Immediately after his appointment as Chief Minister, Manley sought amendments to

the latest federal plan, including the removal of the three British officials who were to be members of the federal executive. The Colonial
Office responded by making clear their determination that their officials must stay.[149] When, during preparations for the next preparatory
conference, Manley's ideas were endorsed by the Governor, Hugh Foot,
suspicions were aroused that the two of them were engaged in a comprehensive project to redesign the federation to suit Jamaica. During a
visit to London in October 1955 Manley received some sympathy for the
specific problems he had in dealing with the scepticism of the Jamaican
public which Bustamante was assiduously cultivating.[150] The real charge
against Manley was that he was stoking his own form of populist anti-
colonial politics by seeking to curtail British influence. In November
Lloyd wrote to Foot about Manley: 'should he insist upon these constitutional amendments he could count on being held in the West Indies
as the champion of constitutional freedom whilst those who felt compelled to oppose him would be branded as reactionaries. If it were true
that he wished to destroy Federation there could be no better or simpler
way . . . of doing it.' Foot replied by stating with surprising bluntness: 'to
suggest that he is so dishonest as to wish to destroy Federation for which
he has stood throughout his political life and so mean as to endeavour to gain political credit by doing so is something which I certainly
can never believe.' Lloyd responded in conciliatory fashion. He praised
Foot's diplomatic skills and urged him to 'get Manley to come here in a
reasonable frame of mind.'[151]

By the time Lloyd's letter arrived in Jamaica, Manley had already
escalated his campaign for revisions in a way that the Colonial Office
regarded as thoroughly unreasonable. On 30 November he presented
seven propositions to the House of Representatives which amounted
to a radical reformulation of the federal scheme. In addition to the
removal of officials from the executive, Manley demanded that the
elected Prime Minister should appoint Senators to the upper house, that
the Governor-General's reserved powers should be circumscribed, that
the federal government should have greater discretion over regional
planning, that the scheme of British financial assistance should be
improved and that the method of constitutional revision should be
altered and reconsideration given to the respective status of unit and
federal ministers. The metropolitan government responded by seeking
to isolate Manley through an appeal to the conservative instincts of
many Caribbean politicians and their apprehensions about Jamaican
hegemony inside the federation. The Colonial Office registered the view
of Manley's opponents, with which they clearly concurred, that the

changes would destabilise the new federation 'by concentrating too great power in the hands of the Prime Minister and by unduly weakening the restraining influence of the British Government.' They opted to convey to Manley, Adams and Gomes the importance of respecting British constitutional requirements and 'to warn them not to disregard these interests' when planning further revisions to the federal plan.[152] As might be expected, Adams, as the author of the CLC federal plan was reported to be 'broadly sympathetic to Manley's ideas'; they therefore had to turn to Gomes, who had been operating in an informal alliance with the Colonial Office since the 1949 SCAC meetings, to lead the opposition to the new Jamaican proposals. The actions of the Colonial Office to undermine Manley prompted Foot to complain about a concerted effort to put the Jamaican delegation 'in the dog house'. Foot claimed that Gomes was attempting to prevent discussion of Manley's ideas 'for his own personal reasons' and emphasised that the circumstances of Jamaican party politics required Manley to campaign for a more advanced constitution. In his conversations with Manley, Stephen Luke found him willing to compromise on the issue of the Governor's reserved powers but not on the exclusion of British officials from a role as voting members of the executive.[153]

It was Eric Williams who came to Manley's aid by subverting Gomes's resistance to constitutional revision during the course of the 1956 Trinidadian election campaign. He regarded the Jamaican proposals for a more advanced federal constitution as admirable on their own terms, but they also provided an opportunity to assault the conservatism of Gomes and the nascent PNM's other electoral opponents. Williams's attack on the federal constitution focused less on the presence of officials in the executive and more on the extensive powers which the Governor-General would exercise. During their ongoing correspondence Williams told Manley that he regarded the mobilisation of support for a new conception of federation as the 'coup de grace' in the PNM's campaign. The Woodford Square lecture which he delivered in January 1956 on the subject of the pros and cons of federation concentrated much more on the pros than the cons, while also providing a critique of both the original Rance proposals and the 1953 London agreement. In contrast to Manley, who often emphasised the spiritual purpose of greater unity, Williams focused on the historical context and the material benefits of federation. He argued that 'Federation is a simple matter of common sense': in a world of large states, the 700,000 inhabitants of Trinidad would be powerless unless they united with the other Anglophone Caribbean territories. What must be prevented was the establishment of a federation

which was a continuation of colonial rule rather than the manifestation of a new autonomous nation. Williams criticised the willingness of
the existing Trinidadian Legislative Council to compromise with British
rule: 'in 1956 we find Trinidadian legislators leading the procession and
waving banners which call for more of the colonialism that has ruined
us, selling our birthright as West Indians for a mess of federal pottage
for themselves.' He concluded by declaring that his audience should
regard themselves as the true legislators of the country and invited
them to pass a resolution opposing any federal constitution in which
a British Governor possessed reserved powers.[154] Just before Gomes and
the Trinidad delegation left for London in February, Williams issued
an open letter denouncing their failure to consult the people and
demanding revisions to the 1953 plan.[155] This bout of populist agitation
occurred while Luke was conducting a survey of regional opinion on
behalf of the Colonial Office. He predicted that the necessity to avoid
giving the impression that they were collaborating with British imperialism during Trinidad's election year would oblige members of their
delegation to support Manley's campaign for revisions and might even
require them to make 'more far reaching points of their own i.e. the setting of a date for Dominion Status and the appointment of indigenous
governors.'[156]

A freezing English February proved an inauspicious environment for
the latest federal conference. Mordecai recalled: 'shivering winds, snow-
storms and icy rains proved lethal to visitors from the sunny West
Indies. The list of casualties, including the main performers, grew daily,
and the jagged tempers of those who resumed gave evidence of their
discomfort.'[157] Despite the pressure Williams was applying from outside
the Trinidad legislature, Gomes courted further unpopularity by acting
as the principal defender of British policy. In response to Lennox-Boyd's
welcoming address, he went as far as to declare 'he was somewhat jeal-
ous of the fact that the Secretary of State had so often been right whereas
West Indians had so often proved wrong.' Manley and Adams followed
this unwelcome testimony by immediately presenting the case for revisions to the 1953 plan; the latter noted 'that HMG had been giving the
units an increasing measure of self-government and that it would not
be appropriate to grant less to the new Federation.' At the ninth meeting on 16 February Manley argued for the first of his seven propositions:
the exclusion of British officials from the Executive Council. Lennox-
Boyd insisted that they should sit as full members because Britain would
remain 'deeply involved both morally and financially in the Federation.' Manley described their presence as 'unnecessary and harmful.' The

following day he moved on to the third of his propositions, the extensive reserved powers of the future Governor-General, which was the
issue on which Williams was campaigning. Manley wondered why such
safeguards were regarded as essential in the Caribbean but not thought
necessary in the new constitution of the Gold Coast. He was told by the
British representative at the session, James McPetrie, that Britain had an
'ultimate interest' in financial matters.[158] The Colonial Office believed
that the federation could not expect to be liberated from British political
control while remaining in a state of financial dependence and, in that
respect, their case was strengthened by Manley's reversion to the fifth
proposition which called for an increase in financial assistance. Despite
their disagreements on other matters, there was almost unanimous support among Caribbean delegates for the Jamaican notion of a federal
consolidated fund backed by a £ 2 million loan from the British Treasury
offered at a nominal rate of interest.[159] Amidst the escalating arguments
Manley achieved some progress: the revisions made to the 1953 plan in
the 1956 conference report included the removal of British officials from
the executive and their replacement with three nominees who would be
unable to vote, a new formula for the exercise of the Governor-General's
reserved powers, a doubling of the Treasury's support for the construction of a federal capital and some vague provisions for British assistance
in raising a loan should circumstances make this necessary.[160] Although
this did not constitute a radical restructuring, the marginalisation of the
official voice in the executive in favour of greater authority for elected
representatives did make the new settlement more palatable to nationalist opinion and ensured that the putative federation began its life closer
to the goal of political independence.

If one side of the conference was concerned with how to wrestle
greater political autonomy and financial assistance from the British, the
other was dominated by unavailing attempts to reconcile the differing
interests of the Caribbean parties. The place where these collisions had
the greatest impact was in the contiguous domains of revenue collection
and customs union. This had always been a battlefield for the conflicting interests of the territories. Sydney Caine began his investigation of
financial issues in June 1955 and three months later produced a report
which sought to resolve the arguments over finance but actually provided the pretext for a new round of disagreements. Caine effectively
overturned the 1953 London plan by rejecting the notion that the federation should be dependent for its revenue on a proportion of the units'
customs income; as an alternative he recommended a return to the original principles outlined at Montego Bay that it should have powers to

raise money through taxes on both consumption and income. Given the political and practical difficulties in establishing a federal income tax, he proposed that for an initial period the new federal government should rely on levies on petrol, cigarettes and alcoholic beverages.[161] When Lennox-Boyd endorsed this idea some delegates objected that new consumption taxes 'might arouse local opposition.'[162] The notion of a customs union was even more controversial. Although the territorial units were expected to harmonise trade policies in the longer term, it was accepted that in the short term they would continue to set their own independent tariffs and duties. It was on the question of any long-term alignment of customs duties that Manley was at his most prickly and uncooperative. The PNP had plans to invest in the Jamaican economy and extend welfare provision which would place additional burdens on the budget of the unit government and there was a possibility of the entire programme being jeopardised by the loss of revenue entailed in the establishment of a federal levy and the gradual harmonisation of duties. On 20 February there was a full-scale row between the Jamaican and other delegations over the issue of customs union. Carl La Corbiniere of St Lucia took the lead in representing the interests of the small islands, who believed that revenues should be diverted away from the unit budgets and towards the federal government so that they could be spent on regional development. He threatened to reserve their position on all other aspects of the federation unless stronger guarantees were offered that customs union would be imposed at an early stage.[163] The final report of the conference stipulated that a Commission on Trade and Tariffs would report on the matter within two years of the establishment of the federation. In a similar vein it was agreed to delay the implementation of the Caine recommendations by making provisional arrangements for funding the first five years of the federation. During this transitional period it would be reliant on profits made from currency trading, a mandatory levy on the units and powers to enforce a limited customs levy of its own.[164] Once again the possibility of a consistent and reliable source of federal income had slipped away. If the constitutional recommendations amounted to moderate progress then the excessively cautious financial provisions constituted a setback; the postponement of a final resolution of the revenue controversy ensured that after the federation was established, arguments about tariffs and taxation would remain a toxic political issue.

A final matter which caused friction between the Caribbean islands and would eventually generate a conflict between the local nationalists and the Anglo-American allies was the question of the site of the federal capital. This had already been hypothetically relocated from Trinidad to Grenada without any actual construction work being undertaken. At the London conference in 1956 delegates from St Lucia, Antigua, St Kitts and Barbados vied with one another in claiming that they would make the best hosts, while spokesmen for Trinidad and Grenada reasserted their claims.[165] The final conference report contained the plaintive admission that after 'lengthy discussion' the delegates had concluded they were 'not in possession of all the information necessary to enable us to reach a final decision'. Responsibility for choosing a location was entrusted to a fact-finding mission chaired by a former member of the Indian Civil Service, Francis Mudie.[166] Six months later the Mudie Commission reported to the Standing Federation Committee (SFC) that it would be more economical for one of the large islands to host the capital. In a maladroit political manoeuvre they argued the case for Jamaica, which had professed the least interest in acting as host, on the grounds that the societies of Barbados and Trinidad were corrupted by racial prejudice. This was typical both of the Colonial Office's attentiveness to racial feeling in the imperial periphery and their insensitivity to nationalist sentiments. Williams exploited the widespread affront caused by Mudie and at the second meeting of the SFC in January 1957 obtained a final decision in favour of Trinidad's claims. Even Williams's opponents repudiated the Mudie Commission and applauded his triumph in securing the capital and Trinidad's participation in the federation.[167] The selection of the precise location of the capital became the responsibility of yet another commission which in April recommended the Northwest peninsula of Trinidad around Chaguaramas as the most suitable of the seven sites examined: it was close to the metropolitan facilities available in Port of Spain and suitable for further development.[168]

One unmistakable difficulty with the choice of Chaguaramas was that the peninsula had been occupied by the American military since the conclusion of the destroyers for bases deal between Roosevelt and Churchill 15 years earlier. The proposal dismayed the British government, infuriated the Eisenhower administration and, paradoxically in view of later developments, irritated Williams's Trinidadian government. Reports from Washington noted that the suggestion that they should evacuate any portion of Chaguaramas constituted 'a painful surprise'. The Eisenhower administration refused to consent to the idea. Partly as a consequence of the moderate stance adopted by Williams's government and partly in deference to British views they did agree to talk to Caribbean politicians about the matter in London.[169] At a time when final preparations were being made for the establishment of the federation, British policymakers hoped that exposure to the intensity of Caribbean sentiment on the issue of the capital's location would moderate Washington's uncompromising refusal to lease any of the site back to Trinidadian jurisdiction.[170] At this initial stage it was Manley who articulated nationalist resentment of American neo-colonialism, which Williams would subsequently elaborate and amplify. In presenting the case for dividing the peninsula between the federal bureaucracy and the US armed forces, Manley complained: 'the Americans held far more land than they really needed; this was the trouble with the US military, they behaved in small islands as if they had the whole of the North American continent to spread themselves in.'[171] However, it was Williams who took the opportunity of his encounter with American officials in London to unleash an indignant denunciation of Anglo-American imperialism and instigate a four-year campaign to regain control of Chaguaramas. The controversy over the capital site, alongside the revenue-raising dilemma, were the two matters which dominated the short life of the federation and will be considered in the next chapter.

Apart from agreeing to return the capital to Trinidad the SFC made few decisions which altered the architecture of the federation. After his election Williams continued to criticise what he later described as 'the disgraceful constitution, colonialist top to bottom', but chose to cooperate because it included provisions for a major review after five years. In a letter of 11 December 1956, Manley attempted to reassure Williams on this point by asserting 'I am absolutely certain that at the end of the first five years if we unitedly wish to we will get Dominion Status for the asking.'[172] Although it meant suspending the campaign he had begun a year earlier, in January 1957 Williams publicly accepted that it was not feasible to seek a more advanced constitution before the establishment of the federation.[173] At the SFC meeting in May 1957, which chose Chaguaramas as the federal capital, delegates also discussed the issue of the review period and agreed that provision should be made to allow for major constitutional changes before the end of the five-year interim period. Other disagreements regarding the powers of the federal government proved irreconcilable. Jamaica remained stoutly opposed to an early customs union and Williams continued Gomes's policy of resisting further liberalisation on the issue of freedom of movement.[174] The disagreements on these vital matters reinforced the lack of authority and independence which were a consequence of British determination to keep the federation under colonial supervision. These constraints did not make the federation an attractive arena for Manley and Williams who opted to remain as Chief Ministers of their local island governments rather than seek federal office. Manley's decision was regarded as particularly shocking because he was perceived to be the leader who could both enthuse Jamaican opinion and mediate between the Eastern Caribbean islands. His friend and biographer Philip Sherlock recalled that he felt 'as though he had struck me in the face' when Manley told him he would stay in Jamaica rather than seek to lead the new federal government in Trinidad.[175] On reflection Sherlock acknowledged that Manley had been needed in Jamaica to combat Bustamante's increasingly destructive anti-federalist rhetoric. Grantley Adams of Barbados became federal Prime Minister but was perceived by many as a third-choice candidate. A further damaging personnel matter was the decision to appoint Patrick Buchan Hepburn as the first Governor General which incensed Manley. Buchan Hepburn, who became Lord Hailes, was a middle-ranking figure in Conservative politics with no experience of the Caribbean. Manley partly blamed the British government for the decision but argued that the appointment of a 'Lord Somebody' who was unknown in the region, rather than a more eminent figure with experience of colonial affairs, was also a consequence of the inability of local actors to effectively convey their views. During the short life of the federation Hailes would be persistently at odds with both Manley and Williams.

Conclusion

For the architects of British decolonisation the 1950s were the age of anxiety: they fretted that the conflict with communism in East Asia would spread to the rest of the empire, that conflicts between black and white people in the remains of the British empire in Africa would taint their record and undermine their moral authority and, most of all, they doubted the capacities of the emerging generation of nationalist leaders to maintain the political equilibrium of the newly independent states of the old imperial periphery. In the Caribbean such neuroses were evident in the hysterical reaction to the return of Ferdinand Smith to Jamaica, the anxious commentary on the heightening of tensions on Barbados and Trinidad caused by the triumphs of African-Caribbean nationalist elites in the era of mass participation elections, and in the earnest application of various curbs and checks on the authority of the electoral element during the process of federal constitution-building. By the time the federation was inaugurated on 3 January 1958, a slightly more reassuring atmosphere prevailed. Despite the precedent set by Gairy none of the small islands had succumbed to mob rule, the handful of Caribbean Marxists had been marginalised and Adams's election seemed to guarantee that the first federal Prime Minister would be the most Anglophile of Caribbean politicians. The medium and longer-term consequences of British strategy were less salutary. Efforts to inhibit the potentially irresponsible behaviour of nationalist politicians in their new regional forum by retaining elements of colonial control encumbered the federation with a constitution which was less advanced than that of the unit territories and this, in turn, contributed to its demise. Furthermore, although British ministers and officials expressed concerns about the latent dictatorial tendencies of local leaders, their own persecution of those who challenged the terms on which decolonisation was being offered set a precedent for the authoritarianism of the postcolonial era. None of this was inevitable or wholly caused by British actions but the obsession of imperial administrators with the politics of dissent narrowed the possibilities available to local nationalists. The optimism of British officials in 1958 that progress was being made was widely shared and the long-term future of fragmentation and political turbulence can only be understood through an examination of the expedients adopted once things started to fall apart.

4
The Triumph of Disorder
1958–1962

Examined in retrospect the demise of the federation lends itself to a teleological explanation in which the constant arguments amongst the principal actors led inevitably to its dissolution amidst much rancour and bitterness in 1962. This was not how it was experienced at the time. Until the Jamaican referendum in September 1961, which most expected Manley and the anti-secessionists to win, it was assumed by the participants that the majority of the inhabitants of the Anglophone Caribbean would attain independence as one nation called The West Indies. Constitutional reform was enacted in 1960 in order to introduce a system of Cabinet government and this appeared to mark the penultimate step in the process of decolonisation. At the Lancaster House conference the following year preparations were made for independence in 1962. It was only once the Jamaican people voted to leave the federation that it became evident that the attempt to achieve political unity across the Anglophone Caribbean had been overly ambitious. Faced with the piecemeal, disorderly constitutional process which they had regarded as the worst possible outcome, British policymakers were inclined to blame the regional leaders for the failure and their views have been endorsed by many later commentators. Whilst it is impossible to ignore the contribution made by local rivalry, this ought not to obscure the culpability of a metropolitan government which was committed theoretically to federalism but which was, at the level of detailed policymaking, unsympathetic to the dilemmas which confronted the people of the Anglophone Caribbean. On the matters of future economic assistance to the region and the contentious question of the relationship between Jamaica and the federal centre, the Colonial Office proved a parsimonious benefactor and a partial umpire. The consistent backing which they offered to Manley and his PNP government when they made the case for a looser federal system was surprising because, in principle, the Colonial Office favoured tighter integration. This was partly explicable in terms of longstanding concerns about small island irresponsibility which the British hoped to contain inside the federation by sponsoring responsible 'big island' leadership, as epitomised by Manley's careful, studious style of politics. Aside from the issue of personalities, a lack of metropolitan generosity relating to the continuance of financial assistance and the introduction of immigration controls in Britain further soured the debate about federation. A greater willingness to compromise on these matters would have entailed costs; it was considerably more straightforward for British policymakers to offer conditional support on the issue of ejecting American forces from the planned federal capital site because concessions from Washington to local demands that they evacuate Chaguaramas would have a negligible effect on British interests. What the escalating controversy over the renegotiation of the American lease illustrated was that overt threats to the orderly process of transferring power continued to command British attention; and this provided a notable contrast with the rather careless way in which they handled the mundane constitutional negotiations about the future of the federation.

The federation against neo-imperialism: Chaguaramas

When thinking about the past, the nationalist leaders who challenged British imperialism in the middle of the twentieth century were transfixed by the destructive legacy of racism and authoritarianism they were about to inherit but when they turned their attention to contemporary circumstances they could not but notice the significance of the Cold War. Figures such as Nkrumah, Nasser and Nehru feared that under the auspices of the superpower conflict, Western domination would continue in a form which was modified by the end of European political control but still underpinned by economic dependency, political influence and military occupation. Unlike the leaders of the Non-Aligned Movement, Eric Williams was an ardent advocate of the West's cause in the Cold War. His critique of slavery and neo-imperialism may have been shaped by Marxism but he was uncomfortable with even the Fabian socialism espoused by most of his peers in the Anglophone Caribbean: members of the People's National Movement (PNM) were briefed to reply to the question 'Is the party socialist?' with the decisive rejoinder, 'No, it is nationalist!'.[1] Williams chose instead to fight American power with great intensity on a very narrow front comprised of the issues of financial aid and military occupation. The ferocity of the campaign which he conducted against the Chaguaramas base from June 1957 attracted the attention of American policymakers and Washington would, for a short period, seek his removal through a covert programme of cooperation with Trinidadian opposition groups. To this extent the emphasis in the historiography on the local reactions to American Cold War policymaking is justified.[2] However, it is incomplete without a fuller account of the way in which ministers and officials in London were discomforted both by Williams's inflammatory rhetoric and the American reaction to his campaign. The materials of Caribbean politics were assessed as highly combustible by the Colonial Office and Chaguaramas appeared to possess the potential to act as a spark for further unrest. While the Colonial Office acknowledged that Williams was willing to fan local discontent when it suited his interests, they recognised that over the longer term he was likely to be an upholder of order in the Anglophone Caribbean.

This origin of the Chaguaramas controversy can be traced to the deal struck between Winston Churchill and Franklin Roosevelt during the Second World War which granted the American armed forces access to bases in the Anglophone Caribbean. In August 1940 the British ambassador to Washington, Lord Lothian, received a list of locations in which the Americans wished to acquire military facilities. Churchill's government subsequently agreed to grant 99-year leases on various territories, including the west coast of Trinidad, in return for the transfer of some almost obsolescent destroyers to the Royal Navy.[3] A Commission was established to advise on the precise location of the bases and their activities drew the attention of George VI who asserted that it was regrettable that 'we may well feel obliged to make concessions and submit to off-hand treatment, such as we should not tolerate in ordinary times.' He expressed the hope that any deal would not affect the conditions of life of his West Indian subjects.[4] The Governor of Trinidad, Hubert Young, initially supported the establishment of an American base on the assumption that it would spur economic development. Once he discovered that the American Navy wanted to locate the base at Chaguaramas on the northwest peninsula, enthusiasm transformed to indignation. Construction on the chosen site, Young argued, would have an exceptionally damaging impact on the social life of Port of Spain because the beaches and countryside in the area were the main source of recreation for the residents of the capital.[5] His objections were overruled and his captiousness drew the attention of Churchill who dismissed him rather than face continued conflict with Washington on the matter.

When Williams discovered the documents itemising Young's criticisms of Anglo-American policy he used them as the basis for an attack on British colonialism and American neo-imperialism.

Prior to the London conference of July 1957 Williams had not objected to hosting the Chaguaramas base and his new PNM admin-istration even suggested that the other federal leaders were endangering local security by seeking to eject the Americans in order to make space for the new capital of The West Indies. His decision to launch a rhetor-ical assault on the American presence in Trinidad during a conference which had been designed to reconcile the parties constituted a com-plete reversal of policy which has never been adequately explained. In the absence of any decisive evidence revealing his motivation, the most convincing hypothesis must be that the initiation of Williams's campaign was partly an expression of genuine fury at the manner in which Trinidad's interests had been swept aside because of wartime exi-gencies in 1940 and partly a product of careful calculation about how to fortify his domestic political position and strengthen his bargaining hand in negotiations with Britain and America about financial aid. From his perspective the underlying cause of the dispute was Washington's unwillingness to reconfigure relations with new nations like Trinidad which appeared to indicate that American hegemonic influence would become a form of neo-colonialism. The campaign against the base served useful political purposes in rallying support for the PNM and he constantly stressed that the Trinidadian public resented the American presence. In his memoirs Williams merely states that he used the 'new information' regarding the Young correspondence as the basis for three demands: the American evacuation of Chaguaramas, a Joint Commis-sion to select a new site to which American facilities could be transferred and the revision of the 1941 treaty under which the base facilities had been granted.[6] The first two-thirds of the memorandum he submitted comprised an analysis of the documentary record which was designed to prove that the base had been imposed on Trinidad despite the objections of the local government; the final third consisted of a condemnation of current American policy. Perhaps the most revealing passage dealt with the global politics of base negotiations in which the retention of military facilities by the Western powers was taken as symbolic of polit-ical subservience. Most strikingly, Williams appeared convinced that his own domestic standing was threatened by the occupation of the northwest peninsula: 'What appears to the Americans as only a base, what the SFC sees as only the capital, I see as an explosion of the first order.'[7]

Reverberations from Williams's explosive contribution to the debate about Chaguaramas eventually led the Eisenhower administration to consider the means of getting rid of Williams altogether. In the shorter term, his memorandum caused something approaching panic at the highest levels of the British and American governments. Throughout the ensuing crises, London constantly urged Washington to appease Williams, because his cooperation was necessary if the federation was to survive with Trinidadian participation. On 19 July, the day after Williams's memorable intervention, the new British Prime Minister, Harold Macmillan suggested to Eisenhower the appointment of a Joint Commission to examine the Chaguaramas issue. The President accepted the proposal the following day despite the reservations of some of his senior advisers.[8] The Chairman of the Joint Chiefs of Staff (JCS), Arthur Radford, was 'excited' by Williams's actions which he interpreted as an attack on American interests in the Caribbean. Evidently with Williams's threat of an explosion in his mind, Eisenhower argued: 'we don't have much of a choice. We are going to be driven out.'[9] After the principle of a Joint Commission consisting of representatives from Trinidad, the West Indies, the United States and Britain had been conceded an argument broke out over its terms of reference. On instructions from Macmillan, who was apprehensive about American reactions, the Parliamentary Under-Secretary at the Colonial Office, John Profumo, steered the Caribbean delegates in London away from an exclusive focus on alternative sites for the American base and towards a wider remit which would encompass an examination of the problems of any relocation.[10] This proved a significant concession because, once the Commission began work under the chairmanship of the former Governor of the Gold Coast, Charles Arden-Clarke, it spent much of its time dealing with the practical difficulties which would arise from any attempt to move American military facilities. Their deliberations were also accompanied by provocative articles in the American and Caribbean press, which illustrated both the proprietorial attitude of the American authorities and the heightening sensitivity of Caribbean leaders to any further infringement on their territorial integrity. On 11 August 1957 the *New York Times* published a story headlined: 'Navy Aims to Keep Base on Trinidad'. The paper reported that American officials were confident they would retain their 'slice of tropical paradise' in Trinidad and that they would soon complete work on a new missile-tracking station which had begun three months earlier.[11] As a consequence of Sputnik and the associated development of intercontinental missile technology such facilities were portrayed as vital to American security. In the

Caribbean American press stories were interpreted as an attempt to prejudice the outcome of the Joint Commission. After the latest reports from the *New York Times* were imparted, the letters pages of the *Gleaner* and *Trinidad Guardian* became clogged with accusations of American insensitivity. The backlash culminated on 19 August when *Gleaner* headlines announced the willingness of the future federal Prime Minister, Grantley Adams, to 'Talk Tough' with the Americans and his view that 'America Holds UK by Throat.'[12] On 7 October the Standing Federation Committee (SFC) passed a resolution regretting the decision to expand the facilities at Chaguaramas before the investigation of alternative sites had been completed.[13]

The Colonial Office had little interest in the intrinsic merit of the American case for keeping Chaguaramas but sought to quell the gathering conflict between Caribbean and American opinion regarding the base. They urged the SFC to show tolerance on the matter of the tracking station while advising the Americans not to issue public rebuttals of the statements made by Manley, Williams and the other Caribbean leaders.[14] Once again it was Williams's intervention which upended the British balancing act and the Colonial Office responded by seeking further concessions from Washington. On 15 January 1958 the *Trinidad Guardian* published an interview with the official responsible for supervising the final construction of the missile station. This prompted the Trinidadian government to issue a memorandum criticising the Americans for what was 'generally interpreted as an attitude of domination to a small friendly neighbour.' Officials at the American embassy in London complained that Williams was hostile and unreasonable and suggested the Colonial Office persuade him to moderate his position. The Governor of Trinidad, Edward Beetham, recorded that the Chaguaramas issue 'has caused us all here a great deal of embarrassment' but that he could do nothing to 'muzzle the press nor the politicians anymore than you in the United Kingdom may do.'[15] News that the impending Joint Commission report would endorse the American argument against the lease of any part of the base to the federation evoked the usual British misgivings about potential political turbulence. The American Under-Secretary of State, Christian Herter, issued advanced warnings about the determination of the American authorities to retain their facilities and urged the Colonial Office to do everything possible to restrain incipient anti-American feeling on the islands. This evoked little sympathy in London where the principal preoccupation was with what the newly installed Governor-General of the Federation, Lord Hailes, described as 'a political storm' which would blow across the region once the news broke that the Joint Commission had decided to frustrate efforts to build the new federal capital on the northwest peninsula of Trinidad. The Foreign Secretary, Selwyn Lloyd, insisted that prophylactic measures designed to circumvent the Caribbean backlash would only have a short term effect and complained: 'the Americans want it both ways, in both encouraging anti-colonialism of all kinds and then lecturing us for not behaving as colonialists.' The British ambassador in Washington, Harold Caccia, was told to explain that they could not expect London to play its role in lowering the political temperature of the Chaguaramas issue while the Americans were expanding their facilities 'which is certain to be noticed and cause further uproar at the precise moment when they themselves want us to keep things as calm as possible.'[16]

The concern in the Eisenhower administration that Williams was pioneering anti-Americanism in the Anglophone Caribbean prompted a covert intervention in Trinidadian politics designed to foster an opposition movement which they hoped would be more sympathetic to their interests. The two principal sponsors of this idea were Admiral Joseph Wellings, who was an American representative on the Joint Commission, and the Consul-General in Port of Spain, William Orebaugh. Both had been exposed to the intensity of Williams's feelings on the subject of the American presence at Chaguaramas and concluded that action should be taken to undermine his political position prior to the first federal elections which were to be held in March 1958. On 10 February State Department officials noted that Wellings wanted to provide 'the opposition to Dr Williams with appropriate materials to combat the latter's stand that Chaguaramas should be released' and indicated that they would support such a proposal on condition that 'any materials provided to the opposition should be disseminated without attribution.' The kind of propaganda with which the opposition were supplied appears to have focused on the details of Williams's acrimonious divorce. In the aftermath of the federal elections Orebaugh noted that Ashford Sinanan of the Democratic Labour Party (DLP) 'has been helpful in many ways. His assistance on Chag in the past and the help we can expect in the future are easily demonstrable.' Reporting that Williams was considering legal action against Sinanan following the latter's personal attacks upon him, Orebaugh offered some explanation for the DLP's success in the federal elections: 'The recounting of his marital problems before the federal election helped and the Sinanan trial can be even more fruitful.' Sinanan was not sued but he did have discussions with Ivan White of the State Department about how best to publicise the $21,000 in alimony payments which it was believed that Williams owed to his first wife who was an American citizen. He promised White that the DLP 'would continue to fight Williams on the Chaguaramas issue.'[17]

Williams's merited suspicions that the American consulate was offering covert support to the opposition only fortified his determination to challenge the report of the Joint Commission when he eventually received a copy on 27 March. They concluded that there was 'no significant portion of the useable area within the Chaguaramas Naval Base that is not essential to the base's mission'.[18] Publication was delayed for two months while the British and American governments pondered how to manage the inevitable adverse local reaction; the former still regarded Williams as a useful partner in the process of decolonisation while the latter suspected he was a threat to hemispheric unity. Orebaugh warned that the 'negro racism' of Williams and the PNM would stimulate 'anti-white and possibly specifically anti-American feeling.'[19] The Eisenhower administration pressed the British to explain in stark terms to the leaders of the new federation that they would have to find somewhere other than Chaguaramas for their capital. Profumo ignored American appeals and instructed his officials to formulate some new potential concessions to 'save West Indian face'.[20] On 7 June Lloyd wrote to the American Secretary of State, John Foster Dulles, requesting that he accept a review of American base facilities in the region after 10 years. This was presented as a means of supporting the 'moderate' stance of the federal Prime Minister, Grantley Adams, whose relative temperance on the issue did not prevent him questioning the Joint Commission's decision. Despite opposition from the Department of Defense, Dulles reluctantly agreed to the idea of a future review which, it was hoped, would assuage anti-American sentiment. In the case of Williams it had no such effect; he and Manley sought an early conference of Caribbean leaders to examine ways in which to challenge the Joint Commission's report. The State Department were 'extremely worried' by Williams's attitude and complained to the British embassy in Washington that he had even gone so far as to have Orebaugh put under surveillance.[21] However, when the British colonial attaché from the embassy visited Trinidad to investigate he placed the blame squarely on Orebaugh who, he noted, was still nostalgic for his role in organising special operations in Italy during the war and now appeared to be adopting a similar approach in Trinidad: 'If he could take to the hills and organise an anti-PNM movement...he would be perfectly happy and would probably do a thoroughly good job.'[22]

Although Orebaugh's collusion with the DLP exacerbated the tensions over the base issue they were not their source, which was located in Williams's belief that the American presence impinged on the sovereign rights of Trinidad at the brink of independence. In order to extract concessions from Britain and the United States before the final demission of power he sought to mobilise the general public. He later admitted: 'I used every possible artifice to keep the Chaguaramas issue alive and before the public and embarked on a relentless campaign to this end.'[23] The most compelling testimony about Williams's attitude was provided by the Jamaican Frank Hill who was broadly sympathetic to the Trinidadian case. He wrote to Manley on 29 October 1958 that Williams 'is bitter and fanatical about the American occupation...he is convinced that the Americans will break under the public strain and clear out. He believes this sincerely and is preparing to heighten the intensity of his campaign.'[24] The danger which Williams did not heed, but which magnified British apprehensions, was that he might force Washington to a point where they would insist on his removal. Philip Rogers, who was the Assistant Under-Secretary responsible for Caribbean affairs in the Colonial Office, warned in October 1958: 'Dr Williams has become almost uncontrollable on this issue...his activities represent a very serious danger to the relations of the West Indies, the United States and the UK.'[25]

At a press conference in September 1958 Williams itemised the malign consequences of the base in terms of its impact on the economy, health and social relations. He particularly emphasised that 2,000 acres of the base were used 'for plantation activity competing with Trinidad farmers.'[26] The next astonishing step in his escalation strategy was to suggest, in a speech on 3 July 1959, that the new technology employed at the secretive missile-tracking station constituted a grave medical risk.[27] Williams's deputy, Patrick Solomon, was dispatched to London to demand an investigation into the health hazards arising from radiation emanating from Chaguaramas.[28] Solomon recalled that the PNM leadership was aware of the consequences which American nuclear testing had for the people of the Pacific and were alerted to a potential local danger by a sudden surge in electrical consumption in the base area. They were conscious of their lack of expertise but indignant that, when practical concerns were raised, American officials treated them with 'all the arrogance and lordly contempt for Trinidad, its peoples and its institutions.'[29] In an effort to propitiate Trinidadian opinion a British scientist from the Royal Radar Establishment visited the island in

August and issued a reassuring report.[30] To deal with the more quotidian gripes which arose from hosting a large American base, Trinidadian officials were offered a series of formal consultations with the American Consulate. One of the most contentious issues in these discussions was the existence of the Macqueripe Club inside the base which had a private members list and which, according to Williams, represented 'one of the worst forms of racial discrimination of any kind'.[31] The racialist policies of the American military had been a source of rancour since the war but the renewal of the accusations was interpreted by Williams's opponents in Washington as a gratuitous incitement.[32] Despite attempts at reassurance by the new Consul-General, Robert McGregor, Williams itemised the broader historical case against the base in what he described as 'one of my best and effective speeches' to an audience at Arima on 17 July 1959. The address was entitled 'From Slavery to Chaguaramas' and it contended that from 1898 the United States government had been attempting to create an American Mediterranean in the Caribbean and that this was an imperial project in the tradition of European expansionism. Having placed the dispute in this context Williams asked the question of the British and Americans 'whether they are for colonialism or not.'[33]

Under the rhetorical barrage which Williams directed at the base many in the Eisenhower administration continued to argue that an act of colonialism, in the form of the removal of a locally elected leader, was precisely what was required in Trinidad. This brought them into conflict with the British, who were eager to appease Caribbean opinion by acceding to the request, which the federal leaders made in June 1959, for a conference to consider amending the terms of the 1941 base agreements.[34] The initial response of the Eisenhower administration was that yet more negotiations about Chaguaramas and the other bases would 'serve no useful purpose'; they also complained that the British government 'despite requests on our part have taken no steps to curb Dr Williams. It is believed that unless he is checked, we will continue to have trouble.'[35] Selwyn Lloyd suggested to his American counterpart, Christian Herter, that the United States would soon be obliged to renegotiate terms with the newly independent governments of the region. On the assumption that some concessions would have to be made either before or after independence, the State Department modified their opposition to an early conference.[36] However, the Department of Defense remained opposed to concessions and stolidly committed to Williams's downfall. At a meeting of State and Defense officials on 21 September Wellings argued on behalf of the Navy that any concessions 'would build up Williams' political strength and degrade the US position in the Caribbean'. During 'a discussion of the possibility of Eric Williams' downfall' spokesmen for the State Department warned that Rudranath Capildeo, who was expected to be the next leader of the opposition DLP, was no better than Williams because he had 'Communist influences in his background'. The argument became so embittered that the Defense Department refused to communicate with the State Department about the issue. Herter resolved the dispute by ignoring Defense objections and informing the British in November that they were willing to attend a revision conference.[37]

To the consternation of the British, Williams continued his escalation strategy during preparations for the latest conference. Matters were complicated by the continuing distrust between Williams and Adams which encouraged the former to demand bilateral negotiations between Trinidad and the United States over Chaguaramas which would exclude federal representatives. The Americans had only agreed to convene a revision conference on the assumption that they would be dealing with the federal rather than the Trinidadian government. Instead of welcoming the American offer of talks, Williams resented the suggestion that federal officials would decide the future of the base without consulting his government. In a message to London he complained: 'We have been left alone to bear the full burden of our struggle to vindicate our rights. Never at any time has HMG given the slightest indication that it considers the cause for which we are struggling a just one.'[38] The new American Consul-General, Edwin Moline, was also the object of Williams's anger even though he was far more sympathetic to Caribbean nationalism than Orebaugh. In March 1960 he offered a partial recantation of his previous belief that it was possible to do business with Williams and suggested 'we can do nothing but seek to exploit every opportunity to bring a degree of sense into the Premier who is congenitally disposed not to be sensible.'[39] Moline complained about the febrile political climate on the island and further evidence of this was provided by the rally which Williams and the PNM organised in April 1960. In contrast to the sweeping overview he had offered in the 'Slavery to Chaguaramas' speech, on this occasion Williams dealt with contemporary politics and focused attention on the 'combination of American resistance, British indifference and Federal hostility' which had prevented the PNM government from regaining control of the northwest peninsula of the island. To this list he added 'domestic sabotage' in the form of the local press, opposition politicians and dissidents in the PNM.[40] He again framed the Chaguaramas controversy in terms of a choice between national independence and neo-colonialism. Before protestors set out on their march from Port of Spain to the base, Williams set fire to a number of historical documents which he claimed represented the seven deadly sins of colonialism. Amongst them were the base agreements of 1941.[41] These incendiary actions infuriated the Governor-General Hailes, who was almost as resentful of Williams as the Americans. The day after the march he complained to the British Colonial Secretary, Iain Macleod, of the 'unpleasant, almost sinister atmosphere in Trinidad.' Williams was blamed for the mephitis on the grounds that it 'is not possible incessantly to preach hatred and discontent without effect.' In a slightly sinister passage of his own, Hailes even speculated: 'The longer this is allowed to continue, the nearer Williams will get to the point of no return.'[42]

Despite Hailes's reservations, most British policymakers still believed they could temper Williams's unalloyed nationalism and that he was the leader most likely to channel local anti-imperialism into a tolerable form. John Marnham of the Colonial Office told Ivan White that 'it was essential to achieve Dr Williams's support of any new agreement if he was not to create further difficulties after independence.' He asked in a new form the old question: 'if it would be possible to squash up somewhat in Chaguaramas to make room for the new federal capital.'[43] Fortunately for the British the person least concerned about the problems of squashing up or even moving out was President Eisenhower. At a National Security Council meeting on 17 March 1960 Eisenhower argued in favour of a more generous approach to Williams and Trinidad. He noted 'Cuba should be a warning to us' and indicated that the abandonment of American military facilities 'would not be a bad thing except for the sums of money we have put into our base there.'[44] This set the tone for a more emollient approach to Williams which was evident in the second half of 1960. The State Department attempted to finesse the controversial issue of bilateral negotiations between Trinidad and the US by suggesting that, following any initial meeting of all parties, delegates from the individual territories, rather than the representatives of the federal government, would be allowed to take the lead in presenting their case to US officials.[45] This idea went through a series of transformations until in June 1960, during his successful trip to the Caribbean, Iain Macleod offered an elaborate proposal for a three-stage negotiation: the first and the third stages would be trilateral and involve the British, American and federal governments. Crucially substantive negotiations would occur in the second stage during which Trinidad would take the lead in bilateral negotiations on the

Chaguaramas issue.[46] Williams accepted this formula and, despite some further friction between all parties, they met for the preliminary first-stage negotiation in London in November. After the formalities were performed the representatives travelled to Trinidad where the various bargaining ploys were played out on Williams's home territory.

The Stage 2 negotiations which began with a preliminary meeting in Port of Spain on 29 November, before the delegates decamped to the more soothing environment of Tobago, proved a convivial affair. Williams accepted that the Americans could retain a portion of the northwest peninsula and in return Washington offered a generous compensatory aid package. Ambler Thomas, who attended the meeting in his capacity as Assistant Under-Secretary at the Colonial Office, suggested that White of the State Department believed the Trinidadian delegation had 'taken the shirt off his back.'[47] Despite some resistance on both points, Williams secured financial assistance in the form of grants rather than loans and the approval of a list of major capital projects which would receive American financial support: the establishment of a liberal arts college, reclamation of land at Caroni, the construction of a new road to Chaguaramas, port modernisation and improvements on the railway.[48] Williams presented the deal as a triumphant success and estimated that the package was worth WI $ 111.7 million. After years of constant campaigning to eject the Americans, the leaders of the DLP and critics on the left of the PNM were critical of the fact that they were to remain on the northwest peninsula. Williams's concession on this point triggered the final and decisive split with C. L. R. James who noted that 'the general opinion among all persons who take any political interest in affairs is that Chaguaramas has been sold out.'[49] In the Legislative Assembly Lionel Seukeran of the DLP ridiculed the 'miserable pittance' which Williams had obtained at Tobago; comparing it unfavourably to the assistance offered to other countries in which the Americans retained bases, he questioned whether the PNM campaign had really been worth the accompanying bitterness and vindictiveness.[50] After the backlash the cordiality of the Tobago conference dissipated and differences emerged over the interpretation of the provisions of the assistance package. Domestic Trinidadian scepticism about the extent of American recompense for the continued occupation of the northwest peninsula motivated Williams to insist upon a maximalist interpretation of the aid agreement which obligated Washington to pay the full costs of the approved projects. In May 1962 the American Consul-General in Port of Spain reported that relations with Williams had 'come full circle again' and that 'Chaguaramas will remain as the whipping boy to stir up agreement at the expense of the United States.'[51] Williams's criticism of American frugality was not merely a matter of gamesmanship or domestic party politics. Given the scarcity of local capital at the moment of political independence, additional development assistance was essential if Trinidad was to attain a measure of economic independence. For Williams this was a question of compensation for the exploitation of the island by the British and the Americans. At a more practical level, uncertainty regarding the extent of future American assistance made effective budgeting exceptionally difficult. A policy paper written in the immediate aftermath of independence explained: 'It would appear that economic assistance for the fundamental projects will be given in small driblets – which makes it impossible for the government to make firm long-range plans.'[52] Fortunately for both parties, in the midst of a much more pressing Caribbean crisis on Cuba, the Kennedy administration agreed to set a figure on future levels of American assistance. Reporting one year into the era of independence the first American ambassador to Trinidad could declare that the new state had established a constructive relationship with Washington.[53]

Independent Trinidad did not become a centre of radical anti-Americanism and Eric Williams proved himself a ferocious critic of the Caribbean left, including Castro, Jagan and the Grenadian political party, the New Jewel Movement (NJM). His attacks on the American presence at Chaguaramas in the late 1950s had elements of crude political utility maximising: it enabled Williams to mobilise PNM support against his enemies in the DLP and provide an effective negotiating card to be played against the old colonial enemy and the new regional hegemonic power. Aside from the dictates of expediency, it allowed Williams and the people of Trinidad to configure some normative principles which would distinguish the era of independence from what had gone before. He argued that, despite continuing inequalities in wealth, political influence and military power between Trinidad and the United States, any true sense of autonomy demanded that the consent of the peoples of the Caribbean must be given in decisions affecting their countries. The occupation of the whole of the northwest peninsula as a consequence of a wartime deal agreed to by Churchill and Roosevelt against the objections of local opinion provided a paradigmatic example of the inequity in colonial relationships; in this sense, Williams chose wisely in prolonging the campaign. However, he also jeopardised his own position because the ongoing protests validated British and American judgements that the newly independent Caribbean territories might become a site of resistance to their authority. For Washington the key threat was that organised political movements under the influence of the left would become imbued with anti-Americanism. The American Defense Department believed Williams and the PNM were guilty of orchestrating regional hostility to their presence. He was defended by the British Colonial Office who had a much greater fear of disorganised lawlessness and anomic protest. They tolerated Williams on the assumption that after independence his leadership would effectively channel the turbulent currents of Caribbean opinion into the less volatile form of party politics and organised campaigning. In this instance, British policymakers were more perceptive, despite the fact that their perceptions were based on the kind of clichés about colonial subjects which had sustained imperial rule. By 1962 they were increasingly concerned that the absence of figures like Williams on the small islands and in British Guiana would disrupt the process of decolonisation.

The federation for itself: aid and immigration

Numerous scholars and participants have conducted post-mortems into the early death of the West Indies federation and most have concluded that either the structural problems associated with regional integration or the inadequacy of nationalist leadership were to blame. British policymakers have escaped relatively unscathed. The structural explanations have tended to focus on the divergent interests of the different territories in the Anglophone Caribbean. In upholding a broad theory designed to explain the successes and failures of a variety of federal systems, Chad Rector utilised the case of the West Indies to demonstrate that larger units, such as Jamaica and Trinidad, will be reluctant to integrate if they can see few material benefits and can obtain those objectives which do require a measure of collaboration through international treaty regimes.[54] What Rector leaves out of account is the context provided by colonialism and the Cold War which are incorporated in Jason Parker's explanation. Having provided a broader framework of analysis Parker also concludes that regional factors were decisive and that the federations of the Cold War era 'fractured along ethno-linguistic lines that long predated the US-Soviet Conflict.' The collapse of the federation of The West Indies occurred because romantic pan-Caribbean sentiments were rejected 'in favor of insular identities.'[55] Such a view is congruent with the conclusions offered by Ashton and Killingray: 'The diversity of islands scattered over a wide area, each with its own institutions and jealously guarded interests and political ambitions, made a federation difficult if not impossible to achieve.'[56] Those writers who have dealt with matters of agency have also focused on the attributes of the periphery. The Caribbean economist, Arthur Lewis, who knew the participants, stated in plain terms, 'the leadership of the Federation was awful.'[57] The writer who has come closest to indicting metropolitan agents is Amanda Sives who has pointed to 'the failure on behalf of all the participants (British and West Indian) to create a strong institutional framework.'[58] On the assumption that the failings on the latter side have been extremely well documented the remainder of this chapter will provide an account of some of the problems which arose from British policy.

A revisionism which attempted to make the case that cooperation between the nationalist leaders of the Anglophone Caribbean during the four years of federation led to some lasting achievements would not get very far. The current historiography has established beyond doubt the divisiveness of regional politics, while successful examples of functional cooperation in the realms of transport or higher education took place outside the federal framework. What can be said is that, despite their differences, the nationalist leaders shared a clear vision of what they wanted to obtain from federation: the overriding goal was to achieve greater economic independence and social equality through the promotion of integration between unit economies and diversification of economic activity across the region. Paradoxically, this meant that, in the interim, they required a greater measure of financial assistance in order to rectify the oversupply of labour and the undersupply of capital. On both fronts they did not secure a sympathetic hearing in the metropolis. The arguments they made against new restrictions on migration to Britain and in favour of the continuation of substantial budgetary assistance from the metropolitan government were discounted in London. For the regional economies the outflow of people to Britain in the 1950s provided a source of remittance income and relieved the problems of unemployment and underemployment which had been a feature of the region since emancipation. Despite labour shortages in Britain, many metropolitan politicians regarded migration from the Caribbean as a threat to the social order of the country which necessitated restrictive legislation. On the financial front, the British Treasury proved unsympathetic to the argument that centuries of imperial neglect had produced a regional economy only just able to maintain its citizens above a subsistence level of consumption. Elected politicians, who began to take over economic ministries from colonial financial secretaries in the decade before 1958, now faced the prospect of the curtailment of British economic assistance at a time when the greatest threat to newly forged democratic systems was the poverty of the majority of the electors. Politicians like Manley and Williams argued that a united Anglophone Caribbean would be better able to secure additional financial assistance during the transitional era between the end of imperial control and the first few years of independence. The disappointing answers which federal leaders received from the metropolitan power on these matters constituted embarrassing evidence of continued impotence; a triumph on either one would certainly have strengthened the position of Adams's federal government and demonstrated the potential material benefits of unity.

Although legislation to control migration into Britain was not introduced until after the Jamaican referendum of 1961, it became one of the most controversial issues in relations between the British and the federal government at a much earlier stage. The disenchantment felt across the Caribbean at the imminence of restrictions soured relations between metropolis and periphery. It was unfortunate for the federal leaders that the first year of the new organisation's existence coincided with racial conflict in British cities. Caribbean migrants in Nottingham and West London were first disconcerted and then alarmed by the hostility of their reception in Britain. Local gangs frequently attacked the conspicuous new black inhabitants of the cities and in August 1958 fighting broke out in St Ann's in Nottingham. According to the Caribbean residents of the area the violence began with an attack by Teddy Boys on a black man who had visited a local chemist shop at night, which was a time when most of the other recent immigrants observed a self-imposed curfew. In Notting Hill the situation was aggravated by the presence of Oswald Mosley's fascist Union Movement which aimed to mobilise white disenchantment and direct it against Caribbean migrants.[59] Street-level tensions in British cities became a problem for Caribbean politicians because they provided a pretext for the campaign to limit Commonwealth immigration at a time when labour mobility was an important means of relieving unemployment and underemployment. *The Times* claimed the disturbances in Nottingham had been triggered by an attack by a black man on a white woman outside a pub. Such reports prompted the MPs for Nottingham North and Nottingham Central to call for controls, while the Conservative MP Cyril Osborne urged a one-year moratorium on all Commonwealth immigration to prevent a British facsimile of the racial conflict at Little Rock in the United States. Alarmed by this vehement reaction, Trevor Huddleston, whose reputation had been established by his recent book about African Apartheid *Naught for Your Comfort*, warned that if the violence was used to justify the tightening of immigration controls 'it will be evident that this country positively desires a colour bar and is prepared to enforce one.' The Marquess of Salisbury, who had assumed the leadership of the Conservative right following his resignation as Lord President of the Council in 1957, replied by declaring himself 'extremely apprehensive of the results, economic and social, for Europeans and Africans alike that are likely to flow from an unrestricted immigration of men and women of African race into Britain.' In a notorious leader on 4 September 1958 *The Times* effectively endorsed Salisbury's arguments and stated 'there is a colour problem in our midst.'[60] Three months later Osborne proposed a motion in the Commons demanding restrictions on the entry of those who could be characterised as 'unfit, idle or criminal' and the repatriation of all recent immigrants who had been found guilty of a criminal offence.[61]

Whilst in the pages of *The Times*, Salisbury had disavowed the notion that the debate had anything to do with racism, around the Cabinet table it had been a different matter. Before his resignation, Salisbury had been the strongest advocates of restrictions. During a discussion on immigration from the Caribbean in November 1955 he stated that he was concerned about the 'effects on racial characteristics of the English people in the long run.' Norman Brook, the Cabinet Secretary, clarified Salisbury's view for the Prime Minister: 'Some ministers, notably the Lord President, favour early legislative action to guard against the long-term threat to the racial character of the English people.'[62] Divisions in the Cabinet led to a deadlock and it was decided to monitor the situation. The tone of this monitoring was self-consciously calm and measured but included analysis of the prevalence of miscegenation. A draft progress report dated 29 June 1957 recorded: 'many coloured men are married to or living with white women of low standing or low morals. The number of half-caste children in these districts is increasing and many are thought to be illegitimate.'[63] The new Prime Minister, Harold Macmillan, responded to what he described as the 'race riots' of August 1958 by authorising a new look at the immigration question. Ministers remained in their entrenched positions on the issue of restrictions but agreed to a less controversial measure which allowed for the deportation of those found guilty of criminal offences. Salisbury had left the Cabinet because of disagreements about policy towards Cyprus but on 13 January 1959 supporters of controls in the Cabinet reiterated the potential threat to domestic tranquillity posed by immigration: 'Though racial disturbances appeared to have subsided for the time being, failure to act might lead to a recurrence, to the formation of extremist groups, and to a demand for more stringent measures of control which could prove to be highly controversial and have serious implications in our relations with other Commonwealth countries.'[64]

Opponents of controls deployed two arguments in these discussions: the evidence that the number of migrants from the Caribbean was decreasing and the outright opposition of Caribbean politicians to new restrictions. After consulting Caribbean leaders, in September 1958 Lennox-Boyd reported to the Home Secretary, 'Rab' Butler that any tightening of the regulations under which passports allowing entry to Britain were issued, 'would lead to a serious loss of faith in the United Kingdom.' Having been insulted by a policeman on Harrow Road on the day of his meeting with Lennox-Boyd, Manley insisted that the problem was not one of economics but 'basic racial hostility' in Britain. He also drew attention to the inflammatory nature of fascist literature being distributed on the streets of London.[65] Manley's objections would almost certainly have been unavailing without a sudden and dramatic reduction in the numbers of Caribbean migrants. New figures revealed that in the last six months of 1958 only 5,000 people had entered Britain from the Caribbean compared to 15,000 in the first half of 1957. At the Home Office, Butler and the Permanent Under-Secretary, Charles Cunningham, were confident that the situation could be managed by measures to improve housing conditions and establish better race relations. On 22 July 1959 the Cabinet Sub-Committee dealing with the issue agreed that no further action should be taken in the short term.[66]

The decision not to act on immigration was provisional and no guarantees were offered regarding future policy. To many in the Caribbean the violence in Nottingham and London tarnished the image of Britain, while the debates which followed seemed to portend the introduction of discriminatory legislation. Negotiations over financial assistance provided another test of whether Britain took the rhetorical commitment to the welfare of the old members of the empire and the new members of the Commonwealth seriously. During the first phase of federal negotiations after the war, British policymakers assumed that any discussion of financial assistance after independence was premature because they intended to retain ultimate authority in the Anglophone Caribbean for many years to come. At the end of 1959, however, pressure from local nationalist governments, and in particular Eric Williams in Trinidad, and a change in personnel, with the replacement of Lennox-Boyd by Macleod at the Colonial Office, led to an acceptance of an abridged timetable for independence. Once it was acknowledged that independence would probably come in two years rather than four or five, a decision on the nature and extent of future British aid became more urgent. The acceleration of decolonisation provided the metropolitan government with considerable leeway in financial negotiations because existing obligations, which amounted to approximately £ 6 million annually, would lapse once a transfer of political power had occurred. If this happened sooner rather than later, the long-term costs to the Exchequer were effectively reduced. A Colonial Office briefing established that any effort to curtail assistance which had already been promised would be wholly unacceptable to Caribbean opinion: despite the absence of any binding obligation, the Federal government believed they had 'a very strong moral claim to the outstanding balance of the £ 8.75 million already negotiated for the first quinquennium of the ten year period (1959–1963); and probably a somewhat lesser but still arguable claim to the money they might have received during the second quinquennium (1964–1968) due to be negotiated in 1963.' On the political side of the equation the Colonial Office also noted 'that unless Federation can successfully move into independence fairly soon there will be a danger that the larger territories, such as Jamaica and Trinidad, will grow impatient and as they, in any case, will have to carry the burden of the other small Islands, they might in the end decide they would "better go it alone" and secede from the Federation.'[67]

Sensitivity to these financial and political considerations ought perhaps to have established the basis for a relatively generous package of financial assistance but Treasury parsimony continued to more than counter-balance the arguments of the Colonial Office. From the outset of the negotiations British policymakers refused to offer any estimate of the levels of assistance to be provided to an independent federation, although they did make clear that they would not agree to an interim increase which is what federal leaders had requested. The visit of Manley to Britain in January 1960 occasioned the first bilateral discussions on financial aid to the federation after independence and proved an inauspicious affair. This was a moment at which disenchantment with federation in Jamaica was growing and Blackburne reported before his arrival that Manley was 'thoroughly depressed' by the continuing squabbles over federal taxation and customs union.[68] As the Colonial Office turned to potential financial inducements the Treasury urged caution. Official briefings for the Chancellor, Derick Heathcoat-Amory, reminded him that it was customary to terminate grant-aid at independence. In this context he urged that 'on purely tactical grounds, it would be undesirable to begin passing encouraging messages to the West Indies at this stage.' The eventual formula agreed to by the Colonial

Office and the Treasury incorporated four rather vague commitments to an independent federation: it would be eligible for Commonwealth assistance loans on the same terms as less developed regions, the British government would promote negotiations for American and Canadian assistance to the federation, it would have access to any committed but unspent development funds and the continuation of grant-in-aid on a tapering basis would be considered for up to a maximum of 10 years.[69] The most significant of these provisions was the fourth which had been authorised by the Chancellor, with the proviso that such assistance would be on a 'strictly tapering off basis.'[70] For Manley the calculation was straightforward: a reduction in British economic assistance, including the proposed tapering, meant a larger financial burden on Jamaica in supporting the less developed territories of the federation after independence; the larger the financial burden on Jamaica, the more difficult it was to sell continued membership to the Jamaican public. An offer of decreasing assistance on an unspecified scale constituted a disincentive to remain in the federation. While expressing resentment at Manley's lack of appreciation for British efforts, Macleod also conceded that the discussions had probably reinforced secessionist sentiment. He expressed disappointment that Manley had responded to the vague offer of 'some transitional assistance' by insisting it 'did not go far enough'. Macleod made the parenthetical comment 'it goes considerably further than HMG have ever gone before in discussion of aid after independence.'[71] Four months later Manley announced his decision to hold a referendum on Jamaican membership of the federation.

A combination of global economic developments, which were redirecting the European economies away from the old imperial periphery, and the fragility of their financial position, in terms of the quotidian task of balancing budgets left federal politicians and the governments of the individual units in the unfortunate position of mendicants with an ever-lengthening list of demands. When Macleod visited the Caribbean in June 1960 he offered general reassurance but was unable to address any of their concerns in detail. In summarising the discussions, the Colonial Office recorded that Chief Ministers from the small islands opposed the potential tapering down of economic assistance and urged that it 'should if possible be increased, while the Federal and Jamaican Ministers also pressed the need for continued help to the Federation.' Two particular sources of vulnerability were the shift in British trading patterns towards Europe and the liberalisation of the dollar, both of which threatened the price which Caribbean exports could obtain in commodity markets. Macleod's interlocutors feared 'Britain was abandoning the system of restrictions and preferences on which the West Indies had built up their economy.' They were also apprehensive that a recent upsurge in Caribbean migration after the downturn of 1958 might prompt the Macmillan government to impose restrictions. Vere Bird of Antigua made some particularly pointed and telling observations in support of their case: 'It was not inconsistent with the concept of sovereignty for a nation to receive assistance, and [he] mentioned the circumstances of the United Kingdom immediately after the Second World War. He also referred to the assistance which had been provided by the United Kingdom to Somalia which was likely to budget for a substantial deficit for years to come.'[72] Caribbean politicians argued that the case for further economic assistance did not amount to an appeal to altruism in response to local infirmity but rested on a moral obligation to help rectify the economic problems which the British empire was handing on to the independent states. Initially, the principal weakness in their argument was its lack of detail; when this was remedied by Eric Williams, British officials became thoroughly alarmed. Williams's analysis indicated that, in order to diversify the economies of the small islands and thus relieve the economic burden on Jamaica and Trinidad, Britain would have to contribute $ 442 million in the decade after independence.[73] G. W. Jamieson, who advised Macleod on economic aspects of colonial affairs, represented this calculation as further evidence of 'self pity' and suggested that Caribbean politicians ought to recognise 'that the West Indies are at least lower middle class in the nations of the world and not... among the under-paid and under-privileged.' This would no doubt have come as a surprise to the unemployed of West Kingston or the underemployed plantation workers of St Kitts. Such attitudes provided a discouraging backdrop to the next round of financial discussions which occurred in London in November 1960. The Minister of State at the Colonial Office, Lord Perth, was informed that the Trinidadian request would amount to an annual subsidy of £ 6.6 million. His brief stated: 'We are in no position to make any additional concessions or promises at this juncture.' Inevitably the resulting talks proved even less satisfactory than Manley's discussions in January. Adams told Perth that the Trinidad estimate was a conservative one and that economic assistance 'should be of a substantial order... they were poorer than any of the dependent territories which had so far achieved independence, most of which, such as Malaya and Ghana, had substantial resources.' Williams emphasised that his recommendations would have to be fully implemented in order to increase local economic productivity. Manley indicated that the need for assistance was 'tremendous', that the Trinidadian estimate was a minimum figure and that, in the absence of support on this scale, the West Indian economy 'would fail to take off, which might lead to total economic collapse, which would inevitably be followed by widespread social disruption.'[74]

The Perth negotiations coincided with the reopening of the ministerial debate about Caribbean immigration which was now marked by a new tone of alarmism. Although fewer people from the region had sought residence in the immediate aftermath of the 1958 disturbances, the scale of unemployment on the islands and the fear that restrictions were pending, led to an increase in numbers two years later which was presented as a serious threat to domestic social peace.[75] On 25 November 1960 Butler presented new figures to the Cabinet. He explained that 43,500 West Indians had arrived in the first 10 months of the year and described the increase in numbers as 'a potential source of serious disturbance.' John Hare, the Minister of Labour, predicted that they might face an annual inflow of 100,000 people and indicated that the 'quality is dropping'.[76] Three months later Macleod warned that the imminence of a final constitutional conference on independence meant that it was a 'specially awkward moment' to tighten immigration regulations but the Cabinet pressed ahead. Finally on 30 May 1961 Macleod acquiesced 'with distaste' to the introduction of legislation to restrict Commonwealth immigration although it was agreed to delay an official announcement and Macmillan advised that Manley should not be told.[77] Despite this apparent secrecy, in the absence of any reassurances from Whitehall, Caribbean politicians became convinced that legislation was imminent and lobbied unsuccessfully to prevent it. The Colonial Office had agreed in December 1960 that the West Indian Commissioner in London, Garnet Gordon, could be informed of the decision to reconsider controls. Consequently, when Macmillan visited the Caribbean in March 1961 there was only one issue which the federal leaders wished to discuss with him: the probability of restrictions on Caribbean workers entering the United Kingdom. The Dominican writer and federal politician, Phyllis Shand, urged him not to take an 'unkind' attitude but the emphasis which Macmillan placed on the high levels of unemployment amongst current migrants clearly signalled the future direction of policy.[78] In a later bilateral meeting with Macmillan, Eric Williams linked economic aid, immigration and the fate of the federation: 'The future depended on the UK, if she were to withdraw her support and stop West Indian immigration there would be a social revolution and a Castro situation in the West Indies. The success of the Federation depended on powerful British intervention; otherwise there would be a break up.' In Barbados, the Premier, Hugh Cummins, told Macmillan 'the main problems in which they were interested were those of Immigration and of the Common Market.' Macmillan's empty-handed response merely confirmed Caribbean suspicions. Adams concluded that private lobbying was counter-productive and in April he publicly aired his belief that the British intended to put an end to West Indian immigration before the end of the year. He warned: 'unless we do something about it God help us in Barbados and Jamaica especially.' The *Barbados Advocate* responded by stating 'Every one of the political parties in Barbados and the West Indies realise that a partial answer to the problem of unemployment and underemployment in the West Indies is to promote emigration to those countries which provide opportunities for West Indians.'[79] Macmillan fumed privately that the Adams statement was 'disgraceful' but the government's press statement could only declare, entirely disingenuously, that there were no current plans for such legislation.[80]

By the time of the stormy Lancaster House conference on federal independence in June 1961, all the key protagonists were aware that legislation restricting the entry of Caribbean people into Britain was imminent. Had the Macmillan government revealed precisely how advanced these plans were the atmosphere might have been worse still but the Adams statement was symbolic of the distrust which now attended any negotiations between the federal leaders and the British government. On 12 June the former united to demand a guarantee that the metropolitan government would maintain access to Caribbean migrants. Macleod was unable to offer any reassurance. The controversy over the likely extent of financial assistance after independence also rumbled on and proved just as difficult for the British to finesse. The refusal to offer any estimate of the amount of financial aid the federation would receive after independence brought Caribbean irritation with British procrastination to a climax. It also became entangled with arguments between the local leaders over plans to establish freedom of movement within the federation; this seemed an essential requirement for any form of political unity but Trinidad feared an influx of small island residents would jeopardise its economic future and continued to play an obstructive role. Bramble from Montserrat recognised that migration within the federation was 'intricately bound up with the most complex problem facing the Federation, namely that of economic aid.' Williams was even blunter and argued that a British guarantee of financial assistance for the small islands, as adumbrated in his government's

paper on the economics of federation, was vital to prevent a potentially catastrophic outflow of labour from the Leewards and Windwards
to the large islands. He insisted: 'the present discussion should begin
with a clear acknowledgement by the United Kingdom Government
that the present economic conditions of all the territories was their
sole responsibility.' Although some delegates were sceptical of Williams's
tactics and urged that the case must be made independently of discussions of freedom of movement, they were united in believing that the
British ought to finally go beyond the vague generalities of the Manley
formula.[81]

In preparing for the conference Macleod had anticipated that the
most difficult issue which would arise 'was likely to be the insistence
of on the part of the smaller islands on discussion of an interim plan for
economic development as the price for their continued support of an
independent federation.'[82] It had been evident since Heathcoat-Amory
had devised the 'tapering down' formula before the discussions with
Manley in January 1960, that there was a conflict between Treasury
frugality and demands emanating from the Caribbean for an interim
increase in aid to lessen the additional burden which would accrue
to the large islands once they assumed responsibility for the poorer
islands inside an independent federation. By June 1961 the gap between
Caribbean expectations and Treasury intentions had grown even wider.
As independence approached and the local actors became more expec-
tant, the Treasury became ever more vigilant. They insisted that no new
commitments should be offered and that even the Manley formula,
which prescribed a decrease in British funding, should also entail a
shift in the form of assistance from grants to loans.[83] Such was the
pressure on Macleod at the outset of the Lancaster House conference
that he sought to test Treasury resolution by advising Macmillan that
some financial inducement might be necessary to prevent the conference from failing.[84] Treasury officials were insistent that 'The West Indies
are already due to get more money than we think their needs justify
after independence' and any additional assistance would have to be
found from money already allocated for development elsewhere.[85] Consequently all Macleod could offer the federal leaders was the promise
of an official mission to the Caribbean to report on the region's economic problems.[86] This did nothing to mitigate fears of future federal
indigency. It was the prospect of having to sustain the economies of the
Eastern Caribbean with the help of their own inconsiderable resources
which opponents of the federation in Jamaica emphasised during the
referendum campaign which began in August. The future JLP Prime

Minister, Edward Seaga, who supported the secession cause, recalled: 'To us, the significant progress which Jamaica was making economically should not be jeopardised by the burdens of the other islands, which were much behind in the race for development.'[87] In a more circuitous manner the secessionists also benefitted from the concessions Manley had extracted from the British during the various squabbles which attended the ongoing constitutional negotiations. In particular the guarantee which Manley obtained, that if Jamaica left the federation it would be allowed to proceed to unilateral independence, gave the impression that continued participation in the apparently endless negotiations about the federal constitution was actually delaying the final liberation of Jamaica from colonial control. The history of British efforts to referee these contests regarding the future shape of the federation also had an influence on its eventual collapse.

The federation against itself: the origins of the Jamaican referendum

For the first couple of years of the federation's life, many nationalists feared that the British would utilise the impulse towards regional unity in order to slow the advance towards independence on each individual island and this fostered scepticism about the federal project. At Montego Bay representatives of the Caribbean labour movement had insisted that constitutional development for the islands should not be hindered in that way but, as the events of the 1950s had demonstrated, Colonial Office procrastination regarding constitutional reform was a persistent feature of the politics of the period. After the federation was established the dominant themes in British policymaking were that the islands should not obtain independence outside the federation and that metropolitan influence over the federation should be retained until the local political leadership had demonstrated their competence in stabilising the finances of the region and containing the dangers of racial or class conflict. This was at variance with the nationalist view that federation would expedite the process of ending colonial control. In this sense the British strategy was self-defeating: the slow progress of federal advance at the centre made the alternative of independence for the units more attractive as the notion that regional political cooperation would ensure an early end to British control became ever more implausible. This situation was exacerbated by the bitter controversies which raged between Adams, Manley and Williams and by the favouritism which the British showed to Manley, which was a consequence of the fact that his desire for a weaker federal centre facilitated the Fabian tactics of the British.

The federal election of 25 March 1958 produced a small majority for the parties of the Caribbean left who were aggregated together as the West Indies Federal Labour Party (WIFLP). Members of the new parliament had so few powers to influence the economic and social affairs of its constituent elements that it was inevitable that the attention of elected representatives should be fixed on its own constitutional future. Although provisions had been made for a review after five years, the first two years of the federation's history were dominated by efforts to strengthen its own position in relation both to the units and to the presiding colonial power. At the outset of the first parliamentary session the former PNP radical Ken Hill introduced a motion proposing that a committee should be established to investigate how the federation could achieve dominion status as rapidly as possible. He was motivated by a mixture of nationalist principle and political expediency. On the one hand, he was returning to the idea of federalism as a vehicle to obtain early independence which had been frustrated by colonial officialdom; on the other, Hill remained resentful at his expulsion from the PNP in 1952 and the PNP was a constituent of the WIFLP government of the federation to which he was now opposed. As Mordecai emphasised in his account, the new federal executive led by Adams 'shrank from the danger of being charged by the Opposition with dragging their heels towards a goal which inevitably must be achieved.' In order to maintain their nationalist credentials Adams's federal government resolved to hold a conference on dominion status by June 1959 at the latest.[88] As a consequence the issue of independence became the most pressing question for the planned Inter-Governmental Conference (IGC), although the conflicting schedules of the various participants required its postponement until September 1959.

In the interim, federal politics were marked by immoderate feuding between the various protagonists but, because historiographical attention has been focused on nationalist divisions, it is often forgotten that this encompassed rows between colonial officials appointed to the federal and unit governments. The most illuminating illustration of this tendency was the quarrel between the Governor-General of the Federation, Lord Hailes, and the Governor of Trinidad, Edward Beetham. Their escalating antipathy was partly fuelled by politics, as Hailes tended to support Adams while Beetham defended Williams during the Chaguaramas controversies, but was greatly aggravated by concerns about protocol and status. Beetham was embittered by his eviction from the Governor's residence in Port of Spain in order to make way for Hailes and a demarcation dispute, concerning the extent of the smaller adjoining property to which he had been relegated, ensued. Hailes was irritated by Beetham's preoccupation with the size of his garden and countered by accusing him of withholding telegraphic correspondence with the Colonial Office. Despite the triviality of the issues involved, the domestic disagreements between the two men had head-scratching political consequences. On 2 July 1958 Hailes censured Beetham and Williams for colluding to prevent him from undertaking a birdwatching visit to Caroni and claimed that the Federal government wanted Beetham sacked. In a concluding sentence which revealed much about his attitudes to his neighbour and to the government of Trinidad, Hailes stated: 'I cannot believe that a Governor who is playing off his own personal wishes with a man like Williams and his Ministers, who have their own dangerous aims and ambitions, is a good thing.' First Beetham and then Hailes had to be recalled to London in order to achieve a reconciliation and establish a more united front amongst British officials in the Caribbean.[89]

Acquaintance with the Beetham–Hailes dispute provides a useful perspective on the tripartite altercations between Manley, Adams and Williams. Colonial bureaucrats were as implicated in the politics of the personal vendetta as the politicians who they were supposed to be mentoring. In the case of the nationalist leaders, Adams's notorious evasiveness, Manley's towering temper and Williams's immoderate sensitivity all played a role in the eventual collapse of the federation but the focus on personality may distract from the economic and political constraints which influenced their policies. Once nationalism had established the basis for a system of democratic politics, an improvement in the living standards of the mass of the population became a necessity. The transcending of the politics of oligarchy and imperialism required politicians to satisfy the material needs of the newly enfranchised. As a consequence the participants in the federal drama were required to formulate policies which would provide more and better-paid employment, rectify the extreme economic inequities of the old imperial system and improve social infrastructure, such as housing. In September 1959 Eric Williams supplied the outline of such a programme in *The Economics of Nationhood* but this document reflected Trinidad's preference for a powerful federal centre. Manley contested such a conception and argued for greater economic autonomy for the units.[90] Jamaica was the island where parochial sentiment was strongest and where the federation seemed least likely to offer economic benefits. As the largest island it would take responsibility for subsidising the small islands of the federation as British economic assistance tapered away. One of the most prominent examples of Jamaican particularist tendencies was Manley's determination to grant tax concessions to the oil company Esso as an incentive to build an oil refinery on the island. This proposal was part of a broader strategy for encouraging capital investment as a means of addressing the most serious social problem on the islands which was joblessness. From the perspective of the Eastern Caribbean islands it illustrated Jamaica's disregard for the longstanding aim of harmonising taxes and customs which was an essential element in the process of regional integration. As the only significant oil producer in the Anglophone Caribbean, it had been expected that Trinidad would monopolise refining and Williams objected to any exemptions designed to encourage a rival industry elsewhere in the federation. On this occasion Adams, in his role as guardian of federal interests, backed Williams and the nature of his backing sparked a furious row which embittered relations between Jamaica and the federal government.[91]

In a press conference on 8 September 1958 Adams emphasised that his government supported the equalisation of trade and investment policies inside the federation and appeared to hint that, should unit governments grant their own tax concessions, such as the one Manley planned to grant Esso, the federal government could act retrospectively to gather the lost revenue by imposing new taxes on the units. Adams's statement infuriated Manley. The two men met in Jamaica on 30 October to discuss the matter. After an apparently amicable conversation Adams held another press conference at which the issue of retrospective taxation again arose, and what followed, as Mordecai put it, was that 'all hell broke loose.'[92] The *Gleaner* reported that Adams had gone as far as to claim 'that the Federal Government, not withstanding any tax holidays granted by Unit Governments, would levy its own income tax after five years, and make it retroactive to the date of Federation.' This entirely transcended debates about industrial tax incentives and summoned up nightmarish visions of an enormous federal levy on Jamaicans as the price of federation. In its editorial on 1 November the *Gleaner* advised: 'Jamaica must endeavour to protect the federation from itself. If the task proves impossible it must take adequate steps to avoid an aftermath involving the sacrifice of its future in a mirage visible only to the eyes of federal dreamers.'[93] Despite his lawyerly fluency Manley found it difficult to find the words to express his anger to Adams and settled for the moderate formula: 'I hope that you would assist in dispelling any confusion that may be created by Gleaner headlines which are at variance with general reporting of yesterday's press conference.'[94] To Williams he was blunter and complained that Adams's press conference had 'undone all the work of the last year in trying to get Jamaica to look at Federation with rational eyes.' He asserted that his opponents 'were beginning to get worried and were looking for something to stop our upward move when this God-given business of more taxation, ransacking of incentive legislation and imposing retroactive taxation was handed out to them.'[95] This was of course a reference to Bustamante who was perhaps the Caribbean politician least likely to decline the opportunity for mischief, which the Adams press conference provided. On 5 November the Jamaica Labour Party secured a front-page headline in the *Gleaner* by taking out an advertisement on its inside pages which demanded that Jamaica should either quit the federation or demand a rewriting of the federal constitution to vitiate the already feeble powers of the central government.[96] Manley publicly disdained Bustamante's threats but, as his letter to Williams demonstrated, he recognised that the taxation controversy had unleashed latent Jamaican hostility to increased control from Port of Spain. The row continued until, following a month of further equivocation on the issue, Adams finally stated unambiguously on 9 December that the federation would not act retroactively in the field of taxation. Despite this concession and the eventual completion of negotiations with Esso, the oil refinery was not constructed until after the Jamaican referendum.[97]

For the British the retroactive taxation affair validated and reinforced three tendencies already evident in their thinking: the belief that Adams was a much less effective federal leader than Manley would have been, the desire to foster private capital investment as a substitute for British aid and the conviction that a further period of British supervision of federal affairs was necessary. This last inclination irritated nationalists in the Eastern Caribbean for whom the process of incremental constitutional reform seemed to involve the indefinite postponement of the final transfer of power from Britain. When in January 1959 Williams set a deadline of 22 April 1960 for federal independence, metropolitan policymakers effectively established a tacit alliance with Manley which was designed to foster delay. For some Conservative ministers in Britain the process of dissolving the empire was proceeding far too rapidly. Men like the Colonial Secretary, Alan Lennox-Boyd, his Parliamentary Under-Secretary, Julian Amery, and the Commonwealth Secretary, Alec Douglas-Home, believed that nationalist politicians should serve an extended apprenticeship before obtaining independence. At the end of October 1958 Home wrote to Lennox-Boyd to insist 'there can be no question of "dominion status" for the West Indies within the next four years.' He feared that any constitutional conference would focus on the independence issue rather than on the dull, difficult task of recalibrating the constitutional relationship between the units and the centre. In response Lennox-Boyd alluded to the weakness of the current federal government which was 'hardly worth the name' and agreed it would be necessary to strengthen the power of the federal centre. He reassured Home that the Colonial Office would utilise the impending conferences as 'an invaluable opportunity of making clear ... just how far they have go before the Federal Government could be considered one that can properly be sponsored for full membership of the Commonwealth.'[98]

Despite these expressions of concern regarding the weaknesses of the federal government, which harmonised with Adams's agenda, British representatives in the Caribbean were still eager to promote Manley, who was the most ardent advocate of a decentralised federation, as a regional leader. In January 1959, Hailes, who had sat alongside Home and Lennox-Boyd inside previous Conservative governments, suggested to the latter that Adams was 'not quite a big enough man' for the job of federal Prime Minister and recorded that Manley and 'most responsible people in Jamaica' would be reluctant to secede from the federation. He argued that the 'line to plug' at the forthcoming Council of Ministers was that independence outside a federation would be politically dangerous and might even produce a series of local dictatorships. Rather than expediting federal independence, British strategists sought to redirect attention towards the need to realign constitutional arrangements in the units and at the centre. This would be the work of the forthcoming conference to revise the political systems of the Leewards and the Windwards, which currently lagged behind those of the other federal territories, and the IGC, which would reconsider the nature of the federal constitution. These conclaves were eventually delayed until June and September 1959 respectively, which proved a relief to British policymakers. In the preceding January Lennox-Boyd had taken up the Fabian theme which reappeared so frequently in British analyses of constitutional advance. He advised: 'delay is all to the good at present; it may allow time for tempers to cool after the Adams–Manley dogfight ... if Adams can manage to put both conferences off (and I do realise this won't be easy) something will have been gained if only time.' His epistle also explained that the British preferred to foster inactivity rather than decisive action until the 'real difficulty with the question of finance' was resolved; only once this had been accomplished could independence be envisaged.[99]

During the summer of 1959, British policymakers, with Hailes in the lead, gradually recognised the necessity to accelerate the timetable for independence. As was the case in almost every instance of decolonisation, it was nationalist pressure which forced the pace. On 26 June 1959 Jamieson, who was the British official most directly involved in the various local negotiations, warned his seniors, that they should 'be prepared at least in our own minds for the worst.' What the worst entailed was that the federal leaders would demand independence by late 1960 or early 1961. In a calculated act of defiance, which exceeded Jamieson's worst expectations, Williams pre-empted the Colonial Office by announcing that British imperial rule in the Anglophone Caribbean would end on 22 April 1960. During late 1959 British resistance to the acceleration of the independence timetable slowly crumbled but ministerial foreboding about the consequence of rapid decolonisation in the Caribbean persisted. Home believed there was 'a strong case for playing for the maximum time' while Amery argued that the very earliest feasible dates were in 1963 or 1964. Hailes was the most sympathetic to the idea of an earlier date for independence, probably because nationalist pressure was felt more acutely in Port of Spain than anywhere else. During his visit to London in August 1959 there was much discussion of how local rivalries might be exploited to encourage delay. On the not entirely secure basis that 'Jamaica was in no particular hurry for independence', Amery predicted that the forthcoming IGC meeting could, with some British steering, agree on an earlier, compromise date 'which might fall not far short of acceptance by HMG.' The Permanent Under-Secretary at the Colonial Office, Hilton Poynton, recorded Hailes' view that further tactical manoeuvres to extend the independence timetable were becoming impractical; the Governor-General doubted whether they would be able to 'put the brakes on for any other than practical reasons'. He did acknowledge, however, that Williams's brazen advocacy of an impractical deadline could 'bring Mr Manley into opposition and result in some compromise that might be more reasonable.' Although they hoped that Jamaican caution would act as a check on Trinidadian recklessness, when the hostility between the participants threatened the federation itself, it became necessary to consider ways to appease nationalist sentiment. Matters were greatly complicated by the continuing rivalry between the centralising Trinidadian vision and the devolutionist Jamaican approach to federation. These differences became more pronounced in May 1959 when the Trinidadian PNM and the Jamaican PNP issued rival manifestos. On the issue of trade, for example, the PNM made the case for early customs union as a prelude to independence

within a year, while the PNP insisted that each unit should retain powers to implement protectionist measures.[100] Although Manley's cautious,
incrementalist approach to federal matters was useful to the British in
tactical terms, and Williams's desire to expedite independence was irritating, the Colonial Office also recognised that the latter had a much
clearer vision of how to ensure federalism produced a viable form of
regional integration. Rivalry between Jamaica and Trinidad was useful
only so long as it did not jeopardise the continuation of the federal
enterprise. As the date for the IGC grew nearer, Amery attempted to
reassure Home that 'they would do nothing to hasten the process' of
constitutional advance, while adding the reservations, which reflected
Hailes's view rather more than his own, that: 'The Federation is still a
delicate plant and any excessive check at this stage to West Indian aspirations could have grave repercussions on the standing of the Federal
Government and even compromise the existence of the Federation.'[101]

These already muddy waters became murkier still as the matter of
racial politics again intruded on British debates about their Caribbean
empire. One of the reasons that Home at the Commonwealth Office
was so determined to delay any announcement on federal independence was that the Jamaican decision to impose trade sanctions against
South Africa had strained relations with the new Verwoerd government
at a time when the British hoped for their cooperation in deciding the
future of the Central African Federation. News reached the Colonial
Office in February 1959 that, at the prompting of the influential PNP
minister, Wills Isaacs, Manley intended to prohibit imports from South
Africa in protest against apartheid. British officials and ministers were
furious at the decision. Although legal advice indicated that they could
not prevent the embargo, Lennox-Boyd told the Governor of Jamaica,
Kenneth Blackburne: 'I cannot do other than deprecate any action to
discriminate against a member of the Commonwealth on account of
that country's domestic politics in another field.' The British secured
some delay in the implementation of the policy. During the short lull
the Commonwealth Relations Office became ever more alarmed by the
'wider repercussions which any definite action by the Jamaica Government might have.' Potential consequences included a South African veto
of Commonwealth membership for The West Indies. Minatory signals
issued from Pretoria about their reaction to a Jamaican boycott led the
British High Commissioner to inform the South African Foreign Minister, Eric Louw, of their opposition to sanctions and to restate their
own position, which was that they had no view on his government's
'native policy'.[102] In June, Manley made clear that the boycott would

proceed. Blackburne complained privately, and with a telling use first of a belittling, commonplace metaphor, and then of distancing quotation marks: 'It is unfortunate that Manley and his boys should have decided to boycott South Africa just at this moment.... We all tried to persuade them against it, but they were determined to show their disapproval of "apartheid" in this way.'[103] Verwoerd responded to the imminence of sanctions by warning that his country's 'excellent relations' with Britain 'would be seriously impaired if Jamaica persisted in her wish to boycott South African imports as a protest against apartheid.'[104] In a series of messages to Manley discouraging him from proceeding with the boycott, Blackburne emphasised that the South African government had 'taken a most serious view' of Jamaican actions.[105] Home continued to fume about the Jamaican policy even after it became a *fait accompli* and disassociated himself with advice from his officials that London had no legal authority to prevent the boycott. He exercised his frustrations by authorising an eventually unissued Cabinet paper which stressed that Britain 'clearly have a responsibility for Jamaica behaving in accordance with good Commonwealth neighbour standards. It is equally clear that Jamaica is now using for avowedly political reasons a power that we delegated to her solely for trade and economic purposes.'[106] One notable aspect of the South African controversy was the continuing tendency of British policymakers to absolve Manley of much of the blame for a policy they despised, and blame demotic local politics as represented by populist and supposedly dangerous figures like Wills Isaacs who was also a sceptic about federation. Amery, who had dissuaded Manley from making the initial announcement in May, insisted that the PNP leader had very little interest in pursuing it and did so only because of party pressure.[107]

Similar instincts governed British reactions to the Inter-Governmental Conference (IGC) of September 1959 which was perhaps the worst-tempered meeting in the entire history of the federation. The participants scrutinised and found wanting almost every aspect of the current federal dispensation but were unable to agree on any remedial measures. Amidst the array of contentious topics, the conflict between the centralising demands of Trinidad and the devolutionist aims of Jamaica constituted the seminal controversy. Before the conference, Manley wrote to Adams to reaffirm the position his government had set out in May, namely that federal jurisdiction should be limited to essential matters, such as trade policy, but 'there would remain a larger field of items which do not come under the jurisdiction of the Federation except with the consent of the Unit than at present exists.'[108] This set the Jamaican delegation on collision course with the Trinidadian party. Williams published *The Economics of Nationhood* before the conference. The principal theme of this document was that: 'Only a powerful and centrally directed economic coordination and interdependence can create the foundations of a new nation.'[109] The expectation of continuing disagreements on the question of centralisation fuelled a separate controversy over the redistribution of seats in the House. It was widely accepted that because its population was roughly half the total of the entire area Jamaica should be allowed to increase its allocation from 37.8%. Unfortunately Bustamante's accusations that the PNP would sell out Jamaican interests encouraged cupidity on Manley's part and he proposed a maximalist formula which would raise the figure to 49.2%.[110] This entailed a significant reduction in representation for the small islands and various alternative means of apportioning the seats were batted backwards and forwards between the many participants in a spirit of increasing bad temper until Adams accepted that a decision would have to be deferred. Two Ministerial committees were established, one to examine representation and the other customs union.

The manner in which the British apportioned blame for the failure of the IGC is instructive. Despite criticisms of Williams's tactics, they were willing to indulge him because of his usefulness as an ally against the forces of disorder in the region. Officials at the Colonial Office did not have to like Williams to recognise that his plans for federal centralisation offered precisely the kind of constitutional template which would promote economic self-sufficiency while keeping in check any more populist politics based on racial or class antagonisms. A full report on Williams's conduct, and those of the other participants, was provided by Philip Rogers, who represented the Colonial Office at the IGC meeting. Rogers' assessment was that Williams 'who, as you know, produced an impressive paper and speech on the economics of nationhood and the need for a strong federation, had overdone it politically.' Although Manley's inflexibility was acknowledged as problematic it was placed in the context of increasing opposition to federalism in Jamaica. As in the case of the South African boycott, Rogers' report blamed the rigidity of Jamaica's position on others and concluded that Manley was 'still a Federationist and though he thinks in terms of a weaker Federation than we believe to be practicable, he is prepared to discuss the degree of power to be given to the Federation.' What Rogers did not mention was that the comparative dilatoriness of the Jamaicans on the independence issue helped to mask indecision in Whitehall about the setting of a date. Despite his intransigence at the IGC, Manley retained his heroic status for British officials who still hoped he would become more involved in federal affairs. It was onto Adams and the small island politicians that most of the blame was heaped. The former was singled out by Rogers as 'unfailingly inept and irritating to all his delegates.' The St Lucian representatives were also censured for producing an astonishing paper which 'frightened the Jamaicans at least as much as the Trinidad paper.'[111] Given their belief in the essentially juvenile nature of small island affairs a Manley-type politician running a Williams-type federation was for the British the perfect solution to the refractory politics of the region but one which it seemed almost impossible to attain.

British disillusionment with Adams's performance at the IGC strengthened Manley's position and had an indirect influence on the seminal decision to guarantee that Jamaica could obtain early independence outside the federation. John Mordecai later claimed that there was 'no question of a plot to oust Sir Grantley.'[112] However, failure at the IGC encouraged the Colonial Office to consider the possibility of a constitutional coup. Nigel Fisher, who was Parliamentary Under-Secretary in the Colonial Office at the time of the federation's demise, recalled that it 'was run by a second eleven from the small islands' and suggested that replacing Adams with either Manley or Williams 'might have made the difference between success and failure for the federation as a whole.'[113] In the weeks after the IGC, Rogers continued to criticise Adams's handling of the meeting and concluded that the inefficiency of the federal government 'stems essentially from the appalling inadequacy of Sir Grantley Adams.'[114] When Manley visited London in January 1960 he discussed with British officials the possibility of replacing Adams. Rogers reported that Manley was willing to consider such a manoeuvre in a couple of years, on condition that Jamaican terms for a revised federal architecture were accepted. Hailes wanted more urgent action and suggested Adams should resign on the grounds of ill health so that Manley could take over as Prime Minister as soon as possible. His reports of Adams's 'decrepitude' also prompted Amery to wonder 'whether M [Manley] could be persuaded to take over without a stop gap.' Immediate action proved impractical but Manley's indispensability was reaffirmed, as was the necessity to help protect him against the continual onslaught of the JLP over the federation issue. From Kingston, Blackburne urged that measures be taken to 'strengthen his hand'.[115] During the London talks in January 1960 Macleod made what turned out to be a damaging concession to Jamaican secessionist sentiment by promising that 'no threat, undue pressure or punitive action was contemplated' should they pursue unilateral independence.[116] Macleod's solicitude was predicated on the entirely accurate perception that Bustamante and the JLP would continue their attacks on the federation and the less justified assumption that concessions to the PNP would help them resist the onslaught. Manley articulated the dilemma in which he felt himself, as a proponent of an incrementalist but pro-integrationist policy, besieged by federal zealots on one side and Jamaican isolationists on the other. He told a meeting of PNP members 'in the long run there are real and great advantages in federation but that those advantages cannot be accepted at the price of anything that would destroy or injure us in a fundamental respect.' Any measures which would retard efforts to alleviate Jamaican poverty and unemployment, Manley declared, would be unacceptable.[117] After returning from London he announced that the Colonial Office had provided him with a 'potential permit to secede.' He explained: 'We have made it clear we cannot and will not remain in a Federation which had the right to take over all the economic controls of the area as soon as it becomes independent.... If we cannot reach early agreement, Jamaica will leave Federation and will seek independence on her own. This is fully understood.'[118]

The continuing concessions made to Jamaican interests did almost nothing to divert Bustamante from his relentless focus on the excessive costs of federation. The committee established after the IGC to deal with the electoral representation of units had already agreed on a formula which increased Jamaican representation to 48.4% of the seats in the House of Representatives, which constituted a clear victory for Manley and the PNP government.[119] Success in resolving that issue with surprising speed gave greater salience to the other matters which had been deferred, namely customs union and taxation policy, and these were taken up again at the next ministerial meeting in Port of Spain in May 1960. These issues still divided opinion between Jamaica and the other members of the federation but the implicit recognition by many of the participants that early customs union was impractical constituted a further attempt to allay Jamaican concerns. No concessions were made to the centralist vision of Trinidad but the mere possibility of them attracted obloquy from the JLP. In a series of messages sent in the midst of the negotiations Bustamante asked: 'What does Federation mean to Jamaica? More direct taxes, tax on consumer goods, interference with our industries, thereby causing reduction in unemployment [*sic*], more hunger to the thousands of already hungry people and more tears.' When Manley brushed aside Bustamante's complaints that he was trying to force the federation down unwilling Jamaican throats, the JLP leader advised: 'If you describe these statements again as "rubbish" or "nonsense", I can only suggest you pay a visit to a good psychiatrist.'[120]

Considerations of party political advantage prompted Bustamante to launch a formal campaign against federation despite the fact that technical arguments about representation, customs union and taxation had been, or seemed likely to be, resolved in Jamaica's favour. He resented the JLP electoral defeats of 1955 and 1959 and feared that the financial backing offered to the PNP by Jamaican business interests who favoured federation would permanently marginalise his party. The future Prime Minister and Bustamante acolyte, Edward Seaga, recalled that the JLP leader was infuriated by his inability to raise any more than £ 60 for an impending by-election in St Thomas. On the evening of 30 May he told Seaga: 'I never liked this damn federation any way. I am going to pull Jamaica out of it.'[121] Within hours of the news of Bustamante's new anti-federation campaign appearing in the *Gleaner* on 31 May, Manley announced that he would hold a referendum on the issue of Jamaica's continuing participation. Manley later suggested that he could not give 'logical reasons' to explain why he made this decision.[122] Although it was a finely poised choice which was widely criticised at the time, the explanation appeared fairly straightforward: it was the only way to decisively resolve the contest with Bustamante which was sucking the life out of federal and Jamaican politics. No definitive compromise on any federal issue was possible while the JLP was threatening to take the first opportunity to secede. Perhaps equally pressing from Manley's perspective was disunity within the PNP. Influential figures such as Wills Isaacs continued to warn of the costs of continuing Jamaican membership of the federation. Gordon Lewis emphasised the importance of the informal coalition between the JLP and the right wing of the PNP 'to foment the victory of Jamaican nationalism with its emphasis more and more on the theme of material benefits.'[123] By transferring the final decision to the Jamaican people, Manley gave himself greater domestic room for manoeuvre but at the cost of gambling with the entire future of the federation.

British policymakers were optimistic that Manley's decision would lead to a favourable resolution of pan-Caribbean, domestic Jamaican and PNP controversies. The amenable attitude shown by Macleod during his visit to the region in June 1960 seemed to establish the basis for improved relations between the metropolis and the periphery. He endorsed the decision to hold a referendum and Manley told C. L. R. James that Macleod was 'completely sincere and determined in sticking to the policy that what we do in the West Indies at this time is our own business.'[124] The Colonial Office approved the referendum largely because they expected a Manley victory. Officials went as far as to suggest that 'there seems to be no doubt at all that Jamaica will vote in favour of Federation' and even contemplated the possibility 'that the "Busta challenge" will peter out to the extent of it becoming unnecessary to hold one.'[125] The one dissenting voice was Hailes who told Macleod: 'I can't be v. happy about the referendum'.[126] On 24 October Blackburne attempted to reassure Hailes following a discussion with Manley: 'I have little doubt that he will be able to bring the referendum off all right when the time comes.'[127] Macleod also initiated a renewed effort to obtain compromises on the vexed question of relations between the federal centre and the units and sought to appease Trinidad over the setting of a date for independence. The long history of British irresolution on this last point, which had continued up to the Home–Amery exchanges in autumn 1959, came to an end with Macleod's discussions with Caribbean leaders in June 1960. He offered both an immediate move towards a Cabinet form of government for the federation, which would allow Adams to preside over meetings of the executive, and a promise that 'as soon as you in the West Indies are agreed on the kind of independent Federation you want you will find us ready and willing to help you achieve it.'[128] He avoided offering any specifically British views on the precise structure of the federation but persuaded Manley and Williams to begin serious consideration of a compromise. As a consequence of all this, the visit has been portrayed as 'a triumph of skill and planning.'[129] Judged from a longer-term perspective Macleod's more accommodating attitude towards the nationalist cause cannot be considered too little but it did occur too late. Fisher, who was a friend of Macleod, noted that 'he always regarded the Caribbean as his main area of failure.'[130]

Efforts to accommodate Jamaican requirements reached their climax at a meeting between Williams and Manley on Antigua in August 1960 but, despite British championing of the resulting agreement, the new deal negotiated outside a federal framework produced a backlash which contributed to the eventual destruction of the federation. During the Antigua talks Williams was more conciliatory than was his custom because of the necessity to finally resolve the controversies which were now the only block to independence and to strengthen the hand of Manley, who was a personal friend and political ally, in the referendum. The two men devised the idea of a 'third list', which later became known as the 'reserve list', the items on which would remain outside the ambit of federal control for a minimum of five years. At the end of this interim period the consent of the Regional Council of Ministers would still be necessary to transfer 'third list' items from unit to federal control. It was agreed that income tax and industrial development policies would definitely be included on the 'third list' and possibly education and government borrowing. Although he later disputed this version of events, the contemporary record of their discussions found in the Manley papers, shows that Williams initially agreed that a majority of two-thirds would be required to transfer items to federal control and the voting formula would be based on representation by population. As Jamaicans constituted roughly half the total population of the federation, under the Antigua formula they would have an effective veto over changes to the content of the 'third list'. Manley also triumphed on the matter of federal revenue. It was provisionally agreed that, in the absence of any powers to tax income, the federal government should continue to depend on a portion of customs revenue from the units. The proportion was to be cut from 30% to 20%. On the issue of freedom of movement, which was the one area in which Trinidad was fearful of federal authority, Manley agreed to give 'sympathetic consideration' to a Trinidadian plan to establish an incremental procedure based on gradually increasing quotas for internal migration.[131]

Despite their influence, Manley and Williams were unable to impose the further dilution of federal authority they envisaged at Antigua. Following Williams's return to Trinidad the new Governor, Solomon Hochoy, witnessed an unusual open confrontation between Williams and his two key lieutenants, Patrick Solomon and John O'Halloran, both of whom objected to the extent of his concessions. Williams's unusually solicitous attitude to Jamaican dilemmas was evident when he explained that, because of his earlier assertiveness on the subject of Jamaican interests, Manley 'now finds himself out on a limb and appreciates that he cannot get back easily.' Solomon was infuriated by the notion of a popular two-thirds majority to have items removed from the 'third list' and claimed it was tantamount to 'Jamaica saying that they will be able to do what they like for as long as they like.' O'Halloran insisted that any provision allowing Jamaica to control its own trade policy independently of federal attempts to promote harmonisation would guarantee a shift in industrial investment out of Trinidad and into Jamaica. In response Williams emphasised his dilemma: 'Either Trinidad goes more than half way to meet Manley and so make it possible for Jamaica to stay in the Federation, or risks a complete breakdown.' Hochoy seconded Williams's arguments and pleaded 'let us try to find a formula which could help Manley.'[132] Although the British had in the past always supported the notion of a stronger federal centre they

now turned their fire on the opponents of a scheme which further vitiated the powers of an already feeble federation. Hailes had an even
more difficult job in dealing with the reactions of Adams and federal
ministers. He claimed that Adams's response was entirely emotional
and based on 'hurt feelings' rather than on the damage done to federal viability. His report to Macleod stated: 'Adams is quite capable,
if his position is assailed, of trying to pull down the pillars of the
temple. In his muddled head he flirts with the idea of a Federation
without Jamaica, in which – so he thinks – he could more easily hold
his own.'[133] On 14 September Adams wrote to Manley to denounce
what he believed to be a conspiracy to undermine him. Despite the
fact that he had discussed this matter with the Colonial Office earlier
in the year, Manley disclaimed any involvement in a plot to unseat
Adams.[134]

Prior to the next IGC in October 1960 Manley was confident that
he and Williams had 'resolved all our differences' and that the only
serious obstacle to the ratification of the Antigua deal was opposition from Williams's senior ministers, who he hoped to appease during
further discussions.[135] The Chaguaramas issue was also apparently near-
ing resolution and, despite Adams's resentment, this was the moment
when there seemed the greatest likelihood of concluding the apparently
never-ending series of controversies which blocked the road to federal
independence. Instead, the second IGC proved almost as bad-tempered
as the first and the old controversies re-emerged in new forms. Under
pressure from his own party Williams gave a captious performance.
He now objected to the idea, which he had endorsed at Antigua, that
Jamaica should have an effective veto over any extension of the powers
of the federal government and rejected various compromise proposals
on freedom of movement on the grounds that Trinidad had conceded
so many other points. By the conclusion of the discussions, as Mordecai
noted, the usual positions had been reversed and Manley ended the conference 'on far better personal terms with the Eastern Caribbean leaders
than did Williams.'[136] The doubt which Williams cast over the Jamaican
veto now made it more difficult to shore up Manley's domestic position in advance of the referendum and this engendered a new period
of fretfulness in the Colonial Office. On his return, Manley confronted
objections to the potential loss of the veto from his own party. Wills
Isaacs demanded that the federation should have no powers to interfere
with the policies which units pursued on industrial development, that
Jamaica should retain a veto over the transfer of powers and that the
introduction of a federal income tax must be prohibited. Unless these
conditions were met, he announced 'he would break with his party and

oppose it.' In response to this news, the Parliamentary Under-Secretary at the Colonial Office, Hugh Fraser, pondered whether the debilitating erosion of federal power could be compensated for by getting rid of Adams and his ministers: 'Once established I hope that a first eleven as opposed to the second eleven team we have at the moment in office can make federation work. But for a long time to come I fear it will be a weak federation and not the sort of federation the theorists would desire.'[137]

In the months before the frequently postponed third IGC of May 1961 three events occurred which have already been discussed: the London talks on financial assistance which ended in disappointment, the Tobago conference which resolved the Chaguaramas issue in a spirit of relative amity and the Macmillan visit to the Caribbean which convinced local leaders that their worst fears about immigration controls were justified. The second development strengthened Williams's hand but for the other participants the events of the winter of 1960–1961 warranted only pessimism about the future. For nationalist politicians, the setbacks in negotiations with the British had particularly serious consequences for the debate about freedom of movement within the federation. On 23 March 1961 Adams warned the federal Cabinet that unless they removed internal barriers to migration 'the case against restriction of West Indian migrants to the UK would be extremely weak and that restrictions would probably be introduced before the end of 1961.'[138] Six weeks later at the IGC Adams pressed the case for freedom of movement but was confounded by Williams's opposition which focused on another aspect of British policy, namely the plans to curtail or taper down British financial assistance. His reasons were reported by the Colonial Office's observer, Ambler Thomas, and were perfectly logical: 'Williams has repeatedly tied Freedom [of] Movement with the question of external aid to the smaller territories. His argument is that if there were to be a tight federation on the lines he has consistently urged there would be adequate powers at the centre to promote capital development over the declared Federation. This would make it possible to tackle the immigration problem at its roots by providing employment opportunities in the smaller territories.'[139] The final compromise proposal recognised the force of these arguments: although granting the federal government nominal control over freedom of movement by including it on the exclusive list, it allowed for a nine-year transitional period during which units would be allowed to prevent the federation from exercising these powers. More ominously, the implementation of the deal was conditional on a new and better offer of financial assistance to the small islands from Britain.[140]

Manley supported federal ministers against Trinidad on the freedom of movement issue but on the questions of the reserve list and the Jamaican veto, he continued to exercise the obstinacy licensed by British policymakers' views of his indispensability. Before the IGC the Deputy Permanent Under-Secretary at the Colonial Office, William Gorell Barnes, estimated that 'our chances of success with a Manley on the scene will never again be higher'. In adopting what he described as a 'back seat driver' role, the British continued to steer the constitutional vehicle down a road of yet more concessions to Jamaican opinion.[141] At the outset of the climactic Lancaster House conference in June, and with evident approval from the British observer, Ambler Thomas, Manley disregarded Adams's objections and insisted that the items included on the 'third list' at Antigua, namely income tax and industrial development, should remain the responsibility of the units.[142] Manley promised to undertake further consultations in Jamaica about the transfer of these items to the federal government but the outcome of these enquiries was never in doubt. At the moment of his arrival back in Kingston, Manley was met by JLP protestors, including Edward Seaga, denouncing him for failing to obtain definitive endorsement of the Jamaican veto at the IGC and demanding an early referendum.[143] Within the PNP, Wills Isaacs also rejected any compromise over the veto issue. On 22 May Manley wrote to Adams to say that the Jamaican veto must be retained, offering only the compensatory prospect that in a few years time the federation could acquire 'law-making powers as far as income tax was concerned provided the percentage of income tax that they could collect was constitutionally limited.'[144]

By the time of the Lancaster House conference both Williams and Adams had grown tired of the requirement to appease Jamaican opinion because of the referendum. Rather than refereeing federal disputes on the federal constitution the Colonial Office openly sided with the Jamaicans in order to secure a victory for Manley in his dispute with the JLP. Patricia Robinson, who was a personal assistant to Williams, concluded that he was exasperated by this attitude: 'he began to blame the British, who were never sure of Williams.... Manley spoke their language.... Manley was really their candidate, and to reassure Manley they were prepared to agree anything. They were really darned irritated when Manley was forced into a corner as they thought.'[145] The most significant aspect of the conference was the isolation of the Trinidadian delegation on the freedom of movement issue. The inability of Macleod to offer any substantial concession regarding financial aid, combined with continuing pressure on Trinidad from the British government and the other delegates to accept unrestricted migration between units, tested Williams's limited patience. He snapped when yet another new formula designed to secure Jamaica's interests was adumbrated. This latest proposal entailed the abolition of the reserve list which had been devised by Williams at Antigua. Items which had been allocated to this list, namely income tax and industrial policy, would be transferred back to the concurrent list. However, the consent of the unit legislatures, as well as the federal legislature, would be necessary before items on the new concurrent list became subject to exclusive federal control. In assuaging Jamaican anxieties the proposal effectively universalised their veto by giving it to every one of the units. In response, Williams effectively withdrew from the negotiations on the grounds that the new formula merely compounded federal feebleness by extending a concession designed to meet Jamaican requirements to all parties. Most of all, the assent given to the British formula by the other delegates 'showed the power of the Colonial Office ... the power and influence of the Colonial Office was never greater than on its death bed. The Colonial Office had merely to crack the whip and all the Territories fell in line – all except Trinidad and Tobago.'[146] Williams did not make public his criticisms of the Lancaster House deal but, because nothing had been done to meet any Trinidadian desiderata, he reserved his position on all the conference proceedings.[147] He also expressed his resentment to Manley in an exchange of bitter letters which, a year on from the Antiguan rapprochement, dissolved the political alliance and personal friendship between the two men.[148]

Having secured a new form of Jamaican veto, Manley began campaigning on the referendum issue immediately after his return from London but waited until 3 August 1961 to announce that polling day would be 19 September. Jamaican control over income tax and industrial incentives had been the dominating features of arguments about federation since Adams's press conference of October 1958. Although the Lancaster House meeting effectively guaranteed that the federation would not be able to impinge on these areas of national life, Manley needed to make a positive case for continuing participation. The promise of early independence for the federation was difficult to exploit because of the guarantee, secured in January 1960, that if the country seceded it could obtain unilateral independence. Even the imposition of Jamaican terms at Lancaster House caused problems for Manley because the sour resentment at the outcome amongst other regional leaders left open the possibility of yet more negotiations which would modify what had been intended as a final settlement. Adams and the federal government openly condemned the Lancaster House formula and seemed eager to commence another round of negotiations after the referendum.[149] The notion that the federation had secured a more generous package of British financial aid than the territories would have obtained through bilateral negotiations also seemed implausible. During the campaign the JLP leaders exploited the economic frustrations of the Jamaican public which were symbolised by the unmistakeable financial chasm between those Seaga characterised as the 'Haves' and the 'Have-nots'.[150] The absence of federal achievements in the three years of its existence made it tricky for Manley to present a convincing case against secession either on narrow financial or broader visionary grounds. The turnout of 60.87% was low by Jamaican standards of the time and indicated a degree of apathy amongst PNP supporters. These abstentions ensured that the secessionist voters outnumbered the pro-federationists by nearly 40,000 or just over 8% of the total who turned up at the polls.[151]

The independence race: Trinidad versus Jamaica

The referendum result did not end the clashes of interest between Jamaica and the smaller islands but reframed them. For Adams and the leaders of the Eastern Caribbean, it was important that the resolution of the constitutional dilemmas posed by secession should await the establishment of a revised federal dispensation. In Jamaica the JLP and the PNP were for once united in demanding immediate independence. From a British perspective there was a case to be made for stalling the process of decolonisation across the region in order to facilitate a federal revival in the East but, based on their past record and on the praise and sympathy evinced for Manley in the aftermath of the referendum, there was little doubt about whom they would favour. Of the many considerate messages Manley received from British officials and politicians, perhaps the most effusive came from Blackburne: 'That the finest man in the history of the West Indies should be treated in this way makes one despair of our democratic theories and practices.'[152] Such solicitations did not temper Manley's usual forceful presentation of the Jamaican case and less than a fortnight later he was exchanging much testier messages with Blackburne regarding Macleod's warnings that he avoid unguarded comments on the future of the federation during a planned trip to New York.[153] The American visit passed off without incident but the PNP government was unyielding in its insistence that the constitutional course now set for Jamaica must be charted on the basis of previous assurances that the country would be granted independence following secession. For Manley, the future of the federation was now irrelevant. The day after the referendum result he told his Cabinet that he would urge the Colonial Office to 'fix the earliest possible date for Independence for Jamaica'. The Cabinet settled on 31 May 1962. A delegation was despatched to London with orders that they 'come back with a record that the demand had been uncompromisingly made and thereafter, if necessary, the Government should fight relentlessly for this objective.'[154] As Mordecai later noted, the talks between Manley and Macleod in October 1961 'destroyed whatever federal hope of an adequate respite could have remained.'[155] Although the Colonial Office believed the 31 May date was impractical, under pressure from Manley, Macleod promised to ensure that enabling legislation was passed through the British parliament by the end of March 1962.[156]

This kind of guarantee to Jamaica was precisely what federal ministers had been desperate to avoid. In the race to save the federation Adams had actually beaten Manley to London by a week. He expressed optimism that a viable federation of the nine remaining states could be constructed but warned 'early Jamaican independence would certainly queer the Trinidad pitch.'[157] His argument that Williams would rather seek unilateral independence, and thus reduce the remaining nine federal states to eight, than allow Jamaica to rush to independence ahead of Trinidad, had considerable force but was rejected by Macleod. The unsympathetic reception given to Adams heralded the arrival of an even tougher line towards the small island leaders. For the British the greatest advantage of federation was that it facilitated a graceful imperial retreat by transferring responsibility for the political and financial good conduct of the small islands to Jamaica and Trinidad. Under Manley's eventual leadership it was expected that continuity would trump revolutionary change, that the British connection would be guaranteed and that orthodox capitalist economics would resolve many of the social and economic problems of the region. In the aftermath of the secession vote they were no longer able to contemplate this uplifting vision and Whitehall policymakers faced what Macleod described to Macmillan as the 'most dismal prospect' of being burdened for the foreseeable future with responsibility for the Leewards and the Windwards, all but one of which ran annual budgetary deficits.[158] Based on assumptions about the incapacities of the local leadership to deal with the social, political and economic problems which would arise at independence, the only remaining options the British were willing to consider were a new federation controlled by Trinidad or should

Trinidad insist on unilateral independence, the retightening of the reins of colonial control. A month after the referendum, Ambler Thomas recommended that local administrators in the Eastern Caribbean should make full use of their constitutional prerogatives in order to counteract the tendency of local politicians to 'act independent'. He concluded: 'I think the more relatively gentle jolts and checks which the small island politicians receive when they overstep the mark from now on the better since sooner or later we are going to have a pretty sharp clash with them.' Local administrators were instructed to prepare for a more uncompromising response to any future importunings from local nationalist leaders. Thomas's sentiments were echoed by Hailes on the other side of the Atlantic who declared, 'a much tougher line will have to be taken with the small territories in future if anything is to be salvaged.'[159]

Although both had been foreshadowed, Macleod's endorsement of Jamaican secession and the Home Office's announcement of legislation to control immigration constituted a double blow to hopes of a federal revival. On 18 September Macleod obtained agreement from the Cabinet that, in view of the precedents in terms of size set by Sierra Leone and Cyprus, they would authorise Jamaican independence. In the midst of the discussion of Jamaica's future, ministers sounded a cautionary note that the other islands in the Caribbean should no longer expect 'full financial support'.[160] Once the decision was made, Poynton expressed Colonial Office concern about 'the likely effect on the possibility of preserving an Eastern Caribbean Federation built around Trinidad.' The impatient and uncompromising approach towards the affairs of the Anglophone Caribbean was also evident over the issue of migration to Britain. Legislation had been expected for at least a year but had been delayed until after the Jamaican referendum. Macleod announced 'I detest the bill' but, despite the ramifications for the federation, accepted that it would have to be included in the Queen's Speech.[161] In Cabinet, Butler admitted that the legislation would be seen to be 'aimed at colour'. During discussions the unsentimental nature of the planned trade-off became clear: 'The Bill would provoke some criticism from other Commonwealth countries but this was preferable to the continuing risk of ill-feeling over incidents in this country involving coloured Commonwealth immigrants.'[162] The parliamentary announcement on 31 October prompted the leader of the Labour Party, Hugh Gaitskell, to declare: 'It is all very well that we wish the West Indies well ... but it is then rather difficult, I think, to take steps which might threaten them economically.' The party's deputy leader, George Brown, interpreted the proposed legislation as a concession to Oswald Mosley's campaign to 'Keep Britain White.'[163]

Immigration controls had economic, political and cultural implications in the Anglophone Caribbean. In political terms they made it more likely that Trinidad would withdraw from the federation. Williams's greatest concern had always been that freedom of movement within a federation would lead to an influx of poor small-islanders to Trinidad. Now that migrants would find it more difficult to gain access to Britain, Trinidad's potential problems were magnified. The racial motivation behind the restrictions was even more perturbing to opinion in the Anglophone Caribbean. In correspondence with the Deputy Prime Minister of the Federation, Carl La Corbiniere, C. L. R. James applauded Adams's efforts to revive the federation but complained that the immigration issue had been badly handled. He wanted to mobilise West Indian people to show that the restrictions were felt 'as a personal blow' and suggested: 'Britain is breaking with a tradition of many centuries. This proposal to limit immigration is part of the new outlook of the new Britain ... it comes in regard to the West Indies at a time when every consideration should be given to them, especially in view of independence and the difficulties of the Federation.' His proposed response was a campaign to demonstrate 'that the West Indian people, the body of the people, see this and feel it as a personal blow.'[164] On 17 November Adams took up the historical theme of the role of free movement of goods and people in a letter of protest to Macmillan and warned him of the consequences of immigration controls. He stated: 'It will in future be difficult for any person from the Commonwealth to accept unreflectingly the oft repeated assertion of multi-racial partnership.' Macmillan's weak propitiatory reply was that the planned measures were non-discriminatory and would apply to independent Commonwealth countries as well as the dependent states of the Anglophone Caribbean.[165]

In contrast to the decisive action undertaken on the issue of immigration, British policymakers were uncertain what policy to adopt in relation to the remaining federation of the nine until Trinidad's position was clarified. Williams's public reticence on federal matters in the final months of 1961 made matters particularly difficult. He refused to speak to Hochoy as the official representative of British colonialism but the intelligence received by the Colonial Office from other sources signalled his continuing resentment over the Lancaster House decisions. Arthur Lewis, who was given the task of redrafting the federal constitution, recorded that Williams was 'full of venom' for those he blamed for the collapse of the federation and that the arguments at Lancaster House 'still rankled and he was absolutely fed up with most of the principal characters.' At various points Williams lashed out personally against Macleod, Manley and Adams. In policy terms he announced he 'would have nothing whatever to do with the Grantley Adams Federation; that must pack up and its leaders disappear.' The only area of ambiguity was whether Williams might participate in the reconstruction of some form of Eastern Caribbean federation on his own terms which would revert to the centralising notions contained in the *Economics of Nationhood*. Such a policy was less attractive because Jamaica's exit seemed certain to augment the economic burdens of integration which would fall on Trinidad. Williams declared the 'Colonial Government had gotten the West Indies into the mess and had the duty to take the initiative to get us out.'[166] The completion of Lewis's report on constitutional reform in November and the decisive electoral victory of the PNM in the Trinidadian election of December enabled Williams to respond to a specific set of proposals from a secure political platform. His own later account emphasised the hostility of the PNM to the new financial arrangements envisaged by Lewis. On his interpretation of the figures, Trinidad would contribute 75% towards the federal budget, while receiving only 50% of the political representation in the legislature.[167]

The key influences behind Williams's decision to take Trinidad out of the federation were self-evident: prestige, in the form of his desire that Trinidad should not lag behind Jamaica in the independence race, and economic calculation, in terms of the likely costs to Trinidad of continuing membership. On both counts British policy was influential: Macleod's agreement to early legislation to facilitate Jamaican independence ensured that the decolonisation race was reaching the final sprint for the line, while the imminence of British immigration controls only increased the disincentive for Trinidad to accept freedom of movement which would, at some point, be an inevitable consequence of federation. However, Williams saw no advantage in committing himself on federal issues while the electoral consequences of such a policy remained uncertain. The battles between the PNM and the DLP had reached a ferocious climax at the end of 1961; both parties were aware that the victor of the December elections would lead Trinidad to independence. The leader of the DLP, Rudranath Capildeo, accused Patrick Solomon of sponsoring a campaign of intimidation; Solomon later claimed Capildeo would 'whip himself into a frenzy of passion reminiscent of Hitler in his heyday.'[168] On 15 October the DLP held an enormous rally at the Queen's Park

Savannah. Capildeo responded to growing evidence that the police were deliberately breaking up his party's meetings by declaring: 'I shall call upon my supporters to arm themselves and protect themselves in such circumstances.'[169] Williams's eventual victory was therefore soured by the intensification of racial antagonism on the island, about which the British had always been nervous, and the animosity generated by the campaign became an almost insuperable obstacle when it came time to negotiating the terms of Trinidad's independence.

Despite their reservations regarding the domestic stability of Trinidad, the British government took Williams's decision, like Manley's, as a *fait accompli*. When the newly elected parliament met on 12 January 1962, Williams unleashed his foaming resentment at Trinidad's isolation at Lancaster House and accused Manley and Macleod of killing 'the bastard federation.' Two days later the General Council of the PNM formulated a motion demanding unilateral independence which was approved by a Special Convention of the party on 28 January. The new Colonial Secretary, Reginald Maudling, arrived in the Caribbean amidst these developments and concluded that 'if people wanted to remove themselves from the federation it would be better to let them go.'[170] He was much less explicit regarding what policy he would adopt towards the rump federation. The discussion which ensued when he returned to London illuminated some of the uncertainties of British policy at this point. Both the 'small island problem' and the racial tensions on Trinidad remained preoccupations. Some ministers argued that it would be possible to 'counteract the rapid growth of the Indian population in Trinidad' by allowing the Windwards and Leewards to establish a unitary state across the Eastern Caribbean under leadership from Port of Spain. This was another reheating of the old arguments about the need for big island management and prompted a radical counter-suggestion that each small island might obtain unilateral independence. The objection to this was predictable: 'the Government could not afford altogether to avoid a moral obligation to avert the chaos and bankruptcy in the smaller islands which might well ensue.' The key to ministerial strategy was the reassertion of British political control in the form of a latitudinarian enabling bill which would allow Maudling to impose his own solutions in the Eastern Caribbean.[171] In an era dominated by global anti-colonial sentiment this set the basis for a renewed confrontation with Caribbean nationalism.

Unfortunately for Adams and his ministers, their attempts to preserve existing federal structures occurred at the same time as a financial scandal caused by the cupidity of the Eric Gairy government in

Grenada which attracted the label 'Squandermania' and which reaffirmed metropolitan contempt for the politics of the small islands. The willingness of British ministers to lump together all the leaders of the Windwards and Leewards was evident from Maudling's dismissive summary: 'they were always having rows those chaps'.[172] By far their greatest row was with Maudling himself. During his discussions with federal ministers on 24 January 1962 he indicated that the current federal system would be formally dissolved within two or three months. Adams responded 'that the people of eight territories wanted Federation.' He argued that Jamaica, Trinidad and the federal eight, consisting of Barbados, Grenada, St Vincent, St Lucia, Dominica, St Kitts, Antigua and Montserrat, should achieve independence simultaneously.[173] Despite continuing to favour federalism in principle, the Colonial Office rejected Adams's pleas, ostensibly because it would be impossible to coordinate timetables. More significantly, they were emphatic that the existing federation would have to be wound up and any replacement which did emerge would do so as a dependent, not an independent, territory.[174] In retrospect, a more frank disclosure of British plans during Maudling's trip to the Caribbean, would have at least vitiated the accusations of betrayal which were made following his statement to Parliament on 6 February 1962. After outlining plans to terminate the existing federation Maudling offered the most tepid of support for its putative replacement. He declared: 'Having seen one Federation of the West Indies collapse in the way we are seeing now, I would be unhappy about setting up another until I was confident that it would last.' Gaitskell pointed out that the people of the Windwards and Leewards would resent being returned to the status of Crown Colonies.[175] This assessment was confirmed by the deluge of telegrams which flooded into the Colonial Office as their administrative outposts on the islands recorded the adverse local reactions to Maudling's announcement.[176] Members of the federal Parliament also queued up to denounce current British policy as well as to anatomise past errors, including the 'exit permit' which Macleod had granted to Manley back in January 1960.[177]

It was two of the most conservative and Anglophile leaders of Caribbean nationalism who led the charge against the dissolution of the federation, namely Grantley Adams and Albert Gomes. Despite his prominence in stimulating Trinidadian nationalism in the 1930s, the latter had become a *bête noire* of his peers and he was usually happiest denouncing the puerile nature of Caribbean politics, which he liked to contrast with the mature attitude evinced by the colonising power.

He later observed 'it was always the influence of the Englishman in the chair that managed the miracle of West Indian unity when it seemed impossible of achievement.'[178] Despite this unusual degree of sympathy for the metropolitan power, Maudling's decision to dissolve the federation shocked Gomes who sponsored a motion in the federal parliament authorising the dispatch of a delegation to London as the first step in a campaign to save the federation. Adams agreed to lead the delegation and denounced Maudling's 'immoral and monstrous act' in the House of Representatives.[179] In his biography of the federal Prime Minister, Hoyos noted that after Maudling's announcement, Adams's 'growing anger with the Colonial Office could no longer be contained'. He condemned British policy in a letter to Maudling on 15 February and began contacting potential allies in the metropolis.[180] All of this activity seems merely to have irritated the Colonial Office. They had their own grievances with federal legislators arising from plans for a financial compensation bill which prioritised payments to politicians rather than civil servants. Maudling described the scheme as 'bordering on the scandalous' and vetoed it through the use of an Order-in-Council.[181] After their unsolicited arrival, the federal delegation were ostentatiously ignored for five days until the Minister of State, Lord Perth, eventually agreed to a short meeting with Adams. When Maudling eventually deigned to see the delegates it was in a spirit of reciprocal resentment. Gomes gave a memorable account of the meeting in which Maudling dismissed their pleas to abandon or at least modify the Enabling Bill which would dissolve the federation: 'the arrangement of the room suggested a lecture by the professor to the students.... When eventually we had been invited to sit Mr Maudling, addressing no one in particular asked: "Well what can I do for you gentlemen?" His anger was ill concealed.' He accused the federal ministers of lying when they claimed that they had not been consulted about the Bill. Gomes expressed his resentment at the overt display of colonial inferiority: 'The political destiny of over 3,500,000 West Indians was just a routine Parliamentary chore to Englishmen.... What I remember most is the bitter humiliation, the sense of being just another item in the Englishman's casual self-preoccupation.'[182]

A further source of Maudling's ire was the suspicion that Adams and Gomes were exploiting their contacts with Labour politicians in order to generate a partisan controversy in British politics.[183] There were marked similarities between the case for the perpetuation of the federation which Adams adumbrated and the criticisms made of government policy in the House of Commons. In a radio address delivered just before he travelled to London, Adams offered an overly optimistic but pointed assessment: 'it is inconceivable that the British would accept the undemocratic nature of the Central African Federation should be given the full backing of Her Majesty's Government while the fully representative West Indian Federation is savaged to the irremediable loss of our people.' Adams took up the matter of the retrogressive nature of the new policy in a final plea to Maudling on 12 March. He complained that the Enabling Bill was 'a retrograde step in the history of the West Indies and will give sweeping powers to Her Majesty to introduce whatever kind of legislation she thinks fit in the West Indies.' It was the basis for 'an absolutely reactionary type of Crown Colony government.'[184] Similar issues were raised by Labour's spokesman on colonial affairs, George Thomson. He claimed it was 'shabby' to introduce the Enabling Bill while the federal delegation was left waiting for an audience with the Colonial Secretary. Like Adams he noted the parallels with the Central African Federation: 'Is it conceivable that had Dr Banda wanted to secede from the Central African Federation the same treatment would have been accorded to Sir Roy Welensky?' On 26 March another Labour frontbencher, Denis Healey, took up both the issue of the discourtesy shown to Adams during his visit and the broader political issues. On the former he secured an apology from Maudling regarding the cold-shouldering of the federal delegation; on the latter Healey attended again to the contrast between British policy towards the Central African Federation, where secessionism was being resisted, and the government's unwillingness to support the integrationist case in the Caribbean. He expressed in more moderate tones the anger of the federal leaders about the terms of a bill which effectively returned them 'to some sort of Crown Colony status.'[185] On this point there was no apology. Colonial Office policy was the logical conclusion of the uncompromising line they decided to take with the smaller territories after the Jamaican vote. The federation was formally dissolved on 23 May 1962.

From a strategic perspective the decision to expedite the dissolution of the federation was a success despite the outbreak of tactical hiccoughs following Maudling's 6 February statement. The unit governments, with whom the British would now deal, had frequently been at loggerheads with the federal executive and offered Adams's ministers no support. For the two largest units, Jamaica and Trinidad, the disbanding of the federation was a liberation in the sense that it facilitated early independence. The disputes which accompanied the final negotiations were of a minor character compared to the tumultuous rows of the previous four years. Given the fiercely partisan nature of Jamaican party politics it was predictable that the most contested aspect of the draft constitution concerned provisions to prevent electoral fraud, which the JLP initially regarded as insufficiently rigorous. During the course of a surprisingly equitable constitutional conference in London in February 1962 a revised formula was agreed to which satisfied both parties.[186] After the conference the British Cabinet endorsed 6 August as the date for independence.[187] Expectations that Manley would be the first Prime Minister of an independent Jamaica were confounded when the PNP lost the election of 10 April and Bustamante formed a new JLP government. British policymakers reflected on the result with equanimity. Although in the 1940s the British had feared Bustamante as a demagogue and a potential dictator he was now 78 and surrounded by business-orientated technocrats like Robert Lightbourne, Donald Sangster, Hugh Shearer and Edward Seaga, the last three of whom would each become Prime Minister. Blackburne went as far as to declare: 'They are a good lot – better in some ways than the last government but it remains to be seen how well Bustamante can lead them and make them into a team.'[188] In July the JLP administration negotiated a financial settlement which wrung from the Treasury a small amount of financial assistance in the form of unspent development funds, loans and grants.[189] Some residual resentment at the consequences of Jamaican secession still lingered. On returning to Jamaica, Foot was saddened by the insularity of local politics, which was evident in 'cheap scoffing at the small islands' and concluded, 'Jamaica had chosen a second best. It was a victory for reaction.'[190] For Jamaicans independence day was the culmination of an arduous journey during which the colonial power had played an obstructive rather than a facilitating role. Even a conservative politician such as Seaga recalled 'the raising of the Jamaican flag in slow tempo to the resounding crescendo of the Jamaican anthem was the emotional highlight of my life.'[191]

Trinidadian politicians were determined to keep pace with their Jamaican counterparts. From Williams's perspective, the British had already frustrated a first attempt to obtain independence on 22 April 1960 and 'we had had enough experience in four years of what was meant by just waiting on the British to make decisions for the West Indies.'[192] The requirement to hustle the British forward and his own concerns about the divisiveness of the 1961 elections caused Williams to adopt a relatively flexible position, even if he did not always adopt a lenitive tone, during the talks which took place in early 1962. When asking the Attorney-General, Ellis Clarke, to draft a constitution he urged: 'I want that Constitution. I want it right away. I want it yesterday.'[193]

However, he did amend Clarke's draft as a consequence of public consultations. During the independence conference which commenced on 29 May he initially resisted further changes proposed by the DLP but, when faced with a potential breakdown, Williams compromised. Maudling recalled that the negotiations were exceptionally difficult. He was alarmed that, in the absence of any agreement, there was 'the real danger of major racial tensions.'[194] However, after days of immobility Williams made a deal with Capildeo which met some of the key demands of the DLP, including additional guarantees of judicial independence and safeguards against electoral malpractice.[195] Even after the conference Trinidad's future relationship with Britain and with the small islands, particularly Grenada, was still not definitively resolved. Discussions with the Chief Minister, Herbert Blaize, about the possibility of Grenada forming part of a unitary state with Trinidad continued into the post-colonial era but eventually proved abortive.[196] Williams effectively abandoned attempts to gain substantial financial assistance from Britain but obtained assurances of continued representation during discussions of British plans to enter the Common Market. Progress was so smooth in the weeks following the London conference that Williams remarked to the latest Conservative Colonial Secretary, Duncan Sandys, on 11 July, 'that people were wondering whether Trinidad might get more attention by being more difficult.'[197] Most British policymakers regarded Williams in quite the opposite light: he was seen as complicated, prickly and persistent, but in ideological terms he was recognised to be conservative and pragmatic. It was difficult for the old imperial power to fault the values which Williams espoused in a speech to an Independence Youth Rally on 30 August 1962, the day before Trinidad gained its independence. He told his audience that as the first post-independence generation they must regard 'Discipline, Production, Tolerance' as their watchwords.[198] This ascetic, utilitarian agenda was a somewhat forbidding start to the new era in Trinidadian history but offered reassurance to British policymakers who were still listening out for sounds of disharmony.

Conclusion

Personal animosities played their part in the decline and fall of the federation. Although the British enjoyed anatomising the complicated rivalries between Adams, Manley and Williams and found the first to be a useful scapegoat, the contretemps between Beetham and Hailes demonstrated that metropolitan policymakers could be as quarrelsome as their Caribbean counterparts. As Hailes pointed out, his dispute with Beetham inflamed the extremely sensitive relations between the Trinidadian and Federal governments. But it was the ill feeling between the British and the West Indian parties which was of greatest significance in bringing about the demise of the federation and was symptomatic of wider conflicts of view. The most important of these was the nationalist belief that economic vulnerability and the exigencies of the Cold War would constrain the liberty they hoped to acquire at independence. On the question of Chaguaramas and the other American bases, the British were willing to tolerate Eric Williams's outspokenness and were not persuaded by Washington's caricature of the Trinidadian leader as a dangerous, anti-American demagogue. Although his barbs could be discomfiting, Williams was a familiar cultural figure for the British and was explicitly committed to regional integration and the propagation of Western economic and political models in the Anglophone Caribbean. The British were inclined to endure criticisms from Caribbean leaders as long as they did not appear to impinge on wider British interests. However, the comprehensive failure of the federal leaders to extract concessions on the linked issues of immigration and aid demonstrated that the ostensible British commitment to Caribbean integration had its limits. On the one hand, the British were concerned that, in the wake of the voyage of Caribbean migrants on the Empire Windrush, disorderliness would travel across the Atlantic with the new arrivals; on the other, they regarded the federation, and in particular a federation dominated by Jamaica and Manley, as a guarantor of regional order. Partly because they overestimated Manley's power to influence Jamaican and federal opinion, and partly because of Treasury frugality, they offered insufficient support to prevent the collapse of the federation. This contributed to the process of chaotic decolonisation in the Caribbean which they had hoped to avoid. For years British policymakers had been denigrating the capacities of the leaders of the small islands and British Guiana, but with the declaration of independence for Jamaica and Trinidad, they now had no alternative other than to devise new strategies for the remnants of empire in the Anglophone Caribbean left behind after the painful demise of the federation.

5
Order and Disorder between Dependence and Independence 1962–1969

As the imperial tide ebbed, the remnants of empire acquired greater prominence in British politics simply because the territories in the Anglophone Caribbean were one of the handful of items left on the colonial agenda. After Trinidad and Jamaica became independent events in the region began to receive more attention at the highest levels of the British government. The introduction of proportional representation in British Guiana, the establishment of an Eastern Caribbean federation, the financial scandals on Grenada and the existence of a separatist movement on the tiny island of Anguilla were all subjects of discussion, and of varying degrees of controversy, amongst Cabinet ministers during the 1960s. Although many of the preconceptions regarding the region, including assumptions about West Indian profligacy and captiousness, were held in common by British elites, divisions did emerge between activists and fatalists. The latter group were conscious of the constant misfiring which had accompanied British policymaking in the region and contended that its leaders ought to be allowed to make their own mistakes rather than have miscalculations forced on them by Whitehall. The activists believed that the moment before decolonisation was completed should be the period of maximum metropolitan vigilance and that the process ought to be directed by the colonial power up to its completion. These differences were evident in the arguments between Denis Healey and Michael Stewart in the case of the British intervention in Anguilla, but had even greater salience during the two years of Conservative government between 1962 and 1964 when the imperial minded activist Duncan Sandys replaced the fatalistic Reginald Maudling, as Colonial Secretary. Sandys promoted the notion of an Eastern Caribbean federation which, if it met British constitutional requirements, was expected to be an effective prophylactic against further instability on the Leewards and Windwards and sought to shield British Guiana from Moscow's overshadowing influence by covertly manipulating Guianese politics. Such activities vindicated the apprehensions of many nationalist politicians in the region, who were alert to the possibility that the terms set by the British for a final political separation could constrain their future as independent countries. Both Errol Barrow, who eventually abandoned the Eastern Caribbean federation in order to seek unilateral independence for Barbados, and Cheddi Jagan, who was the most prominent victim of the activist policy, looked back on the period as one of struggle to obtain true autonomy. Whatever the merits of their arguments, the conflict between metropolitan and peripheral actors remained a prominent feature of the last years of the British Empire.

Decolonisation deferred in British Guiana

Gloomy apprehensions about plans for a smooth transition to independence being unsettled by Cold War machinations were fulfilled in British Guiana. What was surprising and alarming for British policymakers was that the corrupting influence emanated from Washington rather than from Moscow. In contrast to the half-hearted efforts of the communist-dominated WFTU to organise leftist resistance to the British across their Caribbean empire between 1952 and 1954, the American trade union movement in the early 1960s, represented by the American Federation of Labour and the Congress of Industrial Organizations (AFL–CIO), organised a sustained and successful campaign of subversion inside British Guiana with the connivance of the Kennedy administration. In 1963 they sponsored a devastating general strike which sealed tight the racial divisions which had been festering since the multi-racial People's Progressive Party (PPP) had split eight years earlier. Many Colonial Office bureaucrats, British trade unionists and even ministers were initially aghast at American presumption but a faction of the Conservative Party, represented in the Cabinet by Sandys, sought to exploit American Cold War prejudices in order to pursue their own campaign against Cheddi Jagan. Although there is now a mature historiography dealing with this episode, the overwhelming focus on the motives of the Kennedy administration has tended to overshadow the contentious debate about the future of British Guiana within the British government.[1] The initial resistance in London to interference from Washington has been recognised but the role of Sandys' later independent initiatives, which included the deliberate sabotaging of the 1963 constitutional conference, the imposition of a new electoral system and the fostering of sectarian divisions within Guiana, all require further illumination.

The campaign against Jagan can be divided into three phases, each of which was marked by Anglo-American tensions. The first began with Jagan's re-election in August 1961 and was characterised by escalating dissatisfaction in the Kennedy administration with the PPP government's conduct; it climaxed in February 1962 when fires broke out across Georgetown during the course of CIA-sponsored protests against budgetary measures designed to raise revenue from the country's small middle class. In this period the British tolerated American intrusions but rebuffed proposals to unseat Jagan who, they insisted, was a more credible partner in the decolonisation process than the Kennedy administration's protégé, Forbes Burnham. The second phase began with British capitulation to Washington's demands: in September 1962 Macmillan accepted Kennedy's scheme to destabilise the PPP government by cultivating divisions amongst its leaders and supporting opposition parties. Despite the change in policy, British officials still resented the presumption of American agents operating in Guiana and, when the British refused to utilise the strikes of 1963 as a pretext to eject Jagan and restore direct rule, the Kennedy government accused the British of complacency. A new agreement in September 1963 ushered in a third phase which, in some respects, was characterised by a greater emphasis on British subterfuge than more direct American methods, as Sandys contrived a pseudo-constitutional strategy designed to defeat Jagan through the manipulation of the electoral system. During this period the Americans remained impatient to replace Jagan with Burnham but, whereas at the outset the British had doubted the prudence of such a policy, in this third phase the main disagreements concerned the tactics to be adopted to achieve this outcome.

The initial willingness of the British to defend Jagan from his critics inside the Kennedy administration stemmed from their own disappointment and frustration with Burnham. His later reputation has been tarnished by retrospective knowledge of the repressive policies Burnham pursued as Prime Minister of an independent Guyana after 1966. Years of election rigging, the suppression of opposition movements and the corruption of the nation's finances, all appeared to demonstrate the prescience of an alarmist pamphlet, *Beware My Brother Forbes*, written by his sister, Jessie Burnham. Published as an item of PPP propaganda in 1964, it warned: 'His motto is the personal ends of power justify ANY means used to achieve them. His bible is *The Prince* by Machiavelli. And should he come to power we will be only pawns in his endless game of self-advancement.'[2] He was the clever son of Barbadian migrants to Guiana who won a scholarship to study in London where he gained a political education through his participation in the West Indian Students' Union. In 1953 Burnham was identified as the nearest equivalent to a Guianese Manley, capable of constructing an alliance between the middle classes and the workers which would steer the country to a safe, non-Marxist future. His pragmatism on economic issues was all the more pronounced in contradistinction to radicals like Janet Jagan and Sydney King. As Colin Palmer has noted, when his faction split from the PPP it appeared that the cause was political philosophy, rather than race: 'Burnham attracted the more ideologically conservative members of the PPP, a group consisting of both Indians and Africans. Jagan had the support of those who were identified as Marxists.'[3] Over time it became more difficult to discriminate in this way: in terms of mass support, it was evident at the 1957 elections that Burnham was reliant on the African-Guianese population of Georgetown. In the following decade he became more unscrupulous in cultivating this group in order to harry Jagan's PPP government. During the London constitutional conference in March 1960 the Colonial Office concluded that Jagan was the more sincere and Burnham the more duplicitous of the two dominant figures in Guianese politics.[4] This judgement was confirmed when the Governor, Ralph Grey, blamed Burnham rather than Jagan for the racial tensions which accompanied the elections of 1961.[5]

American policy plotted a reverse course to that of the British as they became increasingly enamoured of Burnham and ever more vituperative in their denunciations of Jagan. The State Department had been relatively inattentive to the events of 1953 but the thought of Jagan's return to power as a consequence of the 1957 elections prompted them to question whether the British were taking their Cold War duties in the region seriously. In July 1957, Grey's predecessor as Governor, Patrick Renison, attempted to reassure the State Department that most members of the PPP 'are not communists and do not have any understanding of communism.' He was confident that Cheddi Jagan could be either 'tamed' or, if necessary, in the last resort, 'hung'. American diplomats were unconvinced and, once Jagan had won the election, the Deputy Under-Secretary of State, Robert Murphy, told the British Ambassador to Washington, Harold Caccia, that 'certain Communists would build up Jagan and use British Guiana as a base for penetration of other areas.' From the American perspective an opportunity to bolster Burnham's position was missed when a number of PPP members resigned from the government in 1959. At this point the American Consul-General complained that the Colonial Office were sustaining the Jagan government and 'will go to considerable lengths to avoid making a martyr of him.'[6] The Secretary of State in the new Kennedy administration, Dean Rusk, again raised American concerns about British Guiana in a meeting with the British Foreign Secretary, Alec Douglas-Home, in May 1961. Home insisted that there was no better alternative to Jagan, other than the incorporation of British Guiana into the West Indies federation.[7] Even at this late stage federalism was still seen as the most effective container for Caribbean radicalism. Grey believed 'that British Guiana will have a pretty sad future if it does not join the Federation'. However, he was discreet in promoting the idea on the assumption that any overt attempt at persuasion would be interpreted as colonial meddling and generate an adverse local reaction.[8] In the aftermath of the Jamaican referendum, the always distant likelihood of Guianese accession became entirely fanciful and the British were forced by American pressure to reconsider the policy of domesticating Jagan which they had pursued since the PPP election victory of 1957.

The period between Jagan's third electoral triumph in August 1961 and the February 1962 budget witnessed American policy shift from a position of critical dissent from British policy to one of active determination to remove the PPP from power and replace them with a People's National Congress (PNC)-dominated government led by Burnham. Just before the polls opened, after learning of Colonial Office predictions that Jagan's PPP would win an overall majority with between 20 and 22 seats, Rusk wrote to Home explaining that, given the precedent established by Castro, they were unwilling to tolerate Jagan any longer. Another electoral victory for his party, Rusk warned 'would cause us acute embarrassments with inevitable irritations to Anglo-American relations.' For a brief period, immediately after Jagan's re-election the administration seemed willing to consider sympathetically the reassurances offered by the Parliamentary Under-Secretary at the Colonial Office, Hugh Fraser, in London and Grey in Georgetown and 'to accept as a working premise the British thesis that we should try to "educate" Cheddi Jagan.'[9] Between 11 and 16 September 1961 a State Department delegation attended talks in London which produced an odd compromise. On the one hand, the two parties agreed to 'a wholehearted across the board effort to cooperate with the newly elected administration headed by Jagan'; on the other, a secret programme was initiated to isolate the Guianese left and cultivate politicians who could form an 'alternative leadership', should the policy of collaboration with Jagan fail. In a letter to Macmillan, the Colonial Secretary, Macleod, portrayed this as 'a big advance' in American thinking on British Guiana but was obliged to record that 'its positive elements of friendliness and economic aid will only be implemented subject to our acceptance of their covert programme.'[10] Although much of the official record has been released only with redactions, the contents of Macleod's letter, which essentially recommended acquiescence to American demands, and the subsequent course of events indicate that the Macmillan government reluctantly authorised the commencement of CIA subterfuge in British Guiana at this point.

The most striking indication that the American government was willing to reassess its policy towards the PPP in return for a greater influence over political developments inside British Guiana was Kennedy's offer to meet Jagan in October. Jagan was one of the most ambitious of the Caribbean leaders in his vision of what a post-colonial society could achieve and hoped that the Americans would offer economic assistance which, in the absence of local capital, was essential in order to improve the country's infrastructure and diversify production. The Washington visit proved disillusioning for both parties: the slight tilt in American perceptions towards a more generous view of Jagan was reversed and the prospects of a major American aid programme for Guiana receded into the unforeseeable future. Officials at the British embassy in Washington had such low expectations of the encounter that they were able to declare that the outcome was 'as good as we or Jagan had reason to hope for.' However, they also admitted that Jagan was 'deeply suspicious of US sincerity believing he was once more getting the run around' and that the visit had ended with the Guianese leader telling American officials what he thought of the miserly policies of the administration.[11] It was the disobliging remarks which Jagan made about the Cold War during a sensationalist edition of *Meet the Press* which appear to have been a turning point in American attitudes. When Kennedy saw the broadcast, during which Jagan appeared to defend international communism, he immediately 'got upset about it' according to Under Secretary of State, George Ball. On 20 October, in a telephone conversation with Ball about Jagan, Kennedy recommended 'we ought to go cold with him'.[12] At their meeting four days later Kennedy was forced to defend his country's foreign policy record against Jagan's accusations that the United States persistently meddled in the affairs of the independent states of Latin America.[13] On Jagan's own account he went as far as to accuse Kennedy of overthrowing the short-lived Janio Quadros government in Brazil and of constraining the

actions of his successor, Joao Goulart.[14] After the meeting, the Deputy
Assistant Secretary of State for Inter-American Affairs, Richard Goodwin,
who had been in attendance, concluded 'there is a good chance that this
fellow is a communist' and suggested that 'we can drag our feet as much
as we want on actual implementation' of any economic aid programme.
The overt foot-dragging of his American interlocutors disabused Jagan
of any inclination he had ever possessed to accept reassurances about
Washington's goodwill. He returned to Georgetown disheartened and
embittered or as Ball succinctly put it, 'a very unhappy man'.[15]

Jagan's pessimism was justified by the extent of resistance inside
and outside the country to his efforts to alleviate British Guiana's economic dependency. The finances of the country were wholly reliant on
the overseas markets for bauxite and sugar, which generated employment in mines and on plantations but did not produce sufficient
revenue for investment in policies to relieve the chronic problems of
urban joblessness. Whereas Adams in Barbados and Manley in Jamaica
were able to attract international capital in order to address similar
problems, the Cold War hostility which was a product of Jagan's commitment to Marxism deterred overseas investors and necessitated new
measures to increase government income. He turned to the Cambridge
economist Nicholas Kaldor for assistance and on 31 January 1962 the
PPP government introduced a budget which reflected Kaldor's advice.[16]
The political orientation of the budget speech reflected the priority
which the nationalists gave to autonomy and stated that 'foreign aid
is no substitute for self determination either economic or political.'
The financial details included the introduction of a capital gains tax,
new property taxes and a tax on gifts, as well as compulsory savings
measures to prevent the outflow of capital.[17] Essentially, the Jagan government was turning to the country's small European-Guianese and
African-Guianese middle class as a source of revenue to rectify the
absence of external economic assistance or capital investment. There
was an immediate political backlash from these groups and growing
tensions in Georgetown culminated in an outbreak of mob violence
on 14 February. Grey, who had opposed the budgetary measures from
the outset, initially argued that Jagan should resign in order to forestall
the deployment of troops but, when a series of arson attacks two days
later threatened the destruction of the city, he relented and instructed
the Royal Hampshire regiment to defend key facilities.[18] The disturbances illustrated the fanaticism of Jagan's local opponents and raised
suspicions inside Guiana of CIA complicity. In the evidence it prepared for the international Commission of Enquiry which investigated

the disturbances, the PPP identified poverty, low wages and external manipulation as causal factors. Jagan argued that the withholding of American aid was part of a strategy designed to undermine the stability of his administration. PPP documents testified that 'interference of foreign interests in the internal politics of the country strengthened the opposition to the Government and encouraged the use of violence by groups which had planned to overthrow the democratically elected Government by force.'[19] Grey insisted that this draft submission be sanitised for international consumption and the passages referring to American-sponsored anti-PPP propaganda were removed.[20] Confirmation of CIA culpability was eventually provided by a *New York Times* investigation in 1994. William Howard McCabe, operating under the auspices of the AFL–CIO, was identified as an influential actor in directing and funding opposition activities. Stephen Rabe, who has offered the most detailed account of these events, concluded: 'the Kennedy administration would need the skills of a legendary lawyer like Clarence Darrow or F. Lee Bailey to explain away in a court of law the evidence that the Kennedy administration encouraged and financed the attacks on the Jagan government.'[21]

Alongside its covert campaign of destabilisation, the Kennedy administration made a diplomatic intervention to delay decolonisation. The President was irritated by the British decision to deploy troops because, as the State Department explained to the American Ambassador in London, 'it had effect of shoring up tottering Jagan regime.'[22] His attention now turned to London's willingness to expedite Guianese independence. Partly because they underestimated the deleterious impact of Jagan's Washington visit, British policymakers were still planning to hand over power to the PPP government later in 1962. At a meeting of the Colonial Policy Committee on 20 December 1961, Macleod's successor, Maudling, secured ministerial approval for an acceleration in constitutional advance with a view to meeting Jagan's proposal to obtain independence in May 1962. At this stage, British ministers proposed taking a robust line with Washington and argued that accelerating decolonisation by six months would not make a great deal of difference and that 'even if during that period the Americans' worst fears were substantiated, it would in any case not be within our power to hold British Guiana down by force.'[23] After the incendiarism of February 1962 this was precisely what the British were required to do for four years. Although the arsonists in Georgetown failed to topple the Guianese government, Jagan's opponents in Washington remained eager to disabuse the British of the notion that this would be the end of the matter. Rusk wrote to Home on 20 February to say 'it is not possible for us to put up with an independent British Guiana under Jagan' and instructed the British to organise new elections and to ensure a PPP defeat. Macmillan would eventually endorse exactly such a policy but at this stage he was shocked that Washington should order his government to switch to a strategy of 'pure Machiavellianism'. Home responded by criticising American policy as being a 'prime mover' behind the telescoping of the decolonisation process elsewhere and by suggesting that their anti-colonial prejudices had provided opportunities for communists around the world. It was, on Home's account, not possible to make a sudden exception for British Guiana because 'we cannot now go back on course we have set ourselves of bringing these dependent territories to self-government.'[24] The British government was cognisant of the American government's sponsorship of the Georgetown disturbances. They had licensed a CIA role in the country in September 1961 but only on condition that the Kennedy administration sought a rapprochement with Jagan. From the British perspective, only their half of the deal had been realised. In the aftermath of the disturbances one Colonial Office official noted that Washington had done nothing to help Jagan since September and that 'the Americans bear a load of responsibility for what has happened in British Guiana.'[25] Four years later Fraser recalled that the Macmillan government 'was finding the CIA was sort of trying to stir things up a bit...they wanted to see Jagan was discredited...it may have been that they wanted just to keep us with British rule there permanently.'[26]

British Guiana was becoming a conspicuous irritant in Anglo-American relations and during the next few months, it was discussed during Schlesinger's visit to London, Home and Rusk's meeting in Geneva and Fraser's trip to Washington. The effect of these conversations was a British decision to prolong the process of Guianese independence. Macleod and Maudling were extremely uncomplimentary about Jagan when they spoke to Kennedy's Special Assistant, Arthur Schlesinger, at the end of February; the former dismissed him as an LSE Marxist and the latter called him an 'utter fool & bloody bastard.' In deference to American sensitivities they indicated that independence could be delayed but, despite their reservations about Jagan, they suggested that Burnham's PNC was even more ill-prepared to run Guianese affairs.[27] In Geneva in March, Rusk restated the American position that 'the United States were really terrified of another Cuba on their continent.' Home responded by indicating that the British government preferred to consider the 'overt possibilities of delay' rather than to license any further covert action.[28] During his visit to Washington Fraser tried to persuade Kennedy that he was exaggerating the importance of a territory that was 'really nothing but a mudbank'. He implied that Burnham and the leader of the United Force (UF), Peter D'Aguiar, were responsible for racial tension and characterised Jagan as 'a nice man surrounded by mildly sinister characters some of whom were worst kind of anti-colonialist.'[29] Despite his contempt for the Guianese opposition, Fraser effectively conceded to the Americans that immediate independence was not practicable and that colonial control would continue until another election could be organised.[30] On 3 April 1962 Maudling notified his colleagues that 'it would be desirable to hold fresh elections in the Colony before it finally becomes independent.' This effectively reversed the decision to grant independence, made just four months earlier, but would, Maudling reported, 'be welcome to the Americans.'[31]

The next problem confronting the Anglo-American partners was that in any future poll, Jagan would be likely to repeat his triumphs of 1953, 1957 and 1961. To ensure that this did not happen, the Kennedy administration developed a Political Action Program for British Guiana. Although numerous redactions to the relevant documents have hindered efforts to establish precisely how Kennedy intended to ensure Jagan's defeat, the course of events and the broad strategy which the administration pursued can be detected. The programme comprised a series of measures to ensure Burnham's succession to the Guianese premiership. As early as May 1962, Ralph Dungan, Kennedy's Special Assistant, in response to an urgent appeal on behalf of Burnham by Senator Thomas Dodd, had offered the authoritative statement that future policy 'undoubtedly would have as an element the strengthening of the Burnham forces'.[32] The Political Action Program which was presented to the British Ambassador, David Ormsby-Gore, in July stated explicitly: 'The President has personally studied the problem and come to the conclusion that there is no alternative to developing a program to bring about a suitable coalition and to assure that Jagan does not win a new election.' This was to be accomplished through CIA support for the PNC and the encouragement of new Indian parties who would attract voters away from the PPP. There was unease amongst some members of the administration about this course, most notably from Schlesinger and National Security Advisor, McGeorge Bundy. The latter was convinced that 'Jagan will indeed go the way of Castro if he is not prevented' but was apprehensive about the proposed plan because 'it is unproven that CIA knows how to manipulate an election in British Guiana without a backfire.' Similarly, Schlesinger accepted 'the Burnham risk is less than the Jagan risk' but questioned whether the CIA operations could be organised in a way which 'will leave no visible traces'.[33]

American relentlessness on the subject of British Guiana effectively eroded British scruples on a subject where Macmillan decided that there was nothing very important at stake. The Prime Minister suggested in May 1962 that it would be beneficial to be 'cooperative and forthcoming' in response to American concerns about Guiana.[34] His appointment of Duncan Sandys as Maudling's successor two months later represented a concession to the old imperialist school in the Conservative Party. Sandys' desire to impart a Churchillian robustness to the defence of Britain's global interests extended to aping the wartime Prime Minister's tendency to dictate minutes at odd times during the middle of the night.[35] To the even greater dismay of his officials, Sandys evidently believed that Guiana was a corner of the world where Britain should flex its imperial muscles by ousting Jagan for a second time. In August 1962, he expressed the fear that Jagan would use the 'communist lever' and, in order to prevent this, made the bizarre suggestion that constitutional provision could be made to allow the United States to intervene in Guiana after the country had obtained independence. More consequential were his proposals to introduce a new electoral system which would replace traditional constituencies with a system of proportional representation.[36] Now that key members of the British government were in greater sympathy with American Cold War priorities, in September 1962 the British Ambassador David Ormsby-Gore finally brought forth Macmillan's secret answer to the question of what should be done about Jagan. The contemporary sensitivity, and the subsequent problems for historians in uncovering the full story, are evident from Bundy's message to Schlesinger that Kennedy wanted there to be no written record of Macmillan's response and that its contents should be withheld from the State Department. What is known is that the President regarded it as 'satisfactory'.[37] One detailed element of the programme which can be discerned is the encouragement that was given to potential PPP defectors. It was hoped that if his supporters in the Guianese legislature could be persuaded to abandon him, Jagan might be removed without the need for a further election. When Macmillan enquired about the status of the anti-Jagan programme in March 1963 Sandys reassured him: 'certain plans are being considered which might result in the defeat of the Jagan Government in the British Guiana Legislature. If this occurred, it would of course alter the whole situation.'[38]

The failure to secure enough defections from Jagan's party to bring about his downfall necessitated further temporising on the issue of independence; Fabian tactics were essential in order to give the Americans time to fortify the Guianese opposition. The constitutional conference which had been scheduled for early 1962 was constantly deferred and when it finally did meet in November 1962 it proved wholly inconclusive. Jagan believed that Guianese independence would be delayed for as long as Western policymakers reckoned their economic interests were endangered. After the conference he submitted a critique of Sandys' policy to Grey which amounted to an attack on the British failure to apply notions of government by consent to their colonial empire. He pointed out that recent events in Aden, where the inhabitants of the town had been forced into a federation with the states of the interior, and the evidence from recent Guianese history demonstrated that, even in its last throes, colonialism was anti-democratic. Following a decade of constitutional stagnation he rejected proposals for proportional representation and demanded a constitution as advanced as that of Jamaica or Trinidad, both of which had just become independent.[39] Grey was infuriated by what he regarded as Jagan's lack of realism and reported to the Colonial Office, 'the trouble with this chap is not that he is a Communist or Communist sympathiser etc. but that he just is not cut out to be a Premier or a Minister or anything else of a practical nature.'[40]

The air of jaded resignation in Grey's telegrams was replaced by alarm once it became evident that the PPP's attempt to enact a new Labour Relations Bill was likely to provoke even more turmoil than the budget controversy of the previous year. Burnham's supporters in the Guianese Trades Union Council (TUC) argued that the bill, which was introduced by the Jagan government on 16 April 1963, was designed to undermine the industrial relations supremacy of the Manpower Citizens Association (MPCA), whose rivals in the Guiana Agricultural Workers' Union (GAWU) were affiliated to the PPP. They responded with a series of stoppages which amounted to what has been described as the world's longest general strike.[41] The strike was accompanied by escalating racial violence between African-Guianese supporters of the PNC and MPCA and Indian-Guianese supporters of the PPP and GAWU. Despite continuing metropolitan frustration with Jagan, the colonial authorities in Georgetown were more critical of the inflammatory racial rhetoric employed by Burnham during the strike. As a consequence Anglo-American disagreements about the practicalities of removing Jagan persisted. Sandys initially speculated that the chaos which the strike was causing in Georgetown 'may have weakened Jagan's support significantly' and could therefore facilitate a new election which the PPP would lose. Once Grey disabused the Colonial Secretary of this idea by contrasting the professional competence of the PPP with the disarray inside the PNC, more radical ideas were aired.[42] For a brief moment it appeared that London would appease Washington by reimposing direct rule and arresting Jagan. In May Sandys suggested to the Cabinet that a state of emergency might have to be declared but Grey remained bitterly opposed to such a measure 'until the situation in British Guiana has grown very much worse.'[43] Sandys contented himself with making provisional plans for the suspension of the constitution, while finalising arrangements for a new electoral system which would deny Jagan yet another election victory at some future date.

Whilst Sandys pondered how to bring his new activist strategy to fruition, the differences between the British and American attitudes to the strike on the ground in Georgetown became more pronounced. Grey declared his determination to persist with the plan which had been agreed after the 1961 election 'to make the best of Jagan.'[44] His tolerance of the PPP, at a time when Jagan was attempting to mitigate the effects of the strike by importing oil and flour from the Soviet Union, angered American officials who were covertly backing the strikers. The Consul-General, Melby, warned just before the outbreak of industrial hostilities, that further delay would only make it more difficult to get rid of Jagan and by June was in despair that, despite the escalating chaos in British Guiana, British officials had 'acted thus far only to prop up Jagan which [is] neither short term or [sic] long term answer.'[45] The direction and funding of the strike was at least partly in the hands of the AFL–CIO acting through intermediaries such as McCabe, who had also played a role in the 1962 budget protests and Gene Meakins of the American Newspaper Guild.[46] By contrast, the British TUC was enlisted in an attempt to reconcile Jagan's government and the dissident Guianese unions. Although the British left had demonstrated its Cold War credentials and lack of sympathy for the PPP in 1953, the political nature of the 1963 strike offended the conservative traditions of British unionism. After initially sympathising with the MPCA, the British TUC recognised that their Guianese counterparts were engaged in an attempt to destabilise the government in collaboration with the Americans and Burnham. Their representative, Walter Hood, began by espousing fraternal solidarity with the strikers' cause and in May 1963 solicited an additional £ 1,000 for their relief fund.[47] As he saw himself increasingly marginalised by American unionists and witnessed the extent of the disorder he became more sceptical and complained: 'I keep on arguing that it is not our job...to get rid of the Government...there are many who look on this now as a Jagan must go movement...there is no doubt in my mind that racism is well on the surface.' Robert Willis of the London Typographical Society, who was despatched by the TUC to mediate, was even more critical of the strikers and as a consequence secured the enmity of Burnham. He was perturbed when the Guianese TUC refused to end their action even after Jagan effectively abandoned the controversial industrial relations legislation. Having finally secured an agreement, he reported that the Guianese unions 'were not so much concerned with settling the strike as with getting rid of Dr Jagan and they were obviously expecting the suspension of the constitution.'[48] When Willis was congratulated by the Conservative Minister of State, Nigel Fisher, for resolving the strike, he went as far as to recommend additional economic assistance to the PPP government; Fisher responded that this would give an 'unfair advantage' to Jagan.[49]

Back in Washington, the Kennedy administration was dismayed by British unwillingness to utilise industrial conflict as a pretext to impose direct rule. The meliorist behaviour of Grey and the British TUC seemed like a betrayal of the 'satisfactory' response offered by Macmillan in September 1962. Sandys' criticism of the strike as 'a political action' in Parliament on 18 June 1963 particularly rankled and was said to represent 'the unwillingness of the UK to cope with the Jagan government.'[50] Rusk complained that the British government had disavowed their promises to 'take effective action to remove Jagan' and informed the American embassy in London that the State Department would not accept a policy of early independence, 'leaving the mess on our doorstep.' Yet another round of Anglo-American consultations were undertaken which reaffirmed the goal of defeating Jagan. At Washington's insistence Guianese affairs were the principal subject when Kennedy met Macmillan at the end of June. During the discussions Kennedy was emphatic that the PPP would turn Guiana into a Communist state and urged Macmillan to either impose direct rule or ensure that Jagan was replaced by a coalition between Burnham's PNC and Peter D'Augiar's UF, which was the party of European-Guianese business interests. Sandys responded by predicting that, if there was an early election under the current system, Jagan would win again. He also adverted to the pseudo-constitutional solution he had mentioned to Macmillan in March by specifically suggesting that 'we ought to make a really effective effort to get the two members of the PPP to cross the aisle...this meant that we would have to increase the bribe.'[51] British policymakers preferred to suborn members of the Legislative Council as a means of bringing about Jagan's downfall, rather than resort direct rule, which was Washington's favoured solution. Over the next few months a new strategy was formulated which combined elements of American and British tactics. On 19 September 1963 Kennedy outlined to Macmillan a plan for 'a series of moves in September or October [which] would result in the removal of the Jagan government.' Covert elements of the programme included American action 'to steer Forbes Burnham and Peter D'Aguiar on the right path, creating and launching an alternative East Indian party, and a real economic development programme.' The British were expected to suspend the constitution and introduce a new electoral system based on proportional representation. Hilton Poynton, the Permanent Under-Secretary at the Colonial Office, filled in the remaining details in a subsequent minute: a new constitutional conference would be held in October which would end in stalemate; this would provide a pretext for Sandys to scrap the constituency system which was a measure that they expected to be condemned by Jagan; PPP resistance to electoral reform would then present an opportunity for the British to impose direct rule; and further measures could then be taken to ensure the PPP was defeated in the next elections. The only potential danger, which Macmillan alluded to in his reply to Kennedy, was that Burnham and Jagan might reach a reconciliation despite Anglo-American effort to foster their antipathy. He admitted that they were reliant on American agents 'doing whatever they can to discourage any joint moves either for a coalition or for an outside enquiry, either of which might upset all our plans.'[52]

This Machiavellian scheme established the basis for one of the most extraordinary constitutional conferences in the history of British decolonisation. When the Guianese political parties met at Lancaster House on 22 October 1963 their ostensible purpose was to 'settle the unresolved constitutional issues', most notably whether to continue with the British system of single-member constituencies or implement proportional representation.[53] A compromise seemed necessary in order to end racial violence and establish the basis for early independence. However, the covert purpose of the British hosts and arbitrators was to ensure that the conference would fail. During a discussion with his officials on 7 October, Sandys stated: 'It was important to ensure (both at the conference and in the meantime) that Dr Jagan and Mr Burnham failed to agree either on the terms of reference or on the composition of any good offices commission.' As a guarantee that Burnham made no concessions to Jagan the Colonial Office was ordered to ensure 'that there was someone at the conference to advise Mr Burnham generally.' Once the conference was suspended, the British would exploit the chaotic situation in British Guiana to justify the suspension of the constitution and the imposition of proportional representation which would guarantee an electoral defeat for the PPP.[54] In the event, it was only the surprisingly muted reaction of Jagan to these manoeuvres which robbed the British of the opportunity to remove his government. The expected pretext never arose because on 25 October, having agreed on nothing else, Jagan consented to join with Burnham and D'Aguiar in submitting all the issues in dispute to the Colonial Office. Each party promised to abide by whatever solution was proposed by Sandys. Jagan's capitulation was partly an act of desperation, which he later justified on the basis that he believed that it was the only possible means of securing a final British commitment to set a date for independence.[55] Brindley Benn, who was part of the PPP delegation, claimed that Jagan naively believed reassurances that the Colonial Office would reject proportional representation as alien to British traditions. Even so, Benn thought, on the occasion of his submission, Jagan's demeanour reminded him of 'when you have a bad school report and you are carrying it to show your father.'[56] From the Anglo-American point of view Jagan's unexpected capitulation facilitated the imposition of a new voting system which would favour a coalition between the PNC and UF but it also made the resort to direct rule impractical. Although he had unknowingly circumvented plans to remove his government, Jagan's naivety was exposed by Sandys' announcement on 31 October that Guiana would adopt the Israeli electoral model, which was based on strict proportionality, rather than the mixed German model. Even Burnham later admitted that he would have accepted the German system and accused the Colonial Office of 'really rubbing Dr Jagan's nose in the sand unnecessarily.' On a separate occasion, Burnham indicated that he partly understood that Jagan's reasoning proceeded from a sense of vulnerability: 'one of the reasons for Jagan's signing was that he could not exercise power in a hostile Georgetown which I controlled.'[57]

The rigid proportionality of the Israeli system, which effectively transformed the whole country into a single constituency, was important to Sandys because it ensured greater representation for small parties. The largest of the smaller parties, the UF, was the most hostile to Jagan's regime and was certain to increase its representation under the new dispensation. Despite an almost complete lack of sympathy between Burnham and D'Aguiar, their joint opposition to the PPP was regarded as sufficient basis for the formation of a post-election coalition. But Anglo-American plotting went further than this and envisaged the establishment of new parties who would appeal to Indian-Guianese supporters of the PPP. If such parties could capture a handful of seats they would guarantee Jagan's defeat. One idea taken up by the British was to divide Muslim and Hindu voters and portray the PPP as the party of the latter; another was to encourage former members of the PPP who were discontented with Jagan's leadership to establish parties of their own. Hints from the archives indicate that elements of this strategy were being implemented before the London constitutional conference but most of the evidence proving Anglo-American culpability derives from a later period. On 19 December 1963 Sandys explained to Rusk that Jagan's acquiescence at the London conference had robbed the Colonial Office of any pretext for suspending the constitution. For the purposes of ensuring his electoral defeat, it was best that Jagan stay in office and suffer the economic consequences of a lack of external financial assistance. In the interim British and American agencies would ensure 'everything should be done between now and the elections to encourage the formation of new parties.' There followed some discussion of potential leaders. Scepticism was expressed about the capacities of Balram Singh Rai, who had been expelled from the PPP in 1962 and was mentioned by Rusk as a potential alternative to Jagan. Sandys concluded the meeting by stating 'everything had to be subordinate to the aim of securing Dr Jagan's removal from office through the new elections. To do this one might have to put up with a number of things which one didn't like.' The kind of 'things' envisaged are evident from a short note of a meeting which Sandys held with his officials on 25 February 1964 which illustrates British efforts to encourage confessional divisions. Sandys asked 'what progress had been made in encouraging alternative parties to form.' His officials reported a distinct lack of success but noted that Hussein Ghanie was planning to establish a sectarian party which would become the Guianese United Muslim Party (GUMP). Sandys ordered 'that financial encouragement should be given to Mr Ghanie and no questions asked.'[58]

In Georgetown, the new Governor Richard Luyt utilised the constitutional device of last resort, the issuing of Orders in Council by the British sovereign, to accrue ever greater powers. As a consequence, Jagan was once more effectively an opposition figure campaigning against the implementation of proportional representation by the British colonial authorities. In February 1964 the GAWU launched a strike whose ostensible aim was to obtain recognition from the sugar producers but the issue of conditions on the estates was submerged under the wider political struggle. As Seecharan later commented in his analysis of the action: 'the recognition issue, by 1964, had become the arena for Jagan's anti-PR campaign.'[59] Under the influence of the two rival political parties, the PPP and the PNC, the question of what the most appropriate electoral system was for the country became a pretext for racial violence. Jagan conducted a last counter-offensive against what he regarded as an ersatz programme of independence, which would secure constitutional autonomy but hand control of Guiana over to a Burnham government that would run the country in the interests of American, Canadian and British commercial investors. In one of his final meetings with Grey, who was recalled because of his anger at the way that the covert American alliance between Burnham and the CIA had stoked racial tension, Jagan argued that the country was effectively being governed in the interests of overseas capital. In his first meeting with Luyt he predicted that any attempt to end the violence through the formation of a government of national reconciliation between the PPP and PNC would be vetoed by Washington.[60]

The situation was not quite as clear-cut as Jagan believed: despite the implementation by the Anglo-American partners of a medium-term plan to defeat the PPP government, some British officials were willing to consider a potential grand coalition between Jagan and Burnham. Having long feared that decolonisation in the Anglophone Caribbean would be accompanied by disorder, the Colonial Office remained uneasy about the longstanding American policy of cultivating political stalemate and social unrest. On 25 May 1964, the Indian-Guianese inhabitants of Wismar, who formed a minority of the population in the vicinity of the bauxite mines at McKenzie, were attacked, apparently by African-Guianese workers. On 6 July approximately 40 people were killed when a boat travelling along the Demerara River to Wismar was blown up. Most of the crew and passengers were African-Guianese. In the days that followed five Indian-Guianese residents were murdered in McKenzie. At the end of the month the PPP's headquarters in Georgetown was bombed.[61] Luyt reported: 'The inter-race hatred and fear are quite frightful – worse than anything I saw in Africa.'[62] The extent of the violence provided a justification for further restraints on the PPP government. On 13 June Luyt assumed new emergency powers and arrested the Deputy Prime Minister, Brindley Benn. However, these incidents also caused the British to reconsider their opposition to the formation of a coalition government prior to the election. Luyt hoped that power sharing by the two main parties might attenuate racial tension but the idea caused mystification in Washington and the Johnson administration opposed it. After initially showing some enthusiasm for the proposal, in July Burnham made clear that the PNC would not join any coalition with the PPP. Poynton recorded Colonial Office suspicions 'that Burnham was put up to this by the Americans though, of course, we cannot prove it.'[63]

In terms of domestic British politics Conservatives such as Edward Gardner shared the American view 'that to grant independence to a Communist Government was sheer madness.'[64] He told the Commons that it was a 'beneficial fact' that the PNC was almost certain to come to power under the new electoral system. The last hope for the PPP was that the Labour Party would reverse Sandys' policy after their expected victory in the imminent British election of 1964. The traditional lack of sympathy for the PPP in British labour circles manifested itself once more in the form of rows within the NEC about whether to oppose proposals for proportional representation.[65] As Conservative opinion rallied behind Sandys' activist policies, some Labour MPs cast aside doubts about Jagan, in order to attack the Conservative government's policy. On 27 April 1964 Arthur Bottomley proposed a motion to the Commons opposing the submission of the new electoral system for royal assent. He noted that the only Commonwealth countries with a system of proportional representation were Malta and Australia and neither of them had the inflexible Israeli version imposed by Sandys.[66] However, the Labour Party's show of solidarity with the PPP was perfunctory. Even though Jennie Lee and Fenner Brockway offered support for his motion, Bottomley withdrew it without forcing a division.[67] Janet Jagan was pleased at the evidence of some resistance from the Opposition and concluded that a Labour government would rather 'get a proper solution for our country than tamely follow the Conservatives.'[68] Her confidence proved entirely misplaced. Christopher Mayhew informed the State Department that there was a conflict between Bottomley's critical group and the shadow Foreign Secretary, Patrick Gordon Walker, who 'would be inclined to implement current British policy'. Gordon Walker offered his own assurance that any future Labour government would go no further than considering alternative, less crude versions of proportional representation. He doubted Jagan was the menace which the American administration imagined him to be, but indicated that Labour would not object 'if a way could be found for the US to put its troops into BG.'[69] Given the tepid support for Jagan offered even by the Bottomley

group and the tenacious Atlanticism of Gordon Walker, it was predictable that the Labour government would not abjure Anglo-American
plans to ensure the electoral defeat of the PPP. Wilson met Jagan on
29 October, two weeks after Labour's victory at the polls, and explained
that, although they might have made some changes had they come
to power in June, 'it was now too late and HMG saw no alternative
but to let the elections go forward.' Faced with Jagan's predictions that
Burnham would establish a right-wing dictatorship, Wilson attempted
to offer assurances that Labour would not offer independence to any
government which did not have broad support from both Indian- and
African-Guianese.[70]

Any hopes that the new Labour government might revive the idea
of a PNC–PPP coalition after the Guianese elections in December were
unrealistic: the whole of Anglo-American planning was predicated on
the notion of a post-election PNC–UF coalition and Washington had no
intention of allowing backsliding. During preparations for his impending first visit to Washington, Wilson initially expressed the view that
a Jagan-Burnham coalition 'was the prerequisite for stability in British
Guiana.'[71] He was soon disabused of the idea that the American administration would tolerate the idea of bringing Jagan back into government
when three years of planning to get him out were about to be consum-
mated. In briefing Johnson for his meeting with Wilson the day before
the Guianese elections, George Ball, who had observed the evolution
of policy since the first days of the Kennedy administration, noted that
they offered 'the prospect of replacing the Jagan government with a
non-communist coalition government with which we can cooperate.'
He recommended that Wilson should be told that the US would refuse
to offer economic assistance if Jagan had any place in the next government. Neither Wilson nor Johnson appears to have been eager to
discuss potential differences over Guiana at their first meeting and their
advisers exchanged well-established views: the British again stressed that
the Americans had too favourable an opinion of Burnham and the
Americans reiterated their fears of a communist Guiana.[72] Had Jagan
achieved an electoral miracle, a crisis would have ensued which might
have required the attention of Johnson and Wilson but, although he
did come perilously close to winning an outright majority with over
45% of the vote, the PNC and the UF won a sufficient number of seats
to form a coalition government. One notable aspect of the results was
that Sandys' diligent cultivation of new parties proved fruitless: the Justice Party and the GUMP did not dent support for Jagan and the PPP
amongst Indian-Guianese voters.[73]

The inability of the PPP to secure more than 50% of the vote in the Guianese elections of December 1964 signalled the end of the most ambitious attempt undertaken by a Caribbean leader to challenge the concept of independence propagated by the British. While Williams and Manley quarrelled with London on constitutional issues, their economic and social programmes were approved by the metropolitan authorities. Trade union leaders, such as Bustamante in Jamaica and Butler in Trinidad, aroused British distaste for the demotic character of Caribbean politics but their ideological position was essentially conservative and never went beyond demands for incremental improvements in workers' conditions. Jagan, by contrast, sought to mobilise urban and rural workers behind a programme which challenged the control of the economy by overseas business, including American and Canadian bauxite companies and British sugar interests. The shock to British sensibilities administered by the propagation of such a programme led to Jagan's dismissal in 1953. By 1961 there was some confidence in the Colonial Office that the PPP had been domesticated but once it became evident that Washington was prepared to cause chaos inside the country rather than witness a transfer of power to Jagan, the British were forced to reassess their view of Forbes Burnham. The improvement in Jagan's reputation amongst metropolitan policymakers had been mirrored by a decline in Burnham's but the decision to overthrow the PPP government required some rehabilitation in the image of the PNC leader. After the 1964 election Wilson's government tried to persuade themselves and the international community that Burnham would be a moderate and competent leader of an independent Guyana.

One aspect of this rehabilitation was to further denigrate Jagan and his liberationist ideas and contrast them with Burnham's supposed pragmatism. This approach was facilitated by Jagan's bitterness at what he interpreted as yet another betrayal which led him to adopt a policy of unyielding non-cooperation either with Burnham or the new Colonial Secretary, Anthony Greenwood. After the election, PPP leaders seemed resigned to defeat and Luyt was now able to dismiss Jagan as being 'just like another scrawny little Indian'.[74] Although more moderate in his language, Greenwood complained that Jagan 'constantly harps on the past and on the injustice which he feels himself to have been subject.' In tactical terms, this oppositionism proved advantageous for Burnham. After meeting the local leaders during his trip to the country in March 1965, Greenwood recommended a constitutional conference to arrange the terms of Guianese independence before the end of the year. This harmonised with the views of Luyt who suggested: 'It may be that the time has come not to link internal peace and independence as closely as we have perhaps done in earlier thinking.'[75] Even if this principle was to be abandoned in practice, it was still necessary to accommodate Wilson's previous assurances that Guianese independence would not be granted before progress was made in reconciling the country's racial groups. The tangible element of the British solution was an investigation by the International Commission of Jurists (ICJ), whilst the intangible element consisted of a new interpretation of Burnham's political character which emphasised previously unnoticed elements of discretion. There was some conflict between these two aspects of British strategy. The notion of an ICJ mission to the region was introduced by the Colonial Office to pacify critics in Whitehall and Westminster who resisted Luyt's effort to abandon the linkage between order and independence and wanted Burnham's government to serve a longer apprenticeship under colonial supervision. At the OPD meeting which approved the accelerated programme of independence, Wilson insisted that an ICJ report should be a precondition for a Guianese independence conference.[76] Burnham was eager to expedite the process of decolonisation and interpreted the proposed ICJ investigation as evidence of British prevarication. On 1 June 1965 he told Luyt that the question of the racial imbalance in the police force and other public services was 'an unjustifiable red herring' which the Labour Party had devised to appease its internal critics. He threatened to resign if preparations for an ICJ investigation caused the putative independence conference to be delayed beyond the end of 1965. On the same day, Wilson told the Commons that his government would hold a conference 'as early as practicable' and that he would be disappointed if it did not occur before the start of 1966.[77] This pacified Burnham in the short term and although further squabbling ensued over the precise date, the UF and PNC delegates finally met in London on 2 November 1965. The PPP boycott of the meeting ensured that it was a relatively temperate affair. Burnham agreed to implement the proposals of the ICJ report, which recommended measures to ensure a more balanced representation of Indian- and African-Guianese in public life, in return for a guarantee of independence in 1966.[78]

Despite Burnham's combative approach during the final constitutional negotiations, British and American policymakers felt obligated to express greater optimism about his capacities once independence became imminent. On his visit to Washington in October 1965 Greenwood told a receptive audience of State Department officials that 'he thought Burnham had done very well during the last year all things considered. He hoped that once the United Kingdom could no longer be used as a whipping boy the Africans and Indians would see the necessity of working together'.[79] Burnham's position was further strengthened by additional economic assistance from the US which had been denied to Jagan. The American Consul in Georgetown declared: 'The United States has probably been the greatest single factor in making Burnham successful ... continued US influence and manipulation will be required, although it will probably have to be even more skilful once the Burnham administration is sovereign.'[80] For British policymakers, Guyanese independence on 26 May 1966 marked the end of a decolonisation episode which had caused greater angst than any other in the Anglophone Caribbean. They remained uncertain about the outcome of their machinations. The Joint Intelligence Committee (JIC) provided a mixed view of the likely future of the country, as exemplified by their suggestion that Burnham was 'determined to remain in power at all costs but he will try to do so by constitutional means.' The continuation of a British military presence was described as 'a stabilising influence'. In retrospect the least prescient aspect of the report was its assertion that Burnham was an 'anti-Communist' who would ensure that Guiana would 'lean towards the West.' The only caveat which was entered alongside this judgement related back to Grey's old reports about Burnham's racial sensitivities; the JIC considered that he was 'essentially a nationalist and to some extent anti-white and so is likely to resist United States domination.'[81] In the first decade of independence Burnham would resist American domination to the extent of declaring Guyana a Cooperative Republic, nationalising those industries previously under the control of overseas capital and establishing a friendly relationship with Castro. It was Burnham rather than Jagan who declared: 'I personally think we have a lot of things to learn from Cuba, especially how she has organised her educational system and work and study.'[82] For the Guyanese, the 24 years of PNC government after the United Force was ejected from the coalition in 1968 were marked by continuing racial antagonisms as well as authoritarianism and cronyism. In retrospect it is clear that the British assessment of 1961 that Jagan would prove a better partner in the post-independence period than Burnham was almost certainly correct. The revision of policy undertaken by Sandys and Macmillan and then implemented by Wilson and Greenwood was a failure in its own terms of keeping communism out of South America; and the manipulation of electoral politics and the stimulus given to racial grievances by American and British policymakers mark Guiana out as an exceptional case in the history of the end of Britain's Caribbean empire. The natural proclivity for an orderly transfer of power fell prey to the dictates of the Cold War and, despite the feigned optimism of 1966, under Burnham's leadership Guyana became a troubled post-colonial state.

The Eastern Caribbean federation and Barbadian independence

By the time the saga of Caribbean federalism finally ended, the young politicians who had attended the Kingston and Montego Bay conferences in 1947 had become middle-aged, and the middle-aged politicians had grown old. Although some secondary accounts of events in the region abandon the narrative at the point in 1962 when Jamaica and Trinidad obtained independence, discussions of an Eastern Caribbean federation continued until 1965.[83] The tendency to omit any detailed consideration of the last three years of negotiation is justified on the grounds that ongoing talks about integration amongst the Eastern Caribbean islands had very little consequence; that many of the themes of the period, including most obviously the various rows over the proposed distribution of power between federal centre and unit governments, were continuous in a mundane way with what had gone before; and that the territories involved had much less influence over regional affairs than the larger islands. Nevertheless, the story is incomplete without an account of the demise of plans for a Federation of the Little Eight, the Little Seven, without Grenada, or even the Little Six, without Antigua. Events after 1962 further illuminate aspects of British policy and, in particular, their obsession with 'small island syndrome', the symptoms of which supposedly included financial recklessness, political demagoguery and vulnerability to foreign infections. In addition it is impossible to understand the manner in which Barbados moved directly to independence and the small states travelled indirectly to the same destination via Associated Statehood, without recognising that both these journeys were undertaken as alternatives to the establishment of an Eastern Caribbean federation.

The only comprehensive study of the end of empire in the smaller states of the Eastern Caribbean has argued that the process was best understood in terms of a transatlantic triangle drawn between the region, the United States and Britain. On Cox-Alomar's account the Lesser Antilles were 'an uneasy buffer zone between the British and American empires.'[84] As their actions in British Guiana amply illustrated, Washington was determined to prevent any repetition of events in Cuba in the Anglophone Caribbean and expected the British to take the necessary prophylactic action. In contrast to the Guianese case, however, the low-level nudges from Washington regarding potential security issues in the Leewards or Windwards were supererogatory because officials in London remained constantly alive to the slightest evidence of potential instability in those territories which had been regarded as a source of imperial disorder since the outbreak of labour disturbances on St Kitts in 1935. Following Jamaican secession in 1961, the Colonial Office pursued a punitive policy against the governments of the small islands who, they estimated, had been given too much licence because of the apparent imminence of independence inside a federation controlled by Jamaica and Trinidad. At the outset of the Little Eight negotiations in February 1962 British policymakers insisted that local politicians had only two choices: the continuation and even augmentation of British colonial control or incorporation into a federation with a strong central government capable of responsible supervision of the units. In his initial response to the first meeting of the leaders of Barbados, the Leewards and the Windwards, Maudling admitted that he was taking 'a pretty strict and austere view on the conditions which would need to be satisfied especially before a Federation of the Eight could become independent.' The numerous criteria which needed to be met included a general sense of unity and effective administration but more specifically federal control of economic development and responsibility for law and order.[85]

In addition to an institutional framework, the British required a reliable collaborator who they thought capable of steering the federation in the direction of fiscal rectitude and sound administration. The leader of the Democratic Labour Party (DLP) in Barbados, Errol Barrow, initially appeared to meet this specification. Barrow assumed the role previously enacted by Manley: he was portrayed as the resolute and competent politician against whom the incapacities of the small island politicians could be measured. Hugh Fraser described him as 'outstanding among West Indian politicians. He is both a man of strength and a fixer.' Local Colonial Office officials, such as the Administrator of Antigua, Ian Turbott, were also impressed, and assessed him to be 'head and shoulders above all the other "Little Eight" leaders' and 'the only real hope for the future of the area.'[86] Barrow was the son of a radical Anglican priest who had been attracted to both trade unionism and the black empowerment philosophy of Marcus Garvey. Young Barrow was taken to see Garvey by his father and he later recalled: 'I will never forget that meeting because that was when I heard Garvey say: "The trouble with the black man is that he goes to bed too early and he wakes up too late.'"[87] This was precisely the sort of assiduous black consciousness with which the British could work and Barrow's industriousness was regarded as a welcome alternative to the alleged indolence of Grantley Adams. Like Manley, Barrow's mature ideological orientation was a recognisable form of Fabian socialism.[88] Despite all this, he never generated the same degree of personal affection amongst British policymakers as the Jamaican leader. During the three years of negotiations about the Eastern Caribbean federation, relations deteriorated as Barrow's defence of Barbadian interests was identified by the Colonial Office, and in particular by the official responsible for umpiring the negotiations, John Stow, as a key reason for its declining prospects.

Barrow became Chief Minister of Barbados as a result of the DLP election victory of 1961. In the aftermath of the Jamaican referendum, he disparaged the efforts of his old rival, Grantley Adams, to save the existing federation; his alternative policy of bringing together the leaders of Barbados, the Leewards and the Windwards as a Little Eight grouping, who could create a new federation, appeared to the Colonial Office to have greater merit than the policy of trying to salvage the old constitution. The Barbadian proposals necessitated a rethinking of the balance of power between the federal centre and the units, to the advantage of the former. At the outset, Stow urged the metropolitan government to offer Barrow 'some encouragement'.[89] The notion of resuming federal negotiations was met with a degree of ambivalence in the metropolis but it had the support of three notable Conservative politicians: the outgoing High Commissioner and former Chief Whip, Lord Hailes, the Parliamentary Under-Secretary at the Colonial Office, Hugh Fraser, and even the former Prime Minister, Anthony Eden, who was a regular visitor to the Caribbean. They shared concerns about the potential for racial unrest on Trinidad which made the alternative policy of allowing Eric Williams to incorporate at least some of the Windwards and Leewards into a unitary state an unattractive proposition. Hailes argued that they should do nothing to encourage Williams's Trinidadian expansionism 'so long as there is a chance of forming a viable federation of the Eight, which seems to me now to offer the best chance of avoiding indefinite fragmentation in the Eastern Caribbean and of achieving political and economic stability.'[90] Although the Colonial Office expected opposition to this policy from the Commonwealth Relations Office and the Treasury, their proposals to endorse the idea of a federation of the Eight 'went through the CPC (as the Secretary of State put it) like a dose of salts.' The jovial Secretary of State was Maudling who acknowledged that yet more federal negotiations might 'involve the retention of the present corrupt, inefficient and top heavy administrations in the smaller islands.' Despite this somewhat prejudicial assessment, he persuaded his peers to accept a federation of the Little Eight on the basis that the alternatives would either generate a larger financial burden on Britain, in the event of continued fragmentation, or would endanger the stability of the region, in the event of the islands' incorporation into Trinidad, where 'political conflict' along racial lines was expected.[91]

On 16 April 1962 Maudling informed the Commons that the establishment of a new federation in the Eastern Caribbean 'appears to offer the best solution to the problems of the area, provided that the Constitution of the Federation is such as to provide adequate powers to the Federal Government and to offer a reasonable prospect of economic and financial stability.'[92] The Chief Ministers of Barbados, the Leewards and the Windwards sketched out the general principles of federation during a conference in London the following month.[93] Having achieved substantial progress in the three months since the first Little Eight meeting in February, British officials hoped that, if the new constitutional scheme could be modified in the direction of greater centralisation, rapid progress would be possible, but instead the principles adumbrated at the London conference became the subject of prolonged wrangling between the island governments. Rather than attempt to describe the constantly moving constellation of forces between the eight islands across the three-year negotiation process, it is sufficient to offer a broad outline of three interconnected developments which preceded the collapse of the putative Eastern Caribbean federation in April 1965 and established the basis for unilateral independence for Barbados and Associated Statehood for the Windwards and Leewards. These were the gradual splintering away of some of the small islands from the Little Eight group, the burgeoning sense of dissatisfaction caused by British refusal to clarify the financial settlement and rising demands for unilateral independence on Barbados.

The attitudes of particular islands to federation often reflected their economic interests but it was possible to take different views as to what the interests of an individual territory might be at a time when the economic ground was shifting beneath the feet of policymakers. As a consequence the personal proclivities of political leaders were often decisive. For example, Herbert Blaize and Vere Bird in Grenada and Antigua could find plentiful economic justification for their instinctive anti-federalism. After his election victory in September 1962 Blaize abandoned the new federal project to pursue negotiations with Williams and thus reduced 'the Eight' to 'the Seven'. Trinidad had long been a favoured destination for Grenadian migrants. Following its independence, unitary statehood with Trinidad offered the prospect of employment opportunities for Grenadian labour at a time when the British were imposing immigration controls, a larger market for Grenadian producers and a way for nationalists to achieve early independence. On this basis, Blaize persuaded Grenadian voters to support his proposals for integration into Trinidad.[94] While the other Leeward and Windward islands continued their discussions on federation, the PNM government in Trinidad began ponderously to explore the implications of the effective annexation of Grenada. Williams's prevarication on the issue eroded Blaize's political position. By 1965 negotiations were suspended and Grenada had reached another constitutional dead end, although by a different route to that followed by the Little Seven.[95]

At the other end of the Lesser Antilles, the island of Antigua felt itself remote from Trinidad. Its government had been the most sympathetic to Jamaican reservations about a strong centralised federation. The local labour leader and Chief Minister, Vere Bird, had, unlike Bradshaw in St Kitts, chosen to remain on the island during the federal era and shared the cautious incrementalist approach of Manley. He recalled: 'They would have been better to leave a fair amount of autonomy with the territories and let the people see the benefits of federation and then from year to year strength would have been added and the federation would still be here today.'[96] When Bird made this argument at the Barbados Regional Council of Ministers (RCM) in May 1963 it essentially amounted to a recantation of the more integrationist principles agreed at the original meeting of the Little Eight in February 1962. Bird became the focus for the obloquy of both British administrators and the other Chief Ministers. After a bad-tempered altercation with Bird, the Colonial Office's Parliamentary Under-Secretary, Nigel Fisher, declared 'Argument with him is almost impossible since he is incapable of understanding what federation means.'[97] Such demonstrations of imperial disapproval did not endear the federal concept to Bird who was increasingly confident that Antigua had a greater capacity to stand on its own than any of the other islands because of the revenues generated by its pioneering role in developing the Caribbean tourist industry. After the fractious Barbados conference Bird's eagerness to pursue unilateral constitutional advance became increasingly evident and led to speculation that a Little Six might federate without Antigua. In December 1964 Bird authorised a tacit withdrawal from the federal negotiations and this decision was formalised four months later.[98] Antigua's final exit was influenced by events in St Lucia where John Compton's victory over George Charles in the elections of June 1964 increased Bird's sense of estrangement from the federal process. Whereas Charles had been sympathetic to Antigua's devolutionist stance, Compton was an ardent integrationist and following his appointment as Chief Minister demanded additional powers for the federal centre. When the island leaders gathered for the first and only time as the Little Six in April 1965, Compton denounced the decentralising principles underpinning the gimcrack federal constitution now on offer as unsatisfactory and absented himself from the final meetings.

Despite their differences over the balance of power between the federal centre and the island governments there was one thing which had the potential to unite the Chief Ministers of all the islands and would have greatly encouraged integration, namely an assurance from the metropolitan government that a federation would receive more financial assistance than a miscellany of individual island polities pursuing unilateral independence. However, the prospect of increasing aid to a Caribbean federation generated suspicion and dissension within the metropolitan government. For as long as federal plans remained imprecise, the Colonial Office and the Treasury were able to accommodate one another but the rapprochement between the two departments did not last. At the start of the Little Eight negotiations in April 1962 the Minister of State at the Colonial Office, Lord Perth, suggested that in order to obtain 'strong central powers for the Federation' it would be worth considering a bribe in the form of 'being apparently slightly more generous' over the issue of a British financial subsidy. The Treasury were already committed to providing unit governments with the unspent sums allocated to the now defunct federation for the period up to 1963 and were prepared to extend the same terms to any successor organisation which took up the reins of federal authority. They also adhered to the established notion of a tapering down of grants from that point and adopted Arthur Lewis's suggestion that this should occur at an annual rate of 15%. In order to mitigate the effects of this loss of income it was hoped that international funding for development programmes could be sustained at existing levels for five years after 1963.[99] This calculation was founded on the overly sanguine expectation that British obligations would be displaced by American and Canadian aid. All these conjectures had an air of unreality because Treasury policy was based on an assumption, which turned out to be warranted, that the Eastern Caribbean federation would remain unborn.

It was evident to all parties in the negotiations that the smaller islands in the Eastern Caribbean were vulnerable to fluctuations in commodity prices, that diversification, including the extension of economic activities into tourism and light industry, was a necessity and that capital was urgently required to develop the infrastructure of the region. Once the local leaders asked for specific sums to achieve these objectives, the *modus vivendi* between the Treasury and the Colonial Office collapsed with damaging consequences. A report by the economist, Carleen O'Loughlin, which suggested that the extent of assistance required amounted to £ 59.5 million over a decade, was unanimously endorsed by the RCM in September 1963.[100] The Treasury's horrified response to O'Loughlin's estimates of the requirements of 'the Eight' was continuous with the attitudes on display in reaction to Williams's assessment of the economic needs of 'the Ten' two years earlier. On 4 October William Armstrong, the Treasury's Permanent Secretary, told his opposite number in the Colonial Office, Hilton Poynton, that they 'were far from convinced the gains to be had from such a federation would justify any sizable expenditure of money in order to achieve it.' Armstrong's junior officials were even more strident in their condemnation of the O'Loughlin proposals.[101] The Colonial Office were ambivalent about the details of the programme but were irritated by the outright hostility of the Treasury. While refusing to endorse O'Loughlin's figures, officials believed that an increase in economic assistance was a price worth paying to achieve a viable federation. By contrast, Conservative ministers in the Colonial Office expressed weary indignation about requests emanating from the Caribbean. First, Fisher declared, 'I do not see why we should be blackmailed' and then Sandys asked, 'Why should we bribe these people into the federation? What does it matter to us?'[102]

The reasons why the Caribbean federation mattered in the metropolis had been evident since the 1940s: greater unity amongst the islands offered the best guarantee of the continuance of British cultural, economic and political influence after the inevitable process of decolonisation was complete. It was this assumption which underpinned Sandys' eventual endorsement of the Colonial Office's compromise proposal, under which the Treasury would be more generous and the island politicians would accept less. Sandys' natural combativeness soon manifested itself in sallies against both Treasury stinginess and small island cupidity; he succeeded only in making a minuscule dent in the Treasury's tough line on aid to the putative federation, while completely alienating Errol Barrow, whose influence over the future of the Eastern Caribbean would be decisive. Bureaucratic hostilities on the Whitehall front escalated to ministerial level when Sandys wrote to the Chief Secretary to the Treasury, John Boyd-Carpenter, on 26 November 1963 to respond to the objections which Armstrong had voiced to Poynton. Sandys' principal argument was that Barbados would not assume responsibility for the small islands unless they could be made less of an economic burden during the transitional period prior to independence. Boyd-Carpenter was unimpressed and declared 'it is not good enough for the S of S [Secretary of State] to seek to increase expenditure here unless he give it priority over other areas.' Sandys then enlisted the Foreign Secretary, Butler, to warn that any alternative to federation would cause 'political difficulties' and disappoint the Americans. In the face of an assault from two departments, Boyd-Carpenter and Armstrong decided the best tactical option was to suggest 'an anodyne formula' which gave a superficial appearance of greater generosity without offering any firm commitments. They settled on the suitably bland promise, that they would 'when the time comes, be ready to consider whatever case there may be for increased aid having regard to their other commitments at the time.'[103] Sandys instructed Fisher, who was himself sceptical about the claims of the small islands, to 'press the Chief Secretary hard' for a firmer commitment but he made no progress in persuading the Treasury to move beyond the heavily qualified indication that they might be willing to consider additional funding at a later stage.[104]

In the midst of the Whitehall battle over economic assistance Sandys flew to East Africa where he met Errol Barrow during the Kenyan independence celebrations. Barrow, like many West Indians, had been indignant at the repressive policies adopted by the British during the Mau Mau insurgency and this sentiment was reinforced by discussions with Jomo Kenyatta and other African nationalists. Sandys seemed to be suffering from a combination of apprehensiveness about the likely Caribbean reaction to British equivocations over the O'Loughlin proposals and ongoing irritation at small island impecunity. When the two met, Sandys adopted a censorious tone that lingered in Barrow's mind. Eight months later he was still brooding about Sandys' curt suggestion that Britain was unhappy at the notion of 'buying a federation', to which he had responded bluntly that the people of the Caribbean were not 'selling a federation'.[105] At the time, the confrontation amplified Barrow's reservations about the federal project. He declared that British policy was 'humbug', that it was embarrassing that Zanzibar had achieved independence before Barbados and that Kenyatta had been admirably restrained, given that he 'had ample provocation for "turning all the British out of Kenya".'[106] Although other British policymakers tried to find more diplomatic ways of expressing their reservations than Sandys had managed, the absence of any detailed response to the

O'Loughlin proposals became ever more conspicuous as 1964 wore on. Colonial Office officials were aware that their reticence on finance had become an active disincentive to federate. Barrow calculated that the annual cost to Barbados of subsidising the Leewards and Windwards would be $ 1.4 million. Poynton noted in June 1964 that, in circumstances where the Maltese government was being offered a £ 40 million subsidy over 10 years, 'it will be increasingly difficult to argue that we cannot commit ourselves so far ahead to figures of this degree and magnitude for the West Indies.' He explained the apparent inconsistency by the crude fact that an Eastern Caribbean federation was not worth 'as much money as ten years defence facilities in Malta!'[107] The final offer made to the November 1964 RCM reflected Treasury discretion and comprised a promise to continue international aid at current levels for five years; none of the Caribbean delegates regarded this as an adequate alternative to the expanded 10 year programme of financial assistance outlined by O'Loughlin.[108]

Following his tour of the Caribbean in February 1965 Greenwood conceded that demands for additional aid would play a 'big part' in negotiations and that any federation ought to obtain independence 'within a reasonably short period of time of its being fully established.'[109] His qualified optimism proved wholly unjustified because on both these points the patience of Barrow's government had run out. In British calculations Barbados occupied an intermediate position between Jamaica and Trinidad, who were assumed to be capable of unilateral independence, and the Windwards and Leewards who, they insisted, would have to remain in some form of colonial relationship with Britain should federation fail. From Barrow's perspective, the end of colonial rule in Barbados was necessary to validate the nationalist credentials he had established in the election of 1961. While pressing the case for greater financial assistance to any new federation, the Barbadian government had also insisted that it ought to obtain 'independence at its inception.'[110] This put Barrow at odds with the British who argued that the new federation, like the old, would have to serve a period of colonial apprenticeship. In the aftermath of his conversation with Sandys in Nairobi, Barrow began making provisional plans for unilateral Barbadian independence, while participating in the federal negotiations to ensure that he avoided any appearance of culpability when they collapsed. In February 1965 Stow reported that Barrow was making active preparations for such an eventuality.[111] Once the final break occurred as a consequence of Antigua's withdrawal and the collapse of the Little Six negotiations in April 1965, Barrow found himself in the same situation

as Manley after the Jamaican referendum: both his political reputation as a forthright nationalist and his conception of the national
self-interest required that he expedite the inevitable end of British
authority. He set a timetable which anticipated a constitutional conference in November 1965 and independence by July 1966.[112]

Although the British had few compunctions about the principle of
Barbadian independence, the actuality engendered the habitual feelings of ambivalence and fears for the future. After a period of relative
calm on the domestic front, Barrow's push for a final demission of
power was accompanied by noisy recriminations between the various
factions on the Barbadian political scene. He confronted a split within
the DLP caused by the attachment of more radical Barbadian politicians to the federal idea. The key figures in this group were Erskine
Ward and Wynter Crawford both of whom resigned from the party
in protest at Barrow's unwillingness to make any attempt to revive the
now moribund Eastern Caribbean federation. Crawford believed federalism was a prerequisite for economic specialisation across the region and
for the fostering of a wider market for Barbadian manufactured goods.
He recalled 'the federation meant a lot for Barbados' and that Barrow
had been disingenuous in his support for integration.[113] While Crawford
and Ward regarded the federation as the only means to obtain genuine
political and economic autonomy, Barrow was also challenged by conservative opposition groups, including the Barbados Labour Party and
the Barbados National Party who advocated the continuation of some
form of dependent relationship with Britain for as long as was necessary
to revive the federal arrangements. They demanded a further election
to test public opinion on the matter. This domestic political turmoil
awoke the usual British neuroses and even prompted Greenwood to
wonder whether to endorse the final stage of Barbadian decolonisation.
By October 1965 Stow was complaining that the speeches of the various protagonists in the independence controversy had 'gone down to a
very low level' and predicted that there would be 'some broken heads at
these meetings in the atmosphere of tension in which they take place.'
Barrow feared that the British would procrastinate on the independence
issue and had he known more of the attitude of Greenwood, he would
have found justification for his apprehensions. In a minute written in
November 1965, Greenwood asked his officials 'Are we not prejudging
the issue by talking about an "independence conference"? Surely we
will need a conference which will tell us *what is wanted*? And is there
any point in such a conference unless we know what authority the delegates have?' By this stage, Greenwood's officials were too immersed in

the usual protocols of decolonisation to be diverted by the doubts of the Secretary of State. Poynton explained that they would not have a conference unless there was a demand for independence but if such a conference was called there would be nothing else for it to discuss other than independence.[114]

Greenwood soon made way for Lord Longford and then, in quick succession, Frederick Lee, but the metropolitan authorities maintained a vigilant attitude in overseeing Barbadian politics. As was customary, British reservations were personalised; they focused on the character of Errol Barrow, who had once been seen as a dependable collaborator, with the requisite nous to subdue the volatile politicians of the Leewards and Windwards. By the end of 1965 he had been mentally reallocated to what was more or less the only other conceptual category which colonial bureaucrats used to classify Caribbean nationalists: the volatile demagogue with despotic instincts. In October, officials indicated they were 'going to have serious trouble with Mr Barrow' and, in the following month, his efforts to counter the pro-federalists on Barbados were described in an official memorandum as 'extraordinary'. He was accused by the Colonial Office of displaying 'dictatorial tendencies'.[115] In January 1966, Barrow's motion declaring that his government would seek immediate unilateral independence was passed by the Legislative Council despite protests from the opposition, who insisted that the DLP must seek a new mandate before an irrevocable decision was made. The controversy threatened to wreck the constitutional conference in June, which proved as acrimonious as the famously bad-tempered Trinidad conference four years earlier. Opposition calls for an early election produced a dilemma for the Colonial Office: they were increasingly distrustful of Barrow and his reluctance to give Barbadians an opportunity to vote on the matter seemed to confirm suspicions that his regime would be autocratic, but any refusal to grant independence was certain to lead to a prolonged controversy which would provide him with an opportunity to stimulate nationalist sentiment. Lee insisted on fresh elections before independence but, in order to prevent any public accusations of British interference, secured Barrow's acquiescence in the form of a secret and informal understanding. From Barrow's perspective the grudging attitude of the Colonial Office was continuous with the colonial past. He believed Lee was 'looking for an excuse to say we could not reach agreement on Independence and therefore to postpone it.'[116] The report of the conference proceedings recorded the objections of the opposition groups to various elements of the new constitution but did not contain any reference to Barrow's promise to hold an election.[117]

The covert nature of the deal only generated new anxieties. Lee sought written confirmation of the agreement from Barrow and when none was forthcoming a degree of panic struck Whitehall. It was feared that Barrow was engaged in an act of duplicity. The Parliamentary Under-Secretary at the Colonial Office, John Stonehouse, warned that there was a 'great danger that Barrow will get away with it.' Despite reassurances from Stow, there was a belief in Whitehall that if he was allowed to renege on his promise to hold an election before independence, 'the anti-British trait which has recently been evident in Mr Barrow's statements and actions, would be reinforced by contempt for the British government's actions.' Stow guessed that Barrow would keep to his side of the bargain and in September the minor crisis subsided when he reaffirmed his promise and announced elections for November 1966.[118] The DLP was victorious at the polls and governed Barbados for a decade after the declaration of independence on 30 November. Unlike Duncan Sandys' surrogate, Forbes Burnham in Guyana, Barrow stepped down when defeated by the opposition in a free election in 1976.

The Windwards, the Leewards and Associated Statehood

The constitutional to and fro on the Windwards and Leewards in the two decades after Montego Bay provides plentiful evidence for the notion that the British had very little idea of how to deal with the politics of the two island groups. After 1947 there had been what amounted to a second wave of disturbances on the small islands during which a younger, less bourgeois nationalist leadership had emerged that was treated by the British colonial authorities with a mixture of fear and contempt. Bradshaw, Bird, Gairy and Joshua parlayed trade union activism into political influence and were at the forefront of demands for greater autonomy for the Anglophone Caribbean. The colonial authorities responded by gradually increasing the elected elements in local legislatures and executives on a piecemeal basis until in 1959 they approved a series of coordinated constitutional advances which were implemented in 1960. The conferral of political authority was predicated on the assumption that the supposed impulsiveness of the new popularly elected Chief Ministers would be restrained by the process of Caribbean integration. After the Jamaican secession from the federation, the Colonial Office expressed its determination to retrieve the powers they had just granted. Further constitutional advance for the territories was ruled out for so long as an Eastern Caribbean federation seemed a possibility. Once this project was poisoned by the same toxic mixture of peripheral acrimony and metropolitan dissimulation which had killed the wider federation, it was necessary to make other arrangements. Any new proposals had to deal with two potential causes of instability: small island indigence and the vulnerability of the territories to malign external influences. It was anticipated that the volatility of local politics could yet transform the region into a zone of economic instability, a battlefront in the Cold War or both. In October 1965 the Foreign Office noted that Washington would inevitably be concerned about the emergence of mini-states in such a sensitive region and endorsed Colonial Office apprehensions about the emergence of 'seven potential little Haitis or Cubas'.[119] The imposition of Associated Statehood in early 1967 gave British policymakers greater constitutional influence and hence a greater measure of assurance than the normal procedure of offering internal self-government as a prelude to independence. The two islands which the British concluded were most likely to generate a Duvalier or a Castro were Grenada, where they had failed to extinguish Gairyism, and Anguilla, which was tied to St Kitts and Nevis in what proved to be an unstable union.

Grenada

In a celebrated account of Grenadian politics Arthur Singham characterised the career of Eric Gairy as an archetypical example of the challenge posed to institutional authority by charismatic leadership. Borrowing from Weber, Singham argued that once an alternative emerges to colonial rule in the form of a populist nationalist leader, 'there is almost bound to be a struggle for legitimacy by the actors representing these two authority systems.'[120] The outraged imperial reaction to Gairy's challenge to the norms of decolonisation was validated by his excesses: these were recognised by Singham when he published *The Hero and the Crowd* in 1968 and were corroborated by the appalling authoritarianism of Gairy's government during the following decade. The contemporary distaste colonial bureaucrats felt for Gairy is perhaps best illustrated by a Colonial Office briefing note from April 1966 which described him as 'a man who is almost too bad to be true.'[121] Such British consternation was not specific to the case of Grenada: the extreme example of Gairy's misrule was utilised to illustrate the principle, which the Colonial Office never doubted, that the small island leaders would abuse the authority granted them at the end of empire. The corroboration for this thesis provided by events on Grenada licensed their inattention to the particularities of each case. Gairy's career was taken as only a more startling instance of the volatility of Caribbean nationalism which was also evident in the cases of Barrow on Barbados, Southwell on St Kitts or even Ronald Webster on Anguilla.

Gairy's great achievement had been to force Grenadian commercial interests and the colonial administration to acknowledge the demands of the rural poor for improved working conditions. While the rest of the Anglophone Caribbean had been set aflame by labour protests in the 1930s, the local oligarchy was consoled by the relative calm on Grenada. This bred complacency and it was not until the strikes and disturbances of 1950–1951 that the notion of Grenada as one of the most stable societies in the Caribbean was shattered. Gairy pursued an opportunistic strategy based on the exploitation of rising discontent amongst estate workers but he also played an important role in organising labour and mediating between workers and employers. His success in securing wage increases and new entitlements established a reservoir of popular good will on which he drew for decades. In the immediate aftermath of the strikes he used the momentum generated by the achievements of the Grenada Manual and Mental Workers' Union (GMMWU), and the new opportunities available following the introduction of constitutional reform, to secure representation for popular demands in the legislature. The electoral campaigning of his Grenada United Labour Party (GULP) was entirely personalist and the party offered an even more extreme example of boss rule than Bustamante's domination of the Jamaica Labour Party. The limits of such an approach were evident in the 1957 elections in which the GULP was effectively contained within its agricultural base and won only two of the eight seats which were contested. During the campaign Gairy was accused of disrupting the meetings of his opponents and specifically of leading a steel band through a gathering of supporters of the rival Grenada National Party (GNP); as a consequence he was excluded from the Legislative Council on the grounds of electoral malpractice. Whatever the formal justification for the action, it could be portrayed as a transparent attempt to marginalise the rural interests which he represented and provided a suitable platform for him to develop his favourite anti-colonialist theme. He was so successful that in the election of March 1961 GULP won eight of the 10 seats in the legislature. Although for a short time the British continued to uphold the ban on Gairy, in August they accepted the inevitable: following his readmittance to the legislature he was appointed Chief Minister which was the outcome that the Colonial Office had long hoped to avoid but had long feared.[122]

What added to British perplexity regarding how to deal with Grenadian politics was that the GULP's triumph at the polls occurred after elected politicians had been given greater control of the executive under the reforms enacted across the Leewards and the Windwards in 1960. Furthermore, Gairy's appointment as Chief Minister coincided with the Jamaican referendum vote which ensured the demise of the federation. Now that Norman Manley, or even Grantley Adams, was no longer available to discipline renegade elements in the Eastern Caribbean, the British wanted guarantees of the stability and probity of those territorial governments which remained within the imperial system. Instead, Gairy brought unprecedented levels of patronage and clientelism to the administration of Grenada which inevitably proved intolerable to the colonial bureaucracy. Gordon Lewis provides an effective summary of the charges which were confirmed by the findings of the Commission of Enquiry into the Control of Public Expenditure in Grenada: 'the deliberate and systematic violation of financial regulations, the browbeating of public servants, the deliberate destruction of the morale of the civil service, the illegal purchase with public monies of luxury items, including an expensive piano and a phonograph for the chief minister's residence.'[123] In June 1962 Maudling informed the Commons that the constitution had been suspended and that Gairy had been dismissed on the grounds that 'if he remained in office under the constitution then in force, the same financial malpractices and the same threats against the Civil Service would continue.'[124] The narrow GULP defeat in the new round of elections conducted in September 1962 was more a consequence of the unpopularity of federalism in Grenada, which Herbert Blaize and the GNP exploited by campaigning for unitary statehood with Trinidad, than of disenchantment with Gairy.[125] The wider point about the era of 'Squandermania' was that it incarnated all the fears of political disorder which troubled British policymakers. Three years after the suspension of the constitution, the talks on both federation and unitary statehood with Trinidad had both effectively collapsed and fears of continued malpractice constituted the principal British reservation regarding any advance towards self-government for Grenada and the other small islands.

The great advantage of the novel status of Associated Statehood, which had first been granted to the Cook Islands in 1964 before being considered for the Windwards and Leewards, was that the United Nations recognised it as a legitimate means of ending colonial control but, unlike full independence or even internal self-government, it was sufficiently malleable to allow the metropolitan power to retain some influence. The major disadvantage was that the domain of British control was greatly circumscribed: only in those cases where there was a threat to residual British responsibilities for external affairs and defence could intervention be legitimate.[126] As the Anguilla case would demonstrate this allowed some flexibility in cases where policymakers in London could construe domestic developments as a threat to order, but it manifestly did not apply when financial rectitude was imperilled. When Greenwood discussed the Associated Statehood formula with his officials on 14 September 1965 his main concern was 'the inefficacy of the financial sanction' provided by a constitutional formula in which the grounds for intervention were restricted to security threats. A number of Colonial Office officials were sceptical of the entire enterprise precisely because it offered no means of imposing budgetary restraint, despite the obligation to continue providing British aid. The Deputy Permanent Under-Secretary, A. N. Galsworthy, declared 'it was only in respect of these territories that we had this difficulty about financial maladministration' and suggested that they would be unable to prohibit 'bad financial policy' despite the obligation that the British executive owed to Parliament to account for the spending which they authorised. The counter-argument was that Associated Statehood offered the least offence to nationalist sentiment while guaranteeing some measure of metropolitan control and it prevailed amidst a great deal of grumbling from the Treasury and the Commonwealth Relations Office about the legitimacy of the procedure.[127] At the end of September the Colonial Office began consultations with its local representatives regarding the next stage of constitutional advance, in November the Commissioner for the West Indies, Stephen Luke, toured the islands to judge local reactions and in December the proposals for Associated Statehood were published.[128]

The impossibility of justifying any further overt interventions on the grounds of financial wrongdoing made it urgent to assure the positions of the handful of politicians on the Leewards and Windwards in whom the Colonial Office had some measure of confidence; a list which emphatically excluded Gairy and rather more hesitantly included Herbert Blaize. Fears of what a future Gairy administration might do sharpened the British focus on ensuring the continuation of the GNP administration. The new Administrator of Grenada, Ian Turbott, had outlined a strategy to accomplish this in February 1965. His proposals were underpinned by the straightforward notion that it was 'better to try and assist Blaize than to permit Gairy to return and reintroduce his corrupt practices.' The impediments to successfully implementing the plan were Gairy's charismatic appeal to many Grenadian voters, which contrasted with Blaize who was characterised as 'honest but ineffective', and the economic constraints caused by declining prices for the staples of the Grenadian export trade, including cocoa, nutmeg and bananas. Turbott urged the implementation of a 'package deal' which would include measures of administrative reform and 'certain advances constitutionally patterned on perhaps British Honduras, plus more economic aid but not up to the amount Trinidad is suggesting'.[129] It was the constitutional issue which proved most straightforward for the British to resolve. By the middle of 1965 proposals for unitary statehood between Grenada and Trinidad and the Eastern Caribbean federal negotiations were both in abeyance. Blaize had campaigned for union with Trinidad as the most direct path to independence for Grenada; after the Williams government had effectively eliminated that option, the Colonial Office chose to make constitutional concessions to the GNP which could be presented to the electorate as a success for the politics of pragmatism. In November, Blaize requested the immediate restoration of the 1960 constitution which had been effectively suspended in 1962 and 'pressed very hard' on the issue of additional economic assistance. The Colonial Office approved the idea of giving Blaize 'a "piece of bacon" for him to take back with him' in the form of the full restoration of the 1960 constitution. The only danger they foresaw was that, if the implementation of the Associated Statehood formula was delayed 'and Mr Gairy is returned to power in Grenada, we shall be back in the same awkward position as we were from 1960 to 1962.'[130]

British administrators knew that the ongoing economic problems of Grenada and Blaize's failure to obtain his initial goal of union with Trinidad left him in a vulnerable position and that the restoration of the constitution was unlikely to be decisive in swinging public opinion behind the GNP. Like Barrow in Barbados, Blaize was eager to postpone any general election until after the constitutional issues had been resolved. Although both the GNP government and GULP opposition had reservations about the Associated Statehood formula, it was in Blaize's interest to claim credit first for the restoration of the 1960 constitution and then for any further incremental move towards greater autonomy. Turbott reported before the 1966 Windward Islands constitutional conference, at which both the GULP and the GNP were represented, that Gairy would probably refuse to sign any report without a guarantee of early elections, while Blaize was certain to demand an 18-month postponement. Despite the chequered history of the island's developing democracy, electoral calculations were as important in Grenada as anywhere else and Turbott explained: 'The local scene is fairly simple; if there was an election tomorrow Gairy would probably win and Blaize knows this. But the GNP...feels it would win an election in the latter part of 1967.' As on the issue of the restoration of the constitution, the British sought to accommodate Blaize. Although they acknowledged the precedent set by the secret deal which required Barrow to go to the polls before independence, the Colonial Office stated explicitly 'that they cannot deny the fact that they would not welcome Mr Gairy back in office.... We are therefore not anxious to see early elections.'[131] The controversy rumbled on during the long Windwards conference which commenced on 18 April and ended on 6 May. It was only on the final day that Lee insisted that Gairy sign the report without any formal or informal assurance of early elections. The principal difference between the Associated Statehood proposals for Grenada and the other Windwards Islands was that the former included a special formula on finance which stated: 'The Constitution will contain provision to secure that there is no expenditure from public funds except where there is statutory authority for such expenditure and unless a prescribed procedure has been complied with, which secures full Parliamentary scrutiny.'[132]

Although Gairy was browbeaten at the London conference, as Associated Statehood became imminent he adopted more belligerent tactics to try to force an election. In January1967 the four GULP representatives on the Legislative Council, including Gairy and his wife, resigned. This rendered the legislature barely quorate and necessitated a number of by-elections during which the imposition of Associated Statehood and Blaize's refusal to go to the polls could be used to embarrass the GNP government and the colonial administration. It also gave an opportunity for officials in Whitehall to reaffirm Gairy's status as 'the worst and most unpleasant of all the political figures in the Windwards and Leewards with whom we have ever had dealings.' His rivals and associates were also characterised as dangerous radicals, including the trade union leader, Derek Knight, who was believed to be 'out for destruction', and a new GULP spokesman, Michael Sylvester, who was described by Turbott as having 'one of the worst anti-white chips on his shoulder I have ever seen'.[133] In February 1967 Gairy held a candlelit march from Market Square in St George's to Government House where he submitted a petition demanding a general election and internal self-government rather than Associated Statehood. Turbott was pleased and relieved that the crowd did not resort to violence but reported 'how long one is going to be able to hold them peacefully is difficult to say'.[134] Despite

Turbott's determination to postpone the impending by-elections, Gairy avoided any further provocations on the assumption that it would be unwise to provide the British with an opportunity to intervene before the inevitable general elections which he expected to win. When the polls opened in August 1967, the GULP won seven seats and the GNP three. Charles Roberts, who was Britain's senior representative to the new Associated States, offered an insightful analysis of the result, which focused on economic discontent rather than the mystical appeal of Gairy's charisma. He explained, 'whereas we and senior civil servants in Grenada tend to remember with horror the previous administration of Mr Gairy...the workers on the estates remember that period as one when they received large increases in wages.' Despite British praise for Blaize's industry and common sense, the GNP government 'did not put additional money in the workers' pockets.' Although there was now a tendency to suggest that Gairy was more moderate and malleable than Knight and Sylvester, after visiting Grenada for the opening of the new Parliament, Roberts declared: 'I see no reason to be optimistic'.[135] Roberts' sense of foreboding was entirely justified by the events of the next 10 years, while his analysis of the causes of the GULP victory in 1967 provided a persuasive and uncomfortable explanation for the rise of Gairyism and the ineffectiveness of British counter-measures. Their dismay at these developments did not prevent the metropolitan government from endorsing Grenadian independence, with Gairy as first Prime Minister, in 1974.

St Kitts

The story of the unsuccessful British effort to promote centripetalism in the Anglophone Caribbean reached its dismal conclusion with Anguillan secession from the new Associated State of St Kitts–Nevis–Anguilla. Having failed to preserve the unity of their colonial territories in a regional federation and then failed in their efforts to promote integration between Barbados, the Windwards and the Leewards, the metropolitan government failed even to maintain the association of the three small islands contained within this micro-state. The British were not wholly responsible for this disappointing record; the peculiar constitutional inadhesiveness of the local territories was greatly influenced by the parochial nature of Caribbean politics as promoted by Caribbean politicians and manifest, in this instance, in the uncompromising assertion of Kittitian rights by Robert Bradshaw and the captiousness of the leader of the Anguillan separatists, Ronald Webster. But the British were grudging, suspicious and equivocating partners in the process of decolonisation and their misgivings were more apparent on the small islands. The case of Anguilla was particularly significant because by 1969 the full British Cabinet was devoting its attention to this latest instance of Caribbean secessionism and the resulting invasion of the island by a small force of troops and policemen became front-page news. It was warranted on the basis of the residual rights and obligations which the British had retained under the Associated Statehood formula because of their apprehensions about future mismanagement of the islands' affairs. Although the intervention was intended to subdue the secessionists, it led instead to the permanent separation of Anguilla from St Kitts and, in this respect, symbolised the counter-productive nature of much British policy in the region during the era of decolonisation.

In the middle of October 1965 Greenwood discussed the failure of the Eastern Caribbean federation with Rusk in Washington. He attempted to adopt a reassuring tone but his affirmation that the security situation in the Eastern Caribbean was stable came with the caveat that this might change 'if there was a collapse of the sugar price.'[136] Of all the islands it was St Kitts which still had the greatest dependence on the export of sugar and where the miscarriage of plans for an Eastern Caribbean federation provoked most alarm. The problem of dependence on sugar had both an immediate, provisional aspect in the form of a series of low annual crop yields of cane and a longer-term, intractable aspect in terms of global overproduction which was driving down prices. Between 1961 and 1963 Kittitian governmental revenue declined from BWI $ 8.3 million to BWI $ 5.2 million.[137] As in the case of the wider federation, the economic grievances of nationalist politicians became a prominent feature in negotiations about Associated Statehood. The failure of proposals for an Eastern Caribbean federation in 1965, which occasioned the new round of constitutional negotiations, coincided with a potentially catastrophic financial crisis for Paul Southwell's government on St Kitts. Southwell had taken over the leadership of the Kittitian nationalist movement after Robert Bradshaw had left for Trinidad to participate in the federal government. He was unpopular with British administrators who criticised him both for the stridency of his anti-colonialism and his habit of quoting Shakespeare at the slightest provocation. At the end of 1965 his government was confronted with a particularly disastrous year for sugar production; British intelligence reports in August indicated that the crop would amount to 38,000 tons which was the lowest recorded for many years and that the 'effect on the general economy of the territory and on the finances of the Government is likely to be little short of disastrous.' This prompted a haughty outburst from one Colonial Office official: 'What St Kitts does not seem to realise is that the world does not need their sugar – there is a 2 million ton *surplus* estimated for 1965.'[138]

Alongside the economic emergency, Southwell had to deal with the constitutional crisis attendant on the abandonment of plans for integration in the Eastern Caribbean. It was partly because the island represented such an extreme example of a sugar monoculture that the federation was particularly important to St Kitts. Integration into a wider regional economy, which included wealthier territories, offered the prospect of political independence and economic diversification. At the same time the history of exploitation and conflict during the development of the sugar industry on the island had generated a fierce nationalism which became manifest in the strikes of 1935 and 1948. Even as the federal negotiations proceeded Southwell lobbied for a loosening of colonial control. In January 1964 his suggestion that the establishment of internal self-government for the Bahamas and British Honduras ought to set a precedent for St Kitts was dismissed by the Colonial Office on the grounds that this would lead to an 'awkward stage' in the process of constitutional advance.[139] Once it was certain that the latest federal project would fail, Southwell reiterated his demands for internal self-government. On 12 May 1965 he wrote to the Colonial Office to register his 'great distress' at the abandonment of the federal enterprise and his view that the current Kittitian constitution, which was 'neither fish nor fowl', should be amended. Just as their predecessors in Jamaica, Trinidad and Barbados had been, the nationalist leadership in St Kitts were suspicious of British procrastination and insistent on the need for the rapid devolution of power to locally elected executives. During the summer of 1965 Southwell pressed for a constitutional conference in October; by September it was evident this would not be feasible and he wrote to London again to demand an early demission of power.[140]

Southwell favoured internal self-government as a first step towards independence but British bureaucrats were still thinking in quite different terms; internal self-government was rejected by the Colonial Office precisely because it 'does not work well (if at all), as the example of British Guiana has shown, where a government is behaving badly and where the move to independence is delayed.' The British view of the Windwards and Leewards was that 'unless they federate they should not move to full independence either now or in the foreseeable future.'[141] The Associated Statehood formula was designed to maintain a modicum of British control over events in the Eastern Caribbean for a significant period of time. In particular, the metropolitan government reserved the right to intervene in the case of violent disturbances which would constitute a threat to security. When Greenwood consulted his officials on 14 September 1965 they emphasised that local British representatives ought to have sufficient powers to deal with any significant challenge to the status quo. Stow, who had superintended the aborted federal negotiations, complained 'he could not actually see how the UK representative could cope with public disorder.'[142] The revised proposals for Associated Statehood offered a latitudinarian formula which appeared to cover most eventualities: the British government would be free to legislate 'to prevent circumstances arising or continuing in the territory' which threatened their residual responsibilities for external affairs and defence.[143] When presented with the Associated Statehood formula by Luke in November, Southwell was more suspicious than many of his peers and raised two issues of concern: whether St Kitts might still obtain independence as part of a revived federation and whether financial aid 'would be greater or less'. Questions were inevitable as to why the Leewards and Windwards were being offered this novel solution to the constitutional puzzle as an alternative to internal self-government. Luke reported that Southwell was 'unconvinced that these proposals are preferable to full internal self-government for which he had asked, but he is at least prepared to negotiate on them.' On 3 January 1966 Southwell wrote to Greenwood to insist 'the way should be made abundantly easy either for the proposed constitutional status to be succeeded by complete Independence preferably within a Federation but if necessary, without it.'[144]

Partly as a consequence of further inter-island feuding and partly as a consequence of the fact that, in the Colonial Office's estimation, 'Mr Southwell's approach to these proposals had more reservations in it than almost anybody else's', a separate constitutional conference was held for St Kitts.[145] Alongside the need for British assistance to meet the financial crisis on the island and concerns about the inferiority of the Associated Statehood formula in comparison with internal self-government, a third complicating factor in preparing for the meeting was the status of Anguilla and Nevis, both of which had longstanding constitutional ties to St Kitts. The recent history of political fragmentation conditioned the British to take particular cognisance of secessionist feeling in the two satellite territories where there was greater disquiet about the possibility of Kittitian dominance under the Associated Statehood formula than in the case of equivalent territories such as Carriacou and Barbuda which were destined for unity with Grenada and Antigua.

In order to represent Nevisian and Anguillan sentiment at the constitutional conference, the British insisted that Eugene Walwyn of the United National Movement and Peter Adams of the People's Action Movement were invited to attend as representatives of these islands.[146] By the time negotiations commenced on 12 May 1966, Southwell had resigned himself to separate representation for the satellite islands and to the Associated Statehood formula. Rather than dissipate their energies contesting every issue, the Kittitian delegation focused on the most significant question in dispute which concerned the level of financial aid. British refusal to guarantee additional funding generated great ill feeling and Southwell insisted that their dissatisfaction with current levels of assistance was registered in the final report. The British acknowledged that 'the economy of the Territory would continue to be vulnerable so long as it was almost wholly dependent on sugar production', but practical measures to encourage diversification were limited to an offer of assistance with a technical feasibility project designed to examine the potential role of an airfield in promoting tourism. On the matter of the satellite territories, the delegates agreed to the establishment of 'a system of local self-government in Nevis and in Anguilla' based on the creation of local Councils. Unfortunately, the precise method of selecting the members of the Council was left unspecified. Wilson's last Colonial Secretary, Fred Lee, told the Overseas Policy and Defence Committee that the island councils were 'the main novel feature of the constitutional arrangements' and that, because of the refusal to offer any precise guarantees regarding financial assistance, Southwell had been exceptionally reluctant to sign the final report of the conference.[147]

As was usually the case in the story of decolonisation in the Anglophone Caribbean, the ambiguity which served as an expedient to surmount one constitutional hurdle set the precedent for future controversies: Southwell's misgivings regarding the adequacy of future economic assistance, the vagueness surrounding the devolution of political power to the satellite islands and the controversial nature of the prerogatives retained by the British under the new constitution, each contributed to the two-year crisis over Anguilla which began with the implementation of Associated Statehood in February 1967. From the outset it was evident that the government in Basseterre would not have sufficient revenue to address the economic demands of the Anguillans. Whereas one could easily see Nevis from St Kitts and the two islands had broadly similar levels of development, Anguilla was 70 miles across the sea and had no electrical grid or effective telephone system. The island had initially been settled by Kittitians and Nevisians but the economy had never surpassed basic subsistence conditions. The constitutional history of the territory was chequered but, for the most part, the tie to St Kitts had been preserved in various forms, while conditions on Anguilla were neglected both by British Empire-builders and, in the twentieth century, by the new leaders of Caribbean nationalism, including Bradshaw and Southwell. The islanders themselves were convinced that propinquity and recent history meant that the latter had greater culpability and turned to their more distant masters in Whitehall for redress, unaware of the tendency amongst metropolitan policymakers to assume that the demission of political power signalled the beginning of the end of the short era of financial assistance to the region. Given British concern at the number of micro-states which were emerging following the shattering of plans for an Eastern Caribbean federation, they hoped that the remaining fragments would not be smashed into yet smaller pieces. British parsimony and lack of sympathy for local nationalism once again generated a form of diplomacy which aggravated rather than mitigated the effects of the feuds between island politicians. Aside from the issue of scale, the most significant differences between the collapse of the regional federation in the Anglophone Caribbean and the secession of Anguilla from St Kitts were, firstly, that in the latter case a centralised state with effective authority over the constituent elements of the polity had been established in Basseterre and, secondly, that whereas the larger states had been most sceptical of the benefits of unity in the West Indies federation, in the case of St Kitts–Nevis–Anguilla it was the tiniest unit which was most eager to break away.

The Administrator of St Kitts was the Vincentian, Fred Phillips, and during three visits in the course of 1966 he became increasingly alarmed about the hostility with which the Associated Statehood formula was greeted on Anguilla. He registered the unmissable fact 'that the island was very badly neglected' and noted that 'each time I sensed a greater level of frustration and hopelessness among the islanders about the way they perceived themselves as being treated by St Kitts.'[148] In January 1967 he informed the Colonial Office that a popular campaign in favour of secession from St Kitts and the continuation of colonial status had begun. In the absence of additional assistance from Britain, the new government in Basseterre was planning to begin the new constitutional era with an increase in taxes which, Phillips warned on 27 January, was certain to fuel discontent on Anguilla. He recommended that the possibility of additional financial aid to resolve some of the economic problems should be reconsidered. A week later Phillips's gloomy predictions were vindicated when fighting broke out at a beauty contest which was intended to select an Anguillan candidate to contest the Ms State-hood Queen title with rivals from St Kitts and Nevis. The police force, which consisted of Kittitians, used tear gas on the crowd. The essentially economic motivation behind the protests was confirmed when the Minister for Overseas Development, Arthur Bottomley, visited the island to mark the commencement of the era of Associated Statehood on 27 February. Protestors demanded separation from St Kitts but the individuals who spoke to Bottomley were principally concerned with the poor condition of the roads, the lack of electricity and the inadequacy of medical and educational provision.[149] On the constitutional issue, British efforts to encourage the Kittitian government to expedite the establishment of a local council were met with suspicion by Bradshaw, who had returned to the post of Chief Minister in the interval between the Kittitian constitutional conference and the declaration of Associated Statehood, and now accused Wilson's government of engaging in 'imperial blackmail'. The leaders of the Anguillan secessionists were as suspicious of the Kittitians as Bradshaw was of the British and opted to boycott the nomination process by which the local council was supposed to be chosen.[150]

During the following two years, metropolitan officials persistently criticised Bradshaw for his inability to empathise with the frustrations of the Anguillans and the emerging leaders of the secessionist movement for their recklessness. It was the proclivities of the latter that were seen as posing a greater threat. Since the riots of the 1930s British policymakers were alert to any evidence of local demagoguery or external subversion which might set off a new insurrectionary movement in the region and the Associated Statehood formula had been designed to retain a British right of intervention in such instances. Despite the tiny scale of the Anguillan rebellion the fear remained that, in this very late episode in the decolonisation story, the British would once more be embarrassed by the exposure of an unhappy colonial legacy. On 30 May 1967 the Anguillans ejected the Kittitian police and declared themselves independent. A plebiscite held in July endorsed the decision by 1,813 votes to five. The following month Peter Adams, who had attended the original conference on Associated Statehood, was effectively sidelined by the secessionists after he cooperated with a Commonwealth mission that was attempting to mediate. At the end of the year an interim settlement was reached which entailed the dispatch of a British administrator called Anthony Lee to the island. He was unable to obtain Anguillan consent to a definitive agreement which would recognise Kittitian authority, while devolving a measure of political power to the Anguillan local council.

The crisis escalated when in February 1969 a second referendum was held which was as decisive as the first in proclaiming the Anguillans' desire for independence. On 11 March, the Labour politician, William Whitlock, acting in his capacity as Parliamentary Under-Secretary at the Foreign Office, went to Anguilla with the intention of finally imposing a settlement on the secessionists but was chased off the island by armed gunmen just a few hours after arriving. The Wilson government responded by sending a force of British paratroopers and metropolitan policemen who made an unopposed landing on 19 March.

What prompted the British invasion of Anguilla was the belief that local extremists, in combination with external agents, might turn the island into a centre of corruption in the Caribbean. The role of resident incendiarist was allocated to Ronald Webster and of alien subversives to the American mafia. As a substantial property owner, successful merchant and minister of the Seventh Day Adventist Church, Webster was a very different kind of revolutionary from Cheddi Jagan or Ferdinand Smith. The *New York Times* described him as 'a small dark wiry man of 43 who does not smile or laugh easily' and noticed that he lived in a pink house on the east of the island with his mother, wife and children.[151] British officials in the region portrayed Webster as the uncompromising representative of the Anguillan extremists, who were pitted against a smaller faction of moderates. Lee, who administered the island while negotiations for a final settlement continued, advised in February 1969: 'Webster is completely out of his depth and his sense of proportion and reasoning has deserted him, he has the emotional support of the mass of the people while moderate men recognise he is no longer rational.... Words fail me to describe Webster.'[152] The particular source of Webster's purported extremism was his willingness to embrace shady American investors as partners in the Anguillan independence project. As early as August 1967 the Minister of State at the Foreign Office, Malcolm Shepherd, had declared that Anguilla was 'wide open to strong-arm influences...there are interested bodies who feel there is money to be made from these little islands.'[153] The interests to whom Shepherd was coyly referring were Mayer Lansky and the American mafia who were supposedly looking for alternative locations for money laundering now that they were no longer welcome in Cuba. Webster was alleged to be connected to these groups through his relations with the Anguillan hotelier Jerry Gumbs and an American financial investor, Frank Holcomb.[154] The British embassy in Washington managed to obtain access to FBI files on Holcomb and found evidence that he was a 'disreputable character' but did not have a criminal record.

On 15 February 1969 Holcomb returned to Anguilla and the Foreign Office briefed ministers that he and Webster were engaged in 'group intimidation' of their political opponents whose 'common reaction is disgust at Webster's espousal of a foreigner, Holcom [*sic*], and preference to wash their hands of the whole business.'[155] Reports by British officials in the region predicted that, after the second referendum, Webster would set up a 'one man dictatorship.'[156] Richard Crossman, who sat on the government's Overseas Policy and Defence Committee which took the decision to intervene, compared the Anguillan situation to an Evelyn Waugh farce but, like the majority of Labour ministers, was persuaded by the Foreign Secretary, Michael Stewart, that 'gangsters wanted to turn it into a gambling resort, a casino and make it independent of Britain.'[157]

The uneventful post-invasion history of the island has demonstrated quite how fanciful British ministers were in imagining that Webster's Anguilla would end up looking something like Batista's Cuba. Once exposed to the scrutiny of the world's media the fantastic and nightmarish visions of a new Caribbean dictatorship in powerful alliance with Miami gangsters evaporated. Journalists were united in offering confirmation that Anguilla was not overrun by local gunmen and American hoodlums, and cartoonists and satirists had fun at the Wilson government's expense. What followed was a series of recriminations between Cabinet ministers. Barbara Castle recorded Denis Healey squabbling with Michael Stewart over whether Webster was 'the leader of the Anguillan people', as the former had it, or 'a leading Anguillan', as the latter preferred. It was Stewart who came off worse as ministers protested that they had been misled over the nature of the 'disreputable elements', the role of Webster and the attitude of the Caribbean states towards the use of force.[158] The principal beneficiary of the backlash against Stewart was Webster. Rather than detain him, the government opted to negotiate with him, on the basis that he was, as Healey asserted, the representative of Anguillan opinion. Formulating an interim agreement proved arduous and the task was assigned first to Hugh Foot, who as Lord Caradon was British Ambassador to the United Nations, and then, at a lower level, to John Comber, who replaced Lee after it became clear that his personal differences with Webster were irreconcilable. Every concession to Anguillan opinion aggravated relations with the Kittitian government. The deal which Bradshaw had concluded with Whitlock to restore the unity of the islands was effectively abandoned and on 1 April he denounced British policy in general, and Foot personally in a vituperative letter.[159] Although the British did not talk publicly about endorsing secession, Bradshaw's perception that they had now accepted it as a fait accompli was wholly warranted. Five days after Bradshaw sent his letter to Foot, a Foreign Office briefing note recorded that a consensus had been reached among officials 'that the Anguillans should live under an administration of their own choice and should not be returned to St Kitts' and 'that despite his many and serious inadequacies we shall have to try and work with Webster.'[160] An interim settlement with Webster was reached at the end of April and in December the Wilson government announced that Hugh Wooding had agreed to chair a commission to investigate the long-term future of Anguilla. His report, published a year later, proposed the establishment of a more powerful Anguillan Council which, although maintaining a titular tie to St Kitts, would be effectively autonomous.[161] The Anguilla Acts of 1971 and 1980 first made provision for the separation of the island and then formally dissolved the tie as a prelude to Kittitian independence in 1983.[162] Anguilla remains a British Overseas Territory.

Conclusion

There is almost no evidence that, in the aftermath of the collapse of the original pan-Caribbean federation, the British reconfigured their policies in the region. Instead there was a continual worrying away at the same fixations. Consequently the demise of the Eastern Caribbean federation was almost an exact replica in miniature of the failure of the earlier attempt to unite the whole of the Anglophone Caribbean, with the caveat that in the former case the new political union never came into existence at all. In attempting to arbitrate between the various parties, British policymakers once more assumed that the larger islands, in this case Barbados, would willingly take on the role of financier and policeman of the Leewards and Windwards at a time when external financial support for the fragile economies of the region was to taper away. While publicly endorsing the goals of West Indian nationalism, British policymakers regarded West Indian nationalists as a disreputable crowd. In Grenada there was certainly plenty of corroborating evidence for such a view in the events of Eric Gairy's political career. In the new state of St Kitts–Anguilla–Nevis by contrast, the British elevated a parochial protest into a major international crisis. Lastly, in the most significant episode of all in British Guiana, the same Cold War paranoia which had prompted the frantic containment exercise against Ferdinand Smith a decade earlier, was evident in the Byzantine plotting against Cheddi Jagan. It was true that some British officials did take a more realistic view of Jagan's programme than did the Americans but the focus on the machinations of Kennedy, the CIA and the American trade union movement has somewhat obscured the ardent Cold War campaigning of Duncan Sandys. Much of the disagreement between London and Washington over Guiana concerned methods: the British did not believe that the brutal but decisive action favoured by the Americans was feasible in an era of decolonisation and they resorted to fabled British methods of covert imperial intrigue. Although the Colonial Office had reluctantly allowed the agents of the Kennedy administration to propagate disorder in the name of the Cold War, they retained their distaste for the turmoil of demotic politics; and it was this disposition which had governed their strategy during the years of confrontation with the liberationist demands of the nationalist leaders of the Anglophone Caribbean.

6
Conclusion

Fifty years have passed since Jamaica and Trinidad became the first two territories in the Anglophone Caribbean to obtain political independence from Britain. From a comparative chronological perspective the region lagged behind much of Africa and Asia in the race for freedom from imperial control. The delegates at the Kingston and Montego Bay conferences in 1947 did not expect to wait between 15 and 20 years for independence and in the case of the small islands many waited longer. Nationalist politicians in the region were conscious of developments in West Africa: the attainment of independence for Ghana in 1957 provoked feelings of pride and solidarity amongst African-Caribbean people but also rueful contemplation of their continued subordination. The Indian-Caribbean residents of Guiana and Trinidad were conscious of the fact that, had their ancestors not travelled to the Caribbean to become indentured labourers, they would have been living in the independent state of India. Perhaps the most interesting comparison of all was with an earlier British empire in the Western hemisphere in what became the United States. In the eighteenth century the white slave-owning elite of the 13 colonies on the American mainland launched a successful insurrection against British control, almost two centuries before the black descendants of slaves obtained political power in the Anglophone Caribbean in a relatively peaceful manner. While the American War of Independence provided a heroic story of such potency that it was able to sustain the triumphalist ideology of American exceptionalism, the relatively mundane history of constitutional negotiations during which compromise was a reluctant necessity has had much less of an animating or uplifting effect on the outlook of people living in the Anglophone Caribbean. Indeed the histories of West Indian independence written from the region have been lacerating in their criticisms of the nationalist leadership. It is not surprising that many writers and activists from the region increasingly linked the local struggle to the wider project of black nationalism: the population of the Anglophone Caribbean may have been 200 years behind the British and German colonists of North America in obtaining independence but their drive for liberation was coeval with the civil rights campaigns inside the United States. In both cases attention was drawn to the correlation between darker skin colour and economic subordination and in the Caribbean this fuelled a further re-examination of the relationship between political and economic independence. This had been a concern of the nationalist leadership before the formal transfer of power but the region remains in the economic periphery half a century after it left the political periphery. This conclusion will briefly attend, first to the politics of authoritarianism, liberationism and their connections to broader themes concerning order and disorder, then to notions of developmentalism, external intervention and their connections to the themes of dependence and independence, before returning to a re-examination of the British role in the decolonisation of the Anglophone Caribbean.

Authoritarianism and democratic politics in the Anglophone Caribbean

The violence which accompanied the strikes and protests in the region during the 1930s provoked a crisis of imperial legitimacy: to many in the metropolis they illustrated both the requirement for reform and the dangers inherent in the process of decolonisation. During the next 40 years the British pursued a strategy predicated on the necessity to contain the insurrectionist impulses of the general population, particularly on the apparently less stable small islands. The postcolonial history of the region reveals that aspects of this approach were misguided. The assumption that larger islands could form a stable core for the Anglophone Caribbean appears questionable, given that Jamaican politics has been more turbulent than that of the Windwards and Leewards, with the partial and qualified exception of Grenada. Furthermore, the source of much of the disorder of Jamaican politics has been the authoritarian instincts of the state and the corruption of the Westminster-style two party system by former collaborators in the process of decolonisation inside the JLP and the PNP. During the 1960s the JLP was unsuccessful in providing jobs and improved working conditions for the urban poor. Bustamante's successors survived in power for a decade after independence despite these failures, partly because they were effective in further developing a violent form of clientelist politics, which was manifest in efforts to reshape the infrastructure of West Kingston to suit their electoral interests, and partly because of the fragmentation of the opposition.[1] The small, organised factions of the Marxist left, represented by groups such as the Unemployed Workers' Council, remained divided from the more amorphous, less organised opposition politics of those who were committed to a Garveyite politics of black cultural assertiveness, such as that of the Rastafarians. These tendencies in Jamaican affairs came together in the Rodney riots. The historian Walter Rodney sought to produce an ideological synthesis which recognised the specificities of racial oppression in a Caribbean context, while acknowledging the significance of universal class structures to any genuinely emancipatory project.[2] He promoted his work on the University of West Indies campus at Mona. The JLP government of Hugh Shearer first demanded that the Vice-Chancellor stop Rodney's activities and then, in October 1968, refused to allow him to re-enter the country. Intellectuals, PNP members, trade unionists and the unemployed united to oppose the ban but the march they organised from the university campus ended in violence as first JLP partisans and then the police attacked the protestors.[3] The Rodney riots were a precursor to the urban warfare of the 1970s, during which both parties armed their supporters as the JLP sought to resist the renascent PNP of Michael Manley. These developments reached their nadir in 2010 when the JLP government responded to an American extradition request by launching an armed assault on its own supporters in West Kingston in an attempt to arrest Christopher 'Dudus' Coke.

Trinidad has not witnessed quite the same levels of state violence against the population as Jamaica and British fears of a race war on the island after independence have proven misplaced. Nevertheless the politics of cultural assertiveness also influenced Trinidadian politics, and in 1970 and 1990 they appeared to threaten a revolutionary transformation of the island's politics. The rise of the Black Power movement in the United States was echoed in Trinidad by the formation of the National Joint Action Committee (NJAC) in 1967. Under the direction of Geddes Granger, the NJAC criticised the failures of Williams's economic strategy: on their account his reliance on overseas capital investment had left the country in a position of subservience to external interests. They particularly focused on the role of Canadian investors who, they argued, were exploiting the resources of the country through a form of economic imperialism which left the black majority in penury. Granger assumed a similar role to Rodney in Jamaica in mobilising popular discontent behind a form of liberationist politics which recognised the significance of race. Between 1969 and 1970 the University of Woodford Square, which had been a PNM stronghold, became the forum for protests against the Williams government. After his initial attempts to appease the protestors failed, Williams declared a state of emergency in order to forestall a march by the NJAC on 21 April 1970; this in turn precipitated a mutiny amongst those elements of the army who were discontented with their own conditions. As in Jamaica the postcolonial state proved as robust in defence of its interests as the colonial state. Williams restored his authority by filling Trinidad's jails with his opponents. Ryan estimates that 87 soldiers and 54 political activists were charged with treason, sedition or mutiny between April and November and concludes that the lasting effect of the disturbances was to increase the race consciousness of Trinidadian society.[4] One aspect of the Black Power movement in the United States was to have particular resonance in Trinidad. In both cases a turn away from Christianity and towards Islam was motivated partly by a distaste for the former as the religion of New World slavery and partly by an ideological affinity with Islamic notions of social justice and equality before God. The traditional Muslim population of Trinidad was made up of the descendants of Indian indentured labourers but during the 1970s and 1980s, the conversion of a number of African-Trinidadians to Islam changed the confessional pattern of Trinidad's demography. The converts' organisation, Jamaat al-Muslimeen, initially appeared to be confined to the margins of the island's politics but on 27 July 1990 armed members of the group stormed the Red House Parliament and held the Prime Minister, A. N. R. Robinson, and a number of his ministers, as hostages. The leader of the coup attempt, Yasin Abu Bakr, took over the television station. His broadcast of the news of the revolution astonished the general population and led to outbreaks of looting and arson in Port of Spain. The army remained aligned with the established government and after six tense days Abu Bakr surrendered.[5] Although the precise circumstances in which the aborted coup was conducted were peculiar to Trinidad it was an exceptionally forceful demonstration of the salience of cultural factors in the postcolonial politics of the region.

The response of territorial governments to challenges to the status quo has been coercive and punitive but British expectations that, without a powerful federal centre, the nationalist leaders of the region would establish personalist dictatorships have proven to be misplaced. With the notable exceptions of Grenada under Gairy and Guyana under

Burnham, democratic parliamentary elections have remained a feature of political life in the Anglophone Caribbean after independence.
Despite the violence which has accompanied Jamaican electoral campaigns, outcomes have been largely uncontested and both PNP and JLP
governments have left office to make way for their bitter rivals. In the
Eastern Caribbean, although the political parties that were in the vanguard of the struggle for independence have often proven difficult to
dislodge, most of them have been removed from office as a consequence
of electoral defeat. On Barbados, Errol Barrow, whose supposedly dictatorial tendencies had been advertised within the British government in
the months before independence, was defeated in the 1976 election and
succeeded as Prime Minister by Grantley Adams's son, Tom Adams. Four
years later, the St Kitts and Nevis Labour Party which, following the
deaths of both Bradshaw and Southwell, came under the leadership of
Lee Moore, was defeated by the opposition People's Action Movement of
Kennedy Simmonds who then led the country to independence.[6] It was
on St Vincent that the party of labour went into earliest and steepest
decline. Ebenezer Joshua had been an early *bête noire* of the Colonial
Office but they were unable to prevent him from becoming Chief Minister of the island in 1956. His People's Political Party (PPP) was eventually
defeated by the St Vincent Labour Party in the election of 1967 and in
1979 the PPP lost every seat it contested.[7] The party which proved most
difficult to dislodge was the Antigua Labour Party (ALP) of Vere Bird and
his sons, Vere Jnr and Lester Bird; it spent nearly four decades in office,
with a five-year hiatus in the early 1970s, and was responsible for the
slow corruption of political life on the island.[8] Discontent with the ALP
intensified after an investigation by Louis Blom Cooper and Geoffrey
Robertson in 1990 confirmed that Vere Bird Jnr was implicated in the
transhipment of Israeli arms to the Medellin drug cartel in Columbia.[9]
By the late 1990s many Antiguans had concluded that the ALP were only
able to cling to office because of the manipulation of the voting system. A three-person Commonwealth Observer Group which witnessed
the 1999 election identified malpractice including problems with the
electoral register, ALP dominance of media outlets and the cooption of
the organs of the state for the purposes of party political campaigning.
Even in the case of Antigua, however, the ALP eventually suffered electoral defeat: in 2004 Baldwin Spencer's United Progressive Party won an
election which was again monitored by a Commonwealth team who
declared it 'credible', despite continuing imperfections.[10]

One tradition of thinking which nationalist leaders inherited from the
era of metropolitan control was that, in a place as inherently unstable

as the Anglophone Caribbean, order was best secured through authoritarian politics; this was most starkly illustrated in Guyana and Grenada. In the former case, the politics of electoral fraud reached a higher degree of perfection under the direction of Forbes Burnham than the Birds ever achieved in Antigua. The PNC's electoral triumphs in 1968, 1973 and 1980 appeared to show ever-increasing support for Burnham's premiership; on the last of these occasions his party won 41 seats compared to 10 for Jagan's PPP. The favoured tactic of the governing party was to make fraudulent use of the overseas vote. An investigation by the British Parliamentary Human Rights Group (PHRG) into the 1980 elections found 'massive evidence that large numbers of eligible voters were denied the right to vote.' A further report by the PHRG, in collaboration with Americas Watch, reviewed the entire history of electoral manipulation as well as itemised the PNC's control over the media and intimidation of the opposition.[11] Despite his official adherence to the doctrine of Cooperative Socialism, Burnham outmatched other leaders in the region in his assault on opposition from the left. As well as an expansion in the numbers of the police and army he established paramilitary groups such as the Guyana National Service and the People's Militia, which became known in the demotic as 'kick down the door gangs'.[12] Two events drew international attention to the corrupt and sinister nature of Guyanese politics. In 1978 the entire population of the Jonestown community was murdered or committed suicide. The residents were members of the People's Temple, which was one of a number of bizarre religious sects which Burnham had sponsored and which became an informal part of the Guyanese security state.[13] In 1980, Walter Rodney, who had returned to Guyana to resume his career of political activism, was killed by a car bomb while campaigning as an electoral candidate against the PNC. Rodney had played a key role in the establishment of the Working People's Alliance and was in the midst of preparing a history of Guyanese labour which was published posthumously. Only after Burnham's death in 1985, did the politics of electoral coercion begin to recede sufficiently for a measure of reconciliation between opposition groups and the government to occur which paved the way for the return of Cheddi Jagan and the PPP to power in 1992.[14]

In the aftermath of his election victory in 1967, Eric Gairy embarked on a policy of repression in which any challenges to his personal rule were interpreted as a threat to political order on Grenada. He responded to the spread of Black Power movements across the Anglophone

Caribbean even more violently than Shearer in Jamaica or Williams in Trinidad. Demonstrations in St George's in May 1970 echoed the challenge to Williams in Port of Spain but, whereas in Trinidad the government's efforts to introduce repressive legislation were frustrated by the parliamentary process, in Grenada Gairy was able to force through an Emergency Powers Act. He also established a personal protection unit, which later became known as the Mongoose Gang. These 'police aides' came to regard the role of intimidating the opposition as an essential part of their remit and they particularly targeted the emerging New Jewel Movement (NJM). This new group was a coalition of Marxists, Black Power activists and liberal reformists who demanded independence from residual British control, while also challenging Gairy's autocracy. On 18 November 1973 NJM leaders were attacked by Gairy's police force during a visit to Grenville to consult with local business leaders about a planned strike. Two months later Gairy's thugs murdered Rupert Bishop during an assault on the headquarters of the Seamen and Waterfront Workers' Union.[15] Despite opposition to Gairy's rule from all sections of society, including the church, the independent trade unions and the middle classes as well as the radical left, he was successful in negotiating independence from Britain and won the first elections of the postcolonial era through a mixture of intimidation and fraud. It was in these circumstances that the NJM resorted to extra-Parliamentary methods and, while Gairy was in Barbados, a popular revolution took place in March 1979. The spark which set off the coup was the wholly plausible rumour that Gairy was planning to have the NJM leaders assassinated.[16]

The risk of concentrating on the exceptional moments in the history of the region after independence is that it paints a picture of life in the region that manages to be both too bleak and too flattering. The portrayal can be taken as too bleak because moments of crisis such as the failed coup in Trinidad or the national emergency in Jamaica during the attempt to arrest Coke are untypical; the regimes of Burnham and Gairy are unrepresentative of the general political life of the region and most governments have come and gone in a recognisably democratic process. However, the irregularity of political crises also camouflages the ongoing desperation and poverty of many people who live in the region. An analysis of the place of the Anglophone Caribbean in the structures of international politics and economics, which will be necessarily brief, can at least provide some sense of these conditions.

Development, dependency and overseas intervention in the Anglophone Caribbean

Political autonomy and economic development were prioritised by the nationalist politicians who emerged in the 1930s and 1940s. Since the conquest of the region by the European powers, political activity in the Americas had been constrained by the exigencies of British, French, Spanish and Dutch policy. Although in the case of the Anglophone Caribbean, metropolitan influence had often been limited by the power of the plantocracy and the neglectfulness of the imperial authorities in London, from the middle of the nineteenth century the imposition of Crown Colony government in all the territories, other than Barbados, demonstrated that British interests could be made to prevail. The gradual transfer of legislative and executive authority to locally elected politicians and the diminution of crown influence in the twentieth century amounted to the essence of decolonisation. However, politicians in both the metropolis and the periphery were acutely conscious of the fact that political power was not always exercised through formal constitutional means, as the case of American involvement in British Guiana demonstrated. It had been hoped that the vulnerability of the territories to covert and overt intervention would get remedied by establishing a strong federation which would have a significant voice in regional and international politics, but the disintegrationist effect of island loyalties left the region politically fragmented and susceptible to pressure from overseas. The financial fragility of the newly elected governments was not remedied in the last years of imperial control and the nationalists were conscious that additional capital was essential to achieve the seminal goals of developing and diversifying their economic base. The notion of developmentalism became integral to the politics of the Anglophone Caribbean after the riots of the 1930s. For long periods of its colonial history, economic policy had been directed simply at maintaining the viability of the plantation system. The independent governments inherited a relatively novel responsibility for both ameliorating the worst social effects of economic inequality and expanding the range of productive activities on the islands.[17] Now that legislation and executive action both rested on popular consent this was essential; unlike colonial administrators, democratically elected politicians were obliged to show concern for the social conditions in which economic activities were conducted. However, remedial measures, such as efforts to attract overseas investment and increase exports, inevitably increased dependence on overseas capital and international markets.

One avenue of economic self-help which was available to the governments of the newly independent Caribbean countries was to pool their own internal markets and capital resources, which meant a return to the principles which had underpinned the defunct federation. When the Prime Minister, Grantley Adams spoke in the final adjournment debate of the federal Parliament, he chose to quote one of the Fireside Poets, James Russell Lowell, who provided an imaginary rendering of Oliver Cromwell's views of the likelihood of a republican utopia: 'And doubtless, after us, some purer scheme/ Will be shaped out by wiser men than we.'[18] Prospects for a republican England and a united Caribbean have proven equally unsatisfactory. The history of the Caribbean Community (CARICOM) has not established a basis either for political union or markedly greater regional self-sufficiency. CARICOM was preceded by the Caribbean Free Trade Association (CARIFTA) which, in 1965, took over the task of coordinating regional policy with the aim of liberalising trade policy. It was only with the signing of the Treaty of Chaguaramas in 1973 by the independent states of Jamaica, Trinidad, Guyana and Barbados that a Common Market was established. Although it included agreement to a common external tariff, the treaty allowed numerous exemptions which facilitated the continuation of quotas and unequal duties between the member states. In 1989 CARICOM set itself the more ambitious goal of establishing a Single Market and Economy but it was not until 2006 that the members began phased implementation of a programme which was intended to culminate in the free movement of labour and the harmonisation of tax policies.[19] These were the issues which had caused the demise of the original federation and their enactment by CARICOM has once again been accompanied by acrimony and procrastination.

Given the limits of regional cooperation, national planning became the principal influence on economic policy but, in many respects, the story of political independence has been the story of a loss of local economic control. In the 1950s and 1960s a new generation of economists working on the nearby mainland of South America, including Raul Prebisch and Andre Gunder Frank warned of the dangers which dependency posed to peripheral economies; at the same time Norman Manley, Alexander Bustamante and Eric Williams pursued policies which increased the dependence of the Anglophone Caribbean on overseas capital. Given the absence of local financial resources, the inevitable curtailment of British economic assistance and the necessity of finding jobs for the increasing numbers of unemployed and underemployed, greater reliance on external investment appeared to be a requirement of any programme to diversify production. It was the failure of this strategy which laid the basis for continuing social instability on Jamaica and Trinidad. The new industries which were financed by overseas capital generated an estimated 20,000 additional jobs in the 1950s and 1960s which was wholly inadequate to meet the expansion of the population, which in Jamaica amounted to an increase of 25,000 annually between 1956 and 1968. Had it not been for the Immigration and Nationality Act of 1965, which reopened the American labour market to Caribbean migrants, the social pressures caused by the oversupply of labour would have been even more pronounced. In 1968, which was a peak year, 17,470 Jamaicans and 5,266 Trinidadians emigrated to the United States.[20] The stagnation in economic production during the 1970s made the task of relieving the extremes of poverty which existed on the islands still more onerous. Having gained control of economic strategy from the British in the 1940s and 1950s, nationalist leaders in Trinidad, Barbados and Jamaica were obliged to surrender it to the International Monetary Fund (IMF) as other sources of international credit dried up. The most contentious and extreme instance of this development was in Jamaica where Michael Manley initially resisted proposals which would entail financial retrenchment but in 1977 negotiated a deal with the IMF which required significant reductions in government expenditure.[21]

With the partial exceptions of Antigua and Grenada, on the Windwards and Leewards democratic traditions have largely been upheld but the inequities of the status quo have never been adequately confronted. Significant growth has been achieved but frequently at the expense of substituting or supplementing low-wage employment in the plantation economy with low-wage employment in the service sector. The strategy of continued reliance on agricultural exports and a new foray into services has generated problems of its own. In the case of Antigua, Paget Henry has noted that after 1960 governmental energy, which might have been devoted to encouraging a measure of economic diversity, was wholly transferred to the promotion of tourism. The number of tourist arrivals on the island increased from 12,853 in 1958 to 97,901 in 1980. Henry also itemised the factors which limit the stimulant effect of tourism: employment in the industry tends to be seasonal; the low wage and low status jobs are generally filled by local people, while top managerial and clerical positions are occupied by expatriates; few links have been established with the wider economy; and there is a great deal of financial 'leakage' away from the island in the form of the import of goods and additional services from overseas.[22] Nevertheless,

Antigua and the other islands of the Leewards and Windwards were able to achieve a significant measure of growth in the 1980s, which was the first decade of full independence, as the recovery of the global economy after the crises of the previous decade led to a rise in commodity prices and a boom in international tourism.[23] British scepticism about whether the small islands could be economically viable has proven misplaced but they remain vulnerable and dependent upon the vicissitudes of the international economy.

During the era of political independence the Anglophone Caribbean witnessed fewer examples of overt external meddling and subterfuge directed from outside the region than the Hispanophone Caribbean.[24] The most conspicuous exceptions were the American invasion of Grenada in 1984 and the still unresolved controversy over CIA involvement in the defeat of the Manley government in the 1980 Jamaican election. Reagan's decision to send the marines to Grenada has been justified on the grounds that it took place at the behest of regional governments and prevented the consolidation of a nascent military dictatorship under Hudson Austin in the aftermath of the murder of the Prime Minister, Maurice Bishop.[25] A more convincing interpretation is that the intervention was the logical conclusion of a policy of American confrontation with the civilian administration of Bishop's New Jewel Movement. The emergence of 'another Cuba' in the Anglophone Caribbean had long been anathema to American policymakers and this message was constantly reiterated to the British government during the era of decolonisation, most stridently in the case of Guiana. Evidence of the Marxist inclinations of the NJM leaders inevitably prompted a reaction in Washington. The Reagan administration attempted to prevent the European Economic Community, the World Bank and the IMF from funding various development projects which the Bishop government sought to undertake. They also made a loan to other local governments through the Caribbean Development Bank conditional upon the exclusion of Grenada.[26] Tom Adams of Barbados and Eugenia Charles of Dominica acted as regional cheerleaders for the American invasion but there is little doubt that it would have gone ahead without their support. Despite the reservations of the American Joint Chiefs of Staff, Reagan's new National Security Adviser, Robert McFarlane, had briefed him on the need for a major operation, ostensibly to rescue American nationals, on 17 October, which was after the arrest of Bishop but two days before his execution and Austin's declaration of martial law.[27] The scale of the invasion and its dramatic rendering by Hollywood in Clint Eastwood's film *Heartbreak Ridge* have given the event unmistakeable prominence in the history of America's relations with the Caribbean; by contrast, the question of whether there was an attempt by the CIA to destabilise the Jamaican government in the 1970s remains an ongoing source of controversy. The dissident CIA agent, Philip Agee, claimed that a number of CIA agents were operating in support of the JLP from the American embassy in Kingston and the accusations were given fuller treatment in Jenny Pearce's book *Under the Eagle*.[28] American policymakers denied the accusations and in his recent autobiography Seaga has insisted that the accusations have been fabricated.[29] What is undeniable is that Washington pursued economic policies to undermine Michael Manley's reforms, including drastic cuts in assistance programmes and reductions in bauxite imports from Jamaica, which exacerbated the country's debt crisis.[30] By this point British influence in Jamaica had dissipated and it was the government in Washington which entered a close Cold War alliance with the Seaga government in the 1980s. The new era of American subsidy seemed to confirm that dependency was the price to be paid for a measure of social and political respite.

Britain and the Anglophone Caribbean at the end of empire

The notion that the nationalist leaders of the Anglophone Caribbean were ineffectual in promoting the decolonisation of the region has been propagated both by the defenders of Colonial Office policymaking, in the vindicatory tradition, and critics of the postcolonial governments, in the inculpatory school of historiography, yet it is almost entirely without foundation. In the instance both of the individual territories and the broader federation the British were both grudging and excessively cautious in responding to the demands of nationalist leaders for the demission of authority. In many respects this is what one would expect, given the set of presuppositions which animated metropolitan thinkers in the era of decolonisation. Yet a commentator as sophisticated as Obika Gray identified nationalist rivalry, rather than British procrastination, as the factor which delayed decolonisation. Gray states: 'the native intermediate class seemed unable to free itself from the bane of either xenophobia or loyalty to empire... the local leaders not only became willing apprentices but also pursued the consolidation of their respective organizations with a vigour that detracted from the speedy liquidation of colonial rule.'[31] Although it would have been impossible to find either a nationalist leader or a Colonial Office bureaucrat who by the 1950s did not envisage eventual independence for the Caribbean, there was a difference between them: it was the nationalist leaders of the region who pressed for the transfer of power as rapidly as possible, while the Colonial Office attempted to retain as much of their residual constitutional authority as seemed practicable in an atmosphere of mounting hostility to colonialism. This was true in the case of Manley's attempts to introduce new constitutional reforms in Jamaica in the early 1950s and was still more evident in the reaction to Williams's campaign for a fully independent federation in 1960, which attracted the scorn of the Colonial Office. The British government finally acceded to immediate independence for Jamaica and Trinidad in 1961–1962 which was the point when no other options were available. After that period the usual pattern re-emerged: the Colonial Office effectively vetoed the demands of Barrow and others that an Eastern Caribbean federation should become independent at the moment of its formation and thought in terms of yet another period of colonial apprenticeship. When this project collapsed they refused internal self-government to the Windwards and Leewards and offered instead a new formula of Associated Statehood under which they retained a licence to intervene in local politics, as the case of Anguilla demonstrated.

The question of what the metropolitan authorities hoped to achieve by prolonging the process of decolonisation is sometimes obscured by their repeated insistence that they had no national interests to defend in the region. What was at stake, in their understanding, were the prized values of order and stability. Despite the preoccupation of imperial officials with the shortcomings of the nationalist leadership, in an era of ideological conflict in Southeast Asia, communal violence in South Asia and racial antagonism in East Africa, the Anglophone Caribbean appeared a safe haven for British ideas about a temperate and conservative kind of politics. Whenever a debate broke out within the British government about the next round of constitutional reform, the justification for the policy of cautious incrementalism remained the same: peace and social order were much prized but were endangered by the process of decolonisation which, because it was accompanied by democratisation, gave rise to a form of politics which encouraged the worst demotic instincts of local politicians. This thinking reflected both historical circumstances and contemporary factors. In historical terms, the metropolitan authorities had always confronted the same puzzle in the Anglophone Caribbean because of the stark conflict between the European socio-economic elites and the much larger numbers of African and Indian workers who were brought to the region either as slaves or as indentured workers. Against the colonists' reliance on the threat of force to contain popular hostility, the authorities in London usually favoured a more mixed strategy embracing both coercion and meliorist reform. In the first half of the twentieth century the decline in the political power of the European plantocracy and the rise of an intermediate class of bourgeoisie predominantly African-Caribbean businessmen and professionals, rendered the old dilemmas in a new and even more acute form. Once the latter group began to demand political authority, the Colonial Office inevitably questioned whether they would use it responsibly. In this context the issue of trustworthiness was inextricably tied to the question of how the intermediate class would regulate their relations with the working class. This was a particularly sensitive issue because of the tendency to characterise the general population as truculent and unruly but biddable. The destructive labour disputes on St Kitts, Grenada and some of the other islands or the use made of violence and intimidation during popular elections in Jamaica, Trinidad and Barbados were seen as grim portents for the future. The British acknowledged the dispiriting economic conditions which provided the context for local disorder but found this cause insufficient to account for the extent of the protests, which could only be fully explained by drawing on aggravating, auxiliary factors, including the rebellious inclinations of the population at large and the recklessness of local political leadership.

Fear of insurrection on the islands had been an ingrained part of British thinking about the Caribbean for centuries and the post-war generation of policymakers was fully acquainted with the events of the late 1930s during which almost every territory had seemed in danger of descending into lawlessness. Two novel and conflicting ideological developments entrenched British apprehensions in the era of decolonisation: the first was the rise of Garveyite notions of black empowerment, which seemed to constitute a particular threat in those Eastern Caribbean territories with significant non-African minorities, including Trinidad, Barbados and Guiana; the second was the emergence of prominent Caribbean communists such as Ferdinand Smith, Cheddi Jagan and C. L. R. James. In retrospect it is clear that the British overestimated the extent to which either of these movements endangered the decolonisation settlement. This was most evident on Barbados where the increasing rowdiness which accompanied popular elections was taken as a possible precedent for attacks by the African majority against the formerly dominant European elites who accentuated tensions by their determination to maintain a policy of social segregation, even as white political supremacy was extinguished. In Trinidad the rhetoric of the PNM leadership provided further grounds for British apprehensions. Williams was usually keen to promulgate the notion that racism was an imperialist contamination which had no role in an independent Trinidad but in reacting to the emergence of a pre-dominantly Indian party which was bitterly critical of his government, he began to stray towards the notion that minority populations were potentially disloyal and that this disloyalty emanated from a reluctance to accept African-Trinidadian leadership. Despite the concerns aroused by these developments, the politics of race did not predominate in either Barbados or Trinidad after independence. The generation of nationalist leaders who assumed control of the islands' politics became deeply suspicious of the politics of black empowerment. At the end of the 1960s and the beginning of the 1970s men like Hugh Shearer, Williams and Gairy found ways to circumvent, diffuse or simply suppress popular expressions of cultural discontent. With the exception of Guyana, British expectations that democratic rule in a Caribbean context would lead to widespread racial conflict were confounded. Such predictions had a degree of plausibility because race was a subject over which Caribbean people themselves liked to obsess, but the emphasis given to this feature of life in the region, and more particularly to the supposed 'anti-white racism' of Williams and others, was also a transparent attempt to deflect attention from metropolitan neuroticism. Official files were not generally the place where policymakers would vent their feelings about other races but the quotidian belittlement of Caribbean sensibilities which litter the minutes and memoranda of the day certainly evince an innate sense of superiority. The rhetoric which shaped the debate about immigration is even more suggestive and provides evidence of metropolitan fears about miscegenation. And on one occasion sentiments of racial superiority were made explicit. In October 1962, during a satirical exchange between Colonial Office officials over what the motto of the deceased federation might have been, the Permanent Under-Secretary, Hilton Poynton, suggested 'Ten little nigger boys'.[32]

Overt statements of hostility to communism were common during the Cold War era but in the case of the Caribbean it was frequently the overbearing attitude of the United States rather than subversion by the Soviet Union which was most vexing for British policymakers. As Jason Parker has pointed out the influence of the United States in shaping British policy in the region predated the Cold War era and had an intermittent character: for most of the time Washington would defer to British sensibilities but, on occasions, American interventions proved decisive.[33] The most significant example was in British Guiana. Without

Kennedy's decision to issue a direct challenge to British policy, the country would have become independent in 1962 under the leadership of Cheddi Jagan. It is much more difficult to speculate about how Jagan might have governed but the factual, as opposed to counter-factual, record demonstrates that Anglo-American subterfuge exacerbated the antagonism between Guianese of African and Indian descent. In the later historiographical rush to blame Washington for the calamities which ensued, British policymakers have been fortunate in evading their share of responsibility because, after the initial American 'veto', it was Duncan Sandys who shaped the indirect tactics which led to Jagan's downfall; in pursuing an activist policy, he frequently found himself at odds with American strategists who favoured the blunter instrument of a reversion to direct rule. Even when it was not engaged in overt meddling, the United States cast a long shadow over the region, as the fears about the role of the Florida mafia in Anguilla vividly illustrated. In this late episode in the colonial history of the region, British policymakers became fixated on the influence of American criminal organisations as a potential stimulant for disorder. On more mundane issues such as federalism, financial aid and even constitutional reform, it was common for British officials to engage in swift glances or even long glares at the American colossus when considering problems associated with defence and economic viability. They gazed eastwards towards the Soviet Union less frequently but the notable and instructive exception in this regard was the case of Ferdinand Smith. The British interpreted Smith's return to the region as a Soviet-inspired challenge to their authority and their response echoed the McCarthyism which was prevalent in the United States. Smith's activities provoked anxiety because his plans to collaborate with other Caribbean communists were interpreted as a revolutionary challenge to the norms of decolonisation. Rather than playing the game of party formation, electoral campaigning and a negotiated transfer of power, Smith appeared to be pursuing a populist strategy which, rather than channelling demotic discontent, threatened to inflame it. His efforts were frustrated by a paucity of resources, divisions amongst his potential allies and the overwhelming efforts of the colonial authorities to strangle any popular communist movement at birth. The extent of the counter-measures undertaken by apparently liberal figures like Foot again illustrates the consuming British anxieties about any potential disruption to the smooth transfer of political authority to the periphery of empire.

The other features of British policy were, to a degree, matters of tone but illustrate the narrow conservatism of official thinking: they were personalist, in the sense of being obsessed both with the pernicious influence of anti-colonial critics and also the potential mitigating effect of reliable collaborators; backward looking, in the constant emphasis given to the notion that Caribbean societies were mired by the circumstances of the past in a condition of atrophy; and self-justifying in that, whenever a post-mortem was required into a failed policy or initiative, the culprits were always found amongst elected legislators and activists in the Caribbean rather than in Government House or Whitehall. Another way of explaining the personalism of British policy is to say that it was concerned overwhelmingly with agency rather than structure. Although briefing papers would allude to socio-economic conditions in the region, the real British obsession was with character. This was evident both in the belief that Ferdinand Smith could infect the entire Caribbean with communism and in the lauding of Norman Manley as the guarantor of stability in the region. Universal and unbroken acclaim for Manley did not depend on the long acquaintance of Foot or Creech Jones; the British Prime Minister, Harold Macmillan, who took no great interest in the affairs of the Anglophone Caribbean, also described him as 'head and shoulders above any other politician in the West Indies.' Praise for Manley's superlative qualities usually provided the basis for a sharp contrast with the character flaws of his rivals. Macmillan's short diary entry also contains parenthetical reference to Bustamante as 'old and ruthless but the most attractive demagogue in the area.'[34] Despite the flippancy of his tone, Macmillan's comments were typical of British efforts to distinguish the sober methods of Manley from the vulgar appeal to the masses to which other nationalist leaders resorted. Politicians as different as Jagan, Gairy and Bustamante all attracted condemnation for their willingness to engage in inflammatory rhetoric at a time when they were supposed to be serving as apprentices in the art of government, which, in the British view, required them to distance themselves from the purportedly juvenile politics of popular discontent. While the British were willing to concede that one or two politicians of exceptional rectitude had the requisite guile to circumvent the usual methods by which nationalist leaders obtained influence, on the whole the personalisation of the issues turned out to be another way to express their disapproval of what they perceived as the rowdy and minatory nature of Caribbean politics.

On those occasions when the official analysis of the region's problems proceeded beyond the provocations of Smith or Jagan, or the incapacities of Adams or Bradshaw, it generally alighted on the intrinsically tragic history of the region as a potential explanation for the character of contemporary Caribbean society. The record of natural disaster, grinding poverty and popular rebellion was not one which greatly appealed to the British imagination; as far as orientalist notions had an influence on the British Empire's occident, they were denuded of the romantic associations prevalent in the works of Richard Burton or T. E. Lawrence. The idea that tawdry depths lay beneath the surface of the tropical paradise was so common in British governmental, literary and popular representations of the region that it became a cliché. There was ample objective evidence in favour of such a view to be found in the subsistence living conditions of the unemployed in West Kingston or the degrading environment of the Indian sugar workers in Guiana but it took on a more explicitly ideological character when it was used as underpinning for an unremittingly gloomy prognosis for the region's politics. British scepticism about the transformative projects of the region's nationalists and socialists fell into this category. Manley, Williams and Jagan were all, from their different perspectives, attempting to animate the population of the Anglophone Caribbean with a vision of a more egalitarian and communal society. The hostility they expressed towards British officialdom stemmed from the conservative and obstructive attitudes of metropolitan policymakers who seemed to doubt the viability of almost any form of meliorist action. This was most evident during the course of labour disputes. Although the British were frequently critical of the attitudes of employers, they invariably concluded that strikes were counter-productive and that the workers' case for an improvement in their living conditions was unrealistic. The one significant and qualified exception to this pervading scepticism applied to the largest measure of all which was the establishment of a federation across the Anglophone Caribbean which, it was believed, would provide new economic opportunities and a greater measure of security for the region. Even in this instance, it was more common for metropolitan actors to emphasise the significance of federalism as a prophylactic measure which would mitigate the worst excesses of the new era of popular politics. When they were required to hurriedly reshape the constitutional order in the aftermath of the Jamaican referendum, they did so in an atmosphere of pervasive gloom about the future of the territories in an era of unilateral independence.

The blame for the failure of the federation was, inevitably, laid at the door of the nationalist leadership. In the last words of his detailed account of the negotiations, John Mordecai suggested that what the Caribbean required in order to cultivate a greater sense of unity was 'a new generation of political leaders, more responsive than their predecessors to the demands of restraint and compassion, and better able to nourish that seed and redress the past.'[35] The 'leaders' to whom Mordecai was referring were the nationalist politicians whose inadequacies he had itemised in the preceding text and emphatically not the British governors, ministers and officials whose policies had played an influential role in the demise of the federation. For example, there are no blemishes entered on Hailes's record in Mordecai's account, and this reflects the friendship that developed between the two men when they were both involved in administering the federation.[36] What was missing from Mordecai's otherwise comprehensive narrative was any critical analysis of the debates and quarrels which took place within the portals of British officialdom and which were usually resolved by a series of compromises which only increased the force of centrifugal pressures in the Caribbean. In particular, the majority view inside metropolitan policymaking circles was that the federation, like the individual territories, must proceed towards independence as slowly as feasible. British refusal to expedite the process of decolonisation conflicted with nationalist pressure to accelerate constitutional progress and hindered efforts to promote regional integration. While the Colonial Office assumed that the resulting disenchantment was a consequence of the unit territories moving too fast, the nationalist leadership were convinced that it was caused by the pedestrian pace at which constitutional authority was transferred to the federation. More significant still was the argument over whether the politics of decolonisation entailed a reduction in financial assistance to the region, which pitted peripheral advocacy of a compensatory principle against metropolitan assumptions about the necessity for self-reliance. Even without adjudicating on the merits of either case it is plain that the argument had a destructive effect. While the Colonial Office had some sympathy for the problems which would ensue as a consequence of the rapid curtailment of subsidies to a region which required capital investment in order to address the social problems which the new governments had inherited, it was Treasury parsimony which usually prevailed on the British side of the argument. As a consequence Caribbean disillusionment with the likely economic implications of decolonisation was on the rise even before political independence had been obtained. The neglect of this aspect of decolonisation in the historiography reflects a broader tendency to sweep aside the critical case against the architects of British strategy, made by Eric Williams and others. At the end of empire, democratically elected politicians were expected to rectify problems which had been left wholly unaddressed by generations of imperial policymakers; they took on the remedial task of diversifying economic activity and achieving a measure of social progress in an international environment over which they had almost no influence. Any attempt to tell the story of the transition to political independence in the Anglophone Caribbean which does not take account of these factors is incomplete.

This is not to suggest that it is necessary to reconstruct a heroic model of nationalist leadership such as that contained in Williams's self-laudatory book *Inward Hunger*.[37] The record of the independent governments of the region in the subsequent half-century would make such an enterprise wholly implausible. What is required is some rebalancing of the account which draws attention back to the genuine confrontation which took place between the architects of British decolonisation strategy and the liberationist ideals which emerged in the Anglophone Caribbean in the middle of the twentieth century. The focus of analysis has been on who is to blame for what has gone wrong since and, while the metropolitan party has escaped largely unscathed, the leaders of the anti-colonial movement have been found culpable. Official governmental records and the memoirs of the British protagonists frequently denigrated the nationalist programme and this tendency has been reinforced by a new generation of Caribbean writers which has found fault with its own societies and particularly its political leadership. Yet the attainment of independence in the face of metropolitan indifference and a grim colonial inheritance was an achievement in itself and not just the precursor to years of authoritarian politics and continued inequality. The short era of decolonisation has been sandwiched between a period of unalloyed colonial exploitation and an age of frustration and impotence, and has been almost overwhelmed by its own historical context. This is perhaps not surprising. The first Europeans who followed Columbus to the Caribbean exterminated the indigenous population of the islands through warfare and disease. Their successors repopulated the territory by trading Africans as goods. The survivors and their descendants endured hard labour, malnourishment and physical coercion. After the abolition of the slave trade, a new generation of indentured labourers continued to suffer some of the worst labour conditions of the nineteenth century. In the twenty-first century the independent Caribbean remains an exploitative society in which the resources of the state are called upon to stymie challenges to the status quo. And in this context the actions of the last generation of British imperialists in delaying constitutional progress, restricting personal liberties in pursuit of the Cold War, offering a less-than-generous financial settlement and manipulating the electoral process where it thought necessary, may appear to be venial sins. As well as acquitting metropolitan policymakers of the charges of duplicity, obstruction and equivocation, such an attitude deflects attention from the challenges encountered by the people of the region at a time when they were engaged in a constructive exercise which embraced notions of autonomy, democratisation and egalitarianism. The application of such ideas was imperfect and the failure was not wholly a consequence of the impedimentary approach of the British but that does not necessitate a teleological account of decolonisation in which efforts to obtain independence are merely the prelude to a new era of corrupt and disciplinarian politics. The chances of reviving a liberationist project are not improved either by denigrating even the incomplete achievements of the first nationalist generations in challenging European imperialism and establishing a more democratic system in the Anglophone Caribbean or by underestimating the confrontation between peripheral and metropolitan agents at the end of empire.

Notes

1 Introduction

1. *Jamaica Gleaner*, 13 June 2010 (http://jamaica-gleaner.com).
2. *Barbados Advocate*, 20 February 2011 (http://barbadosadvocate.com).
3. C. Hall, 'What is a West Indian?' in B. Schwarz (ed.), *West Indian Intellectuals in Britain* (Manchester, 2003), 31–50.
4. J. C. Everitt, 'The Growth and Development of Belize City', *Journal of Latin American Studies* 18/1 (1986), 75–111.
5. R. B. Potter, D. Barker, D. Conway and T. Klak, *The Contemporary Caribbean* (Harlow, 2004), Ch. 4.
6. The former Governor, David Taylor, offered a critique of the British government's handling of the crisis. See D. G. P. Taylor, 'British Colonial Policy in the Caribbean', *The Round Table* 355 (2000), 337–344.
7. R. B. Sheridan, *Sugar and Slavery* (Barbados, 1974), Ch. 17.
8. B. Dyde, *Out of the Crowded Vagueness* (Oxford, 2005), 94.
9. J. R. Ward, 'The British West Indies 1748–1815' in P. J. Marshall (ed.), *The Oxford History of the British Empire Vol. 3: The Eighteenth Century* (Oxford, 1998), 432–433.
10. E. Williams and P. Sutton, *Forged From the Love of Liberty* (London, 1981), 329; A. Gomes, *Through a Maze of Colour* (Port of Spain, 1974), Ch. 9.
11. G. E. Eaton, *Alexander Bustamante and Modern Jamaica* (Kingston, 1995), 5.
12. For a study of the role of this group in Jamaican society, see G. Heuman, *Between Black and White* (Westport, 1981).
13. F. Birbalsingh, *The Rise of West Indian Cricket: From Colony to Nation* (London, 1997).
14. See *To Sir With Love* originally published in 1959, *The Mimic Men* from 1967 and *The Hills of Hebron* from 1962. Current editions are published by Vintage, Picador and Ian Randle: E. R. Braithwaite, *To Sir With Love* (London, 2005), V. S. Naipaul, *The Mimic Men* (London, 2011), Sylvia Wynter, *The Hills of Hebron* (Kingston, 2010).
15. M. Craton, *Testing the Chains* (Ithaca, 1982).
16. W. Bell, 'Equality and Social Justice: Foundations of Caribbean Nationalism', *Caribbean Studies* 20/2 (June 1980), 5.
17. For a much more detailed account, see H. McD. Beckles, *A History of Barbados* (Cambridge, 1990).
18. G. Lamming, *In the Castle of My Skin* (London, 1953).
19. H. McD. Beckles, *Natural Rebels* (London, 1989), Ch. 8.
20. Beckles describes the two traditions as 'imperial respectable radicalism and an indigenous revolutionism.' See H. McD. Beckles, 'Radicalism and Errol Barrow in the Political Tradition of Barbados' in G. D. Howe and R. D. Marshall (eds), *The Empowering Impulse* (Kingston, 2001), 222.
21. P. Sherlock, *Norman Manley* (London, 1980), 12–14.

22. *Parliamentary Papers 1934–1935*, Cmd. 4956, Papers relating to the Disturbances in St Christopher, July 1935.
23. J. Rodman and T. Conway, 'The Nexus and the Family Tree' in R. B. Potter, D. Conway and J. Phillips (eds), *The Experience of Return Migration* (Aldershot, 2005), 89–108.
24. G. Brizan, *Grenada: Island of Conflict* (London, 1984), 227.
25. E. Williams, *History of the People of Trinidad and Tobago* (London, 1964), 18.
26. S. Engerman, 'Contract Labour, Sugar and Technology in the Nineteenth Century', *Journal of Economic History* 43/3 (1983), 642.
27. Bolland's essays were collected in O. N. Bolland, *Colonialism and Resistance in Belize* (Belize, 1998).
28. R. Lewis, *Walter Rodney's Economic and Politics Thought* (Kingston, 1998), 189–191.
29. M. St Pierre, *Anatomy of Resistance* (London, 1999), 46–48.
30. The letters can be found at the Churchill Archives Centre, Cambridge: HAIS 4/28.
31. J. Mordecai, *The West Indies: The Federal Negotiations* (London, 1968). A quantitative analysis of Mordecai's index would yield some interesting results: Hailes for example has only six entries, while those for Adams and Manley occupy half a column each. Lennox-Boyd would have appeared on p. 481 had his existence been acknowledged in the text.
32. K. Blackburne, *Lasting Legacy* (London, 1976); H. Foot, *A Start in Freedom* (London, 1964).
33. E. Wallace, *The British Caribbean* (Toronto, 1977), 20–21.
34. S. R. Ashton and D. Killingray (eds), *British Documents on the End of Empire: The West Indies* (B/6), (London, 1999), lxix.
35. The relevant titles are R. Hart, *Rise and Organise* (London, 1989), *Towards Decolonisation* (Kingston, 1999), *Time for a Change* (Kingston, 2004), *The End of Empire* (Kingston, 2006).
36. T. Munroe, *The Politics of Constitutional Decolonization* (Old Woking, 1972), 21–22.
37. O. N. Bolland, *The Politics of Labour in the British Caribbean* (Kingston, 2001).
38. M. Marable, *African Caribbean Politics* (London, 1987), 68.
39. C. Fraser, *Ambivalent Anti-Colonialism* (Westport, 1994).
40. S. Rabe, *US Intervention in British Guiana* (Chapel Hill, 2005); J. C. Parker, *Brother's Keeper* (Oxford, 2008); R. Cox-Alomar, *Revisiting the Transatlantic Triangle* (Kingston, 2009).
41. Crawford and his editor Woodville K. Marshall managed to confine most of the critique of Adams to one chapter, but Solomon's resentment of Gomes proved more difficult to contain within the formal structures of an autobiography. Solomon was perhaps responding to the disobliging remark which Gomes made about him in *Through a Maze of Colour*, although Gomes did not actually mention Solomon by name. See W. Crawford and W. K. Marshall, *I Speak for the People* (Kingston, 2003), Ch. 6, P. Solomon, *Solomon: An Autobiography* (Port of Spain, 1981); A. Gomes, *Through a Maze of Colour* (Port of Spain, 1974), 163.
42. E. Williams, *Inward Hunger* (Princeton, 2006).
43. P. Sherlock, *Norman Manley* (London, 1980); F. A. Hoyos, *Grantley Adams and the Social Revolution* (London, 1974).

44. S. Ryan, *Eric Williams* (Kingston, 2009); K. Boodhoo, *The Elusive Eric Williams* (Kingston, 2002); C. A. Palmer, *Eric Williams and the Making of the Modern Caribbean* (Chapel Hill, 2006).
45. G. K. Lewis, *The Growth of the Modern West Indies* (London, 1968).
46. Ashton and Killingray, *West Indies*, xxxvii–lxxxiii.
47. The National Archives, Kew: CO 1031/356, Blackburne to Wallace, 27 October 1952.
48. Lewis, *Growth*, 269–270.
49. O. Gray, *Radicalism and Social Change in Jamaica* (Knoxville, 1991), 49.
50. Williams and Sutton, *Forged From the Love of Liberty*, 208.
51. FDR Library: Charles Taussig Papers, Box 36, Report of the Visit of Taussig to London, December 1942.

2   The Struggle for Independence 1947–1952

1. *Parliamentary Papers 1947–1948*, Cmd. 7291, Conference on the Closer Association of the British West Indian Colonies, 7–11.
2. M. St Pierre, *Anatomy of Resistance* (London, 1999), 46.
3. O. N. Bolland, *The Politics of Labour in the British Caribbean* (Kingston, 2001), 474–476.
4. G. K. Lewis, *The Growth of the Modern West Indies* (London, 1968), 343.
5. R. Alexander, *A History of Organized Labour in the English Speaking Caribbean* (London, 2004), 424–425.
6. Bolland, *Politics of Labour*, 479.
7. H. Neptune, *Caliban and the Yankees* (Chapel Hill, 2007).
8. G. Horne, *Cold War in a Hot Zone* (Philadelphia, 2007), 104–105.
9. J. Parker, *Brother's Keeper* (Oxford, 2008), 41–52.
10. C. Witham, *Bitter Rehearsal* (London, 2002).
11. The National Archives [Henceforward TNA]: CO 1042/91, Stanley to West Indian Governors, 14 March 1945.
12. TNA: CO 1042/91, Seel to West Indian Governors, 12 February 1947, Governor (Leewards) to Secretary of State, 28 February 1947, Governor (Windwards) to Secretary of State, 6 March 1947, Secretary of State to Governor (Windwards), 15 March 1947, Seel to Arundell, 18 March 1947.
13. G. Lewis, *The Growth of the Modern West Indies* (London, 1968), 348.
14. Horne, *Hot Zone*, 78–80.
15. *Daily Gleaner*, 3 September 1947, 1, 22; 4 September 1947, 1, 8; 8 September 1947, 1; 10 September, 1, 12.
16. A. Gomes, *Through a Maze of Colour* (Port of Spain, 1974), 191–192.
17. TNA: CO 318/484/2, CO Notes for the Conference on Closer Association (ud).
18. *Parliamentary Papers 1947–1948*, Cmd. 7291, Conference on the Closer Association of the British West Indian Colonies, 7.
19. J. Mordecai, *The West Indies: The Federal Negotiations* (London, 1968), 36–38.
20. Gomes, *Maze of Colour*, 195.
21. Richard Hart papers, Institute of Social and Economic Studies, UWI, Mona, CLC 12, Bird to Hart, 9 April 1949.

22. TNA: CO 318/485/5, Rance to Creech Jones, 26 October 1949; CO 318/485/3, Rance to Seel, 30 September 1948.
23. D. Benn, *The Caribbean: An Intellectual History* (Kingston, 2004), Ch. 2.
24. TNA: CO 318/485/5, Extract from meeting of Governors' conference, 7–11 November 1949.
25. TNA: CO 1031/486/2, Summary of Second Meeting of SCAC 17–30 March 1949 with Watt minute, 1 June 1949.
26. TNA: CO 1031/486/2, Summary of Second Meeting of SCAC 24 June–5 July 1949, McPetrie minute, 15 August 1949, Marnham to Rance, 12 September 1949; CO 318/485/5, Rance to Creech Jones, 26 October 1949.
27. TNA: CO 1031/486/1, Extract from Carstairs to Seel, 23 April 1949.
28. S. R. Ashton and D. Killingray (eds), *British Documents on the End of Empire B/6: The West Indies* (London, 1999), Carstairs to Watt, 5 September 1949, 13–14.
29. TNA: CO 318/485/5, Rance to Creech Jones, 26 October 1949, Extract from meeting of Governors' conference, 7–11 November 1949.
30. TNA: CO 318/506/5, Luke to Lloyd, 13 March 1951.
31. TNA: CO 318/506/5, Luke to Rance, 22 May 1951, Foot to Luke, 25 June 1951, Blackburne to Luke, 28 June 1951, Luke to Blackburne, 20 July 1951.
32. TNA: CO 318/506/5, Seel to Beckett, 21 March 1951, Luke minute, 20 April 1951.
33. TNA: CO 318/506/5, Jamaica (Foot) to Secretary of State, 15 August 1951, Luke minute, 18 August 1951, Lloyd minute, 20 August 1951, Griffiths minute 21 August 1951.
34. Kenneth Blackburne Papers, Rhodes House, MSS. Brit. Emp. S. 460, Box 15, Letter from Blackburne to his father, 8 October 1961.
35. H. Foot, *A Start in Freedom* (London, 1964), 140.
36. T. Sealy, *Sealy's Caribbean Leaders* (Kingston, 1991), 145.
37. P. Sherlock, *Norman Manley* (London, 1980), 21.
38. R. Nettleford (ed.), *Manley and the New Jamaica* (London, 1971), xx.
39. The letters are collected in F. Hill (ed.), *Bustamante and his Letters* (Kingston, 1976).
40. Manley was only prepared to accept that Bustamante had lived in the United States, Cuba and Panama. See R. Alexander, *Presidents, Prime Ministers and Governors of the English Speaking Caribbean and Puerto Rico* (London, 1997), 18.
41. Sealy, *Leaders*, 90.
42. Sealy, *Leaders*, 99.
43. Sherlock, *Manley*, 93–96; G. Bustamante, *The Memoirs of Lady Bustamante* (Kingston, 1997), 120.
44. TNA: CO 1031/875/5, Seel minute, 24 April 1947, Note on the Jamaican Political Scene, 16 August 1947.
45. Nettleford, *New Jamaica*, lviii.
46. Alexander, *Presidents*, 22.
47. Bustamante, *Memoirs*, 113.
48. Alexander, *Presidents*, 16.
49. A. Sives, *Elections, Violence and the Democratic Process in Jamaica* (Kingston, 2010), 16.
50. T. Munroe, *The Politics of Constitutional Decolonization* (1972), Ch. 2.

51. G. E. Eaton, *Alexander Bustamante and Modern Jamaica* (Kingston, 1995), 118–120.

52. TNA: CO 137/875/5, Huggins to Creech Jones, 8 April 1947.

53. TNA: CO 137/876/6, Note of a Meeting in Caine's room, 15 July 1948.

54. TNA:CO 137/876/6, Huggins (Jamaica) to Secretary of State, 17 March 1948, CO Note on Revision of the Jamaican Constitution, July 1948, Caine minute, 18 July 1948.

55. R. Hart, *The End of Empire* (Kingston, 2006), 92.

56. Critics include those sympathetic to Manley such as Lewis and Sherlock. See Lewis, *Growth*, 372; Sherlock, *Manley*, 178.

57. Jamaican National Archives: Norman Manley Papers, 4/60/2B/13, Manley to Domingo, 28 July 1948.

58. TNA: CO 137/875/4, Lloyd minute, 6 January 1950, Listowel minute, 9 January 1950.

59. TNA: CO 1031/327, Foot to Luke, 22 October 1951, Lennox-Boyd to Munster, 29 January 1951, Munster minute, 30 January 1951.

60. TNA: CO 1031/327, Heinemann minute, 13 December 1951, Beckett minute, 14 December 1951, Luke minute, 19 December 1951, Lloyd minute, 21 December 1951.

61. Lyttelton was distinguishing the 'true sense' of Fabianism, meaning the employment of skilful delaying tactics, from the ideas of the socialist Fabian Society who were progressive on colonial issues. He almost certainly intended to emphasise the noun rather than the adjective in the deliberately chosen oxymoron 'impartial bias'. TNA: CO 1031/327, Foot to Luke, 12 January 1952, Heinemann minute, 21 January 1952, Note by West India Department, 3 March 1952 with Lyttelton minute (ud).

62. TNA: CO 1031/327, Munster to Lyttelton, 9 April 1952.

63. R. Manley (ed.), *Edna Manley: The Diaries* (London, 1989), entries for 13 March 1952, 6 July 1952, 38–41.

64. Manley Papers, 4/60/2B/15, Manley to Domingo, 24 September 1952.

65. TNA: CO 1031/327, Foot to Luke, 5 May 1952.

66. Nettleford (ed.), *New Jamaica*, Speech to the House of Representatives, 2 July 1952, 123–130.

67. TNA: CO 1031/327, Foot to Luke, 9 July 1952, 11 July 1952, Luke minute, 25 July 1952, Lloyd minute, 26 July 1952.

68. TNA: CO 1031/328, Foot to Wallace, 8 May 1953.

69. O. N. Bolland, *The Politics of Labour in the British Caribbean* (Kingston, 2001); R. J. Alexander, *A History of Organized Labour in the English Speaking West Indies* (London, 2004).

70. Sealy, *Caribbean Leaders*, 52–53.

71. B. Dyde, *Out of the Crowded Vagueness* (Oxford, 2005), 242–243.

72. TNA: CO 1052/529/1, Memorandum on the Labour Situation in St Kitts, 5 September 1947.

73. Bolland, *Politics of Labour*, 491.

74. F. Phillips, *Caribbean Life and Culture* (Kingston, 1991), 96.

75. TNA: CO 152/529/2, Greening to Acting Governor (Leewards), 3 December 1947.

76. These figures are an aggregate for St Kitts, Nevis and Anguilla. The cotton industry was centred on Nevis and the statistics therefore underestimate the

dependence of St Kitts itself on sugar. See *Colonial Office List 1953* (London, 1953), 118.

77. P. Leigh Fermor, *The Traveller's Tree* (London, 1950), 213.
78. TNA: CO 152/529/2, Transcript of Address by Bradshaw, 18 January 1948.
79. TNA: CO 152/529/1, Macnie (Antigua) to Secretary of State, 7 November 1947.
80. TNA: CO 152/529/2, Morgan minute, 24 January 1948.
81. S. W. Mintz, *Sweetness and Power* (New York, 1985), 21.
82. TNA: CO 152/526/, Mathieson minute, 17 January 1949, Soulbury Commission Report on the Organisation of the Sugar Industry.
83. TNA: CO 152/529/2, Leewards (Acting Governor) to Secretary of State, 9 January 1948, 17 January 1948, 22 January 1948, Minute of meeting between Parry and CO officials, 19 March 1948.
84. Richard Hart Papers, SALISES, University of the West Indies, Mona, Caribbean Labour Congress Files [Henceforward CLC] 12, Bradshaw to Hart, 24 February 1948, 9 March 1948.
85. Hart Papers, CLC 12, Hart to Adams, 22 March 1948, Bradshaw to Hart 31 March 1948.
86. TNA: CO 152/529/2, Leewards (Acting Governor) to Secretary of State, 14 March 1948.
87. Arthur Creech Jones Papers, Rhodes House, MSS. Brit. Emp. S332, Box 56, Draft Note on Nationalisation, Note of a Meeting in the Secretary of State's Room, 25 October 1949, Note of a Meeting in Seel's Room, 2 November 1949.
88. *Parliamentary Debates*, 5th series, vol. 450, col. 381, 28 April 1948; TNA: CO 152/529/3, Taylor to Creech Jones, 20 March 1948, Bossom to Morgan, 24 March 1948, Morgan minute, 24 March 1948.
89. *Parliamentary Debates*, 5th series, vol. 441, col. 334–335, 29 July 1947; TNA: CO 152/526/3, Morgan to Creech Jones, 30 January 1949, 14 February 1949.
90. TNA: CO 152/529/2, St Kitts (Greening) to Acting Governor, 17 January 1948, Macnie to Secretary of State, 22 March 1948.
91. TNA: CO 152/527/4, Seel minute, 5 July 1949, Caine minute, 6 July 1949.
92. C. J. Walker, *Oliver Baldwin: A Life of Dissent* (London, 2003), ch. 15.
93. TNA: CO 152/527/4, Baldwin to Secretary of State, 26 June 1948.
94. TNA: CO 152/527/4, Creech Jones to Baldwin, 13 January 1949, Mathieson to Seel, 17 January 1949; CO 152/527/5, Leewards (Acting Governor) to Secretary of State, 1 March 1949, Brown minute, 18 March 1949, Smith minutes, 18 March 1949, 22 March 1949.
95. TNA: CO 152/527/5, Bradshaw to Beckett, 25 November 1949.
96. Kenneth Blackburne Papers, Box 10, Blackburne to his mother, 1 October 1950, 8 October 1950, 22 October 1950.
97. K. Blackburne, *Lasting Legacy* (London, 1976), Ch. 9.
98. Kenneth Blackburne Papers, Box 10, Letters to his mother, September 1951, October 1952, 12, October 1952.
99. A. Payne, P. Sutton and T. Thorndike, *Grenada: Politics, Economics and Society* (London, 1985), Ch. 1; G. Sandford, *Grenada: The Untold Story* (1984); H. O'Shaughnessy, *Grenada: Revolution, Invasion and Aftermath* (1984);

J. Searle, *Grenada: The Struggle Against Destabilisation* (London, 1984), part 1; G. Lewis, *The Jewel Despoiled* (London, 1987), Ch. 4.

100. G. Brizan, *Grenada: Island of Conflict*, Ch. 16.
101. Bolland, *Politics of Labour*, 535–536.
102. A. Singham, *The Hero and the Crowd* (London, 1968); P. A. Noguera, 'The Limits of Charisma' in A. Allahar (ed.), *Caribbean Charisma* (Kingston, 2001), 72–91.
103. Bolland, *Politics of Labour*, 534; Lewis, *Emergence*, 156–157.
104. Lewis, *Growth*, 158.
105. Brizan, *Grenada*, 257–264.
106. TNA: CO 321/428/11, Barltrop to Watson, 24 March 1951.
107. Brizan, *Grenada*, 239–241.
108. Bolland, *Politics of Labour*, 536.
109. TNA: CO 321/428/11, Memorandum by Barltrop, 23 March 1951.
110. Brizan, *Grenada*, 265.
111. TNA: CO 321/428/11, Barltrop to Watson, 24 March 1951.
112. *The Times*, 17 March 1951, 3; *Parliamentary Debates*, 5th series, vol. 485, col. 2422, 21 March 1951.
113. TNA: CO 321/428/11, Watson minute, 6 April 1951.
114. *Parliamentary Debates*, 5th series, vol. 486, col. 191, 4 April 1951.
115. TNA: CO 321/428/11, Note of meeting at Government House, 7 March 1951, Barltrop to Watson, 24 March 1951.
116. TNA: CO 321/428/9, Beamish to Griffiths 9 March 1951, Duncan to Beamish, 8 March 1951.
117. *Parliamentary Debates*, 5th series, vol. 484, col. 1749, 26 February 1951.
118. *Parliamentary Debates*, 5th series, vol. 486, col. 193, 4 April 1951, vol. 488, cols 1005–1006, 6 June 1951; TNA: CO 321/428/9, Bass minute, 25 August 1951, Cook to Legge-Bourke, 28 August 1951. La Rose later migrated to Britain where he founded the first Caribbean publishing house in the country, New Beacon Books. See *The Guardian*, Obituaries, 4 March 2006.
119. TNA: CO 321/428/10, Arundell (Windwards) to Secretary of State, 17 March 1951.
120. TNA: CO 321/429/10, Arundell to Griffiths, 30 April 1951, Arundell (Windwards) to Secretary of State, 4 May 1951, 5 May 1951, 7 May 1951, 17 May 1951.
121. Singham, *Hero*, 117.
122. TNA: CO 321/429/1, Arundell to Secretary of State, 11 March 1951, Noble Smith to Secretary of State, 20 April 1951, Bass minute, 30 April 1951, Luke minutes, 2 May 1951, 9 May 1951, 23 May 1951, 25 May 1951, 20 July 1951, Lloyd minute, 21 July 1951, Luke to Arundell, 27 July 1951, Arundell to Luke, 9 August 1951.
123. Singham, *Hero*, 170–171.

3 Ordering the Islands 1952–1958

1. For an analysis of the significance of Williams' campaign of popular education see G. Lamming, 'The Legacy of Eric Williams', *Callaloo* 20/4 (1997), 731–736.

2. The National Archives, Kew [Henceforward TNA]: CO 968/248, Rance to Luke, 13 November 1952 covering Herbert to Colonial Secretary, 8 November 1952.

3. TNA: CO 968/250, Memorandum on Measures to Combat Communism by Watson (ud), Note of a meeting between Security Liaison Officer and Special Branch Officers, 15 June 1953.

4. T. Munroe, *The Cold War and the Jamaican Left 1950–55* (Kingston, 1992), 11.

5. Munroe, *Left*, 200.

6. R. Nettleford, *Manley and the New Jamaica* (London, 1971), xxv–xxvi.

7. Jamaican National Archives [Henceforward JNA]: Norman Manley Papers, 4/60/2B/15, Manley to Walcott, 11 June 1952.

8. R. Hart, *The End of Empire* (Kingston, 2006), Ch. 16; G. Horne, *Red Seas* (London, 2005), Chs 10–12.

9. TNA: CO 968/250, Lyttelton to West Indian Governors, 12 August 1953 with Memorandum on 'Communist Activities in the British Colonies in the Caribbean Area' (ud).

10. TNA: CAB 158/16, JIC(53)73, Situation in the West Indies, 7 August 1953.

11. TNA: CO 968/248, Jackson to Under-Secretary of State for War, 17 June 1952, Extract from Minutes of Cabinet Official Committee on Communism, 24 September 1952, Jackson to McLeod, 4 November 1952, Luke to McLeod, 30 January 1953.

12. TNA: CO 968/248, Luke minute, 5 December 1952.

13. Munroe, *Left*, 74.

14. TNA: CO 968/250, Measures to Combat Communism in the West Indies, May 1953 by Watson with Jamaica: Repressive Measures against Communism (ud) at Annex.

15. TNA: CO 968/248, Memorandum on a Visit by WFTU Supporters to Barbados (ud).

16. TNA: CO 968/250, Note of a meeting at the Colonial Office, 29 June 1953, Note of Meeting between SLOs and SB representatives in Barbados, 15 June 1953.

17. TNA: CO 968/250, Jamaica (Foot) to Secretary of State, 7 October 1953.

18. TNA: CO 968/248, Jamaica (Foot) to Secretary of State, 17 February 1953, Hopkinson minute (ud), Luke minute, 27 February 1953, Lloyd minute, 2 March 1953.

19. TNA: 968/248, Trinidad (Rance) to Secretary of State, 31 October 1952, 19 November 1952, Shaw minute, 21 October 1952; CO 968/250, Measures to Combat Communism by Watson, May 1953.

20. TNA: CO 968/248, Memorandum on visit of WFTU supporters to Barbados (ud).

21. TNA: CO 968/249, Lloyd minute, 8 April 1953.

22. TNA: CO 1031/1961, Crosswell to Colonial Secretary, 1 December 1954.

23. Hart, *End*, 76.

24. TNA: CO 968/302, Jamaica (Foot) to Secretary of State, 28 December 1953, Renison to Secretary of State, 31 December 1953.

25. TNA: CO 1031/1961, Foot to Wallace, 27 January 1954 covering Foot to Bustamante, 16 January 1954, Wallace to Foot, 5 February 1954, minutes by

Wallace, 21 January 1954, Watson, 22 January 1954, Stacpoole, 29 January 1954, Wallace, 1 February 1954.

26. TNA: CO 1031/1961, Foot to Wallace, 6 March 1954 covering Chief Minister to Governor, 2 March 1954, Foot to Wallace, 11 March 1954 covering transcript of Foot's Speech to the Chambers of Commerce.
27. TNA: CO 968/302, Barton minute, 19 December 1953, Heinemann minute, 29 December 1953, Note of a Meeting in Rogers' room 31 December 1953, Barton minute, 2 January 1954, Wallace minute, 4 January 1954, Lloyd minute, 5 January 1954, Hopkinson minute (ud).
28. TNA: CO 1031/1961, Jamaica (Foot) to Secretary of State, 18 March 1954, 19 March 1954.
29. TNA: CO 1031/1961, Jamaica (Foot) to Secretary of State, 29 March 1954, Wallace minute, 2 April 1954, Watson minute, 3 April 1954, Bennett minute, 7 April 1954, Secretary of State to Jamaica (Foot), 16 April 1954, Jamaica (Foot) to Secretary of State, 4 May 1954, Cruchley memorandum, 19 May 1954, Note of a Meeting in Rogers' room, 9 June 1954, Note of a Discussion with Cundall, 16 June 1954, Wallace minutes, 8 June 1954, 20 August 1954.
30. Hart, *End*, 25.
31. TNA: CO 1031/1961, Crosswell to Jamaican Colonial Secretary, 1 December 1954.
32. Munroe, *Left*, 74.
33. S. Rabe, *American Intervention in British Guiana: A Cold War Story* (Chapel Hill, 2005); C. A. Palmer, *Cheddi Jagan and the Politics of Power* (Chapel Hill, 2010); C. Seecharan, *Sweetening Bitter Sugar* (Kingston, 2005). Specifically on the events of 1953, see C. Fraser, 'The PPP on Trial: British Guiana in 1953', *Small Axe* 8/1 (2004), 21–42.
34. C. Jagan, *The West on Trial* (London, 1966), 17.
35. Jagan, *West*, 22.
36. Walter Rodney Archives, Georgetown, Official Report of the Legislative Council, vol. 23, col. 899, 18 January 1952, col. 906, 23 January 1952.
37. T. Sealy, *Sealy's Caribbean Leaders* (Kingston, 2004), 131–132.
38. V. S. Naipaul, *The Middle Passage* (London 1962), 149.
39. Jagan, *West*, Ch. 3.
40. Rabe, *Intervention*, 24–25.
41. Jagan, *West*, 98.
42. TNA: CO 111/791/4, British Guiana (Woolley) to Secretary of State, 9 August 1948, Woolley to Creech Jones, 4 October 1948.
43. TNA: CO 111/791/4, Secretary of State to Woolley, 11 August 1948.
44. TNA: CO 111/791/4, Note of a meeting on 2 November 1948; CO 111/811/7, Watt minute, 14 April 1950.
45. TNA: CO 111/791/4, Seel minute, 11 August 1948.
46. TNA: CO 111/791/4, Note on Matters Discussed during Woolley's Visit (ud), Minutes by Seel, 9 November 1948, Lloyd, 18 December 1948, Listowel, 20 December 1948, Creech Jones, 21 December 1948, Seel, 22 December 1948, Creech Jones to Woolley, 1 January 1949.
47. TNA: CO 111/791/5, Watt minute, 7 July 1949, Seel minute, 12 July 1949.
48. TNA: CO 111/812/1, Vernon minute, 17 July 1951, Note of a discussion with the Secretary of State, 3 August 1951. This file also contains a copy of

the report: Waddington to Griffiths, 29 June 1951 enclosing Report of the British Guiana Constitutional Commission, 29 June 1951.

49. TNA: CO 111/812/1, British Guiana (Woolley) to Secretary of State, 20 September 1951, Griffiths to Woolley, 6 October 1951.
50. TNA: CO 111/811/7, Watt minute, 14 April 1950; CO 111/812/1, Henning minute, 9 August 1951.
51. TNA: CO 111/791/4, Notes on Matters Discussed during Woolley's visit (ud), Seel minute, 9 November 1948; CO 111/812/1, British Guiana (Woolley) to Secretary of State, 20 September 1951.
52. TNA: CO 1031/128, Memorandum on the PPP by Orrett, 10 April 1951, Vernon minute 28 June 1951.
53. TNA: CO 968/248, Jackson to McLeod, 4 November 1952, Luke minute, 29 November 1952, Lloyd minute, 1 December 1952, Luke to McLeod, 30 January 1953.
54. TNA: CO 1031/128, Intelligence Report for April 1953 by Commissioner of Police, 5 May 1953.
55. TNA: PREM 11/827, Churchill to Colonial Secretary, 2 May 1953, Lyttelton to Prime Minister, 5 May 1953.
56. TNA: CO 1031/128, Intelligence Report for April 1953, Political Reports on British Guiana, 47th (10 June 1953) and 48th (3 July 1953).
57. TNA: CO 1031/119, Governor (British Guiana) to Secretary of State, 25 July 1953 enclosing Rose Memorandum on Internal Security in British Guiana, 16 July 1953.
58. TNA: CO 1031/128, 49th Political Report on British Guiana, 10 August 1953, Vernon minute, 24 August 1953.
59. The Watson report indicated that 'partial interception' had been implemented in British Guiana but that it was not wholly successful. Lloyd had authorised Savage to put PPP ministers under 'discreet surveillance'. See TNA: CO 968/250, Measures to Combat Communism in the West Indies by Watson, May 1953; CO 1031/119, Lloyd to Savage, 30 May 1953.
60. TNA: CO 1031/119, Mayle minute, 14 July 1953.
61. TNA: CO 1031/119, Lloyd to Savage, 1 July 1953, British Guiana (Savage) to Secretary of State, 10 July 1953, minutes by Vernon, 13 July 1953, Mayle, 14 July 1953, Barton, 14 July 1953, Rogers, 15 July 1953, Lloyd, 17 July 1953, Lyttelton, 20 July 1953.
62. TNA: CO 1027/14, Ingram to Peck 13 July 1953 covering Ingram Memo on Information Work in British Guiana, Ingram minute, 13 July 1953, Vernon minute, 5 August 1953, Savage to Lloyd, 24 August 1953, Young to Savage, 27 August 1953 covering Memo on Information Services in British Guiana.
63. TNA: CO 1027/14, Fisher to Young, 19 February 1954, Rogers minute, 21 April 1954, 3 May 1954.
64. TNA: CAB 128/26, CC(53)57th mtg., minute 5, 13 October 1953; CAB 195/11, Brook Notes, CC(57)53, 13 October 1953.
65. TNA: CO 1031/119, Savage to Lloyd, 13 September 1953, Secretary of State to British Guiana (Savage), 24 September 1953.
66. TNA: CAB 128/26, CC(53)54th mtg., minute 4, 2 October 1953; CAB 129/63, C(53)261, 30 September 1953; CAB 195/11, Brook Notes, CC(5)53, 2 October 1953.

67. Lord Moran, *Winston Churchill: The Struggle for Survival* (London, 1968), Ch. 42.
68. TNA: DEFE 4/65, COS(53)110th mtg., minute 3, 30 September 1953.
69. TNA: CAB 128/26, CC(53)55th mtg., minute 1, 6 October 1953. *The Times* had reported as early as 5 October that HMS Superb had been ordered to sale from Kingston 'with sealed orders for an unknown destination' and speculated that its destination might be British Guiana. See *The Times*, 5 October 1953, 8.
70. C. Jagan, *Forbidden Freedom* (3rd ed., London, 1994), Ch. 1.
71. TNA: PREM 11/827, British Guiana (Savage) to Secretary of State, 18 October 1953.
72. *Parliamentary Papers*, Cmd. 8980, British Guiana: Suspension of the Constitution, October 1953, including Broadcast by Savage, 9 October 1953 at Appendix C.
73. F. Brockway, *Towards Tomorrow* (London, 1977), 214–215; Jagan, *Freedom*, Ch. 6; *Parliamentary Debates*, 5th series, vol. 518, col. 2167, 22 October 1953, vol. 521, cols 1631–1634, 1651, 7 December 1953.
74. TNA: CAB 195/11, Brook Notes, CC(54)53, 2 October 1953, CC(55)53, 6 October 1953.
75. O. Lyttelton, *The Memoirs of Lord Chandos* (London, 1962), 429–430.
76. *Parliamentary Debates*, 5th series, vol. 518, cols 2210, 2218, 2234, 2238, 22 October 1953.
77. Jagan, *Freedom*, 64–67.
78. People's History Museum, Manchester, Labour Party Archive, International Department, Box 110, Summary of Statements and Answers to Question given by Guianese politicians, National Council of Labour meeting, 22 October 1953.
79. TNA: PREM 11/827, Secretary of State to British Guiana, 7 October 1953, British Guiana (Savage) to Secretary of State, 7 October 1953, Secretary of State to British Guiana, 8 October 1953.
80. Richard Hart Papers, CLR #41, Janet Jagan to Hart, 28 April 1954.
81. Jagan, *West*, 155–160.
82. *Parliamentary Papers*, Cmd. 9274, Report of the British Guiana Constitutional Commission, September 1954.
83. Rabe, *Intervention*, 53–54; Palmer, *Cheddi Jagan*, 58–59.
84. TNA: CAB 128/30, CM(56)30th mtg., minute 6, 19 April 1956; CAB 129/80, CP(56)100, 17 April 1956; CAB 195/13, Brook Notes, CM(30)56, 19 April 1956; Munroe, *Left*, 84.
85. Jagan, *West*, 188.
86. W. Crawford, *I Speak for the People* (Kingston, 2003), 17.
87. TNA: CO 1031/1695, Arundell to Rogers, 21 November 1955.
88. R. J. Alexander, *Presidents, Prime Ministers and Governors of the English Speaking Caribbean* (Westport, 1997), 142–143.
89. Anthony De V. Phillips, 'Grantley Adams, Asquithian Liberalism and Socialism' in G. D. Howe and R. D. Marshall (eds), *The Empowering Impulse* (Kingston, 2001), 165–185.
90. F. A. Hoyos, *Grantley Adams and the Social Revolution* (London, 1974), 46.
91. *Barbados Advocate*, 15 December 1951, 4.

92. TNA: CO 1031/ 529, Savage (Barbados) to Luke 2 January 1952, Luke minute, 26 January 1952.
93. TNA: CO 1031/305, Notes of Meeting Between Lloyd and Adams, 31 March 1952.
94. H. McD. Beckles, 'Radicalism and Errol Barrow in the Political Tradition of Barbados' in Howe and Marshall (eds), *Empowering Impulse*, 221–231.
95. TNA: CO 1031/305, Adams, Cummins, Cox and Walcott to Governor, 27 May 1952, Luke minute, 18 July 1952, Savage to Luke, 11 September 1952, Luke minute, 22 September 1952, Lloyd minute, 23 September 1952.
96. TNA: CO 1031/305, Luke minutes, 26 November 1952, 3 December 1952, 11 December 1952, 16 December 1952, 18 December 1952, Lloyd minute, 22 December 1952, Turner to Lyttelton, 30 April 1953.
97. TNA: CO 1031/306, Barbados (Arundell) to Secretary of State, 7 October 1953, 8 October 1953, Anderson minute, 12 October 1953, Watt minute, 14 October 1953, Rogers minute, 15 October 1953, Lloyd minute, 15 October 1953, Munster minute, 19 October 1953.
98. Alexander, *Presidents*, 144.
99. TNA: CO 1031/305, Savage to Luke, 19 May 1952, Luke minute, 11 December 1952, Lyttelton to Prime Minister, 22 December 1952, Turner to Luke, 8 April 1953, Lloyd minutes, 21 April 1953, 29 April 1953, Secretary of State to Barbados, 1 May 1953, Arundell to Wallace, 18 June 1953, Barbados (Arundell) to Secretary of State, 22 July 1953, Secretary of State to Barbados, 28 July 1953.
100. TNA: CO 1031/1810, Political Report for January 1956.
101. Alexander, *Presidents*, 148.
102. TNA: CO 1031/1810, Governor to Secretary of State, 9 August 1956, Rogers minute, 27 August 1956; CO 1031/1296, Jenkins minute, 10 December 1956, Rogers minute, 11 December 1956.
103. TNA: CO 1031/2239, Rogers to Arundell, 4 March 1957, Arundell to Rogers, 12 March 1957, Arundell to Lennox Boyd, 27 May 1957, Arundell to Wallace, 10 July 1957, Wallace to Arundel, 29 September 1957, Lennox Boyd to Arundell, 31 July 1957.
104. See the *Colonial Office List 1953* (London, 1953), 182.
105. S. Siewah (ed.), *Lotus and the Dagger* (Tunapuna, 1994), 4–7.
106. Oxaal, *Black Intellectuals Come to Power* (Cambridge, Mass., 1968), 96.
107. Among the most notable contributions to 'Eric Williams Studies' are P. Sutton, 'The Historian as Politician' in A. Hennessy (ed.), *Intellectuals in the Twentieth Century Caribbean: Vol. 1* (London, 1992), 98–114; S. R. Cudjoe, 'Eric Williams and the Politics of Language', *Callaloo* 20/4 (1997), 753–763; K. Boodhoo, *The Elusive Eric Williams* (Kingston, 2001); P. Mohammed, 'A Very Public Private Man' in A. L. Allahar (ed.), *Caribbean Charisma* (Kingston, 2001), 155–191; T. Martin, 'Eric Williams and the Anglo-American Caribbean Commission', *Journal of African-American History* 88/3 (2003), 274–290; R. B. Sheridan, 'Eric Williams and Capitalism and Slavery' in B. L. Solow and S. Engerman (eds), *British Capitalism and Caribbean Slavery* (Cambridge, 2004); C. A Palmer, *Eric Williams and the Making of the Modern Caribbean* (Chapel Hill, 2006); S. Ryan, *Eric Williams: The Myth and the Man* (Kingston, 2009).

108. Ryan, *Myth*, 113–114.
109. W. Mottley, *Trinidad and Tobago Industrial Policy 1959–2008* (Kingston, 2008), 10.
110. Ryan, *Myth*, 110.
111. P. Sutton and E. Williams, *Forged From the Love of Liberty* (1981), Historical Background of Race Relations in the Caribbean, 16 August 1955, 209.
112. Boodhoo, *Elusive*, 26–27.
113. E. Williams, *Capitalism and Slavery* (Chapel Hill, 1994).
114. Eric Williams Memorial Collection, UWI, St Augustine, vol. 39, Williams to Manley, 17 June 1954.
115. R. Manley (ed.), *Edna Manley: The Diaries* (London, 1989), 5 March 1960, 58–59.
116. E. Williams, *Inward Hunger* (Princeton, 2006), Ch. 4.
117. TNA: CO 1031/1302, Trinidad (Beetham) to Secretary of State, 15 September 1956.
118. Ryan, *Myth*, 145.
119. Williams, *Hunger*, 164.
120. TNA: CO 1031/2286, Aide-Memoire to the Governor by Williams (ud), Rogers minute, 24 July 1957, Rogers to Hochoy, 9 August 1957.
121. TNA: CO 1031/2286, Beetham to Rogers, 27 February 1958, Marnham minutes, 3 March 1958, 27 March 1958, Rogers minute, 3 March 1959, MacPherson to Beetham, 14 April 1958.
122. Gomes, *Through a Maze of Colour* (Port of Spain, 1974), 181.
123. Siewah, *Lotus*, Interview with Mohammed, 26 March 1994, 495.
124. Ryan, *Myth*, 180–182.
125. TNA: CO 1031/2490, Beetham to Rogers, 4 April 1958, Beetham to MacPherson, 9 April 1958, Baxter minute, 16 April 1958, Marnham minute, 24 April 1958.
126. TNA: CO 1031/2490, Beetham to Rogers, 5 April 1958, Beetham to MacPherson, 9 April 1958, Baxter minute, 16 April 1958, Marnham minute, 24 April 1958.
127. TNA: CO 1031/2286, Governor (Trinidad) to Secretary of State, 21 June 1958, Baker minutes, 24 June 1958, 4 July 1958, Marnham minute, 7 July 1958, Rogers minute, 9 July 1958.
128. P. Solomon, *Solomon: An Autobiography* (Port of Spain, 1981), 160.
129. TNA: CO 1031/2287, Record of a Meeting on 17 September 1958, Record of a Meeting, 26 September 1958, Lennox-Boyd to Rogers, 5 October 1958, Rogers minute, 20 October 1958, 21 October 1958, 27 October 1958, Whitelegg minute, 20 October 1958, Secretary of State to Trinidad (Acting Governor), 29 October 1958.
130. Churchill Archives Centre: Julian Amery papers, AMEJ 1/5, Governor-General (from Amery) to Secretary of State, 30 June 1959.
131. Williams, *Hunger*, 170–171; Solomon, *Autobiography*, 161–162.
132. *Parliamentary Papers 1947–48*, Cmd. 7291, Conference on the Closer Association of the British West Indian Colonies, Appendix B/a, Report of the Fiscal Sub-Committee.
133. TNA: CO 318/506/2, Seel to Rance, 5 October 1950.
134. TNA: CO 1031/750, Lyttelton to West Indian governments, 6 February 1952.

135. TNA: CO 1031/750, Foot (Jamaica) to Secretary of State, 17 June 1952, 25 July 1952, Note on Jamaica Joint Committee Report, 23 August 1952.
136. TNA: CO 1031/760, Seel to Luke, 2 August 1952, Luke to Seel, 25 August 1952.
137. TNA: CO 1031/750, Trinidad (Rance) to Secretary of State, 13 March 1952, Meeting at the Colonial Office, 4 June 1952, Note of a Discussion with Gomes, 16 September 1952.
138. TNA: CO 1031/760, Luke to Seel, 7 June 1952.
139. TNA: CO 1031/760, Bourdillon report on Visit to the West Indies, Bourdillon to Luke, 17 December 1951, Bourdillon minute, 23 February 1952.
140. TNA: CO 1031/751, Blackburne to Luke, 15 August 1952 covering Blackburne memo on Federation in the British West Indies, 14 August 1952, Luke to Blackburne, 5 September 1952.
141. TNA: CO 1031/761, Note of a Meeting at the Colonial Office, 9 December 1952, Rance to Lloyd, 17 February 1953, covering Gomes to Rance, 14 February 1953, Lloyd to Rance, 20 March 1953.
142. S. R. Ashton and D. Killingray (eds), *British Documents on the End of Empire B/6: The West Indies* (London, 1999), Communique on the West Indian Federation Conference, April 1953, 42–44; *Parliamentary Papers 1952–1953*, Cmd. 8837, Report by the Conference on West Indian Federation, May 1953, Cmd. 8895, The Plan for a British Caribbean Federation, July 1953.
143. TNA: CO 1031/1693, Rance (Trinidad) to Rogers, 1 December 1954, 13 December 1954, 22 January 1954, Minute of a Meeting on Trinidad's Attitude to Federation, 21 December 1954, Secretary of State to Trinidad, 24 January 1955.
144. TNA: CO 1031/1693, Rogers minute, 28 October 1954.
145. TNA: CO 1031/1693, Note of a Colonial Office Meeting, May 1954, Note on the Establishment of a British Caribbean Federation, June 1954, Rogers to Luke, 19 July 1954, Luke to Rogers, 5 August 1954.
146. TNA: CO 1031/1694, Secretary of State to West Indian OAGs, 15 June 1955, Memorandum on the Programme for the British Caribbean Federation, 10 June 1955, Rogers minute, 24 June 1955, Rowlatt to McPetrie, 27 July 1955, McPetrie to Rowlatt, 27 July 1955, McPetrie minute, 27 July 1955, Rogers minute, 4 August 1955, Rogers to Luke, 9 August 1955.
147. Williams, *Hunger*, 115–116.
148. Nettleford, *New Jamaica*, Speech to the CLC, Kingston, 2 September 1947, 165–167.
149. TNA: CO 1031/1694, Luke to Secretary of State, 24 August 1955, Meeting at the Colonial Office, 26 August 1955, Luke to Secretary of State, 24 August 1955, Meeting at the Colonial Office, 26 August 1955, Mayle minute, 1 September 1955.
150. TNA: CO 1031/1694, Lloyd minute, 2 September 1955, Lennox-Boyd minute, 5 October 1955, Foot to Rogers, 27 September 1955, Lloyd minute, 6 October 1955, Rogers minute, 12 October 1955, Lloyd minute, 13 October 1955, Rogers to Jamaica, 2 October 1955; CO 1031/1695, Jamaica (Foot) to Secretary of State, 26 October 1955, Secretary of State to Foot, 29 October 1955, Lloyd to Secretary of State, 31 October 1955. The most interesting document in this surfeit of preparatory paperwork for the 1956 conference

is Lloyd's minute of 6 October; in a passage that has been partially effaced but remains readable, he complains that Foot is cooperating with Manley on proposals which were 'in very great opposition to the policy of HMG.'

151. Ashton and Killingray, *British Documents B6*, Lloyd to Foot, 17 November 1955, Foot to Lloyd, 25 November 1955, Lloyd to Foot, 15 December 1955, 104–114.

152. Ashton and Killingray, *British Documents B6*, Brief on Manley's Seven Propositions, 1 February 1956, 121–125.

153. TNA: CO 1031/1695, Jamaica to Foot, 9 January 1956; CO 1031/1696, Luke to Rogers, 22 January 1956, enclosing Report by Luke.

154. JNA: Manley Papers, 4/60/2a/18, Williams to Manley, 3 January 1956, 27 January 1956; Williams, *Forged*, Pros and Cons of Federation, 284–290.

155. National Archives of Trinidad and Tobago [Henceforward NATT]: Federation Box 1, 2/7/2, Williams to Beetham, 13 January 1956 enclosing Resolution Passed at Woodford Square, Open Letter to Federal Delegation, February 1956.

156. TNA: CO 1031/1695, Jamaica to Foot, 9 January 1956; CO 1031/1696, Luke to Rogers, 22 January 1956, enclosing Report by Luke.

157. J. Mordecai, *The West Indies: The Federal Negotiations* (London, 1968), 54.

158. TNA: CO 1031/1754, BCF(56)1st mtg., 7 February 1956, BCF(56)9th mtg., 16 February 1956, BCF(56)10th mtg., 17 February 1956.

159. TNA: CO 1031/1754, BCF(56) 3rd mtg., 13 February 1956, BCF(56)6th mtg., 15 February 1956, BCF(56)7th mtg., 15 February 1956, BCF(56)8th mtg., 16 February 1956.

160. *Parliamentary Papers 1955–1956*, Cmd. 9733, Report by the Conference on British Caribbean Federation, March 1956.

161. *Parliamentary Papers 1955–1956*, Cmd. 9618, The Plan for a British Caribbean Federation: Report of the Fiscal Commissioner, December 1955.

162. TNA: CO 1031/1754, BCF(56) 3rd mtg., 13 February 1956, BCF(56)4th mtg., 14 February 1956.

163. TNA: CO 1031/1754, BCF(56) 12th mtg., 20 February 1956.

164. *Parliamentary Papers 1955–1956*, Cmd. 9733, Report by the Conference on British Caribbean Federation, March 1956.

165. TNA: CO 1031/1754, BCF(56) 15th mtg., 21 February 1956, BCF(56)16th mtg., 22 February 1956, BCF(56)17th mtg., 22 February 1956.

166. *Parliamentary Papers 1955–1956*, Cmd. 9733, Report by the Conference on British Caribbean Federation, March 1956.

167. See for example Bryan's speech to the Legislative Council, NATT: Debates of the 9th Legislative Council, vol.7, 15 February 1957.

168. TNA: CO 1031/2024, Trinidad (Beetham) to Secretary of State, 8 May 1957; NATT: Federation Box 5, Memo by Mapp, 27 April 1957, Report of Meeting held in Trinidad, 9–12 April 1957.

169. TNA: CO 1031/2024, Washington (Colonial Attache) to Secretary of State, 9 May 1957, 13 May 1957, 14 May 1957, 16 May 1957, 23 May 1957, Note from US Embassy, 13 June 1957.

170. TNA: CO 1031/2024, Wallace minute, 10 May 1957, Secretary of State to Beetham, 13 May 1957, 18 May 1957, 22 May 1957, Trinidad (Beetham) to Secretary of State, 11 May 1957, Wallace minute, 14 May 1957, Secretary of State to SFC Chairman, 4 June 1957.

171. Ashton and Killingray, *British Documents B6*, Huijsman minute, 19 June 1957, 168–169.
172. JNA: Manley Papers, 4/60/2A/18, Williams to Manley, 6 December 1956, Manley to Williams, 11 December 1956; Williams, *Hunger*, p. 174.
173. TNA: CO 1031/2309, Comptroller (Development and Welfare) to Secretary of State, 14 January 1957.
174. Mordecai, *Federal Negotiations*, 63–64.
175. P. Sherlock, *Norman Manley* (London, 1980), 178.

4   The Triumph of Disorder 1958–1962

1. K. Boodhoo, *The Elusive Eric Williams* (Kingston, 2001), 113.
2. C. Palmer, *Eric William and the Making of the Modern Caribbean* (Chapel Hill, 2006), Ch. 3; C. Fraser, *Ambivalent Anti-Colonialism* (Westport, 1994), 147–159; J. Parker, *Brother's Keeper* (Oxford, 2008), Chs 4 and 5.
3. The National Archives [Henceforward TNA]: PREM 3/462/2, Lothian to Foreign Office, 25 August, 30 August, 31 August 1940.
4. TNA: PREM 3/463/1, Hardinge to Secretary of State for Colonies, 31 December 1940.
5. TNA: FO 371/24260, Governor (Trinidad) to Colonial Office, 7 September 1940, 13 September 1940, 9 October 1940, 14 October 1940, 22 October 1940; FO 371/24261, Governor (Trinidad) to Colonial Office, 30 November 1940, 3 December 1940, 10 December 1940; FO 371/24262, Governor (Trinidad) to Colonial Office, 22 October 1940, 21 December 1940.
6. E. Williams, *Inward Hunger* (Princeton, 2006), 206–207.
7. S. Ashton and D. Killingray (eds), *British Documents on the End of Empire B/6: The West Indies* (London, 1999), Memorandum by Williams, 18 July 1957, 178–184.
8. E. Geelhoed and A. Edmonds (eds), *The Macmillan-Eisenhower Correspondence* (Basingstoke, 2004), Macmillan to Eisenhower, 19 July 1957, Eisenhower to Macmillan, 20 July 1957, 72–74.
9. Dwight D. Eisenhower Library [Henceforward DDEL]: Papers of John Foster Dulles, Telephone Calls, Box 7, Telephone calls with Radford, the President and Elbrick, 20 July 1957.
10. TNA: PREM 11/2880, Macmillan to Lennox-Boyd, 21 July 1957, Lennox-Boyd to Macmillan, 24 July 1957. For a record of the conference see CO 1031/2024, Summary Record of Discussion at the Foreign Office 16–23 July 1957.
11. *New York Times*, 11 August 1957, 33.
12. *Daily Gleaner*, 22 August 1958, 7, 30 August 1957, 1.
13. TNA: CO 1031/2025, Jamaica (Acting Governor) to Secretary of State, 24 August 1958, Chairman (SFC) to Secretary of State, 30 August 1957, 10 October 1957.
14. TNA: CO 1031/2025, Jenkins minute, 17 October 1957, Secretary of State to Chairman (SFC), 18 October 1957, Foster to Hankey, 4 November 1957, Leishman to Andrews, 5 November 1957, Andrews to Leishman, 29 November 1957.

15. TNA: CO 1031/2025, Mancini (Joint Commission) to Colonial Secretary (Trinidad), 21 January 1958, enclosing Memorandum by the Trinidad government, Hankey (FO) to Rogers (CO), 5 February 1958, Rogers to Beetham, 11 February 1958, Beetham to Rogers, 19 February 1958.
16. TNA: CO 1031/2025, Caccia (Washington) to FO, 28 February 1958 enclosing aide-memoire from Herter, 26 February 1958, Caccia to Hoyer-Millar, 8 March 1958, Hailes to Colonial Office, 17 March 1958, Hoyer-Millar to Caccia, 21 March 1958, Gore-Booth to Caccia, 20 March 1958.
17. National Archives II, College Park [Henceforward NA]: RG59, Records Relating to Trinidad and Tobago, Lots 64D38/66D43, Box 1, Parsons to Jandrey, 10 February 1958, Orebaugh to Dale, 14 May 1958, Memorandum of a Conversation with Sinanan, White, Willoughby, Swihart, Burn (ud).
18. TNA: CO 1031/2026, Trinidad (Beetham) to Secretary of State, 27 March 1958, Arden-Clarke to Lennox-Boyd, 25 March 1958 enclosing report of the Joint Commission.
19. NA: RG59, Central Decimal Files 1955–1959, Box 3207, Orebaugh to State Department, 16 May 1958.
20. TNA: CO 1031/2027, State Department Press Statement, 14 May 1958, Colonial Attaché (Washington) to Secretary of State, 3 June 1958, Marnham (CO) to Hankey (FO), 3 June 1958, Marnham minutes, 5 June 1958, 6 June 1958.
21. TNA: CO 1031/2027, Williams (Washington) to Rogers, 4 June 1958, Profumo to Lennox-Boyd, 7 June 1958, FO to Washington, 7 June 1958 enclosing Lloyd to Dulles, Caccia (Washington) to FO, 8 June 1958, West Indies (Hailes) to Secretary of State, 8 June 1958, Secretary of State to West Indies, 11 June 1958 enclosing Lloyd to Dulles, 11 June 1958, Dulles to Lloyd, 14 June 1958, Williams (Washington) to Marnham (CO), 24 June 1958.
22. TNA: CO 1031/2028, Williams (Washington) to Marnham (CO), 17 July 1958.
23. Williams, *Hunger*, 213.
24. Jamaican National Archives [Henceforward JNA]: 4/60/2B/19, Hill to Manley, 29 October 1958.
25. TNA: CO 1031/2039, Rogers minute, 15 October 1958.
26. Williams, *Hunger*, 216.
27. *Trinidad Guardian*, 5 July 1959, 1, 8.
28. Eric Williams Memorial Collection [Henceforward EWMC]: vol. 1844, Governor to Secretary of State, 9 June 1959, Appendix 3, Report to Cabinet by Solomon and O'Halloran (ud).
29. P. Solomon, *Solomon: An Autobiography* (Trinidad, 1981), 160–161.
30. EWMC: vol. 1844, Report of Chaguaramas visit by Evans (ud).
31. EWMC: vol. 1557, Transcript of Discussion on 'Day-to-Day' Difficulties, 14 May 1959.
32. H. Neptune, *Caliban and the Yankees* (Chapel Hill, 2007).
33. Williams, *Forged from the Love of Liberty* (1981), 301–308; Williams, *Hunger*, 214.
34. TNA: CO 1031/2039, Trinidad (Beetham) to Secretary of State, 2 April 1959, Beetham to Hailes, 23 April 1959, Hailes to Beetham, 13 May 1959, Hailes to Lennox-Boyd, 5 June 1959.

35. DDEL: White House Central, Subject Series, Box 52, Position Paper on US Bases in the West Indies, 21 August 1959.
36. TNA: CO 1031/2041, Secretary of State to West Indies (Acting Governor-General), 25 August 1959, FO to Logan (Washington), 24 August 1959, Washington (Hood) to FO, 27 August 1959, Record of Conversation between Herter and Lloyd, 28 August 1959.
37. NA: RG 59, Bureau of European Affairs: Records Relating to Caribbean Dependencies 1941–1962, Box 1, Memorandum of a Conversation, 18 September 1959, Willoughby to White, 13 November 1959, Merchant to Herter, 19 November 1959, Memorandum of Conversation, 25 November 1959, Merchant to White, 17 November 1959, Kohler to Merchant, 19 November 1959.
38. TNA: CO 1031/3036, Trinidad (Beetham) to Secretary of State, 11 January 1960, 15 January 1960.
39. NA: RG 59, Bureau of Inter-American Affairs, Lots 64D38–66D43, Box 1, Moline to Swihart, 21 March 1960.
40. Williams, *Forged*, 308–313; Williams, *Hunger*, 225–235.
41. *Trinidad Guardian*, 23 April 1960, 1–2.
42. Churchill Archives Centre [Henceforward CAC]: HAIS 4/31, Hailes to Macleod, 23 April 1960.
43. TNA: CO 1031/3036, Meeting of Foreign and Colonial Office officials with White, 28 March 1960.
44. DDEL: NSC Series, Box 12, Memo of 437th NSC meeting, 17 March 1960.
45. TNA: CO 1031/3036, Secretary of State to West Indies (Hailes), 29 April 1960, Hailes to Secretary of State, 15 May 1960, Secretary of State to Hailes, 31 May 1960, Trinidad (Governor's Deputy) to Secretary of State, 1 June 1960, 3 June 1960.
46. TNA: CO 1031/3036, Meeting of Secretary of State with Trinidad Council of State, 10 June 1960.
47. Ashton and Killingray, *British Documents B6*, Minute by Thomas, 20 December 1960, 385.
48. National Archives of Trinidad and Tobago [Henceforward NATT]: CAB E4, Progress in Implementing Chaguaramas Agreement, October 1962.
49. EWMC: CLR James Collection, Folder 108, James to Arthur, 28 March 1961, 3 April 1961.
50. NATT: Records of the 8th Legislative Assembly, vol. 11, pt. 1, col. 843, 19 December 1960.
51. NA: RG 59, Bureau of Inter-American Affairs, Lots 64D38–66D43, Box 1, Christensen (Trinidad) to Foster (State Department), 29 May 1962, 7 June 1962.
52. NATT: CAB E4, Progress in Implementing Chaguaramas Agreement, October 1962.
53. NA: RG 59, General Records of the State Department, Central Files 1963, Box 4070, US Ambassador (Port of Spain) to State, 19 December 1963.
54. C. Rector, *Federations: The Political Dynamics of Cooperation* (London, 2009), 148–159.
55. J. Parker, 'The Failure of the West Indies Federation' in Wm. R. Louis (ed.), *Ultimate Adventures with Britannia* (London, 2009), 244.
56. Ashton and Killingray, *British Documents B/6*, lxxxi.

57. J. Mordecai, *The West Indies: The Federal Negotiations* (London, 1968), 457.
58. Sives, 'Dwelling Separately' in E. Kavalski and M. Zolkos (eds), *Defunct Federalisms* (Aldershot, 2008), 30.
59. M. Phillips and T. Phillips, *Windrush* (London, 1988), 158–180.
60. *The Times*, 25 August 1958, 8; 27 August 1958, 4; 28 August 1958, 4; 30 August 1958, 7; 2 September 1958, 11; 4 September 1958, 11. For biographical details on the correspondents, see D. Goldsworthy, 'Robert Arthur James Gascoyne-Cecil' and R. Denniston, 'Ernest Urban Trevor Huddleston' in the online *Oxford Dictionary of National Biography* (oxforddnb.com).
61. *Parliamentary Debates*, 5th series, vol. 596, 1552–1561.
62. TNA: CAB 195/14, CM39(55), 3 November 1955; PREM 11/2920, Brook minute, 10 November 1955.
63. TNA: CAB 134/1466, CCI(57)4, 29 June 1957.
64. TNA: PREM 11/2920, Macmillan to Lennox-Boyd, 2 September 1958; CAB 134/1467, CC(59)1st mtg., 13 January 1959.
65. TNA: PREM 11/2920, Note of a Meeting with West Indian leaders, 8 September 1958, Lennox-Boyd to Butler, 10 September 1958; CAB 134/1466, CCI(58)3rd mtg., 6 November 1958, CCI(58)6, 17 October 1958.
66. TNA: CAB 134/1467, CC(59)1st mtg., 13 January 1959, CCI(59)2nd mtg., 22 July 1959, CCI(59)1, 3 July 1959; HO 344/43, Perth to Butler, 22 May 1959, Butler minute, 23 May 1959, Cunningham minute, 25 May 1959.
67. Ashton and Killingray, *British Documents* B/6, CO Note, 6 January 1960 with enclosure, 308–317.
68. TNA: CO 1031/3264, Blackburne to Rogers, 5 January 1960.
69. Ashton and Killingray, *British Documents* B/6, Minutes by Pliatzky and Taylor, 6 January 1960, Official Committee on Development Assistance minutes, 7 January 1960, Treasury note, 11 January 1960, 317–323.
70. TNA: T 220/941, Rickett minute, 8 January 1960, Heathcoat-Amory minute, 9 January 1960.
71. TNA: CO 1031/3264, Secretary of State to Hailes (West Indies), 18 January 1960.
72. TNA: CO 1031/3505, Memorandum of Macleod's Visit, June 1960, Minutes of Meeting Between Macleod, the Federal Prime Minister, Premiers and Chief Ministers, 17 June 1960.
73. TNA: CO 1031/3505, Trinidad Government Paper on Economic Development in the Independent West Indian Federation.
74. Ashton and Killingray, *British Documents* B/6, Minute by Jamieson, 27 October 1960, Memo on Visit of West Indian Leaders: Financial Settlement, 3 November 1960, Record of a Meeting with West Indian Ministers, 8 November 1960, 371–384.
75. R. G. Spencer, *British Immigration Policy Since 1939* (London, 1997), 108–128.
76. TNA: CAB 128/34, CC(60)46th mtg., 26 July 1960, minute 2, CC(60)59th mtg., minute 8, 25 November 1960; CAB 129/102, C(60)128, 19 July 1960; CAB 129/103, C(60)165, 15 November 1960; CAB 195/19, CC59(60), 25 November 1960.
77. TNA: CAB 128/35, CC(61)7th mtg., minute 2, 16 February 1961, CC(61)29th mtg., minute 7, 30 May 1961; CAB 129/105, C(61)67, 26 May 1961, C(61)69, 26 May 1961; CAB 195/19, CC7(61), 16 February 1961,

CC29(61), 30 May 1961; Ashton and Killingray, *British Documents* B/6, Minute by Terry, December 1960, 387–389.

78. WI Federal Archives Centre, Cave Hill [Henceforward WIFAC]: FWI/GG/GA/ 424, Record of Discussion with British Prime Minister, 4 March 1961.

79. *Barbados Advocate*, 23 April 1961, 1, 6.

80. TNA: PREM 11/3238, Record of a Meeting with Williams, 25 March 1961, Record of discussions with the DLP and BNP, 28 March 1961, West Indies (Hailes) to Secretary of State, 20 April 1961, Press Statement by Secretary of State, 21 April 1961, Pearson (CO) to Bligh, 21 April 1961, Macmillan minute (ud). For the British, Macmillan's visit was a source of alarm because of popular protests demanding the release of Jomo Kenyatta which were labelled, in customary fashion, 'racist'. See WIFAC: FWI/GG/GA/427, Stow to Hailes, 10 March 1961 with Reports on Visit by the Prime Minister.

81. WIFAC: FWI-GG-GA-44, Records of the West Indies Constitutional Conference, 7th meeting, 7 June 1961, 8th meeting, 8 June 1961, 10th meeting, 12 June 1961.

82. TNA: CAB 134/1560, CP(61)7th mtg., minute 2, 2 June 1961.

83. Ashton and Killingray, *British Documents B6*, Taylor to Gorell Barnes, 7 February 1961, 391–392.

84. TNA: CAB 21/5051, Macleod to Macmillan, 7 June 1961.

85. TNA: T 296/181, Hayes minutes, 2 June 1961, 9 June 1961.

86. WIFAC: FWI-GG-GA-44, Records of the West Indies Constitutional Conference, 12th meeting, 14 June 1961.

87. E. Seaga, *My Life and Leadership: Vol. 1* (Oxford, 2009), 66.

88. Mordecai, *Federal Negotiations*, 104.

89. There is sufficient material in the Hailes paper for an entire chapter on his dispute with Beetham, which began in December 1957 and was still rumbling on in March 1959. For the bird-watching letter, which also contains derogatory comments about Beetham's wife, who was implicated in the various arguments, see CAC: HAIS 4/14, Hailes to Lennox-Boyd, 2 July 1958.

90. Williams, *Hunger*, 175–178.

91. F. A. Hoyos, *Grantley Adams and the Social Revolution* (London, 1974), 210–211.

92. Mordecai, *Federal Negotiations*, 132.

93. *Daily Gleaner*, 31 October 1958, 1; 1 November, 10.

94. WIFAC: FWI-GG-GA-196, Adams to Manley, 31 October 1958.

95. JNA: 4/60/2A/19, Manley to Williams, 13 November 1958.

96. *Daily Gleaner*, 5 November, 1, 16.

97. Mordecai, *Federal Negotiations*, 149–150.

98. Ashton and Killingray, *British Documents* B/6, Home to Lennox-Boyd, 28 October 1958, 217, Lennox-Boyd to Home, 5 November 1958, 222.

99. CAC: HAIS 4/14, Hailes to Lennox-Boyd, 10 January 1959, Lennox-Boyd to Hailes, 23 January 1959.

100. Mordecai, *Federal Negotiations*, 158–159.

101. Ashton and Killingray, *British Documents* B/6, Minute by Jamieson, 26 June 1959, 261–262, Amery minute, 6 August 1959, 272–273, Record of a Meeting between Amery and Hailes and Poynton minute, 14 August 1959, 273–276, Amery to Home, 27 August 1959.

102. TNA: DO 189/92, Blackburne to Lennox-Boyd, 14 February 1959, Lennox-Boyd to Blackburne, 21 April 1959, Secretary of State to Jamaica (Blackburne) 13 May 1959, Chadwick (CRO) to Marnham, 27 May 1959, Jamaica (Blackburne) to Secretary of State, 22 June 1959, Home minute, 25 June 1959, CRO to Pretoria, 28 June 1959.
103. Rhodes House Library [Henceforward RHL]: Kenneth Blackburne papers, s.460, Box 14, Blackburne to his father, 5 July 1959.
104. TNA: DO 189/82, Pretoria to CRO, 2 July 1959.
105. JNA: 4/60/2B/20, Blackburne to Manley, 12 May 1959, Manley to Blackburne, 13 May 1959, Blackburne to Manley, 13 May 1959, Manley to Blackburne, 14 May 1959, Blackburne to Manley, 8 July 1959.
106. TNA: DO 189/92, CRO to Pretoria, 1 July 1959, Home minute, 6 July 1959, Snelling minute, 7 July 1959, Laithwaite minute, 7 July 1959, Home minute, 8 July 1959, Cole (CRO) to Moreton (CO), 13 July 1959 enclosing draft Cabinet paper.
107. TNA: DO 189/92, Blackburne to Rogers, 26 November 1958, Jamaica (Blackburne) to Secretary of State, 21 May 1959.
108. Mordecai, *Federal Negotiations*, 170–171.
109. Williams, *Hunger*, 177.
110. Mordecai, *Federal Negotiations*, 176–177.
111. Ashton and Killingray, *British Documents* B/6, Rogers to Poynton, 6 October 1959, 287–294.
112. Mordecai, *Federal Negotiations*, 243.
113. N. Fisher, *Iain Macleod* (London, 1973), 186.
114. Ashton and Killingray, *British Documents* B/6, Minute by Rogers, 20 October, 295.
115. CAC: HAIS 4/20, Rogers to Hailes, 18 January 1960; HAIS 4/27, Blackburne to Hailes, 10 January 1960; HAIS 4/35, Thomas to Hailes, 19 February 1960.
116. Ashton and Killingray, *British Documents* B/6, CO Note of a Discussion, 19 January 1960, 328.
117. R. Nettleford, *Manley and the New Jamaica* (London, 1971), Presidential Address to the PNP, 25 October 1959.
118. Mordecai, *Federal Negotiations*, 201.
119. Mordecai, *Federal Negotiations*, 197–198.
120. JNA: 4/60/2A/8, Bustamante to Manley, 4 May 1960, 11 May 1960.
121. Seaga, *Life*, 58.
122. P. Sherlock, *Norman Manley* (London, 1980), 188.
123. G. Lewis, The *Growth of the Modern West Indies* (London, 1968), 382.
124. EWMC: CLR James Collection, Box 5, Folder 105, Manley to James, 6 June 1960.
125. TNA: CO 1031/3505, Memo on Macleod's Visit to the West Indies, June 1960, Thomas minute, 7 July 1960.
126. CAC: HAIS 4/31, Hailes to Macleod (ud).
127. CAC: HAIS 4/27, Blackburne to Hailes, 12 October 1960, 24 October 1960.
128. Ashton and Killingray, *British Documents* B/6, Macleod to Hailes, 15 May 1960, 2 June 1960, 338–341.
129. Mordecai, *Federal Negotiations*, 236.
130. Fisher, *Macleod*, 187.

131. JNA: 4/60/2A/19, Record of a Meeting between the Premiers of Jamaica and Trinidad, 7–8 August 1960.
132. Ashton and Killingray, *British Documents* B/6, Hochoy to Thomas, 22 August 1960, 351–355.
133. CAC: HAIS 4/31, Hailes to Macleod, 3 September 1960.
134. Mordecai, *Federal Negotiations*, 254–257.
135. JNA: 4/60/2B/22, Manley to Blackburne, 12 October 1960.
136. Mordecai, *Federal Negotiations*, 297.
137. Ashton and Killingray, *British Documents* B/6, Minutes by Williams, 18 January 1961, Fraser, 20 January 1961, 389–391.
138. WIFAC: FWI-GG-GA-336, Cabinet Conclusions, 17th meeting, 22 March 1961.
139. TNA: CAB 21/5051, West Indies (Hailes) to Secretary of State, 12 May 1961.
140. Ashton and Killingray, *British Documents* B/6, Statement on Freedom of Movement appended to Record of Proceedings, 413–415.
141. Ashton and Killingray, *British Documents* B/6, Minute by Gorell Barnes, April 1961, 401–405.
142. TNA: CAB 21/5051, West Indies (Hailes) to Secretary of State, 6 May 1961.
143. Seaga, *My Life*, 61.
144. WIFAC: FNI-PM-GA-30, Manley to Adams, 22 May 1961.
145. S. Ryan, *Eric Williams: The Myth and the Man* (Kingston, 2009), 238.
146. Williams, *Hunger*, 199.
147. TNA: CO 1031/4281, Hochoy to Fraser, 15 July 1961.
148. JNA: 4/60/2A/19, Manley to Williams, 4 August 1961, Williams to Manley, 14 August 1961.
149. Mordecai, *Federal Negotiations*, 399–401.
150. Seaga, *Life*, 69–70.
151. Mordecai, *Federal Negotiations*, 411–414.
152. JNA: 4/60/2B/25, Blackburne to Manley, 19 September 1961.
153. JNA: 4/60/2B/24, Blackburne to Manley, 28 September 1961, Manley to Blackburne, 28 September 1961.
154. JNA 4/60/2A/46, Cabinet Decision, 20 September 1961, Cabinet Decision, 28 September 1961.
155. Mordecai, *Federal Negotiations*, 424.
156. Ashton and Killingray, *British Documents* B/6, Williams to Blackburne, 9 October 1961, 454–456.
157. WIFAC:FWI-PM-GA-37, Record of a Meeting at the Colonial Office, 26 September 1961.
158. Ashton and Killingray, *British Documents* B/6, Macleod to Macmillan, 22 September 1961, 438–440.
159. TNA: CO 1031/3278, Thomas minute, 17 October 1961, Hailes to Thomas, 1 November 1961, Thomas to Administrators, 6 November 1961.
160. TNA: CAB 128/35, CC(61)62nd mtg., minute 4, 28 September 1961, CAB 129/106, C(61)142, 26 September 1961.
161. Ashton and Killingray, *British Documents* B/6, Minutes by Poynton and Macleod, 4 October 1961, 452–454.
162. TNA: CAB 128/35, CC(55)61st mtg., minute 3, 10 October 1961; CAB 195/20, CC (55)61, minute 3, 10 October 1961.

163. *Parliamentary Debates*, 5th series, vol. 648, col. 17, 31 October 1961, cols 168–169, 1 November 1961.
164. EWMC: CLR James Papers, Box 5, Folder 105, James to La Corbiniere, 6 November 1961.
165. Ashton and Killingray, *British Documents* B/6, Adams to Macmillan, 17 November 1961 including Macmillan's reply of 25 November at n. 2, 467.
166. For the Colonial Office attempts to unpick Williams' thinking see TNA: CO 1031/ 3278, Hailes to Maudling, 21 October 1961, Fraser minute, 24 October 1961, Hailes to Thomas, 6 November 1961, Grey (Georgetown) to Thomas, 9 November 1961, Note by Arthur Lewis (ud), CO Memo on Fraser's visit, November 1961. For other synoptic accounts of Williams' views which are largely based on the reports by Lewis, see Mordecai, *Federal Negotiations*, 418–421, Ryan, *Myth*, 240–255.
167. Williams, *Hunger*, 277–280.
168. Solomon, *Autobiography*, 177.
169. S. Siewah (ed.), *Lotus and the Dagger* (Tunapuna, 1994), 97–107.
170. *Trinidad Guardian*, 13 January 1962, 7, 16 January 1962, 3, 25 January 1962, 1, 29 January 1962, 1.
171. TNA: CAB 134/1560, CPC(61)13th mtg., minute 2, 20 December 1961, CP(61)36, 18 December 1961; CAB 134/1561, CPC (62)3rd mtg., minute 1, 2 February 1962, CPC(62)5, 31 January 1962.
172. L. Baston, *Reggie: The Life of Reginald Maudling* (Stroud, 2004), 156.
173. WIFAC: FWI-PM-GA-37, Record of Meeting between the Federal Government and Maudling, 24 January 1962.
174. TNA: CO 1031/3374, Hailes to Secretary of State, 22 January 1962, Secretary of State to West Indies (Hailes), 24 January 1962, Thomas minute, 31 January 1962.
175. *Parliamentary Debates*, 5th series, vol. 653, cols 230–235, 6 February 1962.
176. TNA: CO 1031/3374, Antigua to Secretary of State, 9 February 1962, St Vincent to Secretary of State, 10 February 1962, Dominica to Secretary of State, 10 February 1962, St Kitts to Secretary of State, 12 February 1962.
177. Mordecai, *Federal Negotiations*, 449.
178. Gomes, *Through a Maze of Colour* (Port of Spain, 1974), 44.
179. Hoyos, *Adams*, 221–222.
180. TNA: CO 1031/3374, West Indies (Hailes) to Secretary of State, 15 February 1962.
181. TNA: CAB 134/1561, CPC(62)5th mtg., minute 2, 2 March 1962.
182. Gomes, *Maze*, 222.
183. TNA: CO 1031/3374, West Indies (Hailes) to Secretary of State, 14 February 1962.
184. WIFAC: FWI-PM-GA-24, Prime Minister's Address to the Nation (ud), Adams to Maudling, 12 March 1962.
185. *Parliamentary Debates*, 5th series, vol. 655, col. 1103, 13 March 1962, vol. 656, cols 858–871, 26 March 1962.
186. Seaga, *Life*, 83–84.
187. TNA: CAB 128/36, CC(62)12th mtg., minute 1, 8 February 1962. For the constitution, see Parliamentary Papers 1961–1962, Cmnd. 1638, Report of the Jamaica Independence Conference, February 1962.

188. RHL: Blackburne Papers, s. 460, Box 16, Blackburne to his Father, 29 April 1962.
189. Ashton and Killingray, *British Documents* B/6, Fraser to Brooke, 6 July 1962, 541–542 including n. 3.
190. H. Foot, *A Start in Freedom* (London, 1964), 132–133.
191. Seaga, *Life*, 105.
192. Williams, *Forged*, 299.
193. Ryan, *Myth*, 300.
194. RHL: MSS. Brit. Emp. S.484, Transcript of Reginald Maudling Interview.
195. Baston, *Reggie*, 158; Williams, *Hunger*, 284–285. A copy of the constitution is available in *Parliamentary Papers 1961–1962*, Cmnd. 1757, Report of the Trinidad and Tobago Independence Conference, June 1962.
196. Palmer, *Modern*, Ch. 5.
197. CAC: DSND, 8/19, Gilmore minute, 11 July 1962.
198. Williams (ed.), *Forged*, 328.

5   Order and Disorder between Dependence and Independence 1962–1969

1. R. Drayton, 'Anglo-American "Liberal" Imperialism, British Guiana and the World Since September 11' in Wm. R. Louis (ed.), *Yet More Adventures with Britannia* (London, 2005), 321–342; R. Waters and G. Daniels, 'The World's Longest General Strike: The AFL-CIO, the CIA and British Guiana', *Diplomatic History* 29 (2005), 279–307; R. Waters, 'The British Guiana Betrayal', *Journal of Caribbean History* 43/1 (2009), 115–135; C. Fraser, 'The New Frontier of Empire in the Caribbean', *International History Review* 22/3 (2000), 583–610.
2. UWI Library, Mona, Richard Hart Papers, Box 1: Guyana, Beware My Brother Forbes, PPP Pamphlet.
3. C. Palmer, *Cheddi Jagan and the Politics of Power* (Chapel Hill, 2010), 195.
4. S. Rabe, *US Intervention in British Guiana* (Chapel Hill, 2005), 66–67.
5. Palmer, *Power*, 204.
6. National Archives II, College Park [Henceforward NA]: RG59, Central Decimal Files 1955–1959, Box 3205, Memo of Conversation between Renison and Humphrey, 26 July 1957, State Department to London, 16 August 1957, Woods to State Department, 12 May 1959.
7. *Foreign Relations of the United States [Henceforward FRUS] 1961–1963*: vol. 12, Battle memorandum for Bundy, 19 May 1961, 517–518.
8. S. R. Ashton and D. Killingray (eds), *British Documents on the End of Empire B6: The West Indies* (London, 1999), Grey to Hailes, 24 October 1960, 363–367.
9. John F. Kennedy Library [Henceforward JFKL]: NSF Country Files, Box 14a, London (Jones) to Secretary of State, 9 August 1961, State Department to US Embassy (London), 11 August 1961, Bruce (London) to Secretary of State, 17 August 1961, Georgetown (Melby) to Secretary of State, 15 August 1961; *FRUS 1961–1963*: vol. 12 Schlesinger memorandum, 28 August 1961, 30 August 1961, State Department to UK Embassy, 31 August 1961,

2 September 1961, Rusk to Bruce (London), 4 September 1961, 5 September 1961, 523–530.

10. The National Archives, Kew [Henceforward TNA]: DO 161/53, Report of the Anglo-American Working Group on British Guiana, September 1961, Macleod to Macmillan, 19 September 1961, Wakeley minutes, 8 September 1961, 12 September 1961.

11. TNA: FO 371/155724, Washington (Colonial Attaché) to Secretary of State, 27 October 1961.

12. JFKL: George Ball papers, Box 2, Johnson-Ball Telcon, 18 October 1961, Kennedy-Ball Telcon, 20 October 1961.

13. JFKL: NSF Country Files, Box 14a, Memorandum of Conversation between Kennedy and Jagan, 24 October 1961.

14. C. Jagan, *The West on Trial* (London, 1966), 353.

15. JFKL: Richard Goodwin Papers, Box 3, Goodwin to Kennedy, 25 October 1961; George Ball Papers Box 2, Telcon Goodwin-Ball, 25 October 1961; NSF Country Files, Box 14a, Memorandum of Conversation between Jagan and American officials, 26 October 1961.

16. TNA: CO 1031/4028, Grey to Huijsman, 30 January 1962, Budget Speech, 31 January 1962.

17. Palmer, *Power*, 210–213.

18. TNA: CO 1031/4028, Grey to Secretary of State, 14 February 1962, 15 February 1962, 16 February 1962.

19. Cheddi Jagan Research Centre, Georgetown [Henceforward CJRC]: CJ 154A, Memorandum on the Background to the February 1962 Disturbances (ud).

20. TNA: CO 1031/4034, Grey to Jagan, 20 June 1962.

21. Rabe, *Intervention*, 92–93.

22. JFKL: NSF Countries, Box 15, Burdett (State) to Bruce (London), 20 February 1962.

23. TNA: CAB 134/1560, CPC (61) 13th mtg., 20 December 1961.

24. Ashton and Killingray, *British Documents on the End of Empire B6*, Rusk to Home, 20 February 1962 with Macmillan minute, 21 February 1962, Home to Rusk, 26 February 1962, 486–489.

25. TNA: CO 1031/4028, Piper minute, 21 February 1962.

26. JFKL: Oral Histories, Hugh Fraser, 17 September 1966.

27. JFKL: Schlesinger Papers, Box WH 27, Schlesinger memorandum of meeting, 27 February 1962, American Embassy (London) to White House, 6 March 1962.

28. Ashton and Killingray, *British Documents B6*, Record by Home of his Conversation with Rusk, 12 March 1962, 489; JFKL: Schlesinger Papers, Box WH 27, Rusk (Geneva) to Acting Secretary, 13 March 1962.

29. *FRUS 1961–1963*: vol. 12, Memorandum of Conversation with Fraser, 17 March 1962, 558–564; JFKL: Schlesinger papers, Box WH 27, State Department to London, 20 March 1962, Oral Histories, Hugh Fraser, 17 September 1966.

30. TNA: PREM 11/3666, Fraser to Secretary of State, 20 March 1962, de Zulueta minute, 23 March 1963.

31. Ashton and Killingray, *British Documents B6*, Maudling Memorandum, 3 April 1962, 493–497.

32. JFKL: Schlesinger Papers, Box WH27, Dungan to Kennedy, 19 May 1962.

33. *FRUS 1961–1963*: vol. 12, Rusk to Kennedy, 12 July 1962, Bundy to Kennedy, 13 July 1962, Schlesinger to Dungan, 19 July 1962, 575–578.
34. TNA: PREM 11/3666, Macmillan to Brook, 3 May 1962.
35. A full account of Sandys' working methods can be found in the British Diplomatic Oral History Project, Denis Doble, 29 March 2004, 6–11.
36. TNA: DO 200/60, McIndoe minute, 9 August 1962.
37. JFKL: Schlesinger papers, Box WH 27, Bundy to Schlesinger, 19 September 1962.
38. Churchill Archives Centre, University of Cambridge [Henceforward CAC]: DSND 8/13, Sandys to Macmillan, 27 March 1963.
39. CJRC: CJ 154A, Jagan to Grey, 7 December 1962.
40. TNA: CO 1031/4377, Grey to Piper, 8 February 1963.
41. Waters and Daniels, 'Longest', 279–307.
42. TNA: CO 1031/4402, Secretary of State to British Guiana, 23 April 1963, Governor to Secretary of State, 24 April 1963, Thomas minute, 25 April 1963, Fisher minute, 26 April 1963, Milton minute, 26 April 1963.
43. TNA: DO 200/59, Sykes minutes, 24 May 1963, 27 May 1963; CAB 128/37, CC (63) 29th mtg., minute 3, 9 May 1963.
44. TNA: CO 1031/4402, Grey to Sandys, 4 March 1963.
45. JFKL: NSF Country files, Box 15, Melby (Georgetown) to Secretary, 14 March 1963, 16 June 1963, 23 June 1963.
46. Rabe, *Intervention*, 112.
47. University of Warwick Modern Records Centre (Henceforward MRC): TUC Records MSS 292B/972.8/3, Nicholson minute, 15 May 1963, Stacpoole (CO) to Hargreaves (TUC), 16 May 1963.
48. MRC: TUC Records, MSS 292B/972.8/4, Hood to Hargreaves, 17 June 1963, Minutes of TUC General Council, 24 July 1963, Report of Visit by Willis, 22 July 1963.
49. People's History Museum, Manchester [Henceforward PHM]: Labour Party International Department, Box 110, Meeting of the TUC General Council and Fisher, 22 August 1963.
50. *House of Commons Debates*, 5th series, vol. 679, col. 38; JFKL: President's Office, Briefing on British Guiana, 21 June 1963.
51. NA: RG59, Central Foreign Policy Files 1963, Box 3840, Rusk to Bruce, 21 June 1963, Box 3839, Memorandum of Conversation, 30 June 1963. This box contains a fuller record of the conversation than that available in FRUS.
52. TNA: CO 1031/4402, Kennedy to Macmillan, 10 September 1963, de Zulueta to Bundy, 11 September 1963, Poynton to de Zulueta, 16 September 1963, Foreign Office to Washington, 28 September 1963.
53. *Parliamentary Papers 1963–1964*, Cmnd. 2203, British Guiana Conference, November 1963.
54. CAC: DSND 8/20, Record of a Meeting in the Colonial Secretary's Room, 7 October 1963.
55. Jagan, *West*, 279.
56. F. Birbalsingh, *The People's Progressive Party of Guyana* (London, 2007), 68,124.
57. T. Sealy, *Sealy's Caribbean Leaders* (Kingston, 1991), 72.

58. TNA: CO 1031/4411, Minute of Meeting in Secretary's Room, 19 December 1963, Note of Meeting with Secretary of State, 25 February 1964.
59. C. Seecharan, *Sweetening Bitter Sugar* (Kingston, 2005), 577.
60. TNA: CO 1031/4406, Grey to Piper, 29 February 1964, Note of a Meeting with Jagan by Luyt, 26 March 1964.
61. Seecharan, *Sweetening*, 591.
62. CAC: DSND 8/16, Luyt to Sandys, 29 June 1964.
63. TNA: FO 371/173552, Poynton to Secretary of State, 7 July 1964.
64. CAC: DSND 8/14, Osborn to Sandys, 8 July 1963.
65. PHM: Labour Party NEC minutes, 27 November 1963, Minutes of the Overseas Sub-Committee, 12 November 1963, 3 December 1963, Cunningham memorandum, 15 November 1963.
66. *House of Commons Debates*, 5th series, vol. 694, cols. 101, 132.
67. *The Times*, 28 April 1964, 9.
68. Seecharan, *Sweetening*, 581.
69. NA: RG 59, Central Foreign Policy Files 1964–1966, Box 1947, Memorandum of Conversation with Gordon Walker, 19 February 1964, Box 1949, Memorandum of Conversation between Knox and Mayhew, 8 April 1964.
70. Ashton and Killingray, *British Documents B6*, Record of a Conversation between Wilson and Jagan, 29 October 1964, 627–629.
71. Ashton and Killingray, *British Documents B6*, Record of a Ministerial Meeting, 25 November 1964, 633–634.
72. NA: RG 59, Central Foreign Policy Files 1964–1966, Box 1947, Ball to President, 6 December 1964, Box 1948, Memorandum of a Conversation at the White House, 7 December 1964.
73. Both parties garnered fewer than 1,500 votes. See the table available in Palmer, *Power*, 239.
74. NA: RG59, Central Foreign Policy Files 1964–1966, Box 1947, Stevenson to State Department, 22 January 1965.
75. TNA: CO 1031/4408, Luyt to Greenwood, 12 March 1965, Greenwood to Prime Minister, 23 March 1965. Greenwood's personal views are evident from his handwritten interpolations in the text drafted by Piper.
76. TNA: CAB 148/18, OPD (65) 19th mtg., minute 5, 31 March 1965; CAB 148/20, OPD (65) 63, 29 March 1965; CO 1031/4408, Briefing Note by Wallace, 30 March 1965.
77. *Parliamentary Debates*, 5th series, vol. 713, col. 1644, 1 June 1964; TNA: CO 1031/4409, British Guiana (Luyt) to Secretary of State, 1 June 1965, 2 June 1965, Piper to Luyt, 2 June 1965.
78. *Parliamentary Papers 1965–1966*, Cmd. 2849, Report of the British Guiana Conference, December 1965.
79. TNA: CO 1031/4410, Record of a Meeting at the State Department, 19 October 1965.
80. NA: RG59, Central Foreign Policy Files 1964–1966, Box 1947, Carlson to State Department, 17 September 1965.
81. TNA: CAB 158/62, JIC (66) 32, 3 June 1966.
82. Sealy, *Leaders*, 74.
83. E. Wallace, *The British Caribbean* (Toronto, 1977); J. Mordecai, *The West Indies: The Federal Negotiations* (London, 1968).
84. R. Cox-Alomar, *Revisiting the Transatlantic Triangle* (Kingston, 2009), xxi.

85. TNA: CO 1031/3374, Secretary of State to Barbados (Stow), 27 February 1962.
86. TNA: CO 1031/3375, Fraser to Secretary of State, 20 March 1962, Turbott to Thomas, 24 April 1962.
87. Sealy, *Leaders*, 33.
88. H. M. Beckles, 'Radicalism and Errol Barrow in the Political Tradition of Barbados' in G. D. Howe and R. D. Marshall (eds), *The Empowering Impulse* (Kingston, 2001), 228.
89. TNA: CO 1031/3374, Barbados (Stow) to Secretary of State, 13 February 1962.
90. TNA: CO 1031/3375, Hailes to Thomas, 17 March 1962, Fraser to Secretary of State, 20 March 1962, Eden to Macmillan, 11 February 1962.
91. TNA: CAB 134/1561, CPC (62) 8th mtg., 11 April 1962, CO 1031/3375, Thomas to Poynton, 12 April, 1962; Ashton and Killingray, *British Documents on the End of Empire B6*, Memorandum by Maudling, 6 April 1962, CO Brief for Maudling, 6 April 1962, 502–512.
92. *House of Commons Debates*, 5th series, vol. 658, 16 April 1962, col. 19.
93. *Parliamentary Papers 1961–1962*, Cmnd. 1746, Report of the East Caribbean Federation Conference, June 1962.
94. A. Singham, *The Hero and the Crowd in a Colonial Polity* (London, 1968), 279–288.
95. C. Palmer, *Eric Williams and the Making of the Modern Caribbean* (Chapel Hill, 2006), Ch. 5.
96. Sealy, *Leaders*, 45.
97. TNA: CO 1031/4535, Barbados (Stow) to Secretary of State, 23 May 1963, Williams to Thomas, 24 May 1963.
98. Cox-Alomar, *Revisiting*, 175–176.
99. Ashton and Killingray, *British Documents B6*, Williams to Burrett, 21 May 1962, 515–516; TNA: T 317/641, Memoranda by Burrett on Federation of the Eight, 7 May 1962, 23 May 1962.
100. TNA: CO 1031/4537, Stow to Secretary of State, 14 September 1963.
101. TNA: T 317/641, Sharp to Taylor, 4 November 1963, Taylor minute, 6 November 1963.
102. TNA: CO 1031/4537, Williams minute, 24 September 1963, Thomas minute, 26 September 1963, Fisher minute (ud), Poynton minute, 2 October 1963, Fisher minute, 2 October 1963, Poynton minute, 4 October 1963.
103. TNA: T 317/641, Sandys to Boyd-Carpenter, 26 November 1963, Boyd-Carpenter minute (ud), Butler to Boyd-Carpenter, 6 December 1963, Taylor minute, 10 December 1963, Harris minute,17 December 1963, Armstrong minute, 18 December 1963, Boyd-Carpenter minute, 18 December 1963, Boyd-Carpenter to Sandys, 19 December 1963.
104. TNA: CO 1031/4538, Huijsman minute, 5 November 1963.
105. TNA: CO 1031/4540, Bryan (St Lucia) to Williams, 14 August 1964.
106. TNA: CO 1031/4538, Stow to Williams, 30 December 1963.
107. TNA: CO 1031/4539, Stow to Williams, 17 July 1964, Poynton minute, 30 June 1964.
108. TNA: CO 1031/4541, Williams to Mayhew, 11 November 1964.

109. Ashton and Killingray, *British Documents B6*, Greenwood memorandum, 15 March 1965, 642–648.
110. TNA: CO 1031/4537, Stow to Secretary of State, 14 September 1963.
111. TNA: CO 1031/4389, Stow to Williams, 25 February 1965.
112. TNA: CO 1031/4390, Stow to Williams, 20 August 1965.
113. W. Crawford and W. Marshall, *I Speak for the People* (Kingston, 2003), 151–156.
114. TNA: CO 1031/4389, Stow to Vaughan, 16 October 1965, Greenwood minute, 12 November 1965, Poynton minute, 29 November 1965.
115. TNA: CO 1031/4389, Williams minute, 20 October 1965, CO Memorandum on the Political Situation in Barbados, November 1965.
116. Sealy, *Leaders*, 32.
117. TNA: CAB 148/25, OPD (66) 31st mtg., minute 3, 5 July 1966; CAB 148/28, OPD (66) 70, 15 June 1966; *Parliamentary Papers 1966–1967*, Report of the Barbados Constitutional Conference, July 1966.
118. TNA: CO 1031/5225, Wallace to Stow, 12 August 1966, containing Stonehouse to Barrow, 12 August 1966, Whitefield minute, 1 September 1966, Secretary of State to Stow, 3 September 1966, Stow to Barrow, 5 September 1966, Wallace minute, 6 September 1966 with Memorandum on Pre-Independence Election, Barrow to Lee, 6 September 1966, Barrow to Stonehouse, 6 September 1966, Barbados (Stow) to Secretary of State, 14 September 1966.
119. TNA: CO 1031/4483, Burrows to Poynton, 7 October 1965.
120. Singham, *Hero*, 16.
121. TNA: CO 1031/5218, Personality Notes for the Windwards Constitutional Talks, 18 April 1966.
122. For a more detailed account, see Singham, *Hero*, Ch. 4.
123. G. Lewis, *Grenada: The Jewel Despoiled* (London, 1987), 13. For the full report see *Parliamentary Papers 1961–1962*: Cmnd. 1735, Report of the Commission of Enquiry into the Control of Public Expenditure in Grenada, May 1962.
124. *House of Commons Debates*, 5th series, vol. 661, 26 June 1962, col. 947.
125. Singham, *Hero*, 273–296.
126. F. Alexis, 'British Intervention in St Kitts', *Journal of International Law and Politics*, 16/581 (1983–1984), 584–586.
127. TNA: CO 1031/4483, Meeting held in Secretary of State's Room, 14 September 1965, 14 September 1965, Pitblado to Poynton, 11 October 1965, Garner to Poynton, 11 October 1965, Williams to Wallace, 11 October 1965, Note on Constitutional Proposals for the Leewards and Windwards, 22 October 1965.
128. *Parliamentary Papers 1965–1966*, Cmnd. 2865, Constitutional Proposals, December 1965.
129. Bodleian Library, Western Manuscripts: Anthony Greenwood Papers, MS. Eng. s.484, c. 6308, Memo on the Grenada Political Situation, 9 February 1965.
130. TNA: CO 1031/4484, Turbott to Williams, 1 November 1965, Williams minute, 8 November 1965.
131. TNA: CO 1031/5092, Grenada (Administrator) to Secretary of State, 31 March 1966, Secretary of State to Grenada, 1 April 1966, Turbott

to Williams, 4 April 1965, 6 April 1965, Background Note on Grenada Constitutional Proposals (ud).

132. *Parliamentary Papers 1966–1967*, Report of the Windward Islands Constitutional Conference, June 1966.

133. TNA: FCO 43/64, Grenada (Administrator) to Commonwealth Office, 20 January 1967, Hall minute, 24 January 1967, Galsworthy minute, 26 January 1967, Turbott to Hall, 23 January 1967 with Memorandum on the Political Situation, 14 January 1967.

134. TNA: FCO 43/65, Turbott (Grenada) to Hall, 2 February 1967.

135. TNA: FCO 43/67, Roberts to George Thomson, 31 August 1967, Vaughan minute, 3 October 1967, Roberts to Sewell, 5 October 1967.

136. Ashton and Killingray, *British Documents B/6*, Record of a meeting between Rusk and Greenwood, 18 October 1965, 672–676.

137. *Colonial Office List 1966*, 133.

138. TNA: CO 1031/4772, Howard (Administrator) to Secretary of State, 12 August 1965 enclosing intelligence report, Gibbs minute, 24 August 1965, Perry minute, 31 August 1965.

139. TNA: CO 1031/4433, Thomas minute, 30 January 1964, Fisher minute, 30 January 1964.

140. TNA: CO 1031/ 4433, Administrator (St Kitts) to Secretary of State, 12 May 1965, 3 June 1965, 9 August 1965, Eastern Caribbean Commission to Secretary of State, 6 September 1965.

141. TNA: CO 1031/4482, Williams minute, 9 September 1965 with Memorandum on Constitutional Change in the Leeward and Windward Islands.

142. TNA: CO 1031/4483, Meeting in the Secretary of State's Room, 14 September 1965.

143. *Parliamentary Papers 1965–1966*, Cmnd. 2865, Constitutional Proposals, December 1965.

144. TNA: CO 1031/4484, St Kitts (Administrator) to Secretary of State, 18 November 1965, Southwell to Secretary of State, 3 January 1966.

145. TNA: CO 1031/4484, Williams minute, 31 January 1966.

146. TNA: CO 1031/4484, Secretary of State to Administrator (St Kitts), 31 March 1966.

147. TNA: CAB 148/28, OPD (66) 67th mtg, 9 June 1966; *Parliamentary Papers 1966–1967*, Cmnd. 3031, Report of the St Kitts/Nevis/Anguilla Conference, June 1966.

148. F. Phillips, *Caribbean Life and Culture* (Kingston, 1991), 103–104.

149. TNA: FCO 43/78, Phillips to Gibbs, 27 January 1967, 5 February 1967, 27 February 1967.

150. Phillips, *Caribbean*, 116; TNA: FCO 43/78, St Kitts (Administrator) to Secretary of State, 16 February 1967.

151. *New York Times*, 24 March 1969, 8.

152. TNA: FCO 43/180, Lee to Sewell, 13 February 1969.

153. *The Times*, 23 August 1967, 3.

154. D. E. Westlake, *Under an English Heaven* (New York, 1972).

155. TNA: FCO 43/181, Thomas to Glasby, 28 January 1969, FCO Note on Anguilla, 22 February 1969.

156. TNA: FCO 43/180, Lee (Antigua) to Secretary of State, 6 February 1969.

157. R. Crossman and J. Morgan (eds), *Diaries of a Cabinet Minister: Vol. 3* (London, 1977), 14 March 1969, 415; TNA: CAB 148/91, OPD (69) 3rd mtg., 14 March 1969.
158. J. B. Priestley Library, University of Bradford, Barbara Castle Diaries, CAS 1/5, 25 March 1969. Castle expunged the numerous references to Anguilla in the manuscript version of her diaries from the volume published in 1984. For the official Cabinet minutes, see TNA: CAB 128/44, CC (69) 14th mtg., minute 2, 25 March 1969.
159. TNA: FCO 63/199, Bradshaw to Caradon, 1 April 1969.
160. TNA: FCO 63/193, Hayman minute, 6 April 1969 with Briefing Note on Anguilla.
161. *Parliamentary Papers 1970–1971*, Cmd. 4510, Report of the Wooding Commission, October 1970.
162. *Parliamentary Papers 1970–1971: Bills*, A Bill to Make Further Provisions with Respect to Anguilla, 7 July 1971; *Parliamentary Papers 1980–1981: Bills*, A Bill Intituled an Act to Make Further Provision with Respect to Anguilla, 8 December 1980.

6 Conclusion

1. A. Sives, *Elections, Violence and the Democratic Process in Jamaica* (Kingston, 2010), 63–68.
2. R. C. Lewis, *Walter Rodney's Intellectual and Political Thought* (Kingston, 1998).
3. O. Gray, *Radicalism and Social Change in Jamaica* (Knoxville, 1991), Ch. 7.
4. S. Ryan, *Eric Williams: The Myth and the Man* (Kingston, 2009), Ch. 26.
5. For an analysis of the motivation of the Jamaat, see C. Bloeser, 'Deprivation, Rationality and Rebellion: The Case of Trinidad and Tobago', *Caribbean Studies* 25/3 (1992), 277–304.
6. B. Dyde, *Out of the Crowded Vagueness* (Oxford, 2005), 292.
7. V. H. Young, *Becoming West Indian* (Washington, 1993), 69–76.
8. M. W. Collier, *Political Corruption in the Caribbean Basin* (Abingdon, 2005), 110–116.
9. *The Guardian*, 6 December 1990, 9.
10. Commonwealth Observer Group, *The General Election in Antigua and Barbuda* (London, 1999); Commonwealth Expert Team, *Antigua and Barbuda General Election 2004* (available via commonwealth.org).
11. UWI Library, Mona: Richard Hart Papers, Box 1: Guyana, *Political Freedom in Guyana* (1985), *Something to Remember* (1980).
12. S. Rabe, *US Intervention in British Guiana* (Chapel Hill, 2005), 183.
13. D. Harris and A. Waterman, 'To Die for the People's Temple' in R. Moore, A. B. Pinn and M. R. Sawyer (eds), *People's Temple and Black Religion in America* (Bloomington, 2004), 103–122.
14. Lewis, *Thought*, Ch. 9.
15. C. Searle, *Grenada: The Struggle Against Destabilization* (London, 1983), 10–23.
16. G. K. Lewis, *Grenada: The Jewel Despoiled* (Baltimore, 1987), 20.
17. H. Johnson, 'The West Indies and the Conversion of the British Official Classes to the Development Idea', *Journal of Imperial and Commonwealth History* 15/1 (1977), 55–83.

18. T. Sealy, *Sealy's Caribbean Leaders* (Kingston, 1991), 8.
19. For a comprehensive account, see A. Payne, *The Political History of CARICOM* (Kingston, 2007).
20. J. Mandle, *Persistent Underdevelopment* (Amsterdam, 1996), 67–70.
21. M. Marable, *African Caribbean Politics* (London, 1987), 166–167.
22. P. Henry, *Peripheral Capitalism and Underdevelopment in Antigua* (Oxford, 1985), 121–127.
23. Mandle, *Persistent*, 139–142.
24. J. Parker, *Brother's Keeper* (Oxford, 2008), 162.
25. R. Crandall, *Gunboat Democracy* (Oxford, 2006), Ch. 3.
26. Lewis, *Jewel*, 87.
27. G. Williams, 'Prelude to an Intervention: Grenada 1983', *Journal of Latin American Studies* 29/1 (1997), 152–153.
28. J. Pearce, *Under the Eagle* (Boston, 1982).
29. E. Seaga, *My Life and Leadership Vol. 1* (Oxford, 2009), 5.
30. Marable, *African*, 164–165.
31. Gray, *Radicalism*, 45.
32. The National Archives, Kew: CO 1031/3376, Williams minute, 19 October 1962, Poynton minute, 22 October 1962. The suggestion was self-evidently inspired by the Agatha Christie novel and Poynton claimed that it originated with the African politician, Seretse Khama.
33. Parker, *Keeper*, 164.
34. P. Catterall (ed.) and H. Macmillan, *The Macmillan Diaries Vol. 2: Prime Minister and After* (Oxford, 2011), 371.
35. J. Mordecai, *The West Indies: The Federal Negotiations* (London, 1968), 454.
36. For details of the Mordecai-Hailes correspondence, see Churchill Archives Centre: HAIS 4/28.
37. E. Williams, *Inward Hunger* (Princeton, 2006).

Bibliography

Primary sources

Archives

The National Archives, Kew
Cabinet (CAB)
CAB 21 Registered Files 1916–1965.
CAB 128 Cabinet Minutes 1945–1978.
CAB 129 Cabinet Memoranda 1945–1978.
CAB 131 Defence Committee Minutes and Papers 1946–1963.
CAB 134 Miscellaneous Committees Minutes and Papers 1945–1982.
CAB 148 Defence and Overseas Policy Committee Minutes and Papers 1964–1980.
CAB 158 Joint Intelligence Committee Memoranda 1947–1968.
CAB 159 Joint Intelligence Committee Minutes 1947–1968.
CAB 195 Cabinet Secretary's Notebooks 1942–1963.

Colonial Office (CO)
CO 111 British Guiana Original Correspondence 1781–1951.
CO 137 Jamaica Original Correspondence 1689–1951.
CO 152 Leeward Islands Correspondence 1689–1951.
CO 318 West Indies Original Correspondence 1624–1951.
CO 321 Windward Islands Correspondence 1874–1951.
CO 968 Defence Department Original Correspondence 1941–1967.
CO 1027 Information Department Registered Files 1952–1967.
CO 1031 West Indian Department Registered Files 1948–1967.
CO 1042 West Indies Development and Welfare Organisation 1938–1958.
CO 1058 Dependent Territories Constitutions Department 1965–1967.

Commonwealth Relations Office (DO)
DO 35 General Records 1915–1971.
DO 161 Constitutional Department 1960–1963.
DO 189 Economic Relations Division 1960–1967.
DO 200 West Indies Department 1961–1967.

Ministry of Defence (DEFE)
DEFE 4 Chiefs of Staff Committee: Minutes 1947–1979.
DEFE 5 Chiefs of Staff Committee: Memoranda 1947–1977.
DEFE 6 Chiefs of Staff Committee: Reports of the Joint Planning Staff 1947–1968.

DEFE 11 Chiefs of Staff Committee: Registered Files 1946–1983.
DEFE 25 Chief of Defence Staff: Registered Files 1957–1984.

Foreign Office (FO, FCO)
FO 371 Political Departments General Correspondence 1906–1966.
FCO 23- Atlantic Department 1966–1968.
FCO 43- West Indian Department 1967–1968.

Home Office (HO)
HO 213 Aliens Department: General Files 1914–1984.
HO 344 Commonwealth Immigration Files 1949–1979.

Prime Minister (PREM)
PREM 3 Operational Correspondence and Papers 1937–1946.
PREM 8 Correspondence and Papers 1945–1951.
PREM 11 Correspondence and Papers 1951–1964.
PREM 13 Correspondence and Papers 1964–1970.

Treasury (T)
T 220 Imperial and Foreign Division 1914–1961.
T 225 Defence Policy and Materiel Division 1911–1976.
T 296 Foreign and Commonwealth Division 1960–1963.
T 317 Overseas Development Divisions 1960–1977.

Rhodes House, University of Oxford

Kenneth Blackburne (MSS. Brit. Emp. s. 460).
Arthur Creech Jones (MSS. Brit. Emp. s.332).
Reginald Maudling Interview Transcript (MSS. Brit. Emp. s. 484).

Bodleian Library, University of Oxford

Anthony Greenwood (MS. Eng. c. 6308).

Churchill Archives Centre, University of Cambridge

Julian Amery (AMEJ).
Patrick Buchan Hepburn, Lord Hailes (HAIS).
Duncan Sandys (DSND).

J. B. Priestley Library, University of Bradford

Barbara Castle.

People's History Museum, Manchester

Labour Party International Department.
Labour Party NEC Minutes.

Modern Records Centre, University of Warwick
TUC Records.

Jamaican National Archives
Norman Manley.

National Archives of Trinidad and Tobago
Cabinet Records.
Files on Federation.
Legislative Council Debates.

Federal Archives Centre, University of the West Indies, Cave Hill
Records of the Federation of the West Indies.

Eric Williams Memorial Collection, University of the West Indies,
St Augustine
Eric Williams.
C. L. R. James.

Sir Arthur Lewis Institute of Social and Economic Studies, University of
West Indies, Mona
Richard Hart.

Cheddi Jagan Research Centre, Georgetown
Cheddi Jagan.

Walter Rodney Archives (National Archives of Guyana)
Records of the British Guiana High Commission (AC3).
Legislative Council of British Guiana: Official Report (AB4).

National Archives II, College Park
RG59: General Records of the State Department.
Central Decimal Files.
Central Foreign Policy Files.
Bureau of European Affairs: Office of British Commonwealth.
Bureau of Inter-American Affairs: Office of Caribbean and Mexican Affairs.

Franklin D. Roosevelt Presidential Museum and Library
President's Secretary's File.
Charles Fahy.
Charles Taussig.
Sumner Welles.

Harry S. Truman Library and Museum

Oral History: William H. Hastie.
Oral Histories: John H. Tolan.
White House Confidential Files.

Dwight D. Eisenhower Presidential Library and Museum

Papers as President: Admin Series, NSC Series, Dulles-Herter Series.
White House Central.
WHO: Office of the Staff Secretary.
John Foster Dulles.
Dennis A. Fitzgerald.
Christian Herter.

John F. Kennedy Presidential Library and Museum

Central Subject Files.
NSF Country Files.
President's Office Files.
Oral Histories: Hugh Fraser.
George Ball.
Richard Goodwin.
Arthur Schlesinger.

Published documentary sources

British documents on the End of Empire:

Ashton, S. R. and Killingray, D. (eds), *Series B, Vol. 6 The West Indies* (London, 1999).
Goldsworthy, D. (ed.), *Series A, Vol. 3 The Conservative Government and the End of Empire 1951–1957* (London, 1994).
Hyam, R. (ed.), *Series A, Vol. 2 The Labour Government and the End of Empire 1945–1951* (London, 1992).
Hyam, R. and Louis, Wm. R. (eds), *Series A, Vol. 4 The Conservative Government and the End of Empire 1957–1964* (London, 2000).

Colonial Office List 1945–1966
Foreign relations of the United States

1940: Vol. 3 The British Commonwealth, The Soviet Union, The Near East and Africa.
1941: Vol. 3 The British Commonwealth, The Near East and Africa.
1955–1957: Vol. 6 American Republics, Multilateral, Mexico, Caribbean.
1958–1960: Vol. 5 American Republics.
1961–1963: Vol. 12 American Republics.
Geelhoed, E. Bruce & Edmonds, Anthony O. (eds), *The Macmillan-Eisenhower Correspondence* (Basingstoke, 2004).
Madden, Frederick (ed.), *The End of Empire Vol. 8: Dependencies Since 1948, pt. 1* (Westport, 2000).

Nettleford, Rex (ed.) & Manley, Norman, *Manley and the New Jamaica: Selected Speeches and Writings* (London, 1971).

Parliamentary Debates: Official Report, 5ᵗʰ Series 1940–1969.

Parliamentary Papers.

Sutton, Paul K. (ed.) & Williams, Eric, *Forged From the Love of Liberty: Selected Speeches of Dr. Eric Williams* (London, 1981).

Memoirs, autobiographies, diaries and interviews

Alexander, Robert J., *Presidents, Prime Ministers and Governors of the English-Speaking Caribbean and Puerto Rico* (Westport, 2000).

Bell, Hesketh, *Glimpses of a Governor's Life: From Diaries, Letters and Memoranda* (London, 1946).

Birbalsingh, Frank, *The People's Progressive Party of Guyana: An Oral History* (London, 2007).

Blackburne, Kenneth, *Lasting Legacy: A Story of British Colonialism* (London, 1976).

Brockway, Fenner, *Towards Tomorrow: The Autobiography of Fenner Brockway* (London, 1977).

Bustamante, Gladys, *Memoirs of Lady Bustamante* (Kingston, 1997).

Castle, Barbara, *The Castle Diaries 1964–1970* (London, 1984).

Catterall, Peter (ed.) & Macmillan, Harold, *The Macmillan Diaries Vol. 2: Prime Minister and After 1957–1966* (Oxford, 2011).

Colville, John, *The Fringes of Power: Downing Street Diaries 1939–1955* (London, 2004).

Crawford, Wynter, & Marshall, Woodville K. (ed.), *I Speak for the People: The Memoirs of Wynter Crawford* (Kingston, 2003).

Crossman, Richard, *The Diaries of a Cabinet Minister, Vol. 3: Secretary of State for Social Services* (London, 1976).

Foot, Hugh, *A Start in Freedom* (London, 1964).

Gomes, Albert, *Through a Maze of Colour* (Port of Spain, 1974).

Hill, Frank (ed.) & Bustamante, Alexander, *Bustamante and his Letters* (Kingston, 1976).

Jagan, Cheddi, *Forbidden Freedom* (London, 1954).

Jagan, Cheddi, *The West on Trial: My Fight for Guyana's Freedom* (London, 1966).

James, C.L.R., *Beyond a Boundary* (London, 1963).

Kincaid, Jamaica, *A Very Small Place* (London, 1988).

Lamming, George, *The Pleasures of Exile* (London, 1960).

Lyttelton, Oliver, *The Memoirs of Lord Chandos* (London, 1964).

Macmillan, Harold, *Pointing the Way 1959–1961* (London, 1972).

Manley, Rachel (ed.) & Manley, Edna, *Edna Manley: The Diaries* (London, 1989).

Maudling, Reginald, *Memoirs* (London, 1978).

Mitchell, James, *Beyond the Islands: An Autobiography* (Oxford, 2006).

Moran, Lord Charles, *Winston Churchill: The Struggle for Survival* (London, 1968).

Phillips, Fred, *Caribbean Life and Culture* (Kingston, 1991).

Romualdi, Serafino, *Presidents and Peons* (New York, 1967).

Roy, Raj & Young, John (eds), *Ambassador to Sixties London: The Diaries of David Bruce 1961–1969* (Dordrecht, 2009).

Rusk, Dean, *As I Saw It* (New York, 1990).

Schlesinger, Arthur M., *A Thousand Days: John F. Kennedy in the White House* (Boston, 1965).
Seaga, Edward, *My Life and Leadership Vol 1: Clash of Ideologies* (Oxford, 2009).
Sealy, Theodore, *Sealy's Caribbean Leaders* (Kingston, 1991).
Siewah, Samaroo (ed.), *Lotus and the Dagger: The Capildeo Speeches* (Tunapuna, 1994).
Singh, Jai Narine, *Guyana: Democracy Betrayed* (Kingston, 1996).
Solomon, Patrick, *Solomon: An Autobiography* (Port of Spain, 1981).
Stewart, Michael, *Life and Labour: An Autobiography* (London, 1980).
Westlake, Donald E., *Under an English Heaven* (New York, 1972).
Williams, Eric, *Inward Hunger: The Education of a Prime Minister* (Princeton, 2006).
Wilson, Harold, *The Labour Government 1964–1970: A Personal Record* (London, 1971).

Novels and travel writing

Braithwaite, E. R., *To Sir With Love* (London, 2005).
Naipaul, V. S., *The Suffrage of Elvira* (London, 1964).
Naipaul, V. S., *The Middle Passage* (London, 2011).
Naipaul, V. S., *The Mimic Men* (London, 2011).
Thomson, Ian, *The Dead Yard* (London, 2009).
Waugh, Alec, *Sunlit Caribbean* (London, 1948).
Winter, Sylvia, *The Hills of Hebron* (Kingston, 2010).

Newspapers

British Library Newspaper Reading Room, Colindale:

Barbados Advocate (for recent editions, barbadosadvocate.com).
Daily Gleaner (for recent editions, jamaica-gleaner.com).
Trinidad Guardian (for recent editions, guardian.co.tt).

Proquest Historical Newspapers:

New York Times
The Guardian
The Observer

Times Digital Archive:

The Times

Secondary sources

Alexander, Robert J., *A History of Organized Labor in the English-Speaking West Indies* (London, 2004).
Alexis, F., 'British Intervention in St Kitts', *Journal of International Law and Politics*, 16/581 (1983–1984), 584–586.

Bakan, Abigail, *Ideology and Class Conflict in Jamaica: The Politics of Rebellion* (Montreal, 1990).

Baptiste, Fitzroy Andre, *War, Cooperation and Conflict: The European Possessions in the Caribbean 1939–1945* (London, 1988).

Baston, Lewis, *Reggie: The Life of Reginald Maudling* (Stroud, 2004).

Basdeo, Sahadeo, *Labour Organisation and Labour Reform in Trinidad* (St Augustine, 1983).

Beckles, Hilary McD., *Natural Rebels: A Social History of Enslaved Black Women in Barbados* (London, 1989).

Beckles, Hilary McD., *A History of Barbados: From Amerindian Settlement to Nation-State* (Cambridge, 1990).

Beckles, Hilary McD., 'Radicalism and Errol Barrow in the Political Tradition of Barbados' in Howe, Glenford D., & Marshall, Ron D. (eds), *The Empowering Impulse: The Nationalist Tradition of Barbados* (Barbados, 2001), 221–231.

Bell, Wendell, 'Equality and Social Justice: Foundations of Nationalism in the Caribbean', *Caribbean Studies* 20/2 (1980), 5–36.

Benn, Dennis, *The Caribbean: An Intellectual History* (Kingston, 2004).

Birbalsingh, Frank, *The Rise of West Indian Cricket* (London, 1997).

Bloeser, C., 'Deprivation, Rationality and Rebellion: The Case of Trinidad and Tobago', *Caribbean Studies* 25/3 (1992), 277–304.

Blouet, Olwyn, M., *The Contemporary Caribbean: History Life and Culture Since 1945* (London, 2007).

Bolland, O. Nigel, *Colonialism and Resistance in Belize* (Belize, 1998).

Bolland, O. Nigel, 'Democracy and Authoritarianism in the Struggle for National Liberation', *Comparative Studies of South Asia, Africa and the Middle East* 18/1 (1997), 99–117.

Bolland, O. Nigel, *The Politics of Labour in the British Caribbean* (Kingston, 2001).

Boodhoo, Ken, *The Elusive Eric Williams* (Kingston, 2002).

Brendon, Piers, *The Decline and Fall of the British Empire 1781–1987* (London, 2007).

Brereton, Bridget, *A Modern History of Trinidad 1783–1962* (Kingston, 1981).

Brizan, George, *Grenada: Island of Conflict* (London, 1984).

Collier, Michael W., *Political Corruption in the Caribbean Basin: Constructing a Theory to Combat Corruption* (Abingdon, 2005).

Cox-Alomar, Rafael, *Revisiting the Caribbean Triangle: The Constitutional Decolonization of the Eastern Caribbean* (Kingston, 2009).

Crandall, Russell, *Gunboat Democracy: US Interventions in the Dominican Republic, Grenada and Panama* (Oxford, 2006).

Craton, Michael, *Testing the Chains: Resistance to Slavery in the British West Indies* (New York, 1982).

Cross, Malcolm, 'The Political Representation of Organised Labour in Trinidad and Guyana' in Cross, Malcolm & Heuman, Gad (eds), *Labour in the Caribbean* (London, 1988), 285–308.

Curtin, Philip D., *The Atlantic Slave Trade: A Census* (Madison, 1969).

Darwin, John, *Britain and Decolonisation* (Basingstoke, 1988).

Drayton, Richard, 'Anglo-American "Liberal" Imperialism, British Guiana and the World Since September 11' in Wm. R. Louis (ed.), *Yet More Adventures with Britannia* (London, 2005), 321–342.

Dyde, Brian, *A History of Antigua: The Unsuspected Isle* (Oxford, 2001).

Dyde, Brian, *Out of the Crowded Vagueness: A History of the Islands of St. Kitts, Nevis and Anguilla* (Oxford, 2005).

Eaton, George R., *Alexander Bustamante and Modern Jamaica* (Kingston, 1995).

Engerman, S. L., 'Contract Labour, Sugar and Technology in the Nineteenth Century', *Journal of Economic History* 43/3 (1983), 635–659.

Engerman, S. L., 'Economic Change and Contract Labour in the British Caribbean' in Richardson, David (ed.), *Abolition and its Aftermath: The Historical Context 1790–1916* (Abingdon, 1985), 225–244.

Everitt, John C., 'The Growth and Development of Belize City', *Journal of Latin American Studies* 18/1 (1986), 75–111.

Fergus, Howard A., *Montserrat: History of a Caribbean Colony* (2nd ed., Oxford, 2004).

Fisher, Nigel, *Iain Macleod* (London, 1973).

Fraser, Cary, *Ambivalent Anti-Colonialism: The United States and the Genesis of West Indian Independence* (Westport, 1994).

Fraser, Cary, 'The New Frontier of Empire in the Caribbean: The Transfer of Power in British Guiana', *International History Review* 22/3 (2000), 583–610.

Fraser, Cary, 'The PPP on Trial: British Guiana in 1953', *Small Axe* 8/1 (2004), 21–42.

Freeman, Gary P., 'Caribbean Migration to Britain and France' in Levine, Barry B. (ed.), *Caribbean Exodus* (Westport, 1987), 185–203.

French, Patrick, *The World Is What It Is: The Authorised Biography of V. S. Naipaul* (London, 2009).

Furedi, Frank, 'Britain's Colonial Wars: Playing the Ethnic Card', *Commonwealth and Comparative Politics* 28/1 (1990), 70–89.

Furedi, Frank, *Colonial Wars and the Politics of Third World Nationalism* (London, 1998).

Gaztambide-Geigel, Antonio, 'The Forces of Regional Cooperation' in Brereton, Bridget (ed.), *UNESCO General History of the Caribbean Vol. 5: The Caribbean in the Twentieth Century* (London, 2004), 346–368.

Ghany, Hamid A., 'Eric Williams, the Constitutional Scholar and the Introduction of Bicameralism in Trinidad and Tobago', *Journal of Legislative Studies* 3/4 (1997), 92–114.

Gray, Obika, *Radicalism and Social Change in Jamaica* (Knoxville, 1991).

Green, William A, *British Slave Emancipation: The Sugar Colonies and the Great Experiment 1830–1865* (Oxford, 1976).

Gupta, P. S., *Imperialism and the British Labour Movement 1914–1964* (London, 1975).

Hall, Catherine, 'What is a West Indian' in Schwarz, Bill (ed.), *West Indian Intellectuals in Britain* (Manchester, 2003), 31–50.

Hall, Douglas, *Five of the Leewards 1834–1870* (London, 1971).

Harris, D. & Waterman, A., 'To Die for the People's Temple' in Moore, R., Pinn, A. B. & Sawyer, M. R. (eds), *People's Temple and Black Religion in America* (Bloomington, 2004), 103–122.

Harrod, Jeffrey, *Trade Union Foreign Policy: A Study of British and American Trade Union Activity in Jamaica* (London, 1972).

Hart, Richard, *Rise and Organise: The Birth of the Workers and National Movement in Jamaica* (London, 1989).

Hart, Richard, *Towards Decolonisation: Politics, Labour and Economic Developments in Jamaica* (Kingston, 1999).

Hart, Richard, *Time for a Change: Constitutional, Political and Labour Developments in Jamaica and Other Colonies in the Caribbean Region* (Kingston, 2004).

Hart, Richard, *The End of Empire: Transition to Independence in Jamaica and Other Caribbean Colonies* (Kingston, 2006).

Havinden, Michael A. & Meredith, David, *Colonialism and Development: Britain and its Tropical Colonies 1850–1960* (Abingdon, 1993).

Henry, Paget, *Peripheral Capitalism and Underdevelopment in Antigua* (Oxford, 1985).

Henry, Paget, *Caliban's Reason: Introducing Afro-Caribbean Philosophy* (London, 2000).

Heuman, Gad, *Between Black and White: Race, Politics and the Free Coloureds in Jamaica* (Westport, 1981).

Heuman, Gad, 'The British West Indies' in Porter, Andrew (ed.), *The Oxford History of the British Empire: The Nineteenth Century* (Oxford, 1999), 470–494.

Higbie, Janet, *Eugenia: The Caribbean's Iron Lady* (London, 1993).

High, Steven, *Base Colonies in the Western Hemisphere* (Basingstoke, 2009).

Higman, B. W., *Slave Populations in the British Caribbean 1807–1834* (London, 1984).

Hintzen, Percy C., *The Costs of Regime Survival: Racial Mobilization, Elite Domination and Control of the State in Guyana and Trinidad* (Cambridge, 1989).

Holt, Thomas C., *The Problem of Freedom: Race, Labor and Politics in Jamaica and the Caribbean 1832–1938* (London, 1992).

Horne, Gerald, *Red Seas: Ferdinand Smith and Radical Black Sailors in the United States and Jamaica* (London, 2005).

Horne, Gerald, *Cold War in a Hot Zone: The United States Confronts Labor and Independence Struggles in the British West Indies* (Philadelphia, 2007).

Hoyos, F. A., *Grantley Adams and the Social Revolution* (London, 1974).

Hyam, Ronald, *Britain's Declining Empire: The Road to Decolonisation 1918–1968* (Cambridge, 2006).

James, Winston, *Holding Aloft the Banner of Ethiopia: Caribbean Radicalism in Early Twentieth Century America* (London, 1998).

Johnson, Howard, 'The West Indies and the Conversion of the British Official Classes to the Development Idea', *Journal of Imperial and Commonwealth History* (1977), 55–83.

Johnson, Howard, 'The Anglo-American Caribbean Commission and the Extension of American Influence in the British Caribbean', *Journal of Commonwealth and Comparative History* 20/2 (1984), 180–203.

Kiely, Ray, *The Politics of Labour and Development in Trinidad* (Kingston, 1996).

Knight, Franklin W., *The Caribbean: The Genesis of a Fragmented Nationalism* (Oxford, 1990).

Knight, Franklin W., 'The Disintegration of the Caribbean Slave Systems 1772–1886' in Knight, Franklin W. (ed.), *UNESCO General History of the Caribbean Vol. 3: The Slave Societies of the Caribbean* (London, 1997), 322–345.

Lacey, Terry, *Violence and Politics in Jamaica 1960–1970: Internal Security in a Developing Country* (Manchester, 1977).

Lai, Walton Look, 'C. L. R. James and Trinidadian Nationalism' in Henry, Paget & Buhle, Paul (eds), *CLR James's Caribbean* (Durham, NC, 1992).

Lamming, George, 'The Legacy of Eric Williams', *Callaloo* 20/4 (1997), 731–736.

Lawrence, K. O., *A Question of Labour: Indentured Immigration to Trinidad and British Guiana* (Kingston, 1994).

Lewis, Gordon K., *The Growth of the Modern West Indies* (London, 1968).

Lewis, Gordon K., *Main Currents in Caribbean Thought* (Baltimore, 1983).

Lewis, Gordon K., *The Jewel Despoiled* (London, 1987).

Lewis, Rupert Charles, *Walter Rodney's Intellectual and Political Thought* (Kingston, 1998).

MacDonald, S. B., *Trinidad and Tobago: Democracy and Development in the Caribbean* (London, 1986).

McPherson, Alan, *Yankee No: Anti-Americanism in US-Latin American Relations* (Cambridge, MA, 2003).

Magid, Alvin, *Urban Nationalism: A Study of Political Development in Trinidad* (Gainesville, 1988).

Mandle, Jay R., *Persistent Underdevelopment* (Amsterdam, 1996).

Marable, Manning, *African Caribbean Politics: From Kwame Nkrumah to Maurice Bishop* (London, 1987).

Mars, Perry, *Ideology and Change: The Transformation of the Caribbean Left* (Detroit, 1998).

Marshall, Dawn, 'A History of West Indian Migrations' in Levine, Barry B. (ed.), *The Caribbean Exodus* (Westport, 1987).

Martin, Tony, 'Eric Williams: His Radical Side in the Early 1940s', *Journal of Caribbean Studies* 17 (2002).

Martin, Tony, 'Eric Williams and the Anglo-American Caribbean Commission', *Journal of African American History* 88/3 (2003), 274–290.

Midgett, Douglas, 'Icon and Myth in a Caribbean Polity: V.C. Bird and Antiguan Political Culture' in Henke, Holger & Reno, Fred (eds), *Modern Political Culture in the Caribbean* (Kingston, 2003), 181–211.

Milette, James, 'Decolonization, Populist Movements and the Formation of New Nations' in Brereton, Bridget (ed.), *UNESCO General History of the Caribbean Vol. 5: The Caribbean in the Twentieth Century*, 174–223.

Mintz, Sidney W., *Caribbean Transformations* (Chicago, 1974).

Mintz, Sidney W., *Sweetness and Power: The Place of Sugar in Modern History* (New York, 1985).

Mintz, Sidney W., *Three Ancient Colonies* (London, 2010).

Mohammed, Patricia, 'A Very Public Private Man: Trinidad's Eric Eustace Williams' in Allahar, Anton (ed.), *Caribbean Charisma: Reflections on Leadership, Legitimacy and Populist Politics* (Kingston, 2001).

Mordecai, John, *The West Indies: The Federal Negotiations* (London, 1968).

Moskos, Charles C., 'Attitudes Towards Political Independence' in Bell, Wendell (ed.), *The Democratic Revolution in the West Indies* (Cambridge, MA, 1967).

Mottley, Wendell, *Trinidad and Tobago Industrial Policy* (Kingston, 2009).

Munroe, Trevor, *The Politics of Constitutional Decolonization: Jamaica 1944–1962* (Old Woking, 1972).

Munroe, Trevor, *The Cold War and the Jamaican Left: Reopening the Files* (Kingston, 1992).

Murphy, Philip, *Alan Lennox Boyd: A Biography* (London, 1999).

Neptune, Harvey, *Caliban and the Yankees* (Chapel Hill, 2007).

Nicholson, Marjorie, *The TUC Overseas: The Roots of Policy* (London, 1986).

Noguera, Pedro A., *The Imperatives of Power: Political Change and the Social Basis of Regime Support in Grenada* (New York, 1997).

Noguera, Pedro A., 'The Limits of Charisma' in Allahar, Anton (ed.), *Caribbean Charisma: Reflections on Leadership, Legitimacy and Populist Politics* (Kingston, 2001).

Nurse, Lawrence A., *Trade Unionism and Industrial Relations in the Commonwealth Caribbean* (London, 1992).

O'Shaughnessy, Hugh, *Grenada: Revolution, Invasion and Aftermath* (London, 1984).

Oxaal, Ivar, *Black Intellectuals Come to Power: The Rise of Creole Nationalism in Trinidad and Tobago* (Cambridge, MA, 1968).

Palmer, Colin A., 'Identity, Race and Black Power in Independent Jamaica' in Knight, Franklin, W. & Palmer, Colin A. (eds), *The Modern Caribbean* (Chapel Hill, 1989), 111–128.

Palmer, Colin A., *Eric Williams and the Making of the Modern Caribbean* (Chapel Hill, 2006).

Palmer, Colin A., *Cheddi Jagan and the Politics of Power* (Chapel Hill, 2010).

Paravisini-Gebert, Lizabeth, *Phyllis Shand Allfrey: A Caribbean Life* (New Brunswick, 1996).

Parry, J.H., Sherlock, Phillip M. & Maingot, A.P., *A Short History of the West Indies* (3rd ed., London, 1971).

Parker, Jason C., 'Re-Mapping the Cold War in the Tropics', *International History Review* 24/2 (2002), 318–347.

Parker, Jason, C., 'Capital of the Caribbean: The African American- West Indian Harlem Nexus and the Transitional Drive for Black Freedom', *Journal of African-American History* 89/2 (2005), 98–117.

Parker, Jason C., *Brother's Keeper: The United States, Race and Empire in the British Caribbean 1937–1962* (Oxford, 2008).

Parker, Jason C., 'The Failure of the West Indies Federation' in Louis, Wm R. (ed.), *Ultimate Adventures with Britannia* (London, 2009), 235–246.

Payne, Anthony, Sutton, Paul K. & Thorndike, T., *Grenada: Politics, Economics and Society* (London, 1985).

Payne, Anthony J., *The Political History of CARICOM* (Kingston, 2008).

Pearce, Jennie, *Under the Eagle: US Intervention in Central America and the Caribbean* (Boston, 1982).

Phillips, Anthony de V., 'Grantley Adams, Asquithian Liberalism and Socialism' in Howe, Glenford D., & Marshall, Ron D. (eds), *The Empowering Impulse: The Nationalist Tradition of Barbados*, 165–185.

Phillips, Mike & Phillips, Trevor, *Windrush: The Irresistible Rise of Multi-Racial Britain* (London, 1998).

Post, Ken, *Arise Ye Starvelings: The Jamaican Labour Rebellion of 1938 and its Aftermath* (1978).

Potter, Robert B., Barker, David, Conway, Dennis & Klak, Thomas, *The Contemporary Caribbean* (Harlow, 2004).

Rabe, Stephen G., *US Intervention in British Guiana: A Cold War Story* (Chapel Hill, 2005).

Ramdin, Ron, *From Chattel Slave to Wage Earner: A History of Trade Unionism in Trinidad and Tobago* (London, 1982).

Rector, Chad, *Federations: The Political Dynamics of Federation* (London, 2009).

Reddock, Rhoda E., *Women, Labour and Politics in Trinidad and Tobago* (London, 1994).

Rich, Paul, 'Sydney Olivier, Jamaica and the Debate on British Colonial Policy in the West Indies' in Cross, Malcolm & Heuman, Gad (eds), *Labour in the Caribbean* (London, 1988).

Richardson, Bonham C., *Caribbean Migrants: Environment and Human Survival on St Kitts and Nevis* (Knoxville, 1983).

Richardson, Bonham C., *The Caribbean in the Wider World 1492–1992* (Cambridge, 1992).

Richardson, Bonham C., *Igniting the Caribbean's Past: Fire in British West Indian History* (London, 2004).

Rodman, Joseph & Conway, Dennis, 'The Nexus and the Family Tree' in Potter, Robert B., Conway, Dennis & Phillips, Joan (eds), *The Experience of Return Migration: Caribbean Perspectives* (Aldershot, 2005), 89–108.

Ryan, Selwyn, *Race and Nationalism in Trinidad* (Toronto, 1972).

Ryan, Selwyn, *Eric Williams: The Myth and the Man* (Kingston, 2009).

Sandford, Gregory & Vigilante, Richard, *Grenada: The Untold Story* (Lanham, 1984).

Searle, Chris, *Grenada: The Struggle against Destabilization* (London, 1984).

Seecharan, Clem, *Sweetening Bitter Sugar: Jock Campbell, the Booker Reformer in British Guiana 1934–1966* (Kingston, 2005).

Sewell, Sharon C., *Decolonization and the Other: The Case of the British West Indies* (Newcastle, 2010).

Shepherd, Robert, *Iain Macleod: A Biography* (London, 1994).

Sheridan, Richard B., *Sugar and Slavery: An Economic History of the West Indies* (Barbados, 1974).

Sheridan, Richard B., 'Eric Williams and Capitalism and Slavery' in Solow, B. L. & Engerman, S. (eds), *British Capitalism and Caribbean Slavery* (Cambridge, 2004).

Sheridan, Richard B., 'The Formation of British Caribbean Society 1689–1748' in Marshall, P. J. (ed.), *The Oxford History of the British Empire: The Eighteenth Century* (Oxford, 1998).

Sherlock, Philip, *Norman Manley* (London, 1980).

Sherlock, Philip & Bennett, Hazel, *The Story of the Jamaican People* (Kingston, 1998).

Simmonds, Keith C., 'Political and Economic Factors Influencing the St Kitts–Nevis Polity: An Historical Perspective', *Phylon* 48/4 (1987), 277–286.

Singh, Kelvin, *Race and Class Struggles in a Colonial Society in Trinidad* (Calgary, 1994).

Singham, A. W., *The Hero and the Crowd in a Colonial Polity* (London, 1968).

Sives, Amanda, 'Dwelling Separately: The Federation of the West Indies and the Challenge of Insularity' in Kavalski, Emilian & Zolkos, Magdalena (eds), *Defunct Federalisms: Critical Perspectives on Federal Failure* (Abingdon, 2008), 17–30.

Sives, Amanda, *Elections, Violence and the Democratic Process in Jamaica* (Kingston, 2010).

Smith, Gaddis, *Last Years of the Munroe Doctrine* (New York, 1994).

Smith, Raymond, *Kinship and Class in the West Indies: A Genealogical History of Jamaica and Guyana* (Cambridge, 1990).

Spencer, Ian R. G., *British Immigration Policy Since 1939: The Making of Multi-Racial Britain* (London, 1997).

Stewart, Robert J., *Religion and Society in Post-Emancipation Jamaica* (Knoxville, 1992).

St Pierre, Maurice, *Anatomy of Resistance: Anti-Colonialism in Guiana* (London, 1999).

St Pierre, Maurice, 'Diasporan Intellectuals in Post-Independence Guyana, Jamaica and Trinidad and Tobago', *Souls* 10/2 (2008), 138–154.

Sutton, Paul, 'The Historian as Politician: Eric Williams and Walter Rodney' in Hennessy, Alistair (ed.), *Intellectuals in the Twentieth Century Caribbean, Vol. 1: Spectre of the New Class* (London, 1992), 98–114.

Taylor, David G. P., 'British Colonial Policy in the Caribbean', *The Round Table* 355 (2000), 337–344.

Thorpe, D. R., *Alec Douglas-Home* (London, 1997).

Tignor, Robert L., *W. Arthur Lewis and the Birth of Development Economics* (Princeton, 2006).

Walker, Christopher J., *Oliver Baldwin: A Life of Dissent* (London, 2003).

Wallace, Elizabeth, *The British Caribbean: From the Decline of Colonialism to the End of Federation* (Toronto, 1977).

Ward, J. R., *Poverty and Progress in the Caribbean 1800–1960* (Basingstoke, 1985).

Ward, J. R., 'The British West Indies in the Age of Abolition 1748–1815' in Marshall, P. J. (ed.), *The Oxford History of the British Empire: The Eighteenth Century* (Oxford, 1998), 415–439.

Waters, Robert, 'Pre-empting Communism: Kennedy, Johnson and British Guiana', *H-Net* (2002).

Waters, Robert & Daniels, Gordon, 'The World's Longest General Strike', *Diplomatic History* 29 (2005), 279–307.

Waters, R., 'The British Guiana Betrayal', *The Journal of Caribbean History* 43/1 (2009) 115–135.

Williams, Eric, *A History of Trinidad and Tobago* (London, 1964).

Williams, G., 'Prelude to an Intervention: Grenada 1983', *Journal of Latin American Studies* 29/1 (1997), 152–153.

Witham, Charlie, *Bitter Rehearsal: British and American Planning for a Post-War West Indies* (Westport, 2001).

Yerxa, Donald A., *Admirals and Empire: The United States Navy and the Caribbean 1898–1945* (Columbia, 1991).

Young, Virginia Heyer, *Becoming West Indian: Culture, Self and Nation in St Vincent* (Washington, 1993).

WEBSITES

The Commonwealth (thecommonwealth.org).

The Oxford Dictionary of National Biography (oxford.dnb.com).

British Diplomatic Oral History Project (chu.cam.ac.uk/archives/collections/BDOHP).

Index

Note: letter 'n' in brackets refers to notes in the text.